Principles of
Macroeconomics

Karl E. Case • Ray C. Fair • Sharon M. Oster

Principles of Macroeconomics

Custom Edition for Chaffey College

Taken from:
Principles of Macroeconomics, Twelfth Edition
by Karl E. Case, Ray C. Fair, and Sharon M. Oster

0002000010272061062

IS

ISBN 10: 1-323-47967-8
ISBN 13: 978-1-323-47967-4

About the Authors

Karl E. Case is Professor of Economics Emeritus at Wellesley College where he has taught for 34 years and served several tours of duty as Department Chair. He is a Senior Fellow at the Joint Center for Housing Studies at Harvard University and a founding partner in the real estate research firm of Fiserv Case Shiller Weiss, which produces the S&P Case-Shiller Index of home prices. He serves as a member of the Index Advisory Committee of Standard and Poor's, and along with Ray Fair he serves on the Academic Advisory Board of the Federal Reserve Bank of Boston.

Before coming to Wellesley, he served as Head Tutor in Economics (director of undergraduate studies) at Harvard, where he won the Allyn Young Teaching Prize. He was Associate Editor of the *Journal of Economic Perspectives* and the *Journal of Economic Education,* and he was a member of the AEA's Committee on Economic Education.

Professor Case received his B.A. from Miami University in 1968; spent three years on active duty in the Army, and received his Ph.D. in Economics from Harvard University in 1976.

Professor Case's research has been in the areas of real estate, housing, and public finance. He is author or coauthor of five books, including *Principles of Economics, Economics and Tax Policy,* and *Property Taxation: The Need for Reform,* and he has published numerous articles in professional journals.

For the last 25 years, his research has focused on real estate markets and prices. He has authored numerous professional articles, many of which attempt to isolate the causes and consequences of boom and bust cycles and their relationship to regional and national economic performance.

Ray C. Fair is Professor of Economics at Yale University. He is a member of the Cowles Foundation at Yale and a Fellow of the Econometric Society. He received a B.A. in Economics from Fresno State College in 1964 and a Ph.D. in Economics from MIT in 1968. He taught at Princeton University from 1968 to 1974 and has been at Yale since 1974.

Professor Fair's research has primarily been in the areas of macroeconomics and econometrics, with particular emphasis on macroeconometric model building. He also has done work in the areas of finance, voting behavior, and aging in sports. His publications include *Specification, Estimation, and Analysis of Macroeconometric Models* (Harvard Press, 1984); *Testing Macroeconometric Models* (Harvard Press, 1994); *Estimating How the Macroeconomy Works* (Harvard Press, 2004), and *Predicting Presidential Elections and Other Things* (Stanford University Press, 2012).

Professor Fair has taught introductory and intermediate macroeconomics at Yale. He has also taught graduate courses in macroeconomic theory and macroeconometrics.

Professor Fair's U.S. and multicountry models are available for use on the Internet free of charge. The address is http://fairmodel.econ.yale.edu. Many teachers have found that having students work with the U.S. model on the Internet is a useful complement to an introductory macroeconomics course.

Sharon M. Oster is the Frederic Wolfe Professor of Economics and Management and former Dean of the Yale School of Management. Professor Oster joined Case and Fair as a coauthor in the ninth edition of this book. Professor Oster has a B.A. in Economics from Hofstra University and a Ph.D. in Economics from Harvard University.

Professor Oster's research is in the area of industrial organization. She has worked on problems of diffusion of innovation in a number of different industries, on the effect of regulations on business, and on competitive strategy. She has published a number of articles in these areas and is the author of several books, including *Modern Competitive Analysis* and *The Strategic Management of Nonprofits.*

Prior to joining the School of Management at Yale, Professor Oster taught for a number of years in Yale's Department of Economics. In the department, Professor Oster taught introductory and intermediate microeconomics to undergraduates as well as several graduate courses in industrial organization. Since 1982, Professor Oster has taught primarily in the Management School, where she teaches the core microeconomics class for MBA students and a course in the area of competitive strategy. Professor Oster also consults widely for businesses and nonprofit organizations and has served on the boards of several publicly traded companies and nonprofit organizations.

Brief Contents

Contents

PART III   The Core of Macroeconomic Theory 139

8 Aggregate Expenditure and Equilibrium Output 141

9 The Government and Fiscal Policy 162

10 Money, the Federal Reserve, and the Interest Rate 187

PART IV   Further Macroeconomics Issues   264

14 Financial Crises, Stabilization, and Deficits   264

Preface

Our goal in the 12th edition, as it was in the first edition, is to instill in students a fascination with both the functioning of the economy and the power and breadth of economics. The first line of every edition of our book has been "The study of economics should begin with a sense of wonder." We hope that readers come away from our book with a basic understanding of how market economies function, an appreciation for the things they do well, and a sense of the things they do poorly. We also hope that readers begin to learn the art and science of economic thinking and begin to look at some policy and even personal decisions in a different way.

What's New in This Edition?

- The 12th edition has continued the changes in the *Economics in Practice* boxes that we began several editions ago. In these boxes, we try to bring economic thinking to the concerns of the typical student. In many cases, we do this by spotlighting recent research, much of it by young scholars. Some of the many new boxes include:
  - Chapter 3 uses behavioral economics to ask whether having unusually sunny weather increases consumer purchasess of convertible cars.
  - In Chapter 7 we look at new research on how individuals unemployed as a result of a recession spend their time. How much of that new time goes to job search versus other activities?
  - In Chapter 14 we describe recent research on how well recessions can be predicted.
  - In Chapter 20 we describe work that uses children's height in India to examine hunger and gender inequality.
  - Chapter 21, our new chapter, contains three boxes, examining the Moving to Opportunity program, birth weight and infant mortality, and the effects of the minimum wage.

  In other cases we use recent events or common situations to show the power and breadth of economic models. For example:
  - In Chapter 25 we illustrate the role of banks in creating money by describing bank runs in two classic movies and in the legend of Wyatt Earp.

  It is our hope that students will come to see both how broad the tools of economics are and how exciting is much of the new research in the field. For each box, we have also added questions to take students back from the box to the analytics of the textbook to reinforce the underlying economic principles of the illustrations.

- As in the previous edition, we have reworked some of the chapters to streamline them and to improve readability. In this edition, Chapter 20 has been revised to include more of the modern approach to economic development, including discussion of the millennium challenge.

- A major change in macro in the last edition was to replace the LM curve with a Fed interest rate rule, where the money supply now plays a smaller role in the analysis. Continuing in this spirit, in the current edition we have merged the supply of money and demand for money chapters into one chapter, Chapter 10. This streamlines the analysis and eliminates material that is no longer important.

- We have added a new chapter, Chapter 21, "Critical Thinking About Research," which we are quite excited about. It may be the first time a chapter like this has been included in an introductory economics text. This chapter covers the research methodology of economics. We highlight some of the key concerns of empirical economics: selection issues, causality, statistical significance, and regression analysis. Methodology is a key part of economics these days, and we have tried to give the introductory student a sense of what this methodology is.

- All of the macro data have been updated through 2014. The slow recovery from the 2008–2009 recession is still evident in these data, as it was in the 11th edition. This gives students a good idea of what has been happening to the economy since they left high school.
- Many new questions and problems at the end of the chapters have been added.

The Foundation

The themes of *Principles of Macroeconomics*, 12th edition, are the same themes of the first eleven editions. The purposes of this book are to introduce the discipline of economics and to provide a basic understanding of how economies function. This requires a blend of economic theory, institutional material, and real-world applications. We have maintained a balance between these ingredients in every chapter. The hallmark features of our book are as follows:

1. Three-tiered explanations of key concepts (*stories-graphs-equations*)
2. Intuitive and accessible structure
3. International coverage

Three-Tiered Explanations: Stories-Graphs-Equations

Professors who teach principles of economics are faced with a classroom of students with different abilities, backgrounds, and learning styles. For some students, analytical material is difficult no matter how it is presented; for others, graphs and equations seem to come naturally. The problem facing instructors and textbook authors is how to convey the core principles of the discipline to as many students as possible without selling the better students short. Our approach to this problem is to present most core concepts in the following three ways.

First, we present each concept in the context of a simple intuitive **story** or example in words often followed by a table. Second, we use a **graph** in most cases to illustrate the story or example. And finally, in many cases where appropriate, we use an **equation** to present the concept with a mathematical formula.

Macroeconomic Structure

We remain committed to the view that it is a mistake simply to throw aggregate demand and aggregate supply curves at students in the first few chapters of a principles book. To understand the AS and AD curves, students need to know about the functioning of both the goods market and the money market. The logic behind the simple demand curve is wrong when it is applied to the relationship between aggregate demand and the price level. Similarly, the logic behind the simple supply curve is wrong when it is applied to the relationship between aggregate supply and the price level. We thus build up to the AS/AD model slowly.

The goods market is discussed in Chapters 8 and 9 (the IS curve). The money market is discussed in Chapter 10 (material behind the Fed rule). Everything comes together in Chapter 11, which derives the AD and AS curves and determines the equilibrium values of aggregate output, the price level, and the interest rate. This is the core chapter and where the Fed rule plays a major role. Chapter 12 then uses the model in Chapter 11 to analyze policy effects and cost shocks. Chapter 13 then brings in the labor market. The figure at the top of the next page (Figure III.1 on page 139) gives you an overview of this structure.

One of the big issues in the organization of the macroeconomic material is whether long-run growth issues should be taught before short-run chapters on the determination of national income and countercyclical policy. In the last four editions, we moved a significant discussion of growth to Chapter 7, "Unemployment, Inflation, and Long-Run

CHAPTERS 8–9	CHAPTER 11	CHAPTER 13
The Goods-and-Services Market • Planned aggregate expenditure 　Consumption (C) 　Planned investment (I) 　Government (G) • Aggregate output 　(income) (Y)	**Full Equilibrium: AS/AD Model** • Aggregate supply curve • Fed rule • Aggregate demand curve 　Equilibrium interest 　rate (r*) 　Equilibrium output 　(income) (Y*) 　Equilibrium price 　level (P*)	**The Labor Market** • The supply of labor • The demand for labor • Employment and 　unemployment

CHAPTER 10	CHAPTER 12
The Money Market • The supply of money • The demand for money • Interest rate (r)	**Policy and Cost Effects in the AS/AD model**

▲ FIGURE III.1 **The Core of Macroeconomic Theory**

Growth," and highlighted it. However, while we wrote Chapter 16, the major chapter on long-run growth, so that it can be taught before or after the short-run chapters, we remain convinced that it is easier for students to understand the growth issue once they have come to grips with the logic and controversies of short-run cycles, inflation, and unemployment.

International Coverage

As in previous editions, we continue to integrate international examples and applications throughout the text. This probably goes without saying: The days in which an introductory economics text could be written with a closed economy in mind have long since gone.

Tools for Learning

As authors and teachers, we understand the challenges of the principles of economics course. Our pedagogical features are designed to illustrate and reinforce key economic concepts through real-world examples and applications.

Economics in Practice

As described earlier, the *Economics in Practice* feature focuses on recent research or events that support a key concept in the chapter and help students think about the broad and exciting applications of economics to their lives and the world around them. Each box contains a question or two to further connect the material they are learning with their lives.

Graphs

Reading and interpreting graphs is a key part of understanding economic concepts. The Chapter 1 Appendix, "How to Read and Understand Graphs," shows readers how to interpret the 200-plus graphs featured in this book. We use red curves to illustrate the behavior

▶ **FIGURE 3.9 Excess Demand, or Shortage**
At a price of $1.75 per bushel, quantity demanded exceeds quantity supplied. When excess *demand* exists, there is a tendency for price to rise. When quantity demanded equals quantity supplied, excess demand is eliminated and the market is in equilibrium. Here the equilibrium price is $2.00 and the equilibrium quantity is 40,000 bushels.

of firms and blue curves to show the behavior of households. We use a different shade of red and blue to signify a shift in a curve.

Problems and Solutions

Each chapter and appendix ends with a problem set that asks students to think about and apply what they've learned in the chapter. These problems are not simple memorization questions. Rather, they ask students to perform graphical analysis or to apply economics to a real-world situation or policy decision. More challenging problems are indicated by an asterisk. Many problems have been updated. The solutions to all of the problems are available in the *Instructor's Manuals*. Instructors can provide the solutions to their students so they can check their understanding and progress.

Digital features located in MyEconLab

MyEconLab is a unique online course management, testing, and tutorial resource. It is included with the eText version of the book or as a supplement to the print book. Students and instructors will find the following online resources to accompany the twelfth edition:

- **Concept Checks:** Each section of each learning objective concludes with an online Concept Check that contains one or two multiple choice, true/false, or fill-in questions. These checks act as "speed bumps" that encourage students to stop and check their understanding of fundamental terms and concepts before moving on to the next section. The goal of this digital resource is to help students assess their progress on a section-by-section basis, so they can be better prepared for homework, quizzes, and exams.

- **Animations:** Graphs are the backbone of introductory economics, but many students struggle to understand and work with them. Select numbered figures in the text have a supporting animated version online. The goal of this digital resource is to help students understand shifts in curves, movements along curves, and changes in equilibrium values. Having an animated version of a graph helps students who have difficulty interpreting the static version in the printed text. Graded practice exercises are included with the animations. Our experience is that many students benefit from this type of online learning.

- **Learning Catalytics:** Learning Catalytics is a "bring your own device" Web-based student engagement, assessment, and classroom intelligence system. This system generates classroom discussion, guides lectures, and promotes peer-to-peer learning with real-time analytics. Students can use any device to interact in the classroom, engage with content, and even draw and share graphs.

  To learn more, ask your local Pearson representative or visit www.learningcatalytics.com.

- **Digital Interactives:** Focused on a single core topic and organized in progressive levels, each interactive immerses students in an assignable and auto-graded activity. Digital Interactives are also engaging lecture tools for traditional, online, and hybrid courses, many incorporating real-time data, data displays, and analysis tools for rich classroom discussions.

- **Dynamic Study Modules:** With a focus on key topics, these modules work by continuously assessing student performance and activity in real time and using data and analytics, provide personalized content to reinforce concepts that target each student's particular strengths and weaknesses.

- **NEW: Math Review Exercises:** MyEconLab now offers a rich array of assignable and auto-graded exercises covering fundamental math concepts geared specifically to principles and intermediate economics students. Aimed at increasing student confidence and success, our new math skills review Chapter R is accessible from the assignment manager and contains over 150 graphing, algebra, and calculus exercises for homework, quiz, and test use. Offering economics students warm-up math assignments, math remediation, or math exercises as part of any content assignment has never been easier!

- **Graphs Updated with Real-Time Data from FRED:** Approximately 25 graphs are continuously updated online with the latest available data from FRED (Federal Reserve Economic Data), which is a comprehensive, up-to-date data set maintained by the Federal Reserve Bank of St. Louis. Students can display a pop-up graph that shows new data plotted in the graph. The goal of this digital feature is to help students understand how to work with data and understand how including new data affects graphs.

- **Interactive Problems and Exercises Updated with Real-Time Data from FRED:** The end-of-chapter problems in select chapters include real-time data exercises that use the latest data from FRED.

MyEconLab for the Instructor

Instructors can choose how much or how little time to spend setting up and using MyEconLab. Here is a snapshot of what instructors are saying about MyEconLab:

> MyEconLab offers [students] a way to practice every week. They receive immediate feedback and a feeling of personal attention. As a result, my teaching has become more targeted and efficient.—Kelly Blanchard, Purdue University

> Students tell me that offering them MyEconLab is almost like offering them individual tutors.—Jefferson Edwards, Cypress Fairbanks College

> MyEconLab's eText is great—particularly in that it helps offset the skyrocketing cost of textbooks. Naturally, students love that.—Doug Gehrke, Moraine Valley Community College

Each chapter contains two preloaded homework exercise sets that can be used to build an individualized study plan for each student. These study plan exercises contain tutorial resources, including instant feedback, links to the appropriate learning objective in the eText, pop-up definitions from the text, and step-by-step guided solutions, where appropriate. After the initial setup of the course by the instructor, student use of these materials requires no further instructor setup. The online grade book records each student's performance and time spent on the tests and study plan and generates reports by student or chapter.

Alternatively, instructors can fully customize MyEconLab to match their course exactly, including reading assignments, homework assignments, video assignments, current news assignments, and quizzes and tests. Assignable resources include:

- Preloaded exercise assignments sets for each chapter that include the student tutorial resources mentioned earlier
- Preloaded quizzes for each chapter that are unique to the text and not repeated in the study plan or homework exercise sets
- Study plan problems that are similar to the end-of-chapter problems and numbered exactly like the book to make assigning homework easier
- *Real-Time-Data Analysis Exercises*, marked with 🌐, allow students and instructors to use the very latest data from FRED. By completing the exercises, students become familiar with a key data source, learn how to locate data, and develop skills in interpreting data.
- In the eText available in MyEconLab, select figures labeled MyEconLab Real-time data 🌐 allow students to display a pop-up graph updated with real-time data from FRED.
- *Current News Exercises*, provide a turnkey way to assign gradable news-based exercises in MyEconLab. Each week, Pearson scours the news, finds a current microeconomics and macroeconomics article, creates exercises around these news articles, and then automatically adds them to MyEconLab. Assigning and grading current news-based exercises that deal with the latest micro and macro events and policy issues has never been more convenient.
- *Experiments in MyEconLab* are a fun and engaging way to promote active learning and mastery of important economic concepts. Pearson's Experiments program is flexible, easy-to-assign, auto-graded, and available in single- and multiplayer versions.
  - Single-player experiments allow your students to play against virtual players from anywhere at any time so long as they have an Internet connection.
  - Multiplayer experiments allow you to assign and manage a real-time experiment with your class.
  - Pre- and post-questions for each experiment are available for assignment in MyEconLab.
  - For a complete list of available experiments, visit **www.myeconlab.com**.
- Test Item File questions that allow you to assign quizzes or homework that will look just like your exams
- Econ Exercise Builder, which allows you to build customized exercises

Exercises include multiple-choice, graph drawing, and free-response items, many of which are generated algorithmically so that each time a student works them, a different variation is presented.

MyEconLab grades every problem type except essays, even problems with graphs. When working homework exercises, students receive immediate feedback, with links to additional learning tools.

Customization and Communication   MyEconLab in MyLab/Mastering provides additional optional customization and communication tools. Instructors who teach distance-learning courses or very large lecture sections find the MyLab/Mastering format useful because they can upload course documents and assignments, customize the order of chapters, and use communication features such as Document Sharing, Chat, ClassLive, and Discussion Board.

MyEconLab for the Student

MyEconLab puts students in control of their learning through a collection of testing, practice, and study tools tied to the online, interactive version of the textbook and other media resources. Here is a snapshot of what students are saying about MyEconLab:

- It was very useful because it had EVERYTHING, from practice exams to exercises to reading. Very helpful.—student, Northern Illinois University
- I would recommend taking the quizzes on MyEconLab because it gives you a true account of whether or not you understand the material.—student, Montana Tech
- It made me look through the book to find answers, so I did more reading.—student, Northern Illinois University

Students can study on their own or can complete assignments created by their instructor. In MyEconLab's structured environment, students practice what they learn, test their understanding, and pursue a personalized study plan generated from their performance on sample tests and from quizzes created by their instructors. In Homework or Study Plan mode, students have access to a wealth of tutorial features, including:

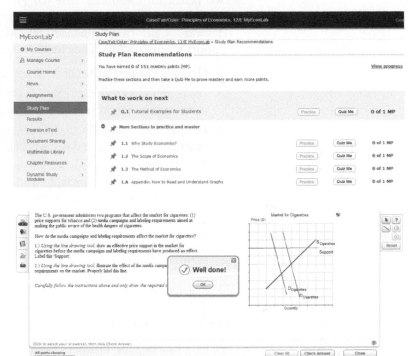

- Instant feedback on exercises that helps students understand and apply the concepts
- Links to the eText to promote reading of the text just when the student needs to revisit a concept or an explanation
- Step-by-step guided solutions that force students to break down a problem in much the same way an instructor would do during office hours
- Pop-up key term definitions from the eText to help students master the vocabulary of economics

- A graphing tool that is integrated into the various exercises to enable students to build and manipulate graphs to better understand how concepts, numbers, and graphs connect

Additional MyEconLab Tools   MyEconLab includes the following additional features:

- **Enhanced eText**—Students actively read and learn, and with more engagement than ever before, through embedded and auto-graded practice, real-time data-graph updates, animations, and more.
- **Print upgrade**—For students who wish to complete assignments in MyEconLab but read in print, Pearson offers registered MyEconLab users a loose-leaf version of the print text at a significant discount.
- **Glossary flashcards**—Every key term is available as a flashcard, allowing students to quiz themselves on vocabulary from one or more chapters at a time.

MyEconLab content has been created through the efforts of Chris Annala, State University of New York–Geneseo; Charles Baum, Middle Tennessee State University; Peggy Dalton, Frostburg State University; Carol Dole, Jacksonville University; David Foti, Lone Star College; Sarah Ghosh, University of Scranton; Satyajit Ghosh, Universtity of Scranton; Woo Jung, University of Colorado; Chris Kauffman, University of Tennessee–Knoxville; Russell Kellogg, University of Colorado–Denver; Katherine McCann, University of Delaware; Daniel Mizak, Frostburg State University; Christine Polek, University of Massachusetts–Boston; Mark Scanlan, Stephen F. Austin State University; Leonie L. Stone, State University of New York–Geneseo; and Bert G. Wheeler, Cedarville University.

Other Resources for the Instructor

The following supplements are designed to make teaching and testing flexible and easy and are available for *Micro, Macro,* and *Economics* volumes.

Instructor's Manuals

Two *Instructor's Manuals,* one for *Principles of Microeconomics* and one for *Principles of Macroeconomics,* were prepared by Tony Lima of California State University, East Bay (Hayward, California). The *Instructor's Manuals* are designed to provide the utmost teaching support for instructors. They include the following content:

- Detailed *Chapter Outlines* include key terminology, teaching notes, and lecture suggestions.
- *Topics for Class Discussion* provide topics and real-world situations that help ensure that economic concepts resonate with students.
- Unique *Economics in Practice* features that are not in the main text provide extra real-world examples to present and discuss in class.
- *Teaching Tips* provide tips for alternative ways to cover the material and brief reminders on additional help to provide students. These tips include suggestions for exercises and experiments to complete in class.
- *Extended Applications* include exercises, activities, and experiments to help make economics relevant to students.
- *Excel Workbooks,* available for many chapters, make it easy to customize numerical examples and produce graphs.
- *Solutions* are provided for all problems in the book.

Four Test Item Files

We have tailored the Test Item Files to help instructors easily and efficiently assess student understanding of economic concepts and analyses. Test questions are annotated with the following information:

- **Difficulty:** 1 for straight recall, 2 for some analysis, 3 for complex analysis
- **Type:** Multiple-choice, true/false, short-answer, essay
- **Topic:** The term or concept the question supports
- **Skill:** Fact, definition, analytical, conceptual
- **AACSB:** See description in the next section.

The Test Item Files include questions with tables that students must analyze to solve for numerical answers. The Test Item Files also contain questions based on the graphs that appear in the book. The questions ask students to interpret the information presented in the graph. Many questions require students to sketch a graph on their own and interpret curve movements.

Microeconomics Test Item File, by Randy Methenitis of Richland College: The Microeconomics Test Item File includes over 2,700 questions. All questions are machine gradable and are either multiple-choice or true/false. This Test Item File is for use with the 12th edition of *Principles of Microeconomics* in the first year of publication. It is available in a computerized format using TestGen EQ test-generating software and is included in MyEconLab.

Microeconomics Test Item File Discussion and Short Answer, by Richard Gosselin of Houston Community College: This second Test Item File includes 1,000 conceptual problems, essay questions, and short-answer questions. Application-type problems ask students to draw graphs and analyze tables. The Word files are available on the Instructor's Resource Center (www.pearsonhighered.com/educator).

Macroeconomics Test Item File by Randy Methenitis of Richland College: The Macroeconomics Test Item File includes over 2,900 questions. All questions are machine gradable and are either multiple-choice or true/false. This Test Item File is for use with the 12th edition of *Principles of Macroeconomics* in the first year of publication. This Test Item File is available in a computerized format using TestGen EQ test-generating software and included in MyEconLab.

Macroeconomics Test Item File: Discussion and Short Answer, by Richard Gosselin of Houston Community College: This second Test Item File includes 1,000 conceptual problems, essay questions, and short-answer questions. Application-type problems ask students to draw graphs and analyze tables. The Word files are available on the Instructor's Resource Center (www.pearsonhighered.com/educator).

The Test Item Files were checked for accuracy by the following professors:

Leon J. Battista, Bronx Community College; Margaret Brooks, Bridgewater State College; Mike Casey, University of Central Arkansas; Mike Cohick, Collin County Community College; Dennis Debrecht, Carroll College; Amrik Dua, California State Polytechnic University, Pomona; Mitchell Dudley, The College of William & Mary; Ann Eike, University of Kentucky; Connel Fullencamp, Duke University; Craig Gallet, California State University, Sacramento; Michael Goode, Central Piedmont Community College; Steve Hamilton, California State Polytechnic University; James R. Irwin, Central Michigan University; Aaron Jackson, Bentley College; Rus Janis, University of Massachusetts, Amherst; Jonatan Jelen, The City College of New York; Kathy A. Kelly, University of Texas, Arlington; Kate Krause, University of New Mexico; Gary F. Langer, Roosevelt University; Leonard Lardaro, University of Rhode Island; Ross LaRoe, Denison University; Melissa Lind, University of Texas, Arlington; Solina Lindahl, California State Polytechnic University; Pete Mavrokordatos, Tarrant County College; Roberto Mazzoleni, Hofstra University; Kimberly Mencken, Baylor University; Ida Mirzaie, Ohio State University; Shahruz Mohtadi, Suffolk University; Mary Pranzo, California State University, Fresno; Ed Price, Oklahoma State University; Robert Shoffner, Central Piedmont Community College; James Swofford, University of South Alabama; Helen Tauchen, University of North Carolina, Chapel Hill; Eric Taylor, Central Piedmont Community College; Henry Terrell, University of Maryland; John Tommasi, Bentley College; Mukti Upadhyay, Eastern Illinois University; Robert Whaples, Wake Forest University; and Timothy Wunder, University of Texas, Arlington.

The Association to Advance Collegiate Schools of Business (AACSB) The authors of the Test Item File have connected select Test Item File questions to the general knowledge and skill guidelines found in the AACSB assurance of learning standards.

What Is the AACSB? AACSB is a not-for-profit corporation of educational institutions, corporations, and other organizations devoted to the promotion and improvement of higher education in business administration and accounting. A collegiate institution offering degrees in business administration or accounting may volunteer for AACSB accreditation review. The AACSB makes initial accreditation decisions and conducts periodic reviews to promote continuous quality improvement in management education. Pearson Education is a proud member of the AACSB and is pleased to provide advice to help you apply AACSB Assurance of Learning Standards.

What Are AACSB Assurance of Learning Standards? One of the criteria for AACSB accreditation is quality of the curricula. Although no specific courses are required, the AACSB expects a curriculum to include learning experiences in areas such as the following:

- Written and Oral Communication
- Ethical Understanding and Reasoning

- Analytic Thinking Skills
- Information Technology
- Diverse and Multicultural Work
- Reflective Thinking
- Application of Knowledge

Questions that test skills relevant to these guidelines are tagged with the appropriate standard. For example, a question testing the moral questions associated with externalities would receive the Ethical Understanding and Reasoning tag.

How Can Instructors Use the AACSB Tags? Tagged questions help you measure whether students are grasping the course content that aligns with the AACSB guidelines noted earlier. This in turn may suggest enrichment activities or other educational experiences to help students achieve these skills.

TestGen

The computerized TestGen package allows instructors to customize, save, and generate classroom tests. The test program permits instructors to edit, add, or delete questions from the Test Item Files; analyze test results; and organize a database of tests and student results. This software allows for extensive flexibility and ease of use. It provides many options for organizing and displaying tests, along with search and sort features. The software and the Test Item Files can be downloaded from the Instructor's Resource Center (**www.pearsonhighered .com/educator**).

PowerPoint® Lecture Presentations

PowerPoint slides for *Principles of Microeconomics* and *Principles of Macroeconomics*, prepared by Jim Lee of Dickinson State University, are available:

- A comprehensive set of PowerPoint slides can be used by instructors for class presentations or by students for lecture preview or review. These slides include all the figures, photos, tables, key terms, and equations in the textbook. Instructors may download these PowerPoint presentations from the Instructor's Resource Center (**www.pearsonhighered.com/educator**).
- A student version of the PowerPoint slides are available as .pdf files. This version allows students to print the slides and bring them to class for note taking. Instructors can download these PowerPoint presentations from the Instructor's Resource Center. (**www.pearsonhighered.com/educator**).

Acknowledgments

We are grateful to the many people who helped us prepare the 12th edition. We thank David Alexander, our editor, and Lindsey Sloan, our program manager, for their help and enthusiasm.

Roberta Sherman, project manager, and Jeffrey Holcomb, our Team Lead of Project Management, ensured that the production process of the book went smoothly. In addition, we also want to thank Stephanie Raga of Integra Software Services, Inc., who kept us on schedule, and Jenell Forschler, who managed the research of the many photographs that appear in the book.

We want to give special thanks to Patsy Balin, Murielle Dawdy, and Tracy Waldman for their research assistance.

We also owe a debt of gratitude to those who reviewed and checked the 12th edition for accuracy. They provided us with valuable insight as we prepared this edition and its supplement package.

Reviewers of the 12th Edition

Bahram Adrangi, University of Portland
Anthony Andrews, Governors State
  University
J Jeffrey Blais, Rhode Island College
Paula M. Cole, University of Denver
Karen Fitzner, DePaul University
James Frederick, UNC at Pembroke
Richard Gearhart, California State
  University, Bakersfield
Wayne Hickenbottom, University of
  Texas at Austin
Janet Koscianski, Shippensburg University
Tim Kwock, University of Hawaii
  West Oahu
Sangjoon Lee, Alfred University
David Lehmkuhl, Lakeland College
Benjamin Liebman, St. Joseph's
  University
Basel Mansour, New Jersey City University
Chris Phillips, Somerset Community
  College
Sarah Quintanar, University of Arkansas
  at Little Rock
Daniel Sichel, Wellesley College
John Solow, University of Iowa
Jadrian Wooten, Penn State University
Linus Yamane, Pitzer College

Reviewers of Previous Editions

The following individuals were of
immense help in reviewing all or part of
previous editions of this book and the
teaching/learning package in various
stages of development:

Cynthia Abadie, Southwest Tennessee
  Community College
Shawn Abbott, College of the Siskiyous
Fatma Abdel-Raouf, Goldey-Beacom
  College
Lew Abernathy, University of North
  Texas
Rebecca Abraham, Nova Southeastern
  University
Basil Adams, Notre Dame de Namur
  University
Jack Adams, University of Maryland
Douglas K. Adie, Ohio University
Douglas Agbetsiafa, Indiana University,
  South Bend
Sheri Aggarwal, University of Virginia
Carlos Aguilar, El Paso Community
  College
Ehsan Ahmed, James Madison University
Ferhat Akbas, Texas A&M University
Sam Alapati, Rutgers University

Terence Alexander, Iowa State
  University
John W. Allen, Texas A&M University
Polly Allen, University of Connecticut
Stuart Allen, University of North
  Carolina at Greensboro
Hassan Aly, Ohio State University
Alex Anas, University at Buffalo, The
  State University of New York
David Anderson, Centre College
Joan Anderssen, Arapahoe Community
  College
Jim Angresano, Hampton-Sydney
  College
Kenneth S. Arakelian, University of
  Rhode Island
Harvey Arnold, Indian River Community
  College
Nick Apergis, Fordham University
Bevin Ashenmiller, Occidental College
Richard Ashley, Virginia Technical
  University
Birjees Ashraf, Houston Community
  College Southwest
Kidane Asmeron, Pennsylvania State
  University
Musa Ayar, University of Texas, Austin
James Aylesworth, Lakeland Community
  College
Moshen Bahmani, University of
  Wisconsin—Milwaukee
Asatar Bair, City College of San
  Francisco
Diana Bajrami, College of Alameda
Mohammad Bajwa, Northampton
  Community College
Rita Balaban, University of North
  Carolina, Chapel Hill
A. Paul Ballantyne, University of
  Colorado, Colorado Springs
Richard J. Ballman, Jr., Augustana
  College
King Banaian, St. Cloud State University
Nick Barcia, Baruch College
Henry Barker, Tiffin University
Robin Bartlett, Denison University
Laurie Bates, Bryant University
Kari Battaglia, University of North Texas
Leon Battista, Bronx Community College
Amanda Bayer, Swarthmore College
Klaus Becker, Texas Tech University
Richard Beil, Auburn University
Clive Belfield, Queens College
Willie J. Belton, Jr., Georgia Institute of
  Technology
Daniel K. Benjamin, Clemson University
Charles A. Bennett, Gannon University
Emil Berendt, Siena Heights University
Daniel Berkowitz, University of
  Pittsburgh

Kurt Beron, University of Texas, Dallas
Derek Berry, Calhoun Community
  College
Tibor Besedes, Georgia Institute of
  Technology
Thomas Beveridge, Durham Technical
  Community College
Anoop Bhargava, Finger Lakes CC
Eugenie Bietry, Pace University
Kelly Blanchard, Purdue University
Mannie Bloemen, Houston Community
  College
Mark Bock, Loyola College in Maryland
Howard Bodenhorn, Lafayette College
Bruce Bolnick, Northeastern University
Frank Bonello, University of
  Notre Dame
Jeffrey Bookwalter, University of
  Montana
Antonio Bos, Tusculum College
Maristella Botticini, Boston University
George Bowling, St. Charles Community
  College
G. E. Breger, University of South Carolina
Dennis Brennan, William Rainey Harper
  Junior College
Anne E. Bresnock, California State
  Polytechnic University, Pomona,
  and the University of California, Los
  Angeles
Barry Brown, Murray State University
Bruce Brown, California State
  Polytechnic University, Pomona
Jennifer Brown, Eastern Connecticut
  State University
David Brownstone, University of
  California, Irvine
Don Brunner, Spokane Falls Community
  College
Jeff Bruns, Bacone College
David Bunting, Eastern Washington
  University
Barbara Burnell, College of Wooster
Alison Butler, Willamette University
Charles Callahan, III, State University of
  New York at Brockport
Fred Campano, Fordham University
Douglas Campbell, University of
  Memphis
Beth Cantrell, Central Baptist College
Kevin Carlson, University of
  Massachusetts, Boston
Leonard Carlson, Emory University
Arthur Schiller Casimir, Western New
  England College
Lindsay Caulkins, John Carroll
  University
Atreya Chakraborty, Boston College
Suparna Chakraborty, Baruch College of
  the City University of New York

Winston W. Chang, University at Buffalo, The State University of New York

Janie Chermak, University of New Mexico

David Ching, University of Hawaii – Honolulu

Harold Christensen, Centenary College

Daniel Christiansen, Albion College

Susan Christoffersen, Philadelphia University

Samuel Kim-Liang Chuah, Walla Walla College

Dmitriy Chulkov, Indiana University, Kokomo

David Colander, Middlebury College

Daniel Condon, University of Illinois at Chicago; Moraine Valley Community College

Karen Conway, University of New Hampshire

Cesar Corredor, Texas A&M University

David Cowen, University of Texas, Austin

Tyler Cowen, George Mason University

Amy Cramer, Pima Community College, West Campus

Peggy Crane, Southwestern College

Barbara Craig, Oberlin College

Jerry Crawford, Arkansas State University

James Cunningham, Chapman University

Scott Cunningham, Baylor University

Elisabeth Curtis, Dartmouth

James D'Angelo, University of Cincinnati

David Dahl, University of St. Thomas

Sheryll Dahlke, Lees-McRae College

Joseph Dahms, Hood College

Sonia Dalmia, Grand Valley State University

Rosa Lea Danielson, College of DuPage

David Danning, University of Massachusetts, Boston

Minh Quang Dao, Eastern Illinois University

Amlan Datta, Cisco Junior College

David Davenport, McLennan Community College

Stephen Davis, Southwest Minnesota State University

Dale DeBoer, Colorado University, Colorado Springs

Dennis Debrecht, Carroll College

Juan J. DelaCruz, Fashion Institute of Technology and Lehman College

Greg Delemeester, Marietta College

Yanan Di, State University of New York, Stony Brook

Amy Diduch, Mary Baldwin College

Timothy Diette, Washington and Lee University

Vernon J. Dixon, Haverford College

Alan Dobrowolksi, Manchester Community College

Eric Dodge, Hanover College

Carol Dole, Jacksonville University

Michael Donihue, Colby College

Leslie Doss, University of Texas San Antonio

Shahpour Dowlatshahi, Fayetteville Technical Community College

Joanne M. Doyle, James Madison University

Robert Driskill, Ohio State University

James Dulgeroff, San Bernardino Valley College

Kevin Duncan, Colorado State University

Yvonne Durham, Western Washington University

Debra Sabatini Dwyer, State University of New York, Stony Brook

Gary Dymski, University of Southern California

David Eaton, Murray State University

Jay Egger, Towson State University

Erwin Ehrhardt, University of Cincinnati

Ann Eike, University of Kentucky

Eugene Elander, Plymouth State University

Ronald D. Elkins, Central Washington University

Tisha Emerson, Baylor University

Michael Enz, Western New England College

Erwin Erhardt III, University of Cincinnati

William Even, Miami University

Ali Faegh, Houston Community College

Noel J. J. Farley, Bryn Mawr College

Mosin Farminesh, Temple University

Dan Feaster, Miami University of Ohio

Susan Feiner, Virginia Commonwealth University

Getachew Felleke, Albright College

Lois Fenske, South Puget Sound Community College

William Field, DePauw University

Deborah Figart, Richard Stockton College

Barbara Fischer, Cardinal Stritch University

Mary Flannery, Santa Clara University

Bill Foeller, State University of New York, Fredonia

Fred Foldvary, Santa Clara University

Roger Nils Folsom, San Jose State University

Mathew Forstater, University of Missouri-Kansas City

Kevin Foster, The City College of New York

Richard Fowles, University of Utah

Sean Fraley, College of Mount Saint Joseph

Johanna Francis, Fordham University

Roger Frantz, San Diego State University

Mark Frascatore, Clarkson University

Amanda Freeman, Kansas State University

Morris Frommer, Owens Community College

Brandon Fuller, University of Montana

David Fuller, University of Iowa

Mark Funk, University of Arkansas, Little Rock

Alejandro Gallegos, Winona State University

Craig Gallet, California State University, Sacramento

N. Galloro, Chabot College

Bill Galose, Drake University

William Ganley, Buffalo State, SUNY

Martin A. Garrett, Jr., College of William and Mary

Tom Gausman, Northern Illinois University

Shirley J. Gedeon, University of Vermont

Jeff Gerlach, Sungkyunkwan Graduate School of Business

Lisa Giddings, University of Wisconsin, La Crosse

Gary Gigliotti, Rutgers University

Lynn Gillette, Spalding University

Donna Ginther, University of Kansas

James N. Giordano, Villanova University

Amy Glass, Texas A&M University

Sarah L. Glavin, Boston College

Roy Gobin, Loyola University, Chicago

Bill Godair, Landmark College

Bill Goffe, University of Mississippi

Devra Golbe, Hunter College

Roger Goldberg, Ohio Northern University

Joshua Goodman, New York University

Ophelia Goma, DePauw University

John Gonzales, University of San Francisco

David Gordon, Illinois Valley College

Richard Gosselin, Houston Community College

Eugene Gotwalt, Sweet Briar College

John W. Graham, Rutgers University

Douglas Greenley, Morehead State University

Thomas A. Gresik, University of Notre Dame

Lisa M. Grobar, California State University, Long Beach

Wayne A. Grove, Le Moyne College

Daryl Gruver, Mount Vernon Nazarene University

Osman Gulseven, North Carolina State University

Mike Gumpper, Millersville University

Benjamin Gutierrez, Indiana University, Bloomington

A. R. Gutowsky, California State University, Sacramento

Anthony Gyapong, Penn State University, Abington

David R. Hakes, University of Missouri, St. Louis

Bradley Hansen, University of Mary Washington

Stephen Happel, Arizona State University

Mehdi Haririan, Bloomsburg University of Pennsylvania

David Harris, Benedictine College

David Harris, San Diego State University

James Hartley, Mount Holyoke College

Bruce Hartman, California Maritime Academy of California State University

Mitchell Harwitz, University at Buffalo, The State University of New York

Dewey Heinsma, Mt. San Jacinto College

Sara Helms, University of Alabama, Birmingham

Brian Hill, Salisbury University

David Hoaas, Centenary College

Arleen Hoag, Owens Community College

Carol Hogan, University of Michigan, Dearborn

Harry Holzer, Michigan State University

Ward Hooker, Orangeburg-Calhoun Technical College

Bobbie Horn, University of Tulsa

John Horowitz, Ball State University

Ali Faegh, Houston Community College

Daniel Horton, Cleveland State University

Ying Huang, Manhattan College

Janet Hunt, University of Georgia

E. Bruce Hutchinson, University of Tennessee, Chattanooga

Creed Hyatt, Lehigh Carbon Community College

Ana Ichim, Louisiana State University

Aaron Iffland, Rocky Mountain College

Fred Inaba, Washington State University

Richard Inman, Boston College

Aaron Jackson, Bentley College

Brian Jacobsen, Wisconsin Lutheran College

Rus Janis, University of Massachusetts

Jonatan Jelen, The City College of New York

Eric Jensen, The College of William & Mary

Aaron Johnson, Missouri State University

Donn Johnson, Quinnipiac University

Paul Johnson, University of Alaska, Anchorage

Shirley Johnson, Vassar College

Farhoud Kafi, Babson College

R. Kallen, Roosevelt University

Arthur E. Kartman, San Diego State University

Hirshel Kasper, Oberlin College

Brett Katzman, Kennesaw State University

Bruce Kaufman, Georgia State University

Dennis Kaufman, University of Wisconsin, Parkside

Pavel Kapinos, Carleton College

Russell Kashian, University of Wisconsin, Whitewater

Amoz Kats, Virginia Technical University

David Kaun, University of California, Santa Cruz

Brett Katzman, Kennesaw State University

Fred Keast, Portland State University

Stephanie Kelton, University of Missouri, Kansas City

Deborah Kelly, Palomar College

Erasmus Kersting, Texas A&M University

Randall Kesselring, Arkansas State University

Alan Kessler, Providence College

Dominique Khactu, The University of North Dakota

Gary Kikuchi, University of Hawaii, Manoa

Hwagyun Kim, State University of New York, Buffalo

Keon-Ho Kim, University of Utah

Kil-Joong Kim, Austin Peay State University

Sang W. Kim, Hood College

Phillip King, San Francisco State University

Barbara Kneeshaw, Wayne County Community College

Inderjit Kohli, Santa Clara University

Heather Kohls, Marquette University

Janet Koscianski, Shippensburg University

Vani Kotcherlakota, University of Nebraska, Kearney

Barry Kotlove, Edmonds Community College

Kate Krause, University of New Mexico

David Kraybill, University of Georgia

David Kroeker, Tabor College

Stephan Kroll, California State University, Sacramento

Joseph Kubec, Park University

Jacob Kurien, Helzberg School of Management

Rosung Kwak, University of Texas at Austin

Sally Kwak, University of Hawaii-Manoa

Steven Kyle, Cornell University

Anil K. Lal, Pittsburg State University

Melissa Lam, Wellesley College

David Lang, California State University, Sacramento

Gary Langer, Roosevelt University

Anthony Laramie, Merrimack College

Leonard Lardaro, University of Rhode Island

Ross LaRoe, Denison University

Michael Lawlor, Wake Forest University

Pareena Lawrence, University of Minnesota, Morris

Daniel Lawson, Drew University

Mary Rose Leacy, Wagner College

Margaret D. Ledyard, University of Texas, Austin

Jim Lee, Fort Hays State University

Judy Lee, Leeward Community College

Sang H. Lee, Southeastern Louisiana University

Don Leet, California State University, Fresno

Robert J. Lemke, Lake Forest College

Gary Lemon, DePauw University

Alan Leonard, Wilson Technical Community College

Mary Lesser, Iona College

Ding Li, Northern State University

Zhe Li, Stony Brook University

Larry Lichtenstein, Canisius College

Benjamin Liebman, Saint Joseph's University

Jesse Liebman, Kennesaw State University

George Lieu, Tuskegee University

Stephen E. Lile, Western Kentucky University

Jane Lillydahl, University of Colorado at Boulder

Tony Lima, California State University, East Bay

Melissa Lind, University of Texas, Arlington

Al Link, University of North Carolina Greensboro

Charles R. Link, University of Delaware

Robert Litro, U.S. Air Force Academy

Samuel Liu, West Valley College

Jeffrey Livingston, Bentley College

Ming Chien Lo, St. Cloud State University

Burl F. Long, University of Florida

Alina Luca, Drexel University

Adrienne Lucas, Wellesley College

Nancy Lutz, Virginia Technical University

Kristina Lybecker, Colorado College

Gerald Lynch, Purdue University

Karla Lynch, University of North Texas

Ann E. Lyon, University of Alaska, Anchorage

Bruce Madariaga, Montgomery College

Michael Magura, University of Toledo

Marvin S. Margolis, Millersville University of Pennsylvania

Tim Mason, Eastern Illinois University

Don Mathews, Coastal Georgia Community College

Don Maxwell, Central State University

Nan Maxwell, California State University at Hayward

Roberto Mazzoleni, Hofstra University

Cynthia S. McCarty, Jacksonville State University

J. Harold McClure, Jr., Villanova University

Patrick McEwan, Wellesley College

Ronnie McGinness, University of Mississippi

Todd McFall, Wake Forest University

Rick McIntyre, University of Rhode Island

James J. McLain, University of New Orleans

Dawn McLaren, Mesa Community College

B. Starr McMullen, Oregon State University

K. Mehtaboin, College of St. Rose

Martin Melkonian, Hofstra University

Alice Melkumian, Western Illinois University

William Mertens, University of Colorado, Boulder

Randy Methenitis, Richland College

Art Meyer, Lincoln Land Community College

Carrie Meyer, George Mason University

Meghan Millea, Mississippi State University

Jenny Minier, University of Miami

Ida Mirzaie, The Ohio State University

David Mitchell, Missouri State University

Bijan Moeinian, Osceola Campus

Robert Mohr, University of New Hampshire

Shahruz Mohtadi, Suffolk University

Amyaz Moledina, College of Wooster

Gary Mongiovi, St. John's University

Terry D. Monson, Michigan Technological University

Barbara A. Moore, University of Central Florida

Joe L. Moore, Arkansas Technical University

Myra Moore, University of Georgia

Robert Moore, Occidental College

Norma C. Morgan, Curry College

W. Douglas Morgan, University of California, Santa Barbara

David Murphy, Boston College

John Murphy, North Shore Community College, Massachusetts

Ellen Mutari, Richard Stockton College of New Jersey

Steven C. Myers, University of Akron

Veena Nayak, University at Buffalo, The State University of New York

Ron Necoechea, Robert Wesleyan College

Doug Nelson, Spokane Community College

Randy Nelson, Colby College

David Nickerson, University of British Columbia

Sung No, Southern University and A&M College

Rachel Nugent, Pacific Lutheran University

Akorlie A. Nyatepe-Coo, University of Wisconsin LaCrosse

Norman P. Obst, Michigan State University

William C. O'Connor, Western Montana College

Constantin Ogloblin, Georgia Southern University

David O'Hara, Metropolitan State University

Albert Okunade, University of Memphis

Ronald Olive, University of Massachusetts, Lowell

Martha L. Olney, University of California, Berkeley

Kent Olson, Oklahoma State University

Jaime Ortiz, Florida Atlantic University

Theresa Osborne, Hunter College

Donald J. Oswald, California State University, Bakersfield

Mete Ozcan, Brooklyn College

Alexandre Padilla, Metropolitan State College of Denver

Aaron Pankratz, Fresno City College

Niki Papadopoulou, University of Cyprus

Walter Park, American University

Carl Parker, Fort Hays State University

Spiro Patton, Rasmussen College

Andrew Pearlman, Bard College

Charlie Pearson, Southern Maine Community College

Richard Peck, University of Illinois at Chicago

Don Peppard, Connecticut College

Elizabeth Perry, Randolph College

Nathan Perry, University of Utah

Joe Petry, University of Illinois-Urbana-Champaign

Joseph A. Petry, University of Illinois

Mary Ann Pevas, Winona State University

Chris Phillips, Somerset Community College

Jeff Phillips, Morrisville Community College

Frankie Pircher, University of Missouri, Kansas City

Tony Pizelo, Spokane Community College

Dennis Placone, Clemson University

Mike Pogodzinski, San Jose State University

Linnea Polgreen, University of Iowa

Elizabeth Porter, University of North Florida

Bob Potter, University of Central Florida

Ed Price, Oklahoma State University

Abe Qastin, Lakeland College

Kevin Quinn, St. Norbert College

Ramkishen S. Rajan, George Mason University

James Rakowski, University of Notre Dame

Amy Ramirez-Gay, Eastern Michigan University

Paul Rappoport, Temple University

Artatrana Ratha, St. Cloud State University

Michael Rendich, Westchester Community College

Lynn Rittenoure, University of Tulsa

Travis Roach, Texas Tech University

Brian Roberson, Miami University

Michael Robinson, Mount Holyoke College

Juliette Roddy, University of Michigan, Dearborn

Michael Rolleigh, University of Minnesota

Belinda Roman, Palo Alto College

S. Scanlon Romer, Delta College

Brian Rosario, University of California, Davis

Paul Roscelli, Canada College

David C. Rose, University of Missouri-St. Louis

Greg Rose, Sacramento City College

Richard Rosenberg, Pennsylvania State University

Robert Rosenman, Washington State University

Robert Rosenthal, Stonehill College

Howard Ross, Baruch College

Paul Rothstein, Washington University

Charles Roussel, Louisiana State University

Jeff Rubin, Rutgers University

Mark Rush, University of Florida

Dereka Rushbrook, Ripon College

Jerard Russo, University of Hawaii

Luz A. Saavedra, University of St. Thomas

William Samuelson, Boston University School of Management

Allen Sanderson, University of Chicago

David Saner, Springfield College – Benedictine University

Ahmad Saranjam, Bridgewater State College

David L. Schaffer, Haverford College

Eric Schansberg, Indiana University – Southeast

Robert Schenk, Saint Joseph's College

Ramon Schreffler, Houston Community College System (retired)

Adina Schwartz, Lakeland College

Jerry Schwartz, Broward Community College

Amy Scott, DeSales University

Gary Sellers, University of Akron

Atindra Sen, Miami University

Chad Settle, University of Tulsa

Jean Shackleford, Bucknell University

Ronald Shadbegian, University of Massachusetts, Dartmouth

Linda Shaffer, California State University, Fresno

Dennis Shannon, Southwestern Illinois College

Stephen L. Shapiro, University of North Florida

Paul Shea, University of Oregon

Geoff Shepherd, University of Massachusetts Amherst

Bih-Hay Sheu, University of Texas at Austin

David Shideler, Murray State University

Alden Shiers, California Polytechnic State University

Gerald Shilling, Eastfield College

Dongsoo Shin, Santa Clara University

Elias Shukralla, St. Louis Community College, Meramec

Anne Shugars, Harford Community College

Richard Sicotte, University of Vermont

William Simeone, Providence College

Scott Simkins, North Carolina Agricultural and Technical State University

Larry Singell, University of Oregon

Priyanka Singh, University of Texas, Dallas

Sue Skeath, Wellesley College

Edward Skelton, Southern Methodist University

Ken Slaysman, York College

John Smith, New York University

Paula Smith, Central State University, Oklahoma

Donald Snyder, Utah State University

Marcia Snyder, College of Charleston

David Sobiechowski, Wayne State University

John Solow, University of Iowa

Angela Sparkman, Itawamba Community College

Martin Spechler, Indiana University

David Spigelman, University of Miami

Arun Srinivasa, Indiana University, Southeast

David J. St. Clair, California State University at Hayward

Sarah Stafford, College of William & Mary

Richard Stahl, Louisiana State University

Rebecca Stein, University of Pennsylvania

Mary Stevenson, University of Massachusetts, Boston

Susan Stojanovic, Washington University, St. Louis

Courtenay Stone, Ball State University

Ernst W. Stromsdorfer, Washington State University

Edward Stuart, Northeastern Illinois University

Chris Stufflebean, Southwestern Oklahoma State University

Chuck Stull, Kalamazoo College

Kenneth Slaysman, York College of Pennsylvania

Della Sue, Marist College

Abdulhamid Sukar, Cameron University

Christopher Surfield, Saginaw Valley State University

Rodney B. Swanson, University of California, Los Angeles

James Swofford, University of Alabama

Bernica Tackett, Pulaski Technical College

Michael Taussig, Rutgers University

Samia Tavares, Rochester Institute of Technology

Timothy Taylor, Stanford University

William Taylor, New Mexico Highlands University

Sister Beth Anne Tercek, SND, Notre Dame College of Ohio

Henry Terrell, University of Maryland

Jennifer Thacher, University of New Mexico

Donna Thompson, Brookdale Community College

Robert Tokle, Idaho State University

David Tolman, Boise State University

Susanne Toney, Hampton University

Karen M. Travis, Pacific Lutheran University

Jack Trierweler, Northern State University

Brian M. Trinque, University of Texas at Austin

HuiKuan Tseng, University of North Carolina at Charlotte

Boone Turchi, University of North Carolina

Kristin Van Gaasbeck, California State University, Sacramento

Amy Vander Laan, Hastings College

Ann Velenchik, Wellesley College

Lawrence Waldman, University of New Mexico

Chris Waller, Indiana University, Bloomington

William Walsh, University of St. Thomas

Chunbei Wang, University of St. Thomas

John Watkins, Westminster

Janice Weaver, Drake University

Bruce Webb, Gordon College

Ross Weiner, The City College of New York

Elaine Wendt, Milwaukee Area Technical College

Walter Wessels, North Carolina State University

Christopher Westley, Jacksonville State University

Joan Whalen-Ayyappan, DeVry Institute of Technology

Robert Whaples, Wake Forest University

Leonard A. White, University of Arkansas

Alex Wilson, Rhode Island College

Wayne Winegarden, Marymount University

Jennifer Wissink, Cornell University

Arthur Woolf, University of Vermont

Paula Worthington, Northwestern University

Bill Yang, Georgia Southern University

Ben Young, University of Missouri, Kansas City
Darrel Young, University of Texas
Michael Youngblood, Rock Valley College
Jay Zagorsky, Boston University

Alexander Zampieron, Bentley College
Sourushe Zandvakili, University of Cincinnati
Walter J. Zeiler, University of Michigan

Abera Zeyege, Ball State University
James Ziliak, Indiana University, Bloomington
Jason Zimmerman, South Dakota State University

We welcome comments about the 12th edition. Please write to us care of David Alexander, Executive Editor, Pearson Economics, 501 Boylston Street, Boston, MA 02116.

Karl E. Case

Ray C. Fair

Sharon M. Oster

Save a Tree!

Many of the components of the teaching and learning package are available online. Online supplements conserve paper and allow you to select and print only the material you plan to use. For more information, please contact your Pearson sales representative.

Principles of
Macroeconomics

The Scope and Method of Economics

1

The study of economics should begin with a sense of wonder. Pause for a moment and consider a typical day in your life. It might start with a bagel made in a local bakery with flour produced in Minnesota from wheat grown in Kansas. After class you drive with a friend on an interstate highway that is part of a system that took 20 years and billions of dollars to build. You stop for gasoline refined in Louisiana from Saudi Arabian crude oil. Later, you log onto the Web with a laptop assembled in Indonesia from parts made in China and Skype with your brother in Mexico City. You use or consume tens of thousands of things. Somebody organized men and women and materials to produce and distribute them. Thousands of decisions went into their completion, and somehow they got to you.

In the United States, about 150 million people—almost half the total population—work at hundreds of thousands of different jobs producing nearly $18 trillion worth of goods and services every year. Some cannot find work; some choose not to work. The United States imports more than $300 billion worth of automobiles and parts and more than $350 billion worth of petroleum and petroleum products each year; it exports around $140 billion worth of agricultural products, including food. In the modern economy, consumers' choices include products made all over the globe.

Economics is the study of how individuals and societies choose to use the scarce resources that nature and previous generations have provided. The key word in this definition is *choose*. Economics is a behavioral, or social, science. In large measure, it is the study of how people make choices. The choices that people make, when added up, translate into societal choices.

economics The study of how individuals and societies choose to use the scarce resources that nature and previous generations have provided.

The purpose of this chapter and the next is to elaborate on this definition and to introduce the subject matter of economics. What is produced? How is it produced? Who gets it? Why? Is the result good or bad? Can it be improved?

1.1 LEARNING OBJECTIVE

Identify three key reasons to study economics. Think of an example from your life in which understanding opportunity costs or the principle of efficient markets could make a difference in your decision making.

Why Study Economics?

There are three main reasons to study economics: to learn a way of thinking, to understand society, and to be an informed citizen.

To Learn a Way of Thinking

Probably the most important reason for studying economics is to learn a way of thinking. Economics has three fundamental concepts that, once absorbed, can change the way you look at everyday choices: opportunity cost, marginalism, and the working of efficient markets.

Opportunity Cost What happens in an economy is the outcome of thousands of individual decisions. People must decide how to divide their incomes among all the goods and services available in the marketplace. They must decide whether to work, whether to go to school, and how much to save. Businesses must decide what to produce, how much to produce, how much to charge, and where to locate. Economic analysis provides a structured way of thinking about these types of decisions.

opportunity cost The best alternative that we forgo, or give up, when we make a choice or a decision.

Nearly all decisions involve trade-offs. A key concept that recurs in analyzing the decision-making process is the notion of *opportunity cost*. The full "cost" of making a specific choice includes what we give up by not making the best alternative choice. The best alternative that we forgo, or give up, when we make a choice or a decision is called the **opportunity cost** of that decision.

When asked how much a movie costs, most people cite the ticket price. For an economist, this is only part of the answer: to see a movie takes not only a ticket but also time. The opportunity cost of going to a movie is the value of the other things you could have done with the same money and time. If you decide to take time off from work, the opportunity cost of your leisure is the pay that you would have earned had you worked. Part of the cost of a college education is the income you could have earned by working full-time instead of going to school.

scarce Limited.

Opportunity costs arise because resources are scarce. **Scarce** simply means limited. Consider one of our most important resources—time. There are only 24 hours in a day, and we must live our lives under this constraint. A farmer in rural Brazil must decide whether it is better to continue to farm or to go to the city and look for a job. A hockey player at the University of Vermont must decide whether to play on the varsity team or spend more time studying.

marginalism The process of analyzing the additional or incremental costs or benefits arising from a choice or decision.

Marginalism A second key concept used in analyzing choices is the notion of **marginalism**. In weighing the costs and benefits of a decision, it is important to weigh only the costs and benefits that arise from the decision. Suppose, for example, that you live in New Orleans and that you are weighing the costs and benefits of visiting your mother in Iowa. If business required that you travel to Kansas City anyway, the cost of visiting Mom would be only the additional, or *marginal*, time and money cost of getting to Iowa from Kansas City.

There are numerous examples in which the concept of marginal cost is useful. For an airplane that is about to take off with empty seats, the marginal cost of an extra passenger is essentially zero; the total cost of the trip is roughly unchanged by the addition of an extra passenger. Thus, setting aside a few seats to be sold at big discounts through www.priceline.com or other Web sites can be profitable even if the fare for those seats is far below the average cost per seat of making the trip. As long as the airline succeeds in filling seats that would otherwise have been empty, doing so is profitable.

Efficient Markets—No Free Lunch   Suppose you are ready to check out of a busy grocery store on the day before a storm and seven checkout registers are open with several people in each line. Which line should you choose? Clearly you should go to the shortest line! But if everyone thinks this way—as is likely—all the lines will be equally long as people move around. Economists often loosely refer to "good deals" or risk-free ventures as *profit opportunities*. Using the term loosely, a profit opportunity exists at the checkout lines when one line is shorter than the others. In general, such profit opportunities are rare. At any time, many people are searching for them; as a consequence, few exist. Markets like this, where any profit opportunities are eliminated almost instantaneously, are said to be **efficient markets**. (We discuss *markets*, the institutions through which buyers and sellers interact and engage in exchange, in detail in Chapter 2.)

> **efficient market**   A market in which profit opportunities are eliminated almost instantaneously.

The common way of expressing the efficient markets concept is "there's no such thing as a free lunch." How should you react when a stockbroker calls with a hot tip on the stock market? With skepticism. Thousands of individuals each day are looking for hot tips in the market. If a particular tip about a stock is valid, there will be an immediate rush to buy the stock, which will quickly drive up its price. This view that very few profit opportunities exist can, of course, be carried too far. There is a story about two people walking along, one an economist and one not. The non-economist sees a $20 bill on the sidewalk and says, "There's a $20 bill on the sidewalk." The economist replies, "That is not possible. If there were, somebody would already have picked it up."

There are clearly times when profit opportunities exist. Someone has to be first to get the news, and some people have quicker insights than others. Nevertheless, news travels fast, and there are thousands of people with quick insights. The general view that large profit opportunities are rare is close to the mark and is powerful in helping to guide decision making.

> The study of economics teaches us a way of thinking and helps us make decisions.

To Understand Society

Another reason for studying economics is to understand society better. Past and present economic decisions have an enormous influence on the character of life in a society. The current state of the physical environment, the level of material well-being, and the nature and number of jobs are all products of the economic system.

At no time has the impact of economic change on a society been more evident than in England during the late eighteenth and early nineteenth centuries, a period that we now call the **Industrial Revolution**. Increases in the productivity of agriculture, new manufacturing technologies, and development of more efficient forms of transportation led to a massive movement of the British population from the countryside to the city. At the beginning of the eighteenth century, approximately 2 out of 3 people in Great Britain worked in agriculture. By 1812, only 1 in 3 remained in agriculture; by 1900, the figure was fewer than 1 in 10. People jammed into overcrowded cities and worked long hours in factories. England had changed completely in two centuries—a period that in the run of history was nothing more than the blink of an eye.

> **Industrial Revolution**   The period in England during the late eighteenth and early nineteenth centuries in which new manufacturing technologies and improved transportation gave rise to the modern factory system and a massive movement of the population from the countryside to the cities.

The discipline of economics began to take shape during this period. Social critics and philosophers looked around and knew that their philosophies must expand to accommodate the changes. Adam Smith's *Wealth of Nations* appeared in 1776. It was followed by the writings of David Ricardo, Karl Marx, Thomas Malthus, and others. Each tried to make sense out of what was happening. Who was building the factories? Why? What determined the level of wages paid to workers or the price of food? What would happen in the future, and what *should* happen? The people who asked these questions were the first economists.

Societal changes are often driven by economics. Consider the developments in the early years of the World Wide Web. Changes in the ways people communicate with one another and with the rest of the world, largely created by private enterprise seeking profits, have affected almost every aspect of our lives, from the way we interact with friends and family to the jobs that we have and the way cities and governments are organized.

> The study of economics is an essential part of the study of society.

To Be an Informed Citizen

A knowledge of economics is essential to being an informed citizen. Between 2008 and 2013 much of the world struggled with a major recession and slow recovery, leaving millions of people around the world out of work. Understanding what happens in a recession and what the government can and cannot do to help in a recovery is an essential part of being an informed citizen.

Economics is also essential in understanding a range of other everyday government decisions at the local and federal levels. Why do governments pay for public schools and roads, but not cell phones? The federal government under President Barack Obama moved toward universal health care for U.S. citizens. What are the pros and cons of this policy? In some states, scalping tickets to a ball game is illegal. Is this a good policy or not? Every day, across the globe, people engage in political decision making around questions like these, questions that depend on an understanding of economics.

> To be an informed citizen requires a basic understanding of economics.

1.2 LEARNING OBJECTIVE

Describe microeconomics, macroeconomics, and the diverse fields of economics.

The Scope of Economics

Most students taking economics for the first time are surprised by the breadth of what they study. Some think that economics will teach them about the stock market or what to do with their money. Others think that economics deals exclusively with problems such as inflation and unemployment. In fact, it deals with all those subjects, but they are pieces of a much larger puzzle. Economists use their tools to study a wide range of topics.

The easiest way to get a feel for the breadth and depth of what you will be studying is to explore briefly the way economics is organized. First of all, there are two major divisions of economics: microeconomics and macroeconomics.

Microeconomics and Macroeconomics

microeconomics The branch of economics that examines the functioning of individual industries and the behavior of individual decision-making units—that is, firms and households.

Microeconomics deals with the functioning of individual industries and the behavior of individual economic decision-making units: firms and households. Firms' choices about what to produce and how much to charge and households' choices about what and how much to buy help to explain why the economy produces the goods and services it does.

Another big question addressed by microeconomics is who gets the goods and services that are produced? Understanding the forces that determine the distribution of output is the province of microeconomics. Microeconomics helps us to understand how resources are distributed among households. What determines who is rich and who is poor?

macroeconomics The branch of economics that examines the economic behavior of aggregates—income, employment, output, and so on—on a national scale.

Macroeconomics looks at the economy as a whole. Instead of trying to understand what determines the output of a single firm or industry or what the consumption patterns are of a single household or group of households, macroeconomics examines the factors that determine national output, or national product. Microeconomics is concerned with *household* income; macroeconomics deals with *national income*.

Whereas microeconomics focuses on individual product prices and relative prices, macroeconomics looks at the overall price level and how quickly (or slowly) it is rising (or falling). Microeconomics questions how many people will be hired (or fired) this year in a particular industry or in a certain geographic area and focuses on the factors that determine how much labor a firm or an industry will hire. Macroeconomics deals with *aggregate* employment and unemployment: how many jobs exist in the economy as a whole and how many people who are willing to work are not able to find work.

ECONOMICS IN PRACTICE

iPod and the World

It is impossible to understand the workings of an economy without first understanding the ways in which economies are connected across borders. The United States was importing goods and services at a rate of more than $2.8 trillion per year in 2014 and was exporting at a rate of more than $2.3 trillion per year.

For literally hundreds of years, the virtues of free trade have been the subject of heated debate. Opponents have argued that buying foreign-produced goods costs Americans jobs and hurts U.S. producers. Proponents argue that there are gains from trade—that all countries can gain from specializing in the production of the goods and services they produce best.

In the modern world, it is not always easy to track where products are made. A sticker that says "Made in China" can often be misleading. Recent studies of two iconic U.S. products, the iPod and the Barbie doll, make this complexity clear.

The Barbie doll is one of Mattel's best and longest selling products. The Barbie was designed in the United States. It is made of plastic fashioned in Taiwan, which came originally from the Mideast in the form of petroleum. Barbie's hair comes from Japan, while the cloth for her clothes mostly comes from China. Most of the assembly of the Barbie is also done in China, using, as we see, pieces from across the globe. A doll that sells for $10 in the United States carries an export value when leaving Hong Kong of $2, of which only 35 cents is for Chinese labor, with most of the rest covering transportation and raw materials. Because the Barbie comes to the United States from assembly in China and transport from Hong Kong, some would count it as being produced in China. Yet, for this Barbie, $8 of its retail value of $10 is captured by the United States![1]

The iPod is similar. A recent study by three economists, Greg Linden, Kenneth Kraemer, and Jason Dedrick, found that once one includes Apple's payment for its intellectual property, distribution costs, and production costs for some components, almost 80 percent of the retail price of the iPod is captured by the United States.[2] Moreover, for some of the

other parts of the iPod, it is not easy to tell exactly where they are produced. The hard drive, a relatively expensive component, was produced in Japan by Toshiba, but some of the components of that hard drive were actually produced elsewhere in Asia. Indeed, for the iPod, which is composed of many small parts, it is almost impossible to accurately tell exactly where each piece was produced without pulling it apart.

So, next time you see a label saying "Made in China" keep in mind that from an economics point of view, one often has to dig a little deeper to see what is really going on.

THINKING PRACTICALLY

1. What do you think accounts for *where* components of the iPod and Barbie are made?

[1] For a discussion of the Barbie see Robert Feenstra, "Integration of Trade and Disintegration of Production in the Global Economy," *Journal of Economic Perspectives*, Fall 1998: 31–50.

[2] Greg Linden, Kenneth Kraemer, and Jason Dedrick, "Who Profits from Innovation in Global Value Chains?" *Industrial and Corporate Change*, 2010: 81–116.

To summarize:

> Microeconomics looks at the individual unit—the household, the firm, the industry. It sees and examines the "trees." Macroeconomics looks at the whole, the aggregate. It sees and analyzes the "forest."

Table 1.1 summarizes these divisions of economics and some of the subjects with which they are concerned.

The Diverse Fields of Economics

Individual economists focus their research and study in many different areas. The subfields of economics are listed in Table 1.2 along with a sample research or policy question that an economist in this subfield might study.

TABLE 1.1 Examples of Microeconomic and Macroeconomic Concerns

Division of Economics	Production	Prices	Income	Employment
Microeconomics	*Production/output in individual industries and businesses* How much steel How much office space How many cars	*Prices of individual goods and services* Price of medical care Price of gasoline Food prices Apartment rents	*Distribution of income and wealth* Wages in the auto industry Minimum wage Executive salaries Poverty	*Employment by individual businesses and industries* Jobs in the steel industry Number of employees in a firm Number of accountants
Macroeconomics	*National production/output* Total industrial output Gross domestic product Growth of output	*Aggregate price level* Consumer prices Producer prices Rate of inflation	*National income* Total wages and salaries Total corporate profits	*Employment and unemployment in the economy* Total number of jobs Unemployment rate

TABLE 1.2 The Fields of Economics

Behavioral economics	Do aggregate household savings increase when we automatically enroll people in savings programs and let them opt out as opposed to requiring them to sign up?
Comparative economic systems	How does the resource allocation process differ in market versus command and control systems?
Econometrics	What inferences can we make based on conditional moment inequalities?
Economic development	Does increasing employment opportunities for girls in developing nations increase their educational achievement?
Economic history	How did the growth of railroads and improvement in transportation more generally change the U.S. banking systems in the nineteenth century?
Environmental economics	What effect would a tax on carbon have on emissions? Is a tax better or worse than rules?
Finance	Is high frequency trading socially beneficial?
Health economics	Do co-pays by patients change the choice and use of medicines by insured patients?
The history of economic thought	How did Aristotle think about just prices?
Industrial organization	How do we explain price wars in the airline industry?
International economics	What are the benefits and costs of free trade? Does concern about the environment change our views of free trade?
Labor economics	Will increasing the minimum wage decrease employment opportunities?
Law and economics	Does the current U.S. patent law increase or decrease the rate of innovation?
Public economics	Why is corruption more widespread in some countries than in others?
Urban and regional economics	Do enterprise zones improve employment opportunities in central cities?

The Method of Economics

Economics asks and attempts to answer two kinds of questions: positive and normative. **Positive economics** attempts to understand behavior and the operation of economic systems *without making judgments* about whether the outcomes are good or bad. It strives to describe what exists and how it works. What determines the wage rate for unskilled workers? What would happen if we abolished the corporate income tax? The answers to such questions are the subject of positive economics.

In contrast, **normative economics** looks at the outcomes of economic behavior and asks whether they are good or bad and whether they can be made better. Normative economics involves judgments and prescriptions for courses of action. Should the government subsidize or regulate the cost of higher education? Should the United States allow importers to sell foreign-produced goods that compete with U.S.-made products? Should we reduce or eliminate inheritance taxes? Normative economics is often called *policy economics*.

Of course, most normative questions involve positive questions. To know whether the government *should* take a particular action, we must know first if it *can* and second what the consequences are likely to be.

Theories and Models

In many disciplines, including physics, chemistry, meteorology, political science, and economics, theorists build formal models of behavior. A **model** is a formal statement of a theory. It is usually a mathematical statement of a presumed relationship between two or more variables.

A **variable** is a measure that can change from time to time or from observation to observation. Income is a variable—it has different values for different people and different values for the same person at different times. The price of a quart of milk is a variable; it has different values at different stores and at different times. There are countless other examples.

Because all models simplify reality by stripping part of it away, they are abstractions. Critics of economics often point to abstraction as a weakness. Most economists, however, see abstraction as a real strength.

The easiest way to see how abstraction can be helpful is to think of a map. A map is a representation of reality that is simplified and abstract. A city or state appears on a piece of paper as a series of lines and colors. The amount of reality that the mapmaker can strip away before the map loses something essential depends on what the map will be used for. If you want to drive from St. Louis to Phoenix, you need to know only the major interstate highways and roads. However, to travel around Phoenix, you may need to see every street and alley.

Like maps, economic models are abstractions that strip away detail to expose only those aspects of behavior that are important to the question being asked. The principle that irrelevant detail should be cut away is called the principle of **Ockham's razor** after the fourteenth-century philosopher William of Ockham.

Be careful—although abstraction is a powerful tool for exposing and analyzing specific aspects of behavior, it is possible to oversimplify. Economic models often strip away a good deal of social and political reality to get at underlying concepts. When an economic theory is used to help formulate actual government or institutional policy, political and social reality must often be reintroduced if the policy is to have a chance of working.

The appropriate amount of simplification and abstraction depends on the use to which the model will be put. To return to the map example: You do not want to walk around San Francisco with a map made for drivers—there are too many very steep hills.

All Else Equal It is usually true that whatever you want to explain with a model depends on more than one factor. Suppose, for example, that you want to explain the total number of miles driven by automobile owners in the United States. Many things might affect total miles driven. More or fewer people may be driving. This number, in turn, can be affected by changes in the driving age, by population growth, or by changes in state laws. Other factors might include the price of gasoline, the household's income, the number and age of children in the household, the distance from home to work, the location of shopping facilities, and the availability and

---

1.3 LEARNING OBJECTIVE

Think about an example of bad causal inference leading to erroneous decision making. Identify the four main goals of economic policy.

positive economics An approach to economics that seeks to understand behavior and the operation of systems without making judgments. It describes what exists and how it works.

normative economics An approach to economics that analyzes outcomes of economic behavior, evaluates them as good or bad, and may prescribe courses of action. Also called *policy economics*.

model A formal statement of a theory, usually a mathematical statement of a presumed relationship between two or more variables.

variable A measure that can change from time to time or from observation to observation.

Ockham's razor The principle that irrelevant detail should be cut away.

quality of public transport. When any of these variables change, the members of the household may drive more or less. If changes in any of these variables affect large numbers of households across the country, the total number of miles driven will change.

Very often we need to isolate or separate these effects. For example, suppose we want to know the impact on driving of a higher tax on gasoline. This increased tax would raise the price of gasoline at the pump, and this could reduce driving.

To isolate the impact of one single factor, we use the device of **ceteris paribus, or all else equal.** We ask, "What is the impact of a change in gasoline price on driving behavior, ceteris paribus, or assuming that nothing else changes?" If gasoline prices rise by 10 percent, how much less driving will there be, assuming no simultaneous change in anything else—that is, assuming that income, number of children, population, laws, and so on, all remain constant? Using the device of ceteris paribus is one part of the process of abstraction. In formulating economic theory, the concept helps us simplify reality to focus on the relationships that interest us.

Expressing Models in Words, Graphs, and Equations   Consider the following statements: Lower airline ticket prices cause people to fly more frequently. Higher gasoline prices cause people to drive less and to buy more fuel-efficient cars. By themselves, these observations are of some interest. But for a firm, government, or an individual to make good decisions, oftentimes they need to know more. How much does driving fall when prices rise? Quantitative analysis is an important part of economics as well. Throughout this book, we will use both graphs and equations to capture the quantitative side of our economic observations and predictions. The appendix to this chapter reviews some graphing techniques.

Cautions and Pitfalls   In formulating theories and models, it is especially important to seperate causation from correlation.

What Is Really Causal?   In much of economics, we are interested in cause and effect. But cause and effect are often difficult to figure out. Recently, many people in the United States have begun to worry about consumption of soda and obesity. Some areas have begun taxing soda, trying to raise the price so that people will drink less of it. Is this working? Answering this question turns out to be hard. Suppose we see that one city raises the tax and at more or less the same time, soda consumption falls. Did the increased tax and price really *cause* all or most of the change in behavior? Or perhaps the city that voted the soda tax increase is more health conscious than its neighbors and it is that health consciousness that accounts for both the town's decision to raise taxes *and* its reduction in soda purchases. In this case, raising taxes in the neighboring towns will not necessarily reduce soda consumption. Sorting out causality from correlation is not always easy, particularly when one wants a quantitative answer to a question.

In our everyday lives, we often confuse causality. When two events occur in a sequence, it seems natural to think A caused B. I walked under a ladder and subsequently stubbed my toe. Did the ladder cause my bad luck? Most of us would laugh at this. But everyday we hear stock market analysts make a similar causal jump. "Today the Dow Jones industrial average rose 100 points on heavy trading due to progress in talks between Israel and Syria." How do they know this? Investors respond to many news events on any given day. Figuring out which one, if any, causes the stock market to rise is not easy. The error of inferring causality from two events happening one after the other is called the ***post hoc, ergo propter hoc*** fallacy ("after this, therefore because of this"). The *Economics in Practice* box describes a causality confusion in looking at peer effects.

Testing Theories and Models: Empirical Economics   In science, a theory is rejected when it fails to explain what is observed or when another theory better explains what is observed. The collection and use of data to test economic theories is called **empirical economics.**

Numerous large data sets are available to facilitate economic research. For example, economists studying the labor market can now test behavioral theories against the actual working experiences of thousands of randomly selected people who have been surveyed continuously since the 1960s. Macroeconomists continuously monitoring and studying the behavior of the national economy at the National Bureau of Economic Research (NBER), analyze thousands of items of data, collected by both government agencies and private companies, over the Internet. Firms like Google, Uber, and Amazon have an enormous amount of data about individual consumers that they analyze with the help of PhD economists to understand consumers' buying

---

ceteris paribus, **or all else equal**   A device used to analyze the relationship between two variables while the values of other variables are held unchanged.

post hoc, ergo propter hoc   Literally, "after this (in time), therefore because of this." A common error made in thinking about causation: If Event A happens before Event B, it is not necessarily true that A caused B.

empirical economics   The collection and use of data to test economic theories.

ECONOMICS IN PRACTICE

Does Your Roommate Matter for Your Grades?

Most parents are concerned about their children's friends. Often they worry that if one of their children has a misbehaving friend, their own child will be led astray. And, in fact, in many areas of life, there are strong indications that *peer effects* matter. The likelihood that a child will be obese, have difficulties in school, or engage in criminal activity all seem to be higher if their friends also have these issues. And yet, in looking at peer effects, it is not hard to see the problem of causality we described in the text. At least to some extent, children choose their own friends. The father worried about the bad influence of his son's friends on his own son should perhaps be equally worried about what his son's choice of friends says about that son's inclinations. Did the friends cause the misbehavior or did an inclination toward mischief cause the son's choice of friends?

Sorting out causality in peer effects, given that peer groups are oftentimes partially a matter of choice, is difficult. But several recent economics studies of the effect of roommates on college grades do a nice job of sorting out the causality puzzle. Dartmouth college, in common with many other schools, randomly assigns roommates to freshmen. In this case, part of a student's peer group—his or her roommate—is not a matter of choice, but a matter of chance. Bruce Sacerdote, a professor at Dartmouth, used data on freshmen academic and social performance, combined with their background data, to test the peer effects from different types of roommates.[1] Sacerdote found that after taking into account many background characteristics, there were strong roommate effects both on grade point average, effort in school, and fraternity membership.

Of course, a roommate is only part of one's peer group. At the U.S. Air Force Academy, students are assigned to 30-person squadrons with whom they eat, study, live, and do intramural sports. Again, these groups were randomly

assigned, so one did not have the problem of similarly inclined people choosing one another. Scott Carrell, Richard Fullerton, and James West found that for this intense peer group, there were strong peer effects on academic effort and performance.[2] The bottom line: Choose your friends wisely!

THINKING PRACTICALLY

1. Would you expect college seniors who choose their own roommates to have more or less similar grades than college freshmen who are assigned as roommates? Why or why not?

[1] Bruce Sacerdote, "Peer Effects with Random Assignment: Results for Dartmouth Roommates," *Quarterly Journal of Economics*, 2001: 681–704.

[2] Scott E. Carrell, Richard L. Fullerton, and James E. West, "Does Your Cohort Matter? Measuring Peer Effects in College Achievement," *Journal of Labor Economics*, 2009: 439–464.

behavior and improve the profitability of their businesses. In doing this analysis, economicsts have learned to be especially careful about causality issues.

In the natural sciences, controlled experiments, typically done in the lab, are a standard way of testing theories. In recent years, economics has seen an increase in the use of experiments, both in the field and in the lab, as a tool to test its theories. One economist, John List of Chicago, tested the effect on prices of changing the way auctions for rare baseball cards were run by sports memorabilia dealers in trade shows. (The experiment used a standard Cal Ripkin Jr. card.) Another economist, Keith Chen of UCLA, has used experiments with monkeys to investigate the deeper biological roots of human decision making.

Economic Policy

Economic theory helps us understand how the world works, but the formulation of *economic policy* requires a second step. We must have objectives. What do we want to change? Why? What is good and what is bad about the way the system is operating? Can we make it better?

Such questions force us to be specific about the grounds for judging one outcome superior to another. What does it mean to be better? Four criteria are frequently applied in judging economic outcomes:

1. Efficiency
2. Equity
3. Growth
4. Stability

Efficiency   In physics, "efficiency" refers to the ratio of useful energy delivered by a system to the energy supplied to it. An efficient automobile engine, for example, is one that uses a small amount of fuel per mile for a given level of power.

efficiency In economics, "efficiency" means "allocative efficiency." An efficient economy is one that produces what people want at the least possible cost.

In economics, **efficiency** means *allocative efficiency*. An efficient economy is one that produces what people want at the least possible cost. If the system allocates resources to the production of goods and services that nobody wants, it is inefficient. If all members of a particular society were vegetarians and somehow half of all that society's resources were used to produce meat, the result would be inefficient.

The clearest example of an efficient change is a voluntary exchange. If you and I each want something that the other has and we agree to exchange, we are both better off and no one loses. When a company reorganizes its production or adopts a new technology that enables it to produce more of its product with fewer resources, without sacrificing quality, it has made an efficient change. At least potentially, the resources saved could be used to produce more of something else.

Inefficiencies can arise in numerous ways. Sometimes they are caused by government regulations or tax laws that distort otherwise sound economic decisions. Suppose that land in Ohio is best suited for corn production and that land in Kansas is best suited for wheat production. A law that requires Kansas to produce only corn and Ohio to produce only wheat would be inefficient. If firms that cause environmental damage are not held accountable for their actions, the incentive to minimize those damages is lost and the result is inefficient.

equity Fairness.

Equity   While efficiency has a fairly precise definition that can be applied with some degree of rigor, **equity** (fairness) lies in the eye of the beholder. To many, fairness implies a more equal distribution of income and wealth. For others, fairness involves giving people what they earn. In 2013, French economist Thomas Piketty's popular new book *Capital in the Twenty-First Century*, brought new historical data to our attention on the extent of inequality across the Western world.

Growth   As the result of technological change, the building of machinery, and the acquisition of knowledge, societies learn to produce new goods and services and to produce old ones better. In the early days of the U.S. economy, it took nearly half the population to produce the required food supply. Today less than 2 percent of the country's population works in agriculture.

economic growth An increase in the total output of an economy.

When we devise new and better ways of producing the goods and services we use now and when we develop new goods and services, the total amount of production in the economy increases. **Economic growth** is an increase in the total output of an economy. If output grows faster than the population, output per person rises and standards of living increase. Rural and agrarian societies become modern industrial societies as a result of economic growth and rising per capita output.

Some policies discourage economic growth, and others encourage it. Tax laws, for example, can be designed to encourage the development and application of new production techniques. Research and development in some societies are subsidized by the government. Building roads, highways, bridges, and transport systems in developing countries may speed up the process of economic growth. If businesses and wealthy people invest their wealth outside their country rather than in their country's industries, growth in their home country may be slowed.

stability A condition in which national output is growing steadily, with low inflation and full employment of resources.

Stability   Economic **stability** refers to the condition in which national output is growing steadily, with low inflation and full employment of resources. During the 1950s and 1960s, the U.S. economy experienced a long period of relatively steady growth, stable prices, and low unemployment. The decades of the 1970s and 1980s, however, were not as stable. The United States experienced two periods of rapid price inflation (more than 10 percent) and two periods of severe unemployment. In 1982, for example, 12 million people (10.8 percent of the work-force) were looking for work. The beginning of the 1990s was another period of instability, with a recession occurring in 1990–1991. In 2008–2009, much of the world, including the United States, experienced a large contraction in output and rise in unemployment, the effects of which lasted until 2013. This was clearly an unstable period.

The causes of instability and the ways in which governments have attempted to stabilize the economy are the subject matter of macroeconomics.

An Invitation

This chapter has prepared you for your study of economics. The first part of the chapter invited you into an exciting discipline that deals with important issues and questions. You cannot begin to understand how a society functions without knowing something about its economic history and its economic system.

The second part of the chapter introduced the method of reasoning that economics requires and some of the tools that economics uses. We believe that learning to think in this powerful way will help you better understand the world.

As you proceed, it is important that you keep track of what you have learned in previous chapters. This book has a plan; it proceeds step-by-step, each section building on the last. It would be a good idea to read each chapter's table of contents at the start of each chapter and scan each chapter before you read it to make sure you understand where it fits in the big picture.

———————— SUMMARY ————————

1. *Economics* is the study of how individuals and societies choose to use the scarce resources that nature and previous generations have provided.

1.1 WHY STUDY ECONOMICS? *p. 2*

2. There are many reasons to study economics, including (a) to learn a way of thinking, (b) to understand society, and (c) to be an informed citizen.

3. The best alternative that we forgo when we make a choice or a decision is the *opportunity cost* of that decision.

1.2 THE SCOPE OF ECONOMICS *p. 4*

4. *Microeconomics* deals with the functioning of individual markets and industries and with the behavior of individual decision-making units: business firms and households.

5. *Macroeconomics* looks at the economy as a whole. It deals with the economic behavior of aggregates—national output, national income, the overall price level, and the general rate of inflation.

6. Economics is a broad and diverse discipline with many special fields of inquiry. These include economic history, international economics, and urban economics.

1.3 THE METHOD OF ECONOMICS *p. 7*

7. Economics asks and attempts to answer two kinds of questions: positive and normative. *Positive economics* attempts to understand behavior and the operation of economies without making judgments about whether the outcomes are good or bad. *Normative economics* looks at the results of economic behavior and asks whether they are good or bad and whether they can be improved.

8. An economic *model* is a formal statement of an economic theory. Models simplify and abstract from reality.

9. It is often useful to isolate the effects of one variable on another while holding "all else constant." This is the device of *ceteris paribus.*

10. Models and theories can be expressed in many ways. The most common ways are in words, in graphs, and in equations.

11. Figuring out causality is often difficult in economics. Because one event happens before another, the second event does not necessarily happen as a result of the first. To assume that "after" implies "because" is to commit the fallacy of *post hoc, ergo propter hoc.*

12. *Empirical economics* involves the collection and use of data to test economic theories. In principle, the best model is the one that yields the most accurate predictions.

13. To make policy, one must be careful to specify criteria for making judgments. Four specific criteria are used most often in economics: *efficiency, equity, growth, and stability.*

REVIEW TERMS AND CONCEPTS

ceteris paribus, or all else equal, p. 8
economic growth, *p. 10*
economics, *p. 1*
efficiency, *p. 10*
efficient market, *p. 3*
empirical economics, *p. 8*
equity, *p. 10*

Industrial Revolution, *p. 3*
macroeconomics, *p. 4*
marginalism, *p. 2*
microeconomics, *p. 4*
model, *p. 7*
normative economics, *p. 7*
Ockham's razor, *p. 7*

opportunity cost, *p. 2*
positive economics, *p. 7*
post hoc, ergo propter hoc, p. 8
scarce, *p. 2*
stability, *p. 10*
variable, *p. 7*

PROBLEMS

All problems are available on MyEconLab.

1.1 WHY STUDY ECONOMICS

LEARNING OBJECTIVE: Identify three key reasons to study economics. Think of an example from your life in which understanding opportunity costs or the principle of efficient markets could make a difference in your decision making.

1.1 One of the scarce resources that constrain our behavior is time. Each of us has only 24 hours in a day. How do you go about allocating your time in a given day among competing alternatives? How do you go about weighing the alternatives? Once you choose a most important use of time, why do you not spend all your time on it? Use the notion of opportunity cost in your answer.

1.2 Every Friday night, Gustavo pays $39.99 to eat nothing but crab legs at the all-you-can-eat seafood buffet at the M Resort in Las Vegas. On average, he consumes 28 crab legs each Friday. What is the average cost of each crab leg to Gustavo? What is the marginal cost of an additional crab leg?

1.3 For each of the following situations, identify the full cost (opportunity cost) involved:
   a. Monique quits her $50,000 per-year job as an accountant to become a full-time volunteer at a women's shelter.
   b. The Agrizone Corporation invests $12 million in a new inventory tracking system.
   c. Taylor receives $500 from his grandmother for his birthday and uses it all to buy shares of stock in Harley-Davidson, Inc.
   d. Hector decides to spend the summer backpacking across Europe after he graduates from Tulane University.
   e. After receiving her master's degree, Molly chooses to enter the doctoral program in Behavioral Science at the University of Texas.
   f. Sanjay chooses to use his vacation time to paint the exterior of his house.
   g. After a night of karaoke, Tiffany forgets to set her alarm and sleeps through her Calculus final exam.

1.4 On the *Forbes* 2015 list of the World's Billionaires, Bill Gates ranks at the top with a net worth of $79.2 billion.

Does this "richest man in the world" face scarcity, or does scarcity only affect those with more limited incomes and lower net worth?

Source: "The World's Billionaires," Forbes, March 2, 2015.

1.2 THE SCOPE OF ECONOMICS

LEARNING OBJECTIVE: Describe microeconomics, macroeconomics, and the diverse fields of economics.

2.1 [**Related to the *Economics in Practice* on p. 5**] Log onto www.census.gov/foreign-trade/statistics/state/. In the State Trade by Commodity and Country section, click on "Exports and Imports", then click on "Exports" for your state. There you will find a list of the top 25 commodities produced in your state which are exported around the world. In looking over that list, are you surprised by anything? Do you know any of the firms that produce these items? Search the Internet to find a company that does. Do some research and write a paragraph about this company: what it produces, how many people it employs, and whatever else you can learn about the firm. You might even call the company to obtain the information.

2.2 Explain whether each of the following is an example of a macroeconomic concern or a microeconomic concern.
   a. The Federal Aviation Administration (FAA) is considering increasing the number of takeoff and landing slots available at Ronald Reagan Washington National Airport.
   b. The president has proposed increasing the marginal tax rate for people whose annual earnings exceed $275,000 and lowering the marginal tax rate for those who earn less than $275,000.
   c. Walmart announced that it will increase its starting wage for employees to $10 per hour by February 2016.
   d. Congress extends the maximum duration for the collection of unemployment benefits from 26 weeks to 52 weeks.

1.3 THE METHOD OF ECONOMICS

LEARNING OBJECTIVE: Think about an example of bad causal inference leading to erroneous decision making. Identify the four main goals of economic policy.

3.1 In the summer of 2007, the housing market and the mortgage market were both in decline. Housing prices in most U.S. cities began to decline in mid-2006. With prices falling and the inventory of unsold houses rising, the production of new homes fell to around 1.5 million in 2007 from 2.3 million in 2005. With new construction falling dramatically, it was expected that construction *employment* would fall and that this would have the potential of slowing the national economy and increasing the general unemployment rate. Go to www.bls.gov and check out the recent data on total employment and construction employment. Have they gone up or down from their levels in August 2007? What has happened to the unemployment rate? Go to www.fhfa.gov and look at the housing price index. Have home prices risen or fallen since August 2007? Finally, look at the latest GDP release at www.bea.gov. Look at residential and nonresidential investment (Table 1.1.5) during the last 2 years. Do you see a pattern? Does it explain the employment numbers? Explain your answer

3.2 Which of the following statements are examples of positive economic analysis? Which are examples of normative analysis?
   a. A devaluation of the U.S. dollar would increase exports from the United States.
   b. Increasing the federal tax on gasoline would cause shipping costs in the United States to increase.
   c. Florida should devote all revenues from its state lottery to improving public education.
   d. Eliminating the trade embargo with Cuba would increase the number of Cuban cigars available in the United States.
   e. As a public safety measure, the state of Texas should not pass legislation that allows people with concealed handgun permits to carry concealed weapons on college campuses.

3.3 In 2012, Colorado and Washington became the first states to legalize marijuana for recreational use, and have since been joined by Oregon, Alaska and Washington, D.C. In 2014, Colorado is reported to have received more than $50 million in tax revenue from the sale of recreational marijuana, much of which was slated to be used for school construction. The potential for increased tax revenues and the benefits these revenues can provide has a number of other states contemplating the possible legalization of recreational-use marijuana.
   a. Recall that efficiency means producing what people want at the least cost. Can you make an efficiency argument in favor of states allowing the recreational use of marijuana?
   b. What nonmonetary costs might be associated with legalizing marijuana use? Would these costs have an impact on the efficiency argument you presented in part a?
   c. Using the concept of equity, argue for or against the legalization of recreational-use marijuana.
   d. What do you think would happen to the flow of tax revenue to state governments if all 50 states legalized marijuana?

3.4 [**Related to the *Economics in Practice* on p. 9**] Most college students either currently have, or at one time have had, roommates or housemates. Think about a time when you have shared your living space with one or more students, and describe the effect this person (or people) had on your college experience, such as your study habits, the classes you took, your grade point average, and the way you spent time away from the classroom. Now describe the effect you think you had on your roommate(s). Were these roommates or housemates people you chose to live with, or were they assigned randomly? Explain if you think this made a difference in your or their behavior?

3.5 Explain the pitfalls in the following statements.
   a. People who eat kale on a regular basis are more likely to exercise every day than people who do not eat kale. Therefore, exercising daily causes people to eat kale.
   b. Whenever the Chicago Cubs are down by 2 runs in the eighth inning, they usually come back to win whenever self-proclaimed Cubs fanatic Cassandra decides to watch the game with her pet ferret Bobo. Last night with the Cubs down by 2 runs in the eighth, Cassandra rushed to grab Bobo and as she expected, the Cubs won the game. Obviously, the Cubs won because Cassandra watched the game with Bobo by her side.
   c. The manager of a large retail furniture store found that sending his least productive salespeople to a week-long motivational training workshop resulted in a 15 percent increase in sales for those employees. Based on this success, the manager decided to spend the money to send all of his other salespeople to this workshop so sales would increase for everyone.

CHAPTER 1 APPENDIX: How to Read and Understand Graphs

LEARNING OBJECTIVE

Understand how data can be graphically represented.

graph A two-dimensional representation of a set of numbers or data.

time series graph A graph illustrating how a variable changes over time.

Economics is the most quantitative of the social sciences. If you flip through the pages of this or any other economics text, you will see countless tables and graphs. These serve a number of purposes. First, they illustrate important economic relationships. Second, they make difficult problems easier to understand and analyze. Finally, they can show patterns and regularities that may not be discernible in simple lists of numbers.

A **graph** is a two-dimensional representation of a set of numbers, or data. There are many ways that numbers can be illustrated by a graph.

Time Series Graphs

It is often useful to see how a single measure or variable changes over time. One way to present this information is to plot the values of the variable on a graph, with each value corresponding to a different time period. A graph of this kind is called a **time series graph**. On a time series graph, time is measured along the horizontal scale and the variable being graphed is measured along the vertical scale. Figure 1A.1 is a time series graph that presents the total disposable personal income in the U.S. economy for each year between 1975 and 2014.[1] This graph is based on

▶ **FIGURE 1A.1** **Total Disposable Personal Income in the United States: 1975–2014 (in billions of dollars)**

Source: See Table 1A.1.

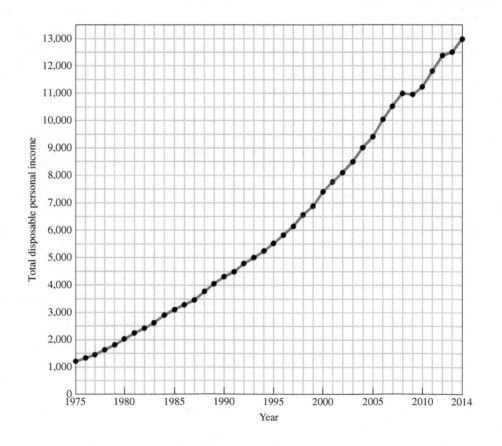

[1] The measure of income presented in Table 1A.1 and in Figure 1A.1 is disposable personal income in billions of dollars. It is the total personal income received by all households in the United States minus the taxes that they pay.

Year	Total Disposable Personal Income	Year	Total Disposable Personal Income
1975	1,219	1995	5,533
1976	1,326	1996	5,830
1977	1,457	1997	6,149
1978	1,630	1998	6,561
1979	1,809	1999	6,876
1980	2,018	2000	7,401
1981	2,251	2001	7,752
1982	2,425	2002	8,099
1983	2,617	2003	8,486
1984	2,904	2004	9,002
1985	3,099	2005	9,401
1986	3,288	2006	10,037
1987	3,466	2007	10,507
1988	3,770	2008	10,994
1989	4,052	2009	10,943
1990	4,312	2010	11,238
1991	4,485	2011	11,801
1992	4,800	2012	12,384
1993	5,000	2013	12,505
1994	5,244	2014	12,981

TABLE 1A.1 Total Disposable Personal Income in the United States, 1975–2014 (in billions of dollars)

Source: U.S. Department of Commerce, Bureau of Economic Analysis.

the data found in Table 1A.1. By displaying these data graphically, we can see that total disposable income has increased every year between 1975 and 2014 except for a small dip in 2009.

Graphing Two Variables

More important than simple graphs of one variable are graphs that contain information on two variables at the same time. The most common method of graphing two variables is a graph constructed by drawing two perpendicular lines: a horizontal line, or **X-axis**, and a vertical line, or **Y-axis**. The axes contain measurement scales that intersect at 0 (zero). This point is called the **origin**. On the vertical scale, positive numbers lie above the horizontal axis (that is, above the origin) and negative numbers lie below it. On the horizontal scale, positive numbers lie to the right of the vertical axis (to the right of the origin) and negative numbers lie to the left of it. The point at which the graph intersects the Y-axis is called the **Y-intercept**. The point at which the graph intersects the X-axis is called the **X-intercept**. When two variables are plotted on a single graph, each point represents a pair of numbers. The first number is measured on the X-axis, and the second number is measured on the Y-axis.

X-axis The horizontal line against which a variable is plotted.

Y-axis The vertical line against which a variable is plotted.

origin The point at which the horizontal and vertical axes intersect.

Y-intercept The point at which a graph intersects the Y-axis.

X-intercept The point at which a graph intersects the X-axis.

Plotting Income and Consumption Data for Households

Table 1A.2 presents data from the Bureau of Labor Statistics (BLS) for 2012. This table shows average income and average spending for households ranked by income. For example, the average income for the top fifth (20 percent) of the households was $167,010 in 2012. The average spending for the top 20 percent was $99,368.

Figure 1A.2 presents the numbers from Table 1A.2 graphically. Along the horizontal scale, the X-axis, we measure average income. Along the vertical scale, the Y-axis, we measure average consumption spending. Each of the five pairs of numbers from the table is represented by a

▶ **FIGURE 1A.2**
Household Consumption and Income

A graph is a simple two-dimensional geometric representation of data. This graph displays the data from Table 1A.2. Along the horizontal scale (*X*-axis), we measure household income. Along the vertical scale (*Y*-axis), we measure household consumption.

Note: At point *A*, consumption equals $22,154 and income equals $9,988. At point *B*, consumption equals $32,632 and income equals $27,585.

Source: See Table 1A.2.

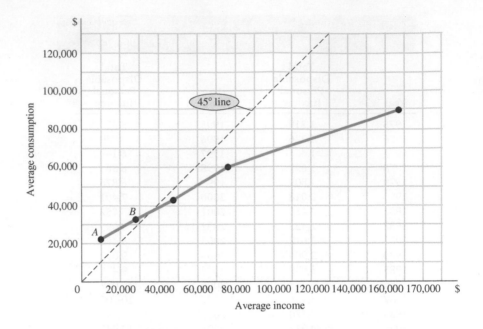

TABLE 1A.2	Consumption Expenditures and Income, 2012	
	Average Income Before Taxes	Average Consumption Expenditures
Bottom fifth	$ 9,988	$ 22,154
2nd fifth	27,585	32,632
3rd fifth	47,265	43,004
4th fifth	75,952	59,980
Top fifth	167,010	99,368

Source: Consumer Expenditures in 2012, U.S. Bureau of Labor Statistics.

positive relationship
A relationship between two variables, *X* and *Y*, in which a decrease in *X* is associated with a decrease in *Y*, and an increase in *X* is associated with an increase in *Y*.

negative relationship
A relationship between two variables, *X* and *Y*, in which a decrease in *X* is associated with an increase in *Y* and an increase in *X* is associated with a decrease in *Y*.

slope A measurement that indicates whether the relationship between variables is positive or negative and how much of a response there is in *Y* (the variable on the vertical axis) when *X* (the variable on the horizontal axis) changes.

point on the graph. Because all numbers are positive numbers, we need to show only the upper right quadrant of the coordinate system.

To help you read this graph, we have drawn a dotted line connecting all the points where consumption and income would be equal. *This 45-degree line does not represent any data.* Instead, it represents the line along which all variables on the *X*-axis correspond exactly to the variables on the *Y*-axis, for example, (10,000, 10,000), (20,000, 20,000), and (37,000, 37,000). The heavy blue line traces the data; the purpose of the dotted line is to help you read the graph.

There are several things to look for when reading a graph. The first thing you should notice is whether the line slopes upward or downward as you move from left to right. The blue line in Figure 1A.2 slopes upward, indicating that there seems to be a **positive relationship** between income and spending: The higher a household's income, the more a household tends to consume. If we had graphed the percentage of each group receiving welfare payments along the *Y*-axis, the line would presumably slope downward, indicating that welfare payments are lower at higher income levels. The income level/welfare payment relationship is thus a **negative relationship**.

Slope

The **slope** of a line or curve is a measure that indicates whether the relationship between the variables is positive or negative and how much of a response there is in *Y* (the variable on the vertical axis) when *X* (the variable on the horizontal axis) changes. The slope of a line between two points is

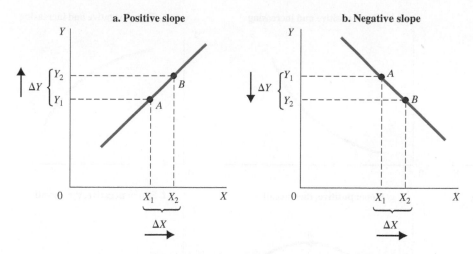

▲ **FIGURE 1A.3   A Curve with (a) Positive Slope and (b) Negative Slope**
A *positive* slope indicates that increases in X are associated with increases in Y and that decreases
in X are associated with decreases in Y. A *negative* slope indicates the opposite—when X increases,
Y decreases; and when X decreases, Y increases.

the change in the quantity measured on the Y-axis divided by the change in the quantity measured
on the X-axis. We will normally use Δ (the Greek letter *delta*) to refer to a change in a variable. In
Figure 1A.3, the slope of the line between points A and B is ΔY divided by ΔX. Sometimes it is easy to
remember slope as "the rise over the run," indicating the vertical change over the horizontal change.

To be precise, ΔX between two points on a graph is simply X_2 minus X_1, where X_2 is the X
value for the second point and X_1 is the X value for the first point. Similarly, ΔY is defined as Y_2
minus Y_1, where Y_2 is the Y value for the second point and Y_1 is the Y value for the first point.
Slope is equal to

$$\frac{\Delta Y}{\Delta X} = \frac{Y_2 - Y_1}{X_2 - X_1}$$

As we move from A to B in Figure 1A.3(a), both X and Y increase; the slope is thus a positive
number. However, as we move from A to B in Figure 1A.3(b), X increases [$(X_2 - X_1)$ is a positive
number], but Y decreases [$(Y_2 - Y_1)$ is a negative number]. The slope in Figure 1A.3(b) is thus a
negative number because a negative number divided by a positive number results in a negative
quotient.

To calculate the numerical value of the slope between points A and B in Figure 1A.2,
we need to calculate ΔY and ΔX. Because consumption is measured on the Y-axis, ΔY is
10,478 [$(Y_2 - Y_1) = (32,632 - 22,154)$]. Because income is measured along the X-axis, ΔX is
17,597 [$(X_2 - X_1) = (27,585 - 9,988)$]. The slope between A and B is

$$\frac{\Delta Y}{\Delta X} = \frac{10,478}{17,597} = +0.60.$$

Another interesting thing to note about the data graphed in Figure 1A.2 is that all the points
lie roughly along a straight line. (If you look very closely, however, you can see that the slope
declines as you move from left to right; the line becomes slightly less steep.) A straight line has
a constant slope. That is, if you pick any two points along it and calculate the slope, you will always get the same number. A horizontal line has a zero slope (ΔY is zero); a vertical line has an
"infinite" slope because ΔY is too big to be measured.

Unlike the slope of a straight line, the slope of a *curve* is continually changing. Consider,
for example, the curves in Figure 1A.4. Figure 1A.4(a) shows a curve with a positive slope that
decreases as you move from left to right. The easiest way to think about the concept of increasing

MyEconLab Visit **www.myeconlab.com** to complete these exercises online and get instant
feedback. Exercises that update with real-time data are marked with art 🌐 .

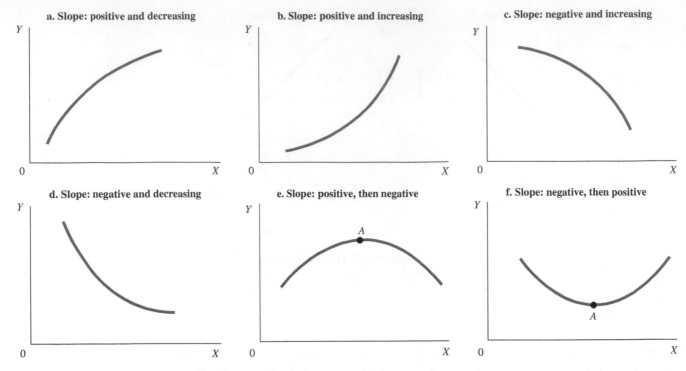

▲ **FIGURE 1A.4   Changing Slopes Along Curves**

or decreasing slope is to imagine what it is like walking up a hill from left to right. If the hill is steep, as it is in the first part of Figure 1A.4(a), you are moving more in the Y direction for each step you take in the X direction. If the hill is less steep, as it is further along in Figure 1A.4(a), you are moving less in the Y direction for every step you take in the X direction. Thus, when the hill is steep, slope ($\Delta Y/\Delta X$) is a larger number than it is when the hill is flatter. The curve in Figure 1A.4(b) has a positive slope, but its slope *increases* as you move from left to right.

The same analogy holds for curves that have a negative slope. Figure 1A.4(c) shows a curve with a negative slope that increases (in absolute value) as you move from left to right. This time think about skiing down a hill. At first, the descent in Figure 1A.4(c) is gradual (low slope), but as you proceed down the hill (to the right), you descend more quickly (high slope). Figure 1A.4(d) shows a curve with a negative slope that *decreases* (in absolute value) as you move from left to right.

In Figure 1A.4(e), the slope goes from positive to negative as X increases. In Figure 1A.4(f), the slope goes from negative to positive. At point A in both, the slope is zero. (Remember, slope is defined as $\Delta Y/\Delta X$. At point A, Y is not changing ($\Delta Y = 0$). Therefore, the slope at point A is zero.)

Some Precautions

When you read a graph, it is important to think carefully about what the points in the space defined by the axes represent. Table 1A.3 and Figure 1A.5 present a graph of consumption and income that is different from the one in Table 1A.2 and Figure 1A.2. First, each point in Figure 1A.5 represents a different year; in Figure 1A.2, each point represented a different group of households at the *same* point in time (2012). Second, the points in Figure 1A.5 represent *aggregate* consumption and income for the whole nation measured in *billions* of dollars; in Figure 1A.2, the points represented average *household* income and consumption measured in dollars.

It is interesting to compare these two graphs. All points on the aggregate consumption curve in Figure 1A.5 lie below the 45-degree line, which means that aggregate consumption is always less than aggregate income. However, the graph of average household income and consumption in Figure 1A.2 crosses the 45-degree line, implying that for some households, consumption is larger than income.

TABLE 1A.3	Aggregate Disposable Personal Income and Consumption for the United States, 1930–2014 (in billions of dollars)	
	Aggregate Disposable Personal Income	Aggregate Consumption
1930	75	70
1940	78	71
1950	215	192
1960	377	332
1970	762	648
1980	2,018	1,755
1990	4,312	3,826
2000	7,401	6,792
2010	11,238	10,202
2011	11,801	10,689
2012	12,384	11,083
2013	12,505	11,484
2014	12,981	11,928

Source: U.S. Department of Commerce, Bureau of Economic Analysis.

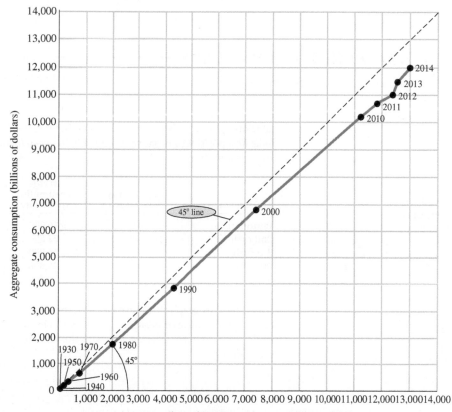

▲ **FIGURE 1A.5   Disposable Personal Income and Consumption**

It is important to think carefully about what is represented by points in the space defined by the axes of a graph. In this graph, we have graphed income with consumption, as in Figure 1A.2, but here each observation point is national income and aggregate consumption in *different years*, measured in billions of dollars.

Source: See Table 1A.3.

MyEconLab Visit **www.myeconlab.com** to complete these exercises online and get instant feedback. Exercises that update with real-time data are marked with art 🌐.

—— APPENDIX SUMMARY ——

1. A *graph* is a two-dimensional representation of a set of numbers, or data. A *time series graph* illustrates how a single variable changes over time.

2. A graph of two variables includes an X (horizontal)-*axis* and a Y (vertical)-*axis*. The points at which the two axes intersect is called the *origin*. The point at which a graph intersects the Y-axis is called the *Y-intercept*. The point at which a graph intersects the X-axis is called the *X-intercept*.

3. The *slope* of a line or curve indicates whether the relationship between the two variables graphed is positive or negative and how much of a response there is in Y (the variable on the vertical axis) when X (the variable on the horizontal axis) changes. The slope of a line between two points is the change in the quantity measured on the Y-axis divided by the change in the quantity measured on the X-axis.

—— APPENDIX REVIEW TERMS AND CONCEPTS ——

graph, *p. 14*

negative relationship, *p. 16*

origin, *p. 15*

positive relationship, *p. 16*

slope, *p. 16*

time series graph, *p. 14*

X-axis, *p. 15*

X-intercept, *p. 15*

Y-axis, *p. 15*

Y-intercept, *p. 15*

—— APPENDIX PROBLEMS ——

All problems are available on MyEconLab.

CHAPTER 1 APPENDIX: HOW TO READ AND UNDERSTAND GRAPHS

LEARNING OBJECTIVE: Understand how data can be graphically represented.

1A.1 Graph each of the following sets of numbers. Draw a line through the points and calculate the slope of each line.

1		2		3		4		5		6	
X	Y	X	Y	X	Y	X	Y	X	Y	X	Y
1	5	1	25	0	0	0	40	0	0	0.1	100
2	10	2	20	10	10	10	30	10	10	0.2	75
3	15	3	15	20	20	20	20	20	20	0.3	50
4	20	4	10	30	30	30	10	30	10	0.4	25
5	25	5	5	40	40	40	0	40	0	0.5	0

1A.2 Plot the income and consumption data in the following table on a graph, with income on the X-axis. Does the data indicate a positive or negative relationship between income and consumption?

Households by Percentage	Average Income Before Taxes	Average Consumption Expenditures
Bottom fifth	$ 5,500	$ 16,000
2nd fifth	12,000	22,500
3rd fifth	37,800	35,000
4th fifth	59,000	46,800
Top fifth	95,000	72,500

1A.3 For each of the graphs in Figure 1, determine whether the curve has a positive or negative slope. Give an intuitive explanation for what is happening with the slope of each curve.

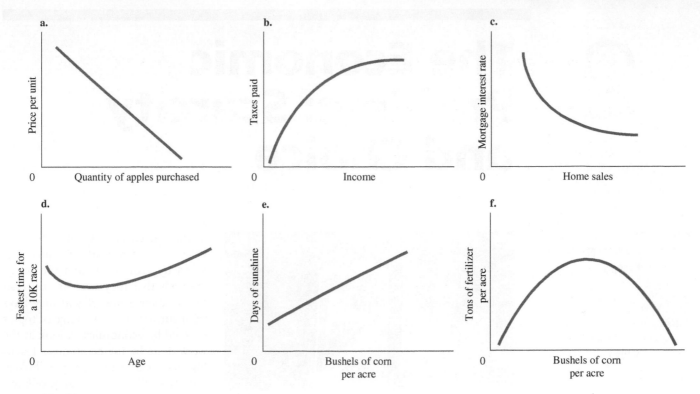

▲ **FIGURE 1**

1A.4 The following table shows the relationship between the price of organic turkeys and the number of turkeys sold by Godfrey's Free-Range Gobblers.
   a. Is the relationship between the price of turkeys and the number of turkeys sold by Godfrey's Free-Range Gobblers a positive relationship or a negative relationship? Explain.
   b. Plot the data from the table on a graph, draw a line through the points, and calculate the slope of the line.

Price per Turkey	Quantity of Turkeys	Month
$ 16	70	September
20	80	October
52	160	November
36	120	December
8	50	January

1A.5 Calculate the slope of the demand curve at point A and at point B in the following figure.

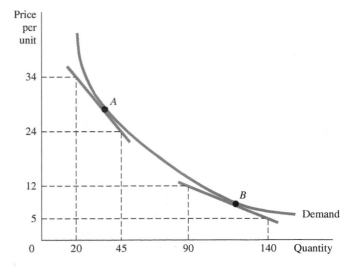

2

The Economic Problem: Scarcity and Choice

In the last chapter we provided you with some sense of the questions asked by economists and the broad methods that they use. As you read that chapter, some of you may have been surprised by the range of topics covered by economics. A look at the work done by the economists teaching at your own university will likely reveal a similarly broad range of interests. Some of your faculty will study how Apple and Samsung compete in smartphones. Others will look at discrimination in labor markets. Still others may be exploring the effects of microfinance in India. On the surface, these issues seem quite different from one another. But fundamental to each of these inquiries is the concern with choice in a world of scarcity. Economics explores how individuals make choices in a world of scarce resources and how those individual's choices come together to determine three key features of their society:

- What gets produced?
- How is it produced?
- Who gets what is produced?

This chapter explores these questions in detail. In a sense, this entire chapter *is* the definition of economics. It lays out the central problems addressed by the discipline and presents a framework that will guide you through the rest of the book. The starting point is the presumption that *human wants are unlimited but resources are not*. Limited or scarce resources force individuals and societies to choose among competing uses of resources—alternative combinations of produced goods and services—and among alternative final distributions of what is produced among households.

These questions are *positive or descriptive*. Understanding how a system functions is important before we can ask the normative questions of whether the system produces good or bad outcomes and how we might make improvements.

Economists study choices in a world of scarce resources. What do we mean by resources? If you look at Figure 2.1, you will see that resources are broadly defined. They include products of nature like minerals and timber, but also the products of past generations like buildings and factories. Perhaps most importantly, resources include the time and talents of the human population.

Things that are produced and then used in the production of other goods and services are called capital resources, or simply **capital**. Buildings, equipment, desks, chairs, software, roads, bridges, and highways are a part of the nation's stock of capital.

The three basic questions:

1. What gets produced? 2. How is it produced? 3. Who gets what is produced?

Mix of output

Resources

Producers

Households

Allocation of resources

Distribution of output

▲ **FIGURE 2.1** **The Three Basic Questions**
Every society has some system or process that transforms its scarce resources into useful goods and services. In doing so, it must decide what gets produced, how it is produced, and to whom it is distributed. The primary resources that must be allocated are land, labor, and capital.

The basic resources available to a society are often referred to as **factors of production, or simply factors.** The three key factors of production are land, labor, and capital. The process that transforms scarce resources into useful goods and services is called **production.** In many societies, most of the production of goods and services is done by private firms. Private airlines in the United States use land (runways), labor (pilots and mechanics), and capital (airplanes) to produce transportation services. But in all societies, some production is done by the public sector, or government. Examples of government-produced or government-provided goods and services include national defense, public education, police protection, and fire protection.

Resources or factors of production are the **inputs** into the process of production; goods and services of value to households are the **outputs** of the process of production.

capital Things that are produced and then used in the production of other goods and services.

factors of production (or factors) The inputs into the process of production. Another term for resources.

production The process that transforms scarce resources into useful goods and services.

Scarcity, Choice, and Opportunity Cost

In the second half of this chapter we discuss the global economic landscape. Before you can understand the different types of economic systems, it is important to master the basic economic concepts of scarcity, choice, and opportunity cost.

Scarcity and Choice in a One-Person Economy

The simplest economy is one in which a single person lives alone on an island. Consider Bill, the survivor of a plane crash, who finds himself cast ashore in such a place. Here individual and society are one; there is no distinction between social and private. *Nonetheless, nearly all the same basic decisions that characterize complex economies must also be made in a simple economy.* That is, although Bill will get whatever he produces, he still must decide how to allocate the island's resources, what to produce, and how and when to produce it.

First, Bill must decide *what* he wants to produce. Notice that the word *needs* does not appear here. Needs are absolute requirements; but beyond just enough water, basic nutrition, and shelter to survive, needs are very difficult to define. In any case, Bill must put his wants in some order of priority and make some choices.

Next, he must look at the *possibilities.* What can he do to satisfy his wants given the limits of the island? In every society, no matter how simple or complex, people are constrained in what they can do. In this society of one, Bill is constrained by time, his physical condition, his knowledge, his skills, and the resources and climate of the island.

Given that resources are limited, Bill must decide *how* to best use them to satisfy his hierarchy of wants. Food would probably come close to the top of his list. Should he spend

2.1 LEARNING OBJECTIVE

Understand why even in a society in which one person is better than a second at all tasks, it is still beneficial for the two to specialize and trade.

inputs *or* resources Anything provided by nature or previous generations that can be used directly or indirectly to satisfy human wants.

outputs Goods and services of value to households.

his time gathering fruits and berries? Should he clear a field and plant seeds? The answers to those questions depend on the character of the island, its climate, its flora and fauna (*are there any fruits and berries?*), the extent of his skills and knowledge (does he know anything about farming?), and his preferences (he may be a vegetarian).

Opportunity Cost The concepts of *constrained choice* and *scarcity* are central to the discipline of economics. They can be applied when discussing the behavior of individuals such as Bill and when analyzing the behavior of large groups of people in complex societies.

Given the scarcity of time and resources, if Bill decides to hunt, he will have less time to gather fruits and berries. He faces a trade-off between meat and fruit. There is a trade-off between food and shelter, too. As we noted in Chapter 1, the best alternative that we give up, or forgo, when we make a choice is the **opportunity cost** of that choice.

> **opportunity cost** The best alternative that we give up, or forgo, when we make a choice or decision.

Bill may occasionally decide to rest, to lie on the beach, and to enjoy the sun. In one sense, that benefit is free—he does not have to buy a ticket to lie on the beach. In reality, however, relaxing does have an opportunity cost. The true cost of that leisure is the value of the other things Bill could have otherwise produced, but did not, during the time he spent on the beach.

The trade-offs that are made in this kind of society are vividly and often comically portrayed in the reality television shows that show groups of strangers competing on some deserted island, all trying to choose whether it is better to fish, hunt for berries, build a hut, or build an alliance. Making one of these choices involves giving up an opportunity to do another, and in many episodes we can see the consequences of those choices.

Scarcity and Choice in an Economy of Two or More

Now suppose that another survivor of the crash, Colleen, appears on the island. Now that Bill is not alone, things are more complex and some new decisions must be made. Bill's and Colleen's preferences about what things to produce are likely to be different. They will probably not have the same knowledge or skills. Perhaps Colleen is good at tracking animals and Bill has a knack for building things. How should they split the work that needs to be done? Once things are produced, the two castaways must decide how to divide them. How should their products be distributed?

The mechanism for answering these fundamental questions is clear when Bill is alone on the island. The "central plan" is his; he simply decides what he wants and what to do about it. The minute someone else appears, however, a number of decision-making arrangements immediately become possible. One or the other may take charge, in which case that person will decide for both of them. The two may agree to cooperate, with each having an equal say, and come up with a joint plan; or they may agree to split the planning as well as the production duties. Finally, they may go off to live alone at opposite ends of the island. Even if they live apart, however, they may take advantage of each other's presence by specializing and trading.

Modern industrial societies must answer the same questions that Colleen and Bill must answer, but the mechanics of larger economies are more complex. Instead of two people living together, the United States has more than 300 million people. Still, decisions must be made about what to produce, how to produce it, and who gets it.

Specialization, Exchange, and Comparative Advantage The idea that members of society benefit by specializing in what they do best has a long history and is one of the most important and powerful ideas in all of economics. David Ricardo, a major nineteenth-century British economist, formalized the point precisely. According to Ricardo's **theory of comparative advantage**, specialization and free trade will benefit all trading parties, even when some are "absolutely" more efficient producers than others. Ricardo's basic point applies just as much to Colleen and Bill as it does to different nations.

> **theory of comparative advantage** Ricardo's theory that specialization and free trade will benefit all trading parties, even those that may be "absolutely" more efficient producers.

To keep things simple, suppose that Colleen and Bill have only two tasks to accomplish each week: gathering food to eat and cutting logs to burn. If Colleen could cut more logs than Bill in one day and Bill could gather more nuts and berries than Colleen could, specialization would clearly lead to more total production. Both would benefit if Colleen only cuts logs and Bill only gathers nuts and berries, as long as they can trade.

ECONOMICS IN PRACTICE

Frozen Foods and Opportunity Costs

In 2012, $44 billion of frozen foods were sold in U.S. grocery stores, one quarter of it in the form of frozen dinners and entrées. In the mid-1950s, sales of frozen foods amounted to only $1 billion, a tiny fraction of the overall grocery store sales. One industry observer attributes this growth to the fact that frozen food tastes much better than it did in the past. Can you think of anything else that might be occurring?

The growth of the frozen dinner entrée market in the last 50 years is a good example of the role of opportunity costs in our lives. One of the most significant social changes in the U.S. economy in this period has been the increased participation of women in the labor force. In 1950, only 24 percent of married women worked; by 2013, that fraction had risen to 58 percent. Producing a meal takes two basic ingredients: food and time. When both husbands and wives work, the opportunity cost of time for housework—including making meals—goes up. This tells us that making a home-cooked meal became more expensive in the last 50 years. A natural result is to shift people toward labor-saving ways to make meals. Frozen foods are an obvious solution to the problem of increased opportunity costs.

Another, somewhat more subtle, opportunity cost story is at work encouraging the consumption of frozen foods. In 1960, the first microwave oven was introduced. The spread of this device into America's kitchens was rapid. The microwave turned out to be a quick way to defrost and cook those frozen entrées. So this technology lowered the opportunity cost of making frozen dinners, reinforcing the advantage these meals had over home-cooked meals. Microwaves made cooking with frozen foods cheaper once opportunity cost was considered while home-cooked meals were becoming more expensive.

The entrepreneurs among you also might recognize that the rise we described in the opportunity cost of the home-cooked meal *contributed* in part to the spread of the microwave, creating a reinforcing cycle. In fact, many entrepreneurs find that the simple tools of economics—like the

idea of opportunity costs—help them anticipate what products will be profitable for them to produce in the future. The growth of the two-worker family has stimulated many entrepreneurs to search for labor-saving solutions to family tasks.

The public policy students among you might be interested to know that some researchers attribute part of the growth in obesity in the United States to the lower opportunity costs of making meals associated with the growth of the markets for frozen foods and the microwave. (See David M. Cutler, Edward L. Glaeser, and Jesse M. Shapiro, "Why Have Americans Become More Obese?" *Journal of Economic Perspectives*, Summer 2003: 93–118.)

THINKING PRACTICALLY

1. Many people think that soda consumption also leads to increased obesity. Many schools have banned the sale of soda in vending machines. Use the idea of opportunity costs to explain why some people think these bans will reduce consumption. Do you agree?

Suppose instead that Colleen is better than Bill both at cutting logs *and* gathering food. In particular, whereas Colleen can gather 10 bushels of food per day, Bill can gather only 8 bushels. Further, while Colleen can cut 10 logs per day, Bill can cut only 4 per day. In this sense, we would say Colleen has an **absolute advantage** over Bill in both activities.

Thinking about this situation and focusing just on the productivity levels, you might conclude that it would benefit Colleen to move to the other side of the island and be by herself. Since she is more productive both in cutting logs and gathering food, would she not be better off on her own? How could she benefit by hanging out with Bill and sharing what they produce? One of Ricardo's lasting contributions to economics has been his analysis of exactly this situation. His analysis, which is illustrated in Figure 2.2, shows both how Colleen and Bill should divide the work of the island and how much they will gain from specializing and exchanging even if, as in this example, one party is absolutely better at everything than the other party.

absolute advantage
A producer has an absolute advantage over another in the production of a good or service if he or she can produce that product using fewer resources (a lower absolute cost per unit).

comparative advantage
A producer has a comparative advantage over another in the production of a good or service if he or she can produce that product at a lower *opportunity cost.*

The key to this question is remembering that Colleen's time is limited: this limit creates an opportunity cost. Though Bill is less able at all tasks than Colleen, having him spend time producing something frees up Colleen's time and this has value. The value from Bill's time depends on his comparative advantage. A producer has a **comparative advantage** over another in the production of a good or service if he or she can produce the good or service at a lower opportunity cost. First, think about Bill. He can produce 8 bushels of food per day, or he can cut 4 logs. To get 8 additional bushels of food, he must give up cutting 4 logs. Thus, *for Bill, the opportunity cost of 8 bushels of food is 4 logs.* Think next about Colleen. She can produce 10 bushels of food per day, or she can cut 10 logs. She thus gives up 1 log for each additional bushel; so *for Colleen, the opportunity cost of 8 bushels of food is 8 logs.* Bill has a comparative advantage over Colleen in the production of food because he gives up only 4 logs for an additional 8 bushels, whereas Colleen gives up 8 logs.

Think now about what Colleen must give up in terms of food to get 10 logs. To produce 10 logs she must work a whole day. If she spends a day cutting 10 logs, she gives up a day of gathering 10 bushels of food. Thus, *for Colleen, the opportunity cost of 10 logs is 10 bushels of food.* What must Bill give up to get 10 logs? To produce 4 logs, he must work 1 day. For each day he cuts logs, he gives up 8 bushels of food. He thus gives up 2 bushels of food for each log; so *for Bill, the opportunity cost of 10 logs is 20 bushels of food.* Colleen has a comparative advantage over Bill in the production of logs because she gives up only 10 bushels of food for an additional 10 logs, whereas Bill gives up 20 bushels.

Ricardo argued that two parties can benefit from specialization and trade even if one party has an absolute advantage in the production of both goods if each party takes advantage of his or her comparative advantage. Let us see how this works in the current example.

Suppose Colleen and Bill both want equal numbers of logs and bushels of food. If Colleen goes off on her own and splits her time equally, in one day she can produce 5 logs and 5 bushels of food. Bill, to produce equal amounts of logs and food, will have to spend more time on the wood than the food, given his talents. By spending one third of his day producing food and two thirds chopping wood, he can produce $2\frac{2}{3}$ *units* of each. In sum, when acting alone $7\frac{2}{3}$ logs and bushels of food are produced by our pair of castaways, most of them by Colleen. Clearly Colleen is a better producer than Bill. Why should she ever want to join forces with clumsy, slow Bill?

The answer lies in the gains from specialization, as we can see in Figure 2.2. In block a, we show the results of having Bill and Colleen each working alone chopping logs and gathering food: $7\frac{2}{3}$ logs and an equal number of food bushels. Now, recalling our calculations indicating that Colleen has a comparative advantage in wood chopping, let's see what happens if we assign Colleen to the wood task and have Bill spend all day gathering food. This system is described in block b of Figure 2.2. At the end of the day, the two end up with 10 logs, all gathered by Colleen and 8 bushels of food, all produced by Bill. By joining forces and specializing, the two have increased their production of both goods. This increased production provides an incentive for Colleen and Bill to work together. United, each can receive a bonus over what he or she could produce separately. This bonus—here $2\frac{1}{3}$ extra logs and $\frac{1}{3}$ bushel of food—represent the gains from specialization. Of course if both Bill and Colleen really favor equal amounts of the two goods, they could adjust their work time to get to this outcome; the main point here is that the total production increases with some specialization.

The simple example of Bill and Colleen should begin to give you some insight into why most economists see value in free trade. Even if one country is absolutely better than another country at producing everything, our example has shown that there are gains to specializing and trading.

A Graphical Presentation of the Production Possibilities and Gains from Specialization   Graphs can also be used to illustrate the production possibilities open to Colleen and Bill and the gains they could achieve from specialization and trade.

Figure 2.3(a) shows all of the possible combinations of food and wood Colleen can produce given her skills and the conditions on the island, acting alone. Panel (b) does the same for Bill. If Colleen spends all of her time producing wood, the best she can do is 10 logs, which we show where the line crosses the vertical axis. Similarly, the line crosses the horizontal axis at 10 bushels of food, because that is what Colleen could produce spending full time producing food. We

a. Daily production with no specialization, assuming Colleen and Bill each want to consume an equal number of logs and food

b. Daily Production with Specialization

◀ FIGURE 2.2

Comparative Advantage and the Gains from Trade
Panel (a) shows the best Colleen and Bill can do each day, given their talents and assuming they each wish to consume an equal amount of food and wood. Notice Colleen produces by splitting her time equally during the day, while Bill must devote two thirds of his time to wood production if he wishes to equalize his amount produced of the two goods. Panel (b) shows what happens when both parties specialize. Notice more units are produced of each good.

have also marked on the graph possibility C, where she divides her time equally, generating 5 bushels of food and 5 logs of wood.

Bill in panel (b) can get as many as 4 logs of wood or 8 bushels of food by devoting himself full time to either wood or food production. Again, we have marked on his graph a point F, where he produces $2\frac{2}{3}$ bushels of food and $2\frac{2}{3}$ logs of wood. Notice that Bill's production line is lower down than is Colleen's. The further to the right is the production line, the more productive is the individual; that is, the more he or she can produce of the two goods. Also notice that the slope of the two lines is not the same. Colleen trades off one bushel of food for one log of wood, while Bill gives up 2 bushels of food for one log of wood. These differing slopes show

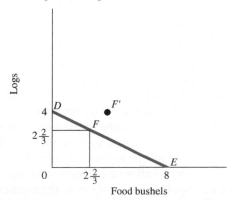

▲ FIGURE 2.3 **Production Possibilities with and without Trade**
This figure shows the combinations of food and wood that Colleen and Bill can each generate in one day of labor, working by themselves. Colleen can achieve independently any point along line ACB, whereas Bill can generate any combination of food and wood along line DFE. Specialization and trade would allow both Bill and Colleen to move to the right of their original lines, to points like C′ and F′. In other words, specialization and trade allow both people to be better off than they were acting alone.

the differing opportunity costs faced by Colleen and Bill. They also open up the possibility of gains from specialization. Try working through an example in which the slopes are the same to convince yourself of the importance of differing slopes.

What happens when the possibility of working together and specializing in either wood or food comes up? In Figure 2.2 we have already seen that specialization would allow the pair to go from production of $7\frac{2}{3}$ *units* of food and wood to 10 logs and 8 bushels of food. Colleen and Bill can split the $2\frac{1}{3}$ extra logs and the $\frac{1}{3}$ extra bushel of food to move to points like C' and F' in Figure 2.3, which were unachievable without cooperation. In this analysis we do not know how Bill and Colleen will divide the surplus food and wood they have created. But because there is a surplus means that both of them can do better than either would alone.

Weighing Present and Expected Future Costs and Benefits

Very often we find ourselves weighing benefits available today against benefits available tomorrow. Here, too, the notion of opportunity cost is helpful.

While alone on the island, Bill had to choose between cultivating a field and just gathering wild nuts and berries. Gathering nuts and berries provides food now; gathering seeds and clearing a field for planting will yield food tomorrow if all goes well. Using today's time to farm may well be worth the effort if doing so will yield more food than Bill would otherwise have in the future. By planting, Bill is trading present value for future value.

The simplest example of trading present for future benefits is the act of saving. When you put income aside today for use in the future, you give up some things that you could have had today in exchange for something tomorrow. Because nothing is certain, some judgment about future events and expected values must be made. What will your income be in 10 years? How long are you likely to live?

We trade off present and future benefits in small ways all the time. If you decide to study instead of going to the dorm party, you are trading present fun for the expected future benefits of higher grades. If you decide to go outside on a very cold day and run 5 miles, you are trading discomfort in the present for being in better shape later.

Capital Goods and Consumer Goods

A society trades present for expected future benefits when it devotes a portion of its resources to research and development or to investment in capital. As we said previously in this chapter, *capital* in its broadest definition is anything that has already been produced that will be used to produce other valuable goods or services over time.

Building capital means trading present benefits for future ones. Bill and Colleen might trade gathering berries or lying in the sun for cutting logs to build a nicer house in the future. In a modern society, resources used to produce capital goods could have been used to produce **consumer goods**—that is, goods for present consumption. Heavy industrial machinery does not directly satisfy the wants of anyone, but producing it requires resources that could instead have gone into producing things that do satisfy wants directly—for example, food, clothing, toys, or golf clubs.

consumer goods Goods produced for present consumption.

Capital is everywhere. A road is capital. Once a road is built, we can drive on it or transport goods and services over it for many years to come. A house is also capital. Before a new manufacturing firm can start up, it must put some capital in place. The buildings, equipment, and inventories that it uses comprise its capital. As it contributes to the production process, this capital yields valuable services over time.

Capital does not need to be tangible. When you spend time and resources developing skills or getting an education, you are investing in human capital—your own human capital. This capital will continue to exist and yield benefits to you for years to come. A computer program produced by a software company and available online may cost nothing to distribute, but its true intangible value comes from the ideas embodied in the program itself. It too is capital.

investment The process of using resources to produce new capital.

The process of using resources to produce new capital is called **investment**. (In everyday language, the term *investment* often refers to the act of buying a share of stock or a bond, as in "I invested in some Treasury bonds." In economics, however, investment *always* refers to the creation of capital: the purchase or putting in place of buildings, equipment, roads, houses, and the like.) A wise investment in capital is one that yields future benefits that are more valuable than the present cost. When you spend money for a house, for example, presumably you value its future benefits. That is, you expect to gain more in shelter services than you would from the things you could buy today with the same money. Because resources are scarce, the opportunity cost of every investment in capital is forgone present consumption.

The Production Possibility Frontier

A simple graphic device called the **production possibility frontier (ppf)** illustrates the principles of constrained choice, opportunity cost, and scarcity. The ppf is a graph that shows all the combinations of goods and services that can be produced if all of a society's resources are used efficiently. Figure 2.4 shows a ppf for a hypothetical economy. We have already seen a simplified version of a ppf in looking at the choices of Colleen and Bill in Figure 2.3. Here we will look more generally at the ppf.

On the Y-axis, we measure the quantity of capital goods produced. On the X-axis, we measure the quantity of consumer goods. All points below and to the left of the curve (the shaded area) represent combinations of capital and consumer goods that are possible for the society given the resources available and existing technology. Points above and to the right of the curve, such as point G, represent combinations that cannot currently be realized. You will recall in our example of Colleen and Bill that new trade and specialization possibilities allowed them to expand their collective production possibilities and move to a point like G. If an economy were to end up at point A on the graph, it would be producing no consumer goods at all; all resources would be used for the production of capital. If an economy were to end up at point B, it would be devoting all its resources to the production of consumer goods and none of its resources to the formation of capital.

While all economies produce some of each kind of good, different economies emphasize different things. About 13 percent of gross output in the United States in 2012 was new capital. In Japan, capital has historically accounted for a much higher percent of gross output, while in the Congo, the figure is about 7 percent. Japan is closer to point A on its ppf, the Congo is closer to B, and the United States is somewhere in between.

Points that are actually on the ppf are points of both full resource employment and production efficiency. (Recall from Chapter 1 that an efficient economy is one that produces the things that people want at the least cost. *Production efficiency* is a state in which a given mix of outputs is produced at the least cost.) Resources are not going unused, and there is no waste. Points that lie within the shaded area but that are not on the frontier represent either unemployment of resources or production inefficiency. An economy producing at point D in Figure 2.4 can produce more capital goods and more consumer goods, for example, by moving to point E. This is possible because resources are not fully employed at point D or are not being used efficiently.

production possibility frontier (ppf) A graph that shows all the combinations of goods and services that can be produced if all of society's resources are used efficiently.

◀ FIGURE 2.4
Production Possibility Frontier
The ppf illustrates a number of economic concepts. One of the most important is *opportunity cost*. The opportunity cost of producing more capital goods is fewer consumer goods. Moving from E to F, the number of capital goods increases from 550 to 800, but the number of consumer goods decreases from 1,300 to 1,100.

Negative Slope and Opportunity Cost   Just as we saw with Colleen and Bill, the slope of the ppf is negative. Because a society's choices are constrained by available resources and existing technology, when those resources are fully and efficiently employed, it can produce more capital goods only by reducing production of consumer goods. The opportunity cost of the additional capital is the forgone production of consumer goods.

The fact that scarcity exists is illustrated by the negative slope of the ppf. (If you need a review of slope, see the Appendix to Chapter 1.) In moving from point E to point F in Figure 2.4, capital production *increases* by 800 − 550 = 250 units (a positive change), but that increase in capital can be achieved only by shifting resources out of the production of consumer goods. Thus, in moving from point E to point F in Figure 2.4, consumer goods production *decreases* by 1,300 − 1,100 = 200 units (a negative change). The slope of the curve, the ratio of the change in capital goods to the change in consumer goods, is negative.

marginal rate of transformation (MRT)
The slope of the production possibility frontier (ppf).

The value of the slope of a society's ppf is called the **marginal rate of transformation (MRT)**. In Figure 2.4, the MRT between points E and F is simply the ratio of the change in capital goods (a positive number) to the change in consumer goods (a negative number). It tells us how much society has to give up of one output to get a unit of a second.

The Law of Increasing Opportunity Cost   The negative slope of the ppf indicates the trade-off that a society faces between two goods. In the example of Colleen and Bill, we showed the ppf as a straight line. What does it mean that the ppf here is bowed out?

In our simple example, Bill gave up two bushels of food for every one log of wood he produced. Bill's per-hour ability to harvest wood or produce food didn't depend on how many hours he spent on that activity. Similarly Colleen faced the same trade off of food for wood regardless of how much of either she was producing. In the language we have just introduced, the marginal rate of transformation was constant for Bill and Colleen; hence the straight line ppf. But that is not always true. Perhaps the first bushel of food is easy to produce, low-hanging fruit for example. Perhaps it is harder to get the second log than the first because the trees are farther away. The bowed out ppf tells us that the more society tries to increase production of one good rather than another, the harder it is. In the example in Figure 2.4, the opportunity cost of using society's resources to make capital goods rather than consumer goods increases as we devote more and more resources to capital goods. Why might that be? A common explanation is that when society tries to produce only a small amount of a product, it can use resources—people, land and so on—most well-suited to those goods. As a society spends a larger portion of its resources on one good versus all others, getting more production of that good often becomes increasingly hard.

Let's look at the trade-off between corn and wheat production in Ohio and Kansas as an example. In a recent year, Ohio and Kansas together produced 510 million bushels of corn and 380 million bushels of wheat. Table 2.1 presents these two numbers, plus some hypothetical combinations of corn and wheat production that might exist for Ohio and Kansas together. Figure 2.5 graphs the data from Table 2.1.

Suppose that society's demand for corn dramatically increases. If this happens, farmers would probably shift some of their acreage from wheat production to corn production. Such a shift is represented by a move from point C (where corn = 510 and wheat = 380) up and to the left along the ppf toward points A and B in Figure 2.5. As this happens, it becomes more difficult to produce additional corn. The best land for corn production was presumably already in corn, and the best land for wheat production was already in wheat. As we try to produce more corn, the land is less well-suited to that crop. As we take more land out of wheat production, we are taking increasingly better wheat-producing land. In other words, the opportunity cost of more corn, measured in terms of wheat foregone, increases.

Moving from point E to D, Table 2.1 shows that we can get 100 million bushels of corn (400 − 300) by sacrificing only 50 million bushels of wheat (550 − 500)—that is, we get 2 bushels of corn for every bushel of wheat. However, when we are already stretching the ability of the land to produce corn, it becomes harder to produce more and the opportunity cost increases. Moving from point B to A, we can get only 50 million bushels of corn (700 − 650) by sacrificing 100 million bushels of wheat (200 − 100). For every bushel of wheat, we now get only half a bushel of corn. However, if the demand for *wheat* were to increase substantially and we were to move down and to the right along the ppf, it would become increasingly difficult to produce wheat and the opportunity cost of wheat, in terms of corn foregone, would increase. This is the *law of increasing opportunity cost*.

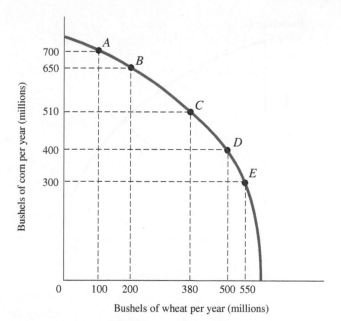

▲ **FIGURE 2.5   Corn and Wheat Production in Ohio and Kansas**
The ppf illustrates that the opportunity cost of corn production increases as we shift resources from wheat production to corn production. Moving from point *E* to *D*, we get an additional 100 million bushels of corn at a cost of 50 million bushels of wheat. Moving from point *B* to *A*, we get only 50 million bushels of corn at a cost of 100 million bushels of wheat. The *cost per bushel* of corn—measured in lost wheat—has increased.

TABLE 2.1	Production Possibility Schedule for Total Corn and Wheat Production in Ohio and Kansas	
Point on ppf	Total Corn Production (Millions of Bushels per Year)	Total Wheat Production (Millions of Bushels per Year)
A	700	100
B	650	200
C	510	380
D	400	500
E	300	550

Unemployment   During the Great Depression of the 1930s, the U.S. economy experienced prolonged unemployment. Millions of workers found themselves without jobs. In 1933, 25 percent of the civilian labor force was unemployed. This figure stayed above 14 percent until 1940. More recently, between the end of 2007 and 2010, the United States lost more than 8 million payroll jobs and unemployment rose to higher than 15 million.

In addition to the hardship that falls on the unemployed, unemployment of labor means unemployment of capital. During economic downturns or recessions, industrial plants run at less than their total capacity. When there is unemployment of labor and capital, we are not producing all that we can.

Periods of unemployment correspond to points inside the ppf, points such as *D* in Figure 2.4. Moving onto the frontier from a point such as *D* means achieving full employment of resources.

Inefficiency   Although an economy may be operating with full employment of its land, labor, and capital resources, it may still be operating inside its ppf (at a point such as *D* in Figure 2.4). It could be using those resources *inefficiently*.

Waste and mismanagement are the results of a firm operating below its potential. If you are the owner of a bakery and you forget to order flour, your workers and ovens stand idle while you figure out what to do.

Sometimes inefficiency results from mismanagement of the economy instead of mismanagement of individual private firms. Suppose, for example, that the land and climate in Ohio are

▶ **FIGURE 2.6**

Inefficiency from Misallocation of Land in Farming

Inefficiency always results in a combination of production shown by a point inside the ppf, like point A. Increasing efficiency will move production possibilities toward a point on the ppf, such as point B.

best-suited for corn production and that the land and climate in Kansas are best-suited for wheat production. If Congress passes a law forcing Ohio farmers to plant 50 percent of their acreage with wheat and Kansas farmers to plant 50 percent with corn, neither corn nor wheat production will be up to potential. The economy will be at a point such as A in Figure 2.6—inside the ppf. Allowing each state to specialize in producing the crop that it produces best increases the production of both crops and moves the economy to a point such as B in Figure 2.6.

The Efficient Mix of Output   To be efficient, an economy must produce what people want. This means that in addition to operating *on* the ppf, the economy must be operating at the *right point* on the ppf. This is referred to as *output efficiency*, in contrast to production efficiency. Suppose that an economy devotes 100 percent of its resources to beef production and that the beef industry runs efficiently using the most modern techniques. If everyone in the society were a vegetarian and there were no trade, resources spent on producing beef would be wasted.

It is important to remember that the ppf represents choices available within the constraints imposed by the current state of agricultural technology. In the long run, technology may improve, and when that happens, we have *growth*.

economic growth   An increase in the total output of an economy. Growth occurs when a society acquires new resources or when it learns to produce more using existing resources.

Economic Growth   **Economic growth** is characterized by an increase in the total output of an economy. It occurs when a society acquires new resources or learns to produce more with existing resources. New resources may mean a larger labor force or an increased capital stock. The production and use of new machinery and equipment (capital) increase workers' productivity. (Give a man a shovel, and he can dig a bigger hole; give him a steam shovel, and wow!) Improved productivity also comes from technological change and *innovation*, the discovery and application of new, more efficient production techniques.

In the past few decades, the productivity of U.S. agriculture has increased dramatically. Based on data compiled by the Department of Agriculture, Table 2.2 shows that yield per acre in corn production has increased sixfold since the late 1930s, and the labor required to produce it has dropped significantly. Productivity in wheat production has also increased, at only a slightly less remarkable rate: Output per acre has more than tripled, whereas labor requirements are down nearly 90 percent. These increases are the result of more efficient farming techniques, more and better capital (tractors, combines, and other equipment), and advances in scientific knowledge and technological change (hybrid seeds, fertilizers, and so on). As you can see in Figure 2.7, changes such as these shift the ppf up and to the right.

Sources of Growth and the Dilemma of Poor Countries   Economic growth arises from many sources. The two most important over the years have been the accumulation of capital and technological advances. For poor countries, capital is essential; they must build

TABLE 2.2	Increasing Productivity in Corn and Wheat Production in the United States, 1935–2009			
	Corn		Wheat	
	Yield per Acre (Bushels)	Labor Hours per 100 Bushels	Yield per Acre (Bushels)	Labor Hours per 100 Bushels
1935–1939	26.1	108	13.2	67
1945–1949	36.1	53	16.9	34
1955–1959	48.7	20	22.3	17
1965–1969	78.5	7	27.5	11
1975–1979	95.3	4	31.3	9
1981–1985	107.2	3	36.9	7
1985–1990	112.8	NA[a]	38.0	NA[a]
1990–1995	120.6	NA[a]	38.1	NA[a]
1998	134.4	NA[a]	43.2	NA[a]
2001	138.2	NA[a]	43.5	NA[a]
2006	145.6	NA[a]	42.3	NA[a]
2007	152.8	NA[a]	40.6	NA[a]
2008	153.9	NA[a]	44.9	NA[a]
2009	164.9	NA[a]	44.3	NA[a]

[a] Data not available.

Source: U.S. Department of Agriculture, Economic Research Service, Agricultural Statistics, Crop Summary.

the communication networks and transportation systems necessary to develop industries that function efficiently. They also need capital goods to develop their agricultural sectors.

Recall that capital goods are produced only at a sacrifice of consumer goods. The same can be said for technological advances. Technological advances come from research and development that use resources; thus, they too must be paid for. The resources used to produce capital

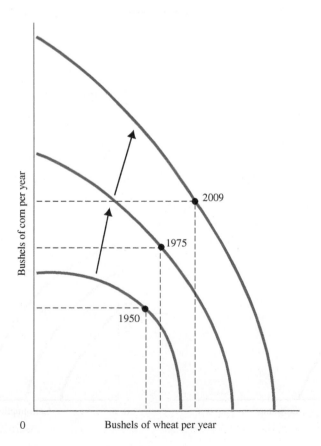

◀ **FIGURE 2.7 Economic Growth Shifts the PPF Up and to the Right**
Productivity increases have enhanced the ability of the United States to produce both corn and wheat. As Table 2.2 shows, productivity increases were more dramatic for corn than for wheat. Thus, the shifts in the ppf were not parallel.

goods—to build a road, a tractor, or a manufacturing plant—*and* to develop new technologies could have been used to produce consumer goods.

When a large part of a country's population is poor, taking resources out of the production of consumer goods (such as food and clothing) is difficult. In addition, in some countries, people wealthy enough to invest in domestic industries choose instead to invest abroad because of political turmoil at home. As a result, it often falls to the governments of poor countries to generate revenues for capital production and research out of tax collections.

All these factors have contributed to the growing gap between some poor and rich nations. Figure 2.8 shows the result using ppfs. On the bottom left, the rich country devotes a larger portion of its production to capital, whereas the poor country on the top left produces mostly consumer goods. On the right, you see the results: The ppf of the rich country shifts up and out further and faster.

The importance of capital goods and technological developments to the position of workers in less-developed countries is well-illustrated by Robert Jensen's study of South India's industry. Conventional telephones require huge investments in wires and towers and, as a result, many less developed areas are without landlines. Mobile phones, on the other hand, require a lower investment; thus, in many areas, people upgraded from no phones directly to cell phones. Jensen found that in small fishing villages, the advent of cell phones allowed fishermen to determine on any given day where to take their catch to sell, resulting in a large decrease in fish wasted and an increase in fishing profits. The ability of newer communication technology to aid development is one of the exciting features of our times. (See Robert Jensen, "The Digital Provide: Information Technology, Market Performance, and Welfare in the South Indian Fisheries Sector," *Quarterly Journal of Economics*, 2007: 879–924.)

Although it exists only as an abstraction, the ppf illustrates a number of important concepts that we will use throughout the rest of this book: scarcity, unemployment, inefficiency, opportunity cost, the law of increasing opportunity cost, economic growth, and the gains from trade.

▶ **FIGURE 2.8 Capital Goods and Growth in Poor and Rich Countries**
Rich countries find it easier than poor countries to devote resources to the production of capital, and the more resources that flow into capital production, the faster the rate of economic growth. Thus, the gap between poor and rich countries has grown over time.

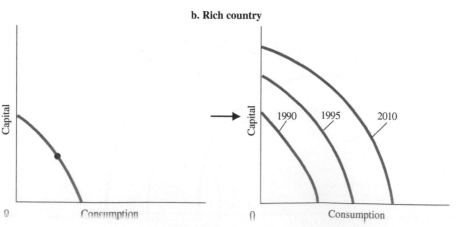

ECONOMICS IN PRACTICE

Trade-Offs among the Rich and Poor

In all societies, for all people, resources are limited relative to people's demands. There are, however, quite large differences in the kinds of trade-offs individuals face in rich versus poor countries.

In 1990, the World Bank defined the extremely poor people of the world as those earning less than $1 a day. Among development economists and policy makers, this figure continues to be used as a rough rule of thumb. In a recent survey, Abhijit Banerjee and Esther Duflo, two MIT economists, surveyed individuals living at this level in 13 countries across the world.[1] What did they learn about the consumption trade-offs faced by these individuals versus consumers in the United States?

It should not surprise you to learn that for the extremely poor, food is a much larger component of the budget. On average over the 13 countries, between 56 percent and 78 percent of consumption was spent on food. In the United States, just under 10 percent of the average budget goes to food. Even for the poorest consumers, however, biological need is not all determining. The Banerjee and Duflo study finds that in Udaipur, India, almost 10 percent of the typical food budget goes to sugar and processed foods rather than more nutritionally valuable grains. So even at these low levels of income, some choice remains. Perhaps more interestingly, almost 10 percent of the budget of those surveyed goes to weddings, funerals, and other festivals. In societies with very few entertainment outlets, Banerjee and Duflo suggest we

may see more demand for festivals, indicating that even in extremely poor societies, household choice plays a role.

THINKING PRACTICALLY

1. Why might we see a greater demand for festivals in poor countries than in rich ones? How might this be affected by choices available?

[1] Abhijit Banerjee and Esther Duflo, "The Economic Lives of the Poor," *Journal of Economic Perspective*, Winter 2007: 141–167.

The Economic Problem

Recall the three basic questions facing all economic systems: (1) What gets produced? (2) How is it produced? and (3) Who gets it?

When Bill was alone on the island, the mechanism for answering those questions was simple: He thought about his own wants and preferences, looked at the constraints imposed by the resources of the island and his own skills and time, and made his decisions. As Bill set about his work, he allocated available resources quite simply, more or less by dividing up his available time. Distribution of the output was irrelevant. Because Bill was the society, he got it all.

Introducing even one more person into the economy—in this case, Colleen—changed all that. Cooperation and coordination may give rise to gains that would otherwise not be possible. When a society consists of millions of people, coordination and cooperation become more challenging, but the potential for gain also grows. In large, complex economies, specialization can grow dramatically. The range of products available in a modern industrial society is beyond anything that could have been imagined a hundred years ago, and so is the range of jobs. Specialization plays a role in this.

The amount of coordination and cooperation in a modern industrial society is almost impossible to imagine. Yet something seems to drive economic systems, if sometimes clumsily and inefficiently, toward producing the goods and services that people want. Given scarce resources, how do large, complex societies go about answering the three basic economic questions? This is the economic problem, which is what this text is about.

2.2 LEARNING OBJECTIVE

Understand the central difference in the way command
economies and market economies decide what is produced.

Economic Systems and the Role of Government

Thus far we have described the questions that the economic system must answer. Now we turn to the mechanics of the system. What is the role played by government in deciding what and how things are produced? There are many circumstances in which the government may be able to improve the functioning of the market.

Command Economies

command economy An economy in which a central government either directly or indirectly sets output targets, incomes, and prices.

In a pure **command economy**, like the system in place in the Soviet Union or China some years ago, the basic economic questions are answered by a central government. Through a combination of government ownership of state enterprises and central planning, the government, either directly or indirectly, sets output targets, incomes, and prices.

At present, for most countries in the world, private enterprise plays at least some role in production decisions. The debate today is instead about the extent and the character of government's role in the economy. Government involvement, in theory, may improve the efficiency and fairness of the allocation of a nation's resources. At the same time, a poorly functioning government can destroy incentives, lead to corruption, and result in the waste of a society's resources.

Laissez-Faire Economies: The Free Market

laissez-faire economy Literally from the French: "allow [them] to do." An economy in which individual people and firms pursue their own self-interest without any government direction or regulation.

market The institution through which buyers and sellers interact and engage in exchange.

At the opposite end of the spectrum from the command economy is the **laissez-faire economy**. The term *laissez-faire*, which translated literally from French means "allow [them] to do," implies a complete lack of government involvement in the economy. In this type of economy, individuals and firms pursue their own self-interest without any central direction or regulation; the sum total of millions of individual decisions ultimately determines all basic economic outcomes. The central institution through which a laissez-faire system answers the basic questions is the **market**, a term that is used in economics to mean an institution through which buyers and sellers interact and engage in exchange.

In short:

> Some markets are simple and others are complex, but they all involve buyers and sellers engaging in exchange. The behavior of buyers and sellers in a laissez-faire economy determines what gets produced, how it is produced, and who gets it.

The following chapters explore market systems in great depth. A quick preview is worthwhile here, however.

consumer sovereignty The idea that consumers ultimately dictate what will be produced (or not produced) by choosing what to purchase (and what not to purchase).

Consumer Sovereignty In a free, unregulated market, goods and services are produced and sold only if the supplier can make a profit. In simple terms, making a *profit* means selling goods or services for more than it costs to produce them. You cannot make a profit unless someone wants the product that you are selling. This logic leads to the notion of **consumer sovereignty**: The mix of output found in any free market system is dictated ultimately by the tastes and preferences of consumers who "vote" by buying or not buying. Businesses rise and fall in response to consumer demands. No central directive or plan is necessary.

Individual Production Decisions: Free Enterprise Under a free market system, individual producers must also determine how to organize and coordinate the actual production of their products or services. In a free market economy, producers may be small or large. One person who is good with computers may start a business designing Web sites. On a larger scale, a group of furniture designers may put together a large portfolio of sketches, raise several million dollars, and start a bigger business. At the extreme are huge corporations such as Microsoft, Mitsubishi, Apple, and Intel, each of which sells tens of billions of dollars' worth of products every year. Whether the firms are large or small, however, production decisions in a market economy are made by separate private organizations acting in what they perceive to be their own interests.

Proponents of free market systems argue that the use of markets leads to more efficient production and better response to diverse and changing consumer preferences. If a producer is inefficient, competitors will come along, fight for the business, and eventually take it away. Thus, in a free market economy, competition forces producers to use efficient techniques of production and to produce goods that consumers want.

Distribution of Output In a free market system, the distribution of output—who gets what—is also determined in a decentralized way. To the extent that income comes from working for a wage, it is at least in part determined by individual choice. You will work for the wages available in the market only if these wages (and the products and services they can buy) are sufficient to compensate you for what you give up by working. You may discover that you can increase your income by getting more education or training.

Price Theory The basic coordinating mechanism in a free market system is price. A price is the amount that a product sells for per unit, and it reflects what society is willing to pay. Prices of inputs—labor, land, and capital—determine how much it costs to produce a product. Prices of various kinds of labor, or *wage rates*, determine the rewards for working in different jobs and professions. Many of the independent decisions made in a market economy involve the weighing of prices and costs, so it is not surprising that much of economic theory focuses on the factors that influence and determine prices. This is why microeconomic theory is often simply called *price theory*.

In sum:

> In a free market system, the basic economic questions are answered without the help of a central government plan or directives. This is what the "free" in free market means—the system is left to operate on its own with no outside interference. Individuals pursuing their own self-interest will go into business and produce the products and services that people want. Other individuals will decide whether to acquire skills; whether to work; and whether to buy, sell, invest, or save the income that they earn. The basic coordinating mechanism is price.

Mixed Systems, Markets, and Governments

The differences between command economies and laissez-faire economies in their pure forms are enormous. In fact, these pure forms do not exist in the world; all real systems are in some sense "mixed." That is, individual enterprise exists and independent choice is exercised even in economies in which the government plays a major role.

Conversely, no market economies exist without government involvement and government regulation. The United States has basically a free market economy, but government purchases accounted for slightly more than 18 percent of the country's total production in 2014 Governments in the United States (local, state, and federal) directly employ about 14 percent of all workers (15 percent including active duty military). They also redistribute income by means of taxation and social welfare expenditures, and they regulate many economic activities.

One of the major themes in this book, and indeed in economics, is the tension between the advantages of free, unregulated markets and the desire for government involvement. Identifying what the market does well, and where it potentially fails, and exploring the role of government in dealing with market failure is a key topic in policy economics. We return to this debate many times throughout this text.

Looking Ahead

This chapter described the economic problem in broad terms. We outlined the questions that all economic systems must answer. We also discussed broadly the two kinds of economic systems. In the next chapter, we analyze the way market systems work.

SUMMARY

1. Every society has some system or process for transforming into useful form what nature and previous generations have provided. Economics is the study of that process and its outcomes.

2. *Producers* are those who take resources and transform them into usable products, or *outputs*. Private firms, households, and governments all produce something.

2.1 SCARCITY, CHOICE, AND OPPORTUNITY COST *p. 23*

3. All societies must answer *three basic questions*: What gets produced? How is it produced? Who gets what is produced? These three questions make up the *economic problem*.

4. One person alone on an island must make the same basic decisions that complex societies make. When a society consists of more than one person, questions of distribution, cooperation, and specialization arise.

5. Because resources are scarce relative to human wants in all societies, using resources to produce one good or service implies *not* using them to produce something else. This concept of *opportunity cost* is central to understanding economics.

6. Using resources to produce *capital* that will in turn produce benefits in the future implies *not* using those resources to produce consumer goods in the present.

7. Even if one individual or nation is absolutely more efficient at producing goods than another, all parties will gain if they specialize in producing goods in which they have a *comparative advantage*.

8. A *production possibility frontier* (ppf) is a graph that shows all the combinations of goods and services that can be produced if all of society's resources are used efficiently. The ppf illustrates a number of important economic concepts: scarcity, unemployment, inefficiency, increasing opportunity cost, and economic growth.

9. *Economic growth* occurs when society produces more, either by acquiring more resources or by learning to produce more with existing resources. Improved productivity may come from additional capital or from the discovery and application of new, more efficient techniques of production.

2.2 ECONOMIC SYSTEMS AND THE ROLE OF GOVERNMENT *p. 36*

10. In some modern societies, government plays a big role in answering the three basic questions. In pure *command economies*, a central authority directly or indirectly sets output targets, incomes, and prices.

11. A *laissez-faire economy* is one in which individuals independently pursue their own self-interest, without any central direction or regulation, and ultimately determine all basic economic outcomes.

12. A *market* is an institution through which buyers and sellers interact and engage in exchange. Some markets involve simple face-to-face exchange; others involve a complex series of transactions, often over great distances or through electronic means.

13. There are no purely planned economies and no pure laissez-faire economies; all economies are mixed. Individual enterprise, independent choice, and relatively free markets exist in centrally planned economies; there is significant government involvement in market economies such as that of the United States.

14. One of the great debates in economics revolves around the tension between the advantages of free, unregulated markets and the desire for government involvement in the economy. Free markets produce what people want, and competition forces firms to adopt efficient production techniques. The need for government intervention arises because free markets are characterized by inefficiencies and an unequal distribution of income and experience regular periods of inflation and unemployment.

REVIEW TERMS AND CONCEPTS

absolute advantage, *p. 25*

capital, *p. 22*

command economy, *p. 36*

comparative advantage, *p. 26*

consumer goods, *p. 28*

consumer sovereignty, *p. 36*

economic growth, *p. 32*

factors of production (or factors), *p. 23*

inputs *or* resources, *p. 23*

investment, *p. 28*

laissez-faire economy, *p. 36*

marginal rate of transformation (MRT), *p. 30*

market, *p. 36*

opportunity cost, *p. 24*

outputs, *p. 23*

production, *p. 23*

production possibility frontier (ppf), *p. 29*

theory of comparative advantage, *p. 24*

PROBLEMS

All problems are available on MyEconLab.

2.1 SCARCITY, CHOICE, AND OPPORTUNITY COST

LEARNING OBJECTIVE: Understand why even in a society in which one person is better than a second at all tasks, it is still beneficial for the two to specialize and trade.

1.1 For each of the following, describe some of the potential opportunity costs:
  a. Going home for Thanksgiving vacation
  b. Riding your bicycle 20 miles every day
  c. The federal government using tax revenue to purchase 10,000 acres in Florida for use as a bird sanctuary
  d. A foreign government subsidizes its national airline to keep airfares down
  e. Upgrading to a balcony suite for your cruise around the Mediterranean Sea
  f. Staying up all night to watch season 5 of *Game of Thrones*

1.2 "As long as all resources are fully employed and every firm in the economy is producing its output using the best available technology, the result will be efficient." Do you agree or disagree with this statement? Explain your answer.

1.3 You are an intern to the editor of a small-town newspaper in Mallsburg, Pennsylvania. Your boss, the editor, asks you to write the first draft of an editorial for this week's paper. Your assignment is to describe the costs and the benefits of building a new bridge across the railroad tracks in the center of town. Currently, most people who live in this town must drive 2 miles through thickly congested traffic to the existing bridge to get to the main shopping and employment center. The bridge will cost the citizens of Mallsburg $25 million, which will be paid for with a tax on their incomes over the next 20 years. What are the opportunity costs of building this bridge? What are the benefits that citizens will likely receive if the bridge is built? What other factors might you consider in writing this editorial?

1.4 Alexi and Tony own a food truck that serves only two items, street tacos and Cuban sandwiches. As shown in the table, Alexi can make 80 street tacos per hour but only 20 Cuban sandwiches. Tony is a bit faster and can make 100 street tacos or 30 Cuban sandwiches in an hour. Alexi and Tony can sell all the street tacos and Cuban sandwiches that they are able to produce.

Output Per Hour

	Street Tacos	Cuban Sandwiches
Alexi	80	20
Tony	100	30

  a. For Alexi and for Tony, what is the opportunity cost of a street taco? Who has a comparative advantage in the production of street tacos? Explain your answer.
  b. Who has a comparative advantage in the production of Cuban sandwiches? Explain your answer.
  c. Assume that Alexi works 20 hours per week in the business. Assuming Alexi is in business on his own, graph the possible combinations of street tacos and Cuban sandwiches that he could produce in a week. Do the same for Tony.
  d. If Alexi devoted half of his time (10 out of 20 hours) to making street tacos and half of his time to making Cuban sandwiches, how many of each would he produce in a week? If Tony did the same, how many of each would he produce? How many street tacos and Cuban sandwiches would be produced in total?
  e. Suppose that Alexi spent all 20 hours of his time on street tacos and Tony spent 17 hours on Cuban Sandwiches and 3 hours on street tacos. How many of each item would be produced?
  f. Suppose that Alexi and Tony can sell all their street tacos for $2 each and all their Cuban Sandwiches for $7.25 each. If each of them worked 20 hours per week, how should they split their time between the production of street tacos and Cuban sandwiches? What is their maximum joint revenue?

1.5 Briefly describe the trade-offs involved in each of the following decisions. Specifically, list some of the opportunity costs associated with each decision, paying particular attention to the trade-offs between present and future consumption.
  a. After a stressful senior year in high school, Sherice decides to take the summer off instead of working before going to college.
  b. Frank is overweight and decides to work out every day and to go on a diet.
  c. Mei is diligent about taking her car in for routine maintenance even though it takes 2 hours of her time and costs $100 four times each year.
  d. Jim is in a hurry. He runs a red light on the way to work.

***1.6** The countries of Orion and Scorpius are small mountainous nations. Both produce granite and blueberries. Each nation has a labor force of 800. The following table gives production per month for each worker in each country. Assume productivity is constant and identical for each worker in each country.

	Tons of Granite	Bushels of Blueberries
Orion workers	6	18
Scorpius workers	3	12

Productivity of one worker for one month

  a. Which country has an absolute advantage in the production of granite? Which country has an absolute advantage in the production of blueberries?
  b. Which country has a comparative advantage in the production of granite? of blueberries?
  c. Sketch the ppf's for both countries.

    d. Assuming no trading between the two, if both countries wanted to have equal numbers of tons of granite and bushels of blueberries, how would they allocate workers to the two sectors?

    e. Show that specialization and trade can move both countries beyond their ppf's.

*1.7 Match each diagram in Figure 1 with its description here. Assume that the economy is producing or attempting to produce at point *A* and that most members of society like meat and not fish. Some descriptions apply to more than one diagram, and some diagrams have more than one description.

    a. Inefficient production of meat and fish

    b. Productive efficiency

    c. An inefficient mix of output

    d. Technological advances in the production of meat and fish

    e. The law of increasing opportunity cost

    f. An impossible combination of meat and fish

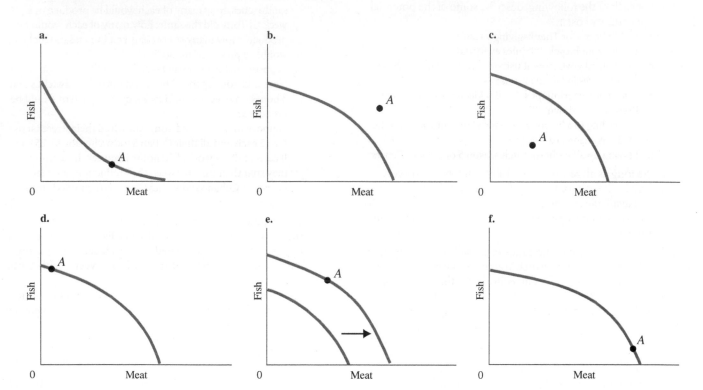

▲ **FIGURE 1**

1.8 A nation with fixed quantities of resources is able to produce any of the following combinations of carpet and carpet looms:

Yards of carpet (Millions)	Carpet looms (Thousands)
0	45
12	42
24	36
36	27
48	15
60	0

These figures assume that a certain number of previously produced looms are available in the current period for producing carpet.

    a. Using the data in the table, graph the ppf (with carpet on the vertical axis).

    b. Does the principle of "increasing opportunity cost" hold in this nation? Explain briefly. (*Hint:* What happens to the opportunity cost of carpet—measured in number of looms—as carpet production increases?)

    c. If this country chooses to produce both carpet and looms, what will happen to the ppf over time? Why?

Now suppose that a new technology is discovered that allows an additional 50 percent of yards of carpet to be produced by each existing loom.

    d. Illustrate (on your original graph) the effect of this new technology on the ppf.

    e. Suppose that before the new technology is introduced, the nation produces 15 thousand looms. After the new technology is introduced, the nation produces 27 thousand looms. What is the effect of the new technology on the production of carpet? (Give the number of yards before and after the change.)

*Note: Problems with an asterisk are more challenging.

1.9 [Related to the *Economics in Practice* on p. 25] An analysis of a large-scale survey of consumer food purchases by Mark Aguiar and Erik Hurst indicates that retired people spend less for the same market basket of food than working people do. Use the concept of opportunity cost to explain this fact.

*1.10 Betty Lou has a car washing and detailing business. She charges $20 to wash a car, a process that takes her 20 minutes and requires no help or materials. For car detailing, a process requiring 1 hour, she charges $50 net of materials. Again, no help is required. Is anything puzzling about Betty Lou's pricing pattern? Explain your answer.

1.11 At the end of the 2014 NFL regular season, the Louisiana Lottery allowed customers to enter their non-winning New Orleans Saints scratch-off lottery game tickets in a final second-chance drawing, with a chance to win the 2015 Saints Season Prize Package Experience. This package includes 4 Plaza Sideline tickets and field passes to every 2015 Saints home game, a season parking pass, and overnight accommodations for each home game. Suppose you entered this second-chance drawing and won this Season Prize Package Experience for the Saints' 2015 season. Would there be a cost to you to attend the Saints' games during the 2015 season?

1.12 High school football is arguably more popular in West Texas than in any other region of the country. During football season, small towns seem to shut down on Friday nights as local high school teams take to the field, and for the following week the results of the games are the talk of each town. Taking into consideration that many of these towns are one hundred or more miles away from any medium-sized or large cities, what might be an economic explanation for the extreme popularity of high school football in these small West Texas towns?

1.13 The nation of Billabong is able to produce surfboards and kayaks in combinations represented by the data in the following table. Each number represents thousands of units. Plot this data on a production possibilities graph and explain why the data shows that Billabong experiences increasing opportunity costs.

	A	B	C	D	E
Surfboards	0	20	40	60	80
Kayaks	28	24	18	10	0

1.14 Explain how each of the following situations would affect a nation's production possibilities curve.
   a. A law is passed which makes community college tuition-free for all U.S. citizens.
   b. An unexpectedly mild spring results in a bumper crop of citrus fruit in both Florida and California.
   c. A change in immigration laws significantly increases the number of immigrant workers entering the country.
   d. The amount of time that unemployed workers can collect unemployment insurance is increased from 26 weeks to 96 weeks during a recession, resulting in workers remaining unemployed for a longer period of time.
   e. An innovation in desalinization technology allows for the more efficient conversion of salt water to fresh water.
   f. A radiation leak at a nuclear power plant results in the long-term evacuation of a 10,000 square-mile area, which significantly reduces the nation's productive capacity.

2.2 ECONOMIC SYSTEMS AND THE ROLE OF GOVERNMENT

LEARNING OBJECTIVE: Understand the central difference in the way command economies and market economies decide what is produced.

2.1 Describe a command economy and a laissez-faire economy. Do any economic systems in the world reflect the purest forms of command or laissez-faire economies? Explain.

2.2 Suppose that a simple society has an economy with only one resource, labor. Labor can be used to produce only two commodities—X, a necessity good (food), and Y, a luxury good (music and merriment). Suppose that the labor force consists of 100 workers. One laborer can produce either 5 units of necessity per month (by hunting and gathering) or 10 units of luxury per month (by writing songs, playing the guitar, dancing, and so on).
   a. On a graph, draw the economy's ppf. Where does the ppf intersect the Y-axis? Where does it intersect the X-axis? What meaning do those points have?
   b. Suppose the economy produced at a point *inside* the ppf. Give at least two reasons why this could occur. What could be done to move the economy to a point *on* the ppf?
   c. Suppose you succeeded in lifting your economy to a point on its ppf. What point would you choose? How might your small society decide the point at which it wanted to be?
   d. Once you have chosen a point on the ppf, you still need to decide how your society's production will be divided. If you were a dictator, how would you decide? What would happen if you left product distribution to the free market?

3

Demand, Supply, and Market Equilibrium

Chapters 1 and 2 introduced the discipline, methodology, and subject matter of economics. We now begin the task of analyzing how a market economy actually works. This chapter and the next present an overview of the way individual markets work, introducing concepts used in both microeconomics and macroeconomics.

In the simple island society discussed in Chapter 2, Bill and Colleen solved the economic problem directly. They allocated their time and used the island's resources to satisfy their wants. Exchange occurred in a relatively simple way. In larger societies, with people typically operating at some distance from one another, exchange can be more complex. *Markets* are the institutions through which exchange typically takes place.

This chapter begins to explore the basic forces at work in market systems. The purpose of our discussion is to explain how the individual decisions of households and firms together, without any central planning or direction, answer the three basic questions: What gets produced? How is it produced? Who gets what is produced? We begin with some definitions.

Firms and Households: The Basic Decision-Making Units

3.1 LEARNING OBJECTIVE

Understand the roles of firms, entrepreneurs, and households in the market.

Throughout this book, we discuss and analyze the behavior of two fundamental decision-making units: *firms*—the primary producing units in an economy—and *households*—the consuming units in an economy. Both are made up of people performing different functions and playing different roles. Economics is concerned with how those people behave, and the interaction among them.

A **firm** exists when a person or a group of people decides to produce a product or products by transforming *inputs*—that is, resources in the broadest sense—*into outputs*, the products that are sold in the market. Some firms produce goods; others produce services. Some are large, many are small, and some are in between. All firms exist to transform resources into goods and services that people want. The Colorado Symphony Orchestra takes labor, land, a building, musically talented people, instruments, and other inputs and combines them to produce concerts. The production process can be extremely complicated. For example, the first flautist in the orchestra combines training, talent, previous performance experience, score, instrument, conductor's interpretation, and personal feelings about the music to produce just one contribution to an overall performance.

firm An organization that transforms resources (inputs) into products (outputs). Firms are the primary producing units in a market economy.

Most firms exist to make a profit for their owners, but some do not. Columbia University, for example, fits the description of a firm: It takes inputs in the form of labor, land, skills, books, and buildings and produces a service that we call *education*. Although the university sells that service for a price, it does not exist to make a profit; instead, it exists to provide education and research of the highest quality possible.

Still, most firms exist to make a profit. They engage in production because they can sell their product for more than it costs to produce it. The analysis of a firm's behavior that follows rests on the assumption that *firms make decisions to maximize profits*. Sometimes firms suffer losses instead of earning profits. When firms suffer losses, we will assume that they act to minimize those losses.

An **entrepreneur** is someone who organizes, manages, and assumes the risks of a firm. When a new firm is created, someone must organize the new firm, arrange financing, hire employees, and take risks. That person is an entrepreneur. Sometimes existing firms introduce new products, and sometimes new firms develop or improve on an old idea, but at the root of it all is entrepreneurship.

entrepreneur A person who organizes, manages, and assumes the risks of a firm, taking a new idea or a new product and turning it into a successful business.

The consuming units in an economy are **households**. A household may consist of any number of people: a single person living alone, a married couple with four children, or 15 unrelated people sharing a house. Household decisions are based on individual tastes and preferences. The household buys what it wants and can afford. In a large, heterogeneous, and open society such as the United States, wildly different tastes find expression in the marketplace. A six-block walk in any direction on any street in Manhattan or a drive from the Chicago Loop south into rural Illinois should be enough to convince anyone that it is difficult to generalize about what people do and do not like.

households The consuming units in an economy.

Even though households have wide-ranging preferences, they also have some things in common. All—even the very rich—have ultimately limited incomes, and all must pay in some way for the goods and services they consume. Although households may have some control over their incomes—they can work more hours or fewer hours—they are also constrained by the availability of jobs, current wages, their own abilities, and their accumulated and inherited wealth (or lack thereof).

Input Markets and Output Markets: The Circular Flow

3.2 LEARNING OBJECTIVE

Understand the role of households as both suppliers to firms and buyers of what firms produce.

Households and firms interact in two basic kinds of markets: product (or output) markets and input (or factor) markets. Goods and services that are intended for use by households are

product *or* output markets
The markets in which goods and services are exchanged.

input *or* factor markets
The markets in which the resources used to produce goods and services are exchanged.

labor market The input/factor market in which households supply work for wages to firms that demand labor.

capital market The input/factor market in which households supply their savings, for interest or for claims to future profits, to firms that demand funds to buy capital goods.

land market The input/factor market in which households supply land or other real property in exchange for rent.

factors of production
The inputs into the production process. Land, labor, and capital are the three key factors of production.

exchanged in **product *or* output markets**. In output markets, firms *supply* and households *demand*.

To produce goods and services, firms must buy resources in **input *or* factor markets**. Firms buy inputs from households, which supply these inputs. When a firm decides how much to produce (supply) in output markets, it must simultaneously decide how much of each input it needs to produce the desired level of output. To produce smart phones Samsung and Apple need many inputs, including hardware and software and a variety of types of labor, both skilled and unskilled.

Figure 3.1 shows the *circular flow* of economic activity through a simple market economy. Note that the flow reflects the direction in which goods and services flow through input and output markets. For example, real goods and services flow from firms to households through output—or product—markets. Labor services flow from households to firms through input markets. Payment (most often in money form) for goods and services flows in the opposite direction.

In input markets, households *supply* resources. Most households earn their incomes by working—they supply their labor in the **labor market** to firms that demand labor and pay workers for their time and skills. Households may also loan their accumulated or inherited savings to firms for interest or exchange those savings for claims to future profits, as when a household buys shares of stock in a corporation. In the **capital market**, households supply the funds that firms use to buy capital goods. Households may also supply land or other real property in exchange for rent in the **land market**.

Inputs into the production process are also called **factors of production**. Land, labor, and capital are the three key factors of production. Throughout this text, we use the terms *input* and *factor of production* interchangeably. Thus, input markets and factor markets mean the same thing.

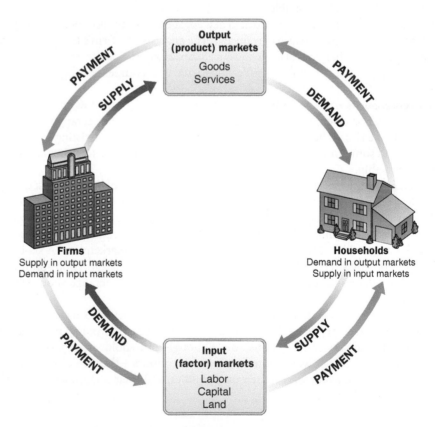

▲ **FIGURE 3.1 The Circular Flow of Economic Activity**
Diagrams like this one show the circular flow of economic activity, hence the name *circular flow diagram*. Here goods and services flow clockwise: Labor services supplied by households flow to firms, and goods and services produced by firms flow to households. Payment (usually money) flows in the opposite (counterclockwise) direction: Payment for goods and services flows from households to firms, and payment for labor services flows from firms to households.

Note: Color Guide-In Figure 3.1 households are depicted in *blue* and firms are depicted in *red*. From now on all diagrams relating to the behavior of households will be blue or shades of blue and all diagrams relating to the behavior of firms will be red or shades of red. The green color indicates a monetary flow.

The supply of inputs and their prices ultimately determine household income. Thus, the amount of income a household earns depends on the decisions it makes concerning what types of inputs it chooses to supply. Whether to stay in school, how much and what kind of training to get, whether to start a business, how many hours to work, whether to work at all, and how to invest savings are all household decisions that affect income.

As you can see:

> Input and output markets are connected through the behavior of both firms and households. Firms determine the quantities and character of outputs produced and the types and quantities of inputs demanded. Households determine the types and quantities of products demanded and the quantities and types of inputs supplied.[1]

In 2015 a 12-pack of 12 oz. soda costs about $5, and many of you likely have one somewhere in your dormitory room. What determines the price of that soda? How can I explain how much soda you will buy in a given month or year? By the end of this chapter you will see the way in which prices in the market are determined by the interaction of buyers like you and suppliers like soda manufacturers. The model of supply and demand covered in this chapter is the most powerful tool of economics. By the time you finish this chapter we hope you will look at shopping in a different way.

Demand in Product/Output Markets

3.3 LEARNING OBJECTIVE

Understand what determines the position and shape of the demand curve and what factors move you along a demand curve and what factors shift the demand curve.

Every week you make hundreds of decisions about what to buy. Your choices likely look different from those of your friends or your parents. For all of you, however, the decision about what to buy and how much of it to buy ultimately depends on six factors:

- The *price of the product* in question.
- The *income available* to the household.
- The household's *amount of accumulated wealth*.
- The *prices of other products* available to the household.
- The household's *tastes and preferences*.
- The household's *expectations* about future income, wealth, and prices.

Quantity demanded is the amount (number of units) of a product that a household would buy in a given period *if it could buy all it wanted at the current market price*. Of course, the amount of a product that households finally purchase depends on the amount of product actually available in the market. The expression *if it could buy all it wanted* is critical to the definition of quantity demanded because it allows for the possibility that quantity supplied and quantity demanded are unequal.

quantity demanded   The amount (number of units) of a product that a household would buy in a given period if it could buy all it wanted at the current market price.

Changes in Quantity Demanded versus Changes in Demand

In our list of what determines how much you buy of a product the price of that product comes first. This is no accident. The most important relationship in individual markets is between market price and quantity demanded. So that is where we will start our work. In fact, we begin by looking

---

[1] Our description of markets begins with the behavior of firms and households. Modern orthodox economic theory essentially combines two distinct but closely related theories of behavior. The "theory of household behavior," or "consumer behavior," has its roots in the works of nineteenth-century utilitarians such as Jeremy Bentham, William Jevons, Carl Menger, Leon Walras, Vilfredo Parcto, and F. Y. Edgeworth. The "theory of the firm" developed out of the earlier classical political economy of Adam Smith, David Ricardo, and Thomas Malthus. In 1890, Alfred Marshall published the first of many editions of his *Principles of Economics*. That volume pulled together the main themes of both the classical economists and the utilitarians into what is now called *neoclassical economics*. Although there have been many changes over the years, the basic structure of the model that we build can be found in Marshall's work.

at what happens to the quantity a typical individual demands of a product when all that changes is its price. Economists refer to this device as *ceteris paribus*, or "all else equal." We will be looking at the relationship between quantity demanded of a good by an individual or household when its price changes, holding income, wealth, other prices, tastes, and expectations constant. If the price of that 12-pack of soda were cut in half, how many more cases would you buy in a given week?

In thinking about this question it is important to focus on the price change alone and to maintain the all else equal assumption. If next week you suddenly found yourself with more money than you expected (perhaps a windfall from an aunt), you might well find yourself buying an extra 12-pack of soda even if the price did not change at all. To be sure that we distinguish clearly between changes in price and other changes that affect demand, throughout the rest of the text we will be precise about terminology. Specifically:

Changes in the price of a product affect the *quantity demanded* per period. Changes in any other factor, such as income or preferences, affect *demand*. Thus, we say that an increase in the price of Coca-Cola is likely to cause a decrease in the *quantity of Coca-Cola demanded*. However, we say that an increase in income is likely to cause an increase in the *demand* for most goods.

Price and Quantity Demanded: The Law of Demand

demand schedule   Shows how much of a given product a household would be willing to buy at different prices for a given time period.

A **demand schedule** shows how much of a product a person or household is willing to purchase per time period (each week or each month) at different prices. Clearly that decision is based on numerous interacting factors. Consider Alex who just graduated from college with an entry-level job at a local bank. During her senior year, Alex got a car loan and bought a used Mini Cooper. The Mini gets 25 miles per gallon of gasoline. Alex lives with several friends in a house 10 miles from her workplace and enjoys visiting her parents 50 miles away.

How often Alex will decide to drive herself to work and parties, visit her family, or even go joy riding depends on many things, including her income and whether she likes to drive. But the price of gasoline also plays an important role, and it is this relationship between price and quantity demanded that we focus on in the law of demand. With a gasoline price of $3.00 a gallon, Alex might decide to drive herself to work every day, visit her parents once a week, and drive another 50 miles a week for other activities. This driving pattern would add up to 250 miles a week, which would use 10 gallons of gasoline in her Mini. The demand schedule in Table 3.1 thus shows that at a price of $3.00 per gallon, Alex is willing to buy 10 gallons of gasoline. We can see that this demand schedule reflects a lot of information about Alex including where she lives and works and what she likes to do in her spare time.

Now suppose an international crisis in the Middle East causes the price of gasoline at the pump to rise to $5.00 per gallon. How does this affect Alex's demand for gasoline, assuming that everything else remains the same? Driving is now more expensive, and we would not be surprised if Alex decided to take the bus some mornings or share a ride with friends. She might visit her parents less frequently as well. On the demand schedule given in Table 3.1, Alex cuts her desired consumption of gasoline by half to 5 gallons when the price goes to $5.00. If,

TABLE 3.1	Alex's Demand Schedule for Gasoline
Price (per Gallon)	Quantity Demanded (Gallons per Week)
$ 8.00	0
7.00	2
6.00	3
5.00	5
4.00	7
3.00	10
2.00	14
1.00	20
0.00	26

◀ FIGURE 3.2 Alex's Demand Curve
The relationship between price (P) and quantity demanded (q) presented graphically is called a demand curve. Demand curves have a negative slope, indicating that lower prices cause quantity demanded to increase. Note that Alex's demand curve is blue; demand in product markets is determined by household choice.

instead, the price of gasoline fell substantially, Alex might spend more time driving, and that is in fact the pattern we see in the table. This same information presented graphically is called a **demand curve**. Alex's demand curve is presented in Figure 3.2. You will note in Figure 3.2 that *quantity* (q) is measured along the horizontal axis and *price* (P) is measured along the vertical axis. This is the convention we follow throughout this book.

demand curve A graph illustrating how much of a given product a household would be willing to buy at different prices.

Demand Curves Slope Downward
The data in Table 3.1 show that at lower prices, Alex buys more gasoline; at higher prices, she buys less. Thus, there is a *negative, or inverse, relationship between quantity demanded and price*. When price rises, quantity demanded falls, and when price falls, quantity demanded rises. Thus, demand curves always slope downward. This negative relationship between price and quantity demanded is often referred to as the **law of demand**, a term first used by economist Alfred Marshall in his 1890 textbook.

Some people are put off by the abstraction of demand curves. Of course, we do not actually draw our own demand curves for products. When we want to make a purchase, we usually face only a single price and how much we would buy at other prices is irrelevant. However, demand curves help analysts understand the kind of behavior that households are *likely* to exhibit if they are actually faced with a higher or lower price. We know, for example, that if the price of a good rises enough, the quantity demanded must ultimately drop to zero. The demand curve is thus a tool that helps us explain economic behavior and predict reactions to possible price changes.

Marshall's definition of a social "law" captures the idea:

law of demand The negative relationship between price and quantity demanded: *Ceteris paribus*, as price rises, quantity demanded decreases; as price falls, quantity demanded increases during a given period of time, all other things remaining constant.

> The term "law" means nothing more than a general proposition or statement of tendencies, more or less certain, more or less definite…a *social law* is a statement of social tendencies; that is, that a certain course of action may be expected from the members of a social group under certain conditions.[2]

It seems reasonable to expect that consumers will demand more of a product at a lower price and less of it at a higher price. Households must divide their incomes over a wide range of goods and services. At $3.00 per gallon and 25 miles to a gallon, driving the 20 miles round trip to work costs Alex $2.40. It may look like a good deal relative to taking a bus. At $5.00 per gallon, the trip now costs $4.00. With the higher prices, Alex may have to give up her morning latte if she drives, and that may turn out to be too big a sacrifice for her. Now the bus may look better. As the price of gasoline rises, the opportunity cost of driving in terms of other types of consumption also rises and that is why Alex ends up driving less as the price of gasoline rises. Goods compete with one another for our spending.

---

[2] Alfred Marshall, *Principles of Economics*, 8th ed. (New York: Macmillan, 1948), p. 33. (The first edition was published in 1890.)

Economists use the concept of *utility* to explain the slope of the demand curve. We consume goods and services because they give us utility or satisfaction. As we consume more of a product within a given period of time, it is likely that each additional unit consumed will yield successively less satisfaction. The utility you gain from a second ice cream cone is likely to be less than the utility you gained from the first, the third is worth even less, and so on. This *law of diminishing marginal utility* is an important concept in economics. If each successive unit of a good is worth less to you, you are not going to be willing to pay as much for it. Thus, it is reasonable to expect a downward slope in the demand curve for that good.

Thinking about the ways that people are affected by price changes also helps us see what is behind the law of demand. Consider this example: Luis lives and works in Mexico City. His elderly mother lives in Santiago, Chile. Last year the airlines servicing South America got into a price war, and the price of flying between Mexico City and Santiago dropped from 20,000 pesos to 10,000 pesos. How might Luis's behavior change?

First, he is better off. Last year he flew home to Chile three times at a total cost of 60,000 pesos. This year he can fly to Chile the same number of times, buy exactly the same combination of other goods and services that he bought last year, and have 30,000 pesos left over. Because he is better off—his income can buy more—he may fly home more frequently. Second, the opportunity cost of flying home has changed. Before the price war, Luis had to sacrifice 20,000 pesos worth of other goods and services each time he flew to Chile. After the price war, he must sacrifice only 10,000 pesos worth of other goods and services for each trip. The trade-off has changed. Both of these effects are likely to lead to a higher quantity demanded in response to the lower price.

In sum:

> It is reasonable to expect quantity demanded to fall when price rises, ceteris paribus, and to expect quantity demanded to rise when price falls, ceteris paribus. Demand curves have a negative slope.

Other Properties of Demand Curves   Two additional things are notable about Alex's demand curve. First, it intersects the Y, or price, axis. This means that there is a price above which she buys no gasoline. In this case, Alex simply stops driving when the price reaches $8 per gallon. As long as households have limited incomes and wealth, all demand curves will intersect the price axis. For any commodity, there is always a price above which a household will not or cannot pay. Even if the good or service is important, all households are ultimately constrained, or limited, by income and wealth.

Second, Alex's demand curve intersects the X, or quantity, axis. Even at a zero price, there is a limit to how much she will drive. If gasoline were free, she would use 26 gallons, but not more. That demand curves intersect the quantity axis is a matter of common sense. Demand in a given period of time is limited, if only by time, even at a zero price.

To summarize what we know about the shape of demand curves:

1. They have a negative slope. An increase in price is likely to lead to a decrease in quantity demanded, and a decrease in price is likely to lead to an increase in quantity demanded.
2. They intersect the quantity (X) axis, a result of time limitations and diminishing marginal utility.
3. They intersect the price (Y) axis, a result of limited income and wealth.

That is all we can say; it is not possible to generalize further. The actual shape of an individual household demand curve—whether it is steep or flat, whether it is bowed in or bowed out—depends on the unique tastes and preferences of the household and other factors. Some households may be sensitive to price changes; other households may respond little to a change in price. In some cases, plentiful substitutes are available; in other cases, they are not. Thus, to fully understand the shape and position of demand curves, we must turn to the other determinants of household demand.

Other Determinants of Household Demand

Of the many factors likely to influence a household's demand for a specific product, we have considered only the price of the product. But household income and wealth, the prices of other goods and services, tastes and preferences, and expectations also matter to demand.

Income and Wealth   Before we proceed, we need to define two terms that are often confused, *income* and *wealth*. A household's **income** is the sum of all the wages, salaries, profits, interest payments, rents, and other forms of earnings received by the household *in a given period of time*. Income is thus a *flow* measure: We must specify a time period for it—income *per month* or *per year*. You can spend or consume more or less than your income in any given period. If you consume less than your income, you save. To consume more than your income in a period, you must either borrow or draw on savings accumulated from previous periods.

Wealth is the total value of what a household owns minus what it owes. Another word for wealth is **net worth**—the amount a household would have left if it sold all of its possessions and paid all of its debts. Wealth is a *stock* measure: It is measured at a given point in time. If, in a given period, you spend less than your income, you save; the amount that you save is added to your wealth. Saving is the flow that affects the stock of wealth. When you spend more than your income, you *dissave*—you reduce your wealth.

Households with higher incomes and higher accumulated savings or inherited wealth can afford to buy more goods and services. In general, we would expect higher demand at higher levels of income/wealth and lower demand at lower levels of income/wealth. Goods for which demand goes up when income is higher and for which demand goes down when income is lower are called **normal goods**. Movie tickets, restaurant meals, and shirts are all normal goods.

However, generalization in economics can be hazardous. Sometimes demand for a good falls when household income rises. When a household's income rises, it is likely to buy higher-quality meats—its demand for filet mignon is likely to rise—but its demand for lower-quality meats—chuck steak, for example—is likely to fall. At higher incomes, people can afford to fly. People who can afford to fly are less likely to take the bus long distances. Thus, higher income may *reduce* the number of times someone takes a bus. Goods for which demand tends to fall when income rises are called **inferior goods**.

Prices of Other Goods and Services   No consumer decides in isolation on the amount of any one commodity to buy. Instead, each decision is part of a larger set of decisions that are made simultaneously. Households must apportion their incomes over many different goods and services. As a result, the price of any one good can and does affect the demand for other goods. This is most obviously the case when goods are substitutes for one another. For Alex the bus is an alternative that she uses when gasoline gets expensive.

When an *increase* in the price of one good causes demand for another good to *increase* (a positive relationship), we say that the goods are **substitutes**. A *fall* in the price of a good causes a *decline* in demand for its substitutes. Substitutes are goods that can serve as replacements for one another.

To be substitutes, two products do not need to be identical. Identical products are called **perfect substitutes**. Japanese cars are not identical to American cars. Nonetheless, all have four wheels, are capable of carrying people, and use fuel. Thus, significant changes in the price of one country's cars can be expected to influence demand for the other country's cars. Restaurant meals are substitutes for meals eaten at home, and flying from New York to Washington, D.C., is a substitute for taking the train. The *Economics in Practice* box describes substitution in the textbook market.

Often two products "go together"—that is, they complement each other. Bacon and eggs are **complementary goods**, as are cars and gasoline. When two goods are **complements**, a *decrease* in the price of one results in an *increase* in demand for the other and vice versa. For iPads and Kindles, for example, the availability of content at low prices stimulates demand for the devices.

Tastes and Preferences   Income, wealth, and prices of goods available are the three factors that determine the combinations of goods and services that a household is *able* to buy. You know that you cannot afford to rent an apartment at $1,200 per month if your monthly income is only

income   The sum of all a household's wages, salaries, profits, interest payments, rents, and other forms of earnings in a given period of time. It is a flow measure.

wealth *or* net worth   The total value of what a household owns minus what it owes. It is a stock measure.

normal goods   Goods for which demand goes up when income is higher and for which demand goes down when income is lower.

inferior goods   Goods for which demand tends to fall when income rises.

substitutes   Goods that can serve as replacements for one another; when the price of one increases, demand for the other increases.

perfect substitutes   Identical products.

complements, complementary goods   Goods that "go together"; a decrease in the price of one results in an increase in demand for the other and vice versa.

ECONOMICS IN PRACTICE

Have You Bought This Textbook?

As all of you know full well, college textbooks are expensive. And, at first, it may seem as though there are few substitutes available for the cash-strapped undergraduate. After *all*, if your professor assigns Smith's *Principles of Biology* to you, you cannot go out and see if Jones' *Principles of Chemistry* is perhaps cheaper and buy it instead. As it turns out, as some recent work by Judy Chevalier and Austan Goolsbee[1] discovered, even when instructors require particular texts, when prices are high students have found substitutes. Even in the textbook market student demand does slope down!

Chevalier and Goolsbee collected data on textbooks from more than 1600 colleges for the years 1997–2001 to do their research. For that period, the lion's share of both new and used college textbooks was sold in college bookstores. Next, they looked at class enrollments for each college in the large majors, economics, biology, and psychology. In each of those classes they were able to learn which textbook had been assigned. At first, one might think that the total number of textbooks, used plus new, should match the class enrollment. After all, the text is required! In fact, what they found was the higher the textbook price, the more text sales fell below class enrollments.

So what substitutes did students find for the required text? While the paper has no hard evidence on this, students themselves gave them lots of suggestions. Many decide to share books with roommates. Others use the library more. These solutions are not perfect, but when the price is high enough, students find it worth their while to walk to the library!

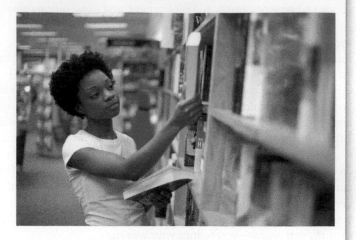

THINKING PRACTICALLY

1. If you were to construct a demand curve for a required text in a course, where would that demand curve intersect the horizontal axis?

2. And this much harder question: In the year before a new edition of a text is published, many college bookstores will not buy the older edition. Given this *fact*, what do you think happens to the gap between enrollments and new plus used book sales in the year before a new edition of a text is expected?

[1] Judith Chevalier and Austan Goolsbee, "Are Durable Goods Consumers Forward Looking? Evidence From College Textbooks," *Quarterly Journal of Economics*, 2009: 1853–1884.

$400, but within these constraints, you are more or less free to choose what to buy. Your final choice depends on your individual tastes and preferences.

Changes in preferences can and do manifest themselves in market behavior. Thirty years ago the major big-city marathons drew only a few hundred runners. Now tens of thousands enter and run. The demand for running shoes, running suits, stopwatches, and other running items has greatly increased.

Within the constraints of prices and incomes, preference shapes the demand curve, but it is difficult to generalize about tastes and preferences. First, they are volatile: Five years ago more people smoked cigarettes and fewer people had smartphones. Second, tastes are idiosyncratic: Some people like to text, whereas others still prefer to use e-mail; some people prefer dogs, whereas others are crazy about cats. The diversity of individual demands is almost infinite.

One of the interesting questions in economics is why, in some markets, diverse consumer tastes give rise to a variety of styles, whereas in other markets, despite a seeming diversity in tastes, we find only one or two varieties. All sidewalks in the United States are a similar gray color, yet houses are painted a rainbow of colors. Yet it is not obvious on the face of it that people would not prefer as much variety in their sidewalks as in their houses. To answer this type of question, we need to move beyond the demand curve. We will revisit this question in a later chapter.

ECONOMICS IN PRACTICE

On Sunny Days People Buy Convertibles!

Cars are a durable good. Most people who buy new cars expect to keep them for a number of years. Cars also have many different features, including size, power, and styling. These features in turn influence consumer demand for one type of car or another. As economists we might well expect people to choose the type of car they buy thinking about which features of those cars they will enjoy over the next few years. A four-wheel-drive car is likely to be more attractive if I expect a lot of snow in the next months or years. A convertible would be fun if it is likely to be clear and sunny on average in my region of the country.

On the other hand, given that cars are durable, we would be surprised if the weather *on a particular day* influenced car purchases. If a potential car buyer wakes up to an unseasonably warm and sunny day in November, we might be surprised if he or she all of a sudden decides to buy a convertible. A sunny day is a good reason to take a hike, but not a good reason to buy a durable good like a convertible that depends for its enjoyment on a string of sunny days. And, yet, in recent work, Meghan Busse, an economist at Northwestern, and her co-authors found after examining more than 40 million car transactions that car purchasers were heavily influenced in their choice of cars by temporary weather fluctuations at the time of purchase.[1] A snow storm increased the likelihood of buying a four-wheel drive vehicle within the next week by 6 percent, holding constant the average snow in that area of the country. An increase of 10-degrees on a fall or spring day over the norm increased purchase of convertibles by almost 3 percent.

Behavioral economists looking at this case would argue that the snow or sun makes one feature of a car—its four-wheel drive feature or soft top—more **salient** or important to the consumer's decision to purchase.

THINKING PRACTICALLY

1. Economists predict that my interest in purchasing a convertible also depends on how much I think other people like convertibles. How is this prediction related to the durability of cars?

[1] Meghan Busse, Devon Pope, Jaron Pope, and Jorge Silva-Russo, "The Psychological Effect of Weather on Car Purchases," *Quarterly Journal of Economics,* February, 2015.

Expectations What you decide to buy today certainly depends on today's prices and your current income and wealth. You also have expectations about what your position will be in the future. You may have expectations about future changes in prices too, and these may affect your decisions today.

There are many examples of the ways expectations affect demand. When people buy a house or a car, they often must borrow part of the purchase price and repay it over a number of years. In deciding what kind of house or car to buy, they presumably must think about their income today, as well as what their income is likely to be in the future.

As another example, consider a student in the final year of medical school living on a scholarship of $25,000. Compare that student with another person earning $12 an hour at a full-time job, with no expectation of a significant change in income in the future. The two have virtually identical incomes. But even if they have the same tastes, the medical student is likely to demand different goods and services, simply because of the expectation of a major increase in income later on.

Increasingly, economic theory has come to recognize the importance of expectations. We will devote a good deal of time to discussing how expectations affect more than just demand. For the time being, however, it is important to understand that demand depends on more than just *current* incomes, prices, and tastes.

TABLE 3.2	Shift of Alex's Demand Schedule Resulting from an Increase in Income	
	Schedule D_0	Schedule D_1
Price (per Gallon)	Quantity Demanded (Gallons per Week at an Income of $500 per Week)	Quantity Demanded (Gallons per Week at an Income of $700 per Week)
$ 8.00	0	3
7.00	2	5
6.00	3	7
5.00	5	10
4.00	7	12
3.00	10	15
2.00	14	19
1.00	20	24
0.00	26	30

Shift of Demand versus Movement along a Demand Curve

Recall that a demand curve shows the relationship between quantity demanded and the price of a good. Demand curves are constructed while holding income, tastes, and other prices constant. If income, tastes, or other prices change, we would have to derive an entirely new relationship between price and quantity.

Let us return once again to Alex. (See Table 3.1 and Figure 3.2 on pp. 46 and 47.) Suppose that when we derived the demand curve in Figure 3.2 Alex was receiving a salary of $500 per week after taxes. If Alex faces a price of $3.00 per gallon and chooses to drive 250 miles per week, her total weekly expenditure works out to be $3.00 per gallon times 10 gallons or $30 per week. That amounts to 6.0 percent of her income.

Suppose now she were to receive a raise to $700 per week after taxes. Alex's higher income may well raise the amount of gasoline being used by Alex *regardless* of what she was using before. The new situation is listed in Table 3.2 and graphed in Figure 3.3. Notice in Figure 3.3 that Alex's entire curve has shifted to the right—at $3.00 a gallon the curve shows an increase in the quantity demanded from 10 to 15 gallons. At $5.00, the quantity demanded by Alex increases from 5 gallons to 10 gallons.

The fact that demand *increased* when income increased implies that gasoline is a *normal good* to Alex.

▶ **FIGURE 3.3** **Shift of a Demand Curve Following a Rise in Income**

When the price of a good changes, we move *along* the demand curve for that good. When any other factor that influences demand changes (income, tastes, and so on), the demand curve shifts, in this case from D_0 to D_1. Gasoline is a normal good so an income increase shifts the curve to the right.

The conditions under which we drew Alex's original demand curve have now changed. One of the factors affecting Alex's demand for gasoline (in this case, her income) has changed, creating a new relationship between price and quantity demanded. This is referred to as a **shift of a demand curve**.

It is important to distinguish between a change in quantity demanded—that is, some movement *along* a demand curve—and a shift of demand. Demand schedules and demand curves show the relationship between the price of a good or service and the quantity demanded per period, ceteris paribus. If price changes, quantity demanded will change—this is a **movement along a demand curve**. When any of the *other* factors that influence demand change, however, a new relationship between price and quantity demanded is established—this is a *shift of a demand curve*. The result, then, is a *new demand curve*. Changes in income, preferences, or prices of other goods cause a demand curve to shift:

Change in price of a good or service leads to
└────➤ change in *quantity demanded* (**movement along a demand curve**).
Change in income, preferences, or prices of other goods or services leads to
└────➤ change in *demand* (**shift of a demand curve**).

Figure 3.4 illustrates the differences between movement along a demand curve and shifting demand curves. In Figure 3.4(a), an increase in household income causes demand for hamburger (an inferior good) to decline, or shift to the left from D_0 to D_1. (Because quantity is measured on the horizontal axis, a decrease means a *shift to the left*.) In contrast, demand for steak (a normal good) increases, or *shifts to the right*, when income rises.

In Figure 3.4(b), an increase in the price of hamburger from $1.49 to $3.09 a pound causes a household to buy less hamburger each month. In other words, the higher price causes the *quantity demanded* to decline from 10 pounds to 5 pounds per month. This change represents a movement *along* the demand curve for hamburger. In place of hamburger, the household buys more chicken. The household's demand for chicken (a substitute for hamburger) rises—the demand curve shifts to the right. At the same time, the demand for ketchup (a good that complements hamburger) declines—its demand curve shifts to the left.

From Household Demand to Market Demand

So far we have been talking about what determines an individual's demand for a product. We ask the question: How many 12-packs of soda are you willing to buy per week when the price of that 12-pack is $5. This is a question you answer often in your life, whenever you go to the local store. We see the answer depends on how much money you have, how much you like soda, and what else is available to you at what price. Next time you go to the store and see a price change, we hope you think a bit more about your buying reaction.

Individual reactions to price changes are interesting, especially to the individual. But for us to be able to say something more general about prices in the market, we need to know about market demand.

Market demand is simply the sum of all the quantities of a good or service demanded per period by all the households buying in the market for that good or service. Figure 3.5 shows the derivation of a market demand curve from three individual demand curves. (Although this market demand curve is derived from the behavior of only three people, most markets have thousands, or even millions of demanders.) As the table in Figure 3.5 shows, when the price of a pound of coffee is $3.50, both household A and household C would purchase 4 pounds per month, while household B would buy none. At that price, presumably, B drinks tea. Market demand at $3.50 would thus be a total of 4 + 4, or 8 pounds. At a price of $1.50 per pound, however, A would purchase 8 pounds per month; B, 3 pounds; and C, 9 pounds. Thus, at $1.50 per pound, market demand would be 8 + 3 + 9, or 20 pounds of coffee per month.

The total quantity demanded in the marketplace at a given price is the sum of all the quantities demanded by all the individual households shopping in the market *at that price*. A market demand curve shows the total amount of a product that would be sold at each price if

---

shift of a demand curve The change that takes place in a demand curve corresponding to a new relationship between quantity demanded of a good and price of that good. The shift is brought about by a change in the original conditions.

movement along a demand curve The change in quantity demanded brought about by a change in price.

market demand The sum of all the quantities of a good or service demanded per period by all the households buying in the market for that good or service.

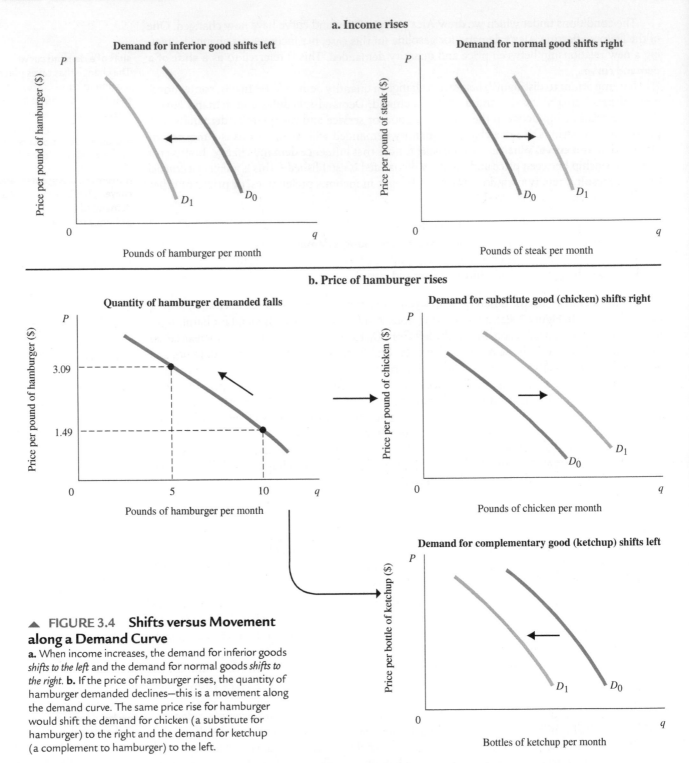

a. Income rises

Demand for inferior good shifts left

Price per pound of hamburger ($)

D_1 D_0

Pounds of hamburger per month

Demand for normal good shifts right

Price per pound of steak ($)

D_0 D_1

Pounds of steak per month

b. Price of hamburger rises

Quantity of hamburger demanded falls

Price per pound of hamburger ($)

3.09

1.49

0   5   10   q

Pounds of hamburger per month

Demand for substitute good (chicken) shifts right

Price per pound of chicken ($)

D_0 D_1

Pounds of chicken per month

Demand for complementary good (ketchup) shifts left

Price per bottle of ketchup ($)

D_1 D_0

Bottles of ketchup per month

▲ **FIGURE 3.4** **Shifts versus Movement along a Demand Curve**
a. When income increases, the demand for inferior goods *shifts to the left* and the demand for normal goods *shifts to the right*. **b.** If the price of hamburger rises, the quantity of hamburger demanded declines—this is a movement along the demand curve. The same price rise for hamburger would shift the demand for chicken (a substitute for hamburger) to the right and the demand for ketchup (a complement to hamburger) to the left.

households could buy all they wanted at that price. As Figure 3.5 shows, the market demand curve is the sum of all the individual demand curves—that is, the sum of all the individual quantities demanded at each price. Thus, the market demand curve takes its shape and position from the shapes, positions, and number of individual demand curves. If more people are in a market, more demand curves must be added and the market demand curve will shift to the right. Market demand curves may also shift as a result of preference changes, income changes, or changes in the price of substitutes or complements.

▲ **FIGURE 3.5   Deriving Market Demand from Individual Demand Curves**
Total demand in the marketplace is simply the sum of the demands of all the households shopping in a particular market. It is the sum of all the individual demand curves—that is, the sum of all the individual quantities demanded at each price.

As a general rule throughout this book, capital letters refer to the entire market and lowercase letters refer to individual households or firms. Thus, in Figure 3.5, Q refers to total quantity demanded in the market, while q refers to the quantity demanded by individual households.

An interesting feature of the demand curve in Figure 3.5 is that at different prices, the *type* of people demanding the product may change. When Apple halved the price of its iPhone in fall 2007, it announced that it wanted to make the iPhone available to a broader group of people. When prices fall, people like those in household B in Figure 3.5 move into markets that are otherwise out of their reach. When Apple introduced a new, improved, but much more expensive iPhone in the fall of 2014, its first sales were likely made to people who both had more resources and were more tech-savvy than the average old model iPhone user. Early adopters of products often look different from later users.

Supply in Product/Output Markets

3.4 LEARNING OBJECTIVE

Be able to distinguish between forces that shift a supply curve and changes that cause a movement along a supply curve.

We began our exploration of supply and demand some pages back with a simple question: Why is the average price of a 12-pack of soda $5 in 2015? So far we have seen one side of the answer: Given the tastes, incomes, and substitute products available in the United States, there are a lot of people willing to pay at least $5 for a 12-pack of soda! Now we turn to the other half of the market: How can we understand the behavior of the many firms selling that soda? What determines their willingness to sell soda? We refer to this as the supply side of the market.

Firms build factories, hire workers, and buy raw materials because they believe they can sell the products they make for more than it costs to produce them. In other words, firms supply goods and services like soda because they believe it will be profitable to do so. Supply decisions thus depend on profit potential. Because **profit** is the difference between revenues and costs, supply is likely to react to changes in revenues and changes in production costs. If the prices of soda are high, each 12-pack produces more revenue for suppliers because revenue is simply price per unit times units sold. So, just as in the case of buyers, the price will be important in explaining the behavior of suppliers in a market. It also typically costs suppliers something to produce whatever product they are bringing to market. They have to hire workers, build factories, and buy inputs. So the supply behavior of firms will also depend on costs of production.

profit The difference between revenues and costs.

In later chapters, we will focus on how firms decide *how* to produce their goods and services and explore the cost side of the picture more formally. For now, we will begin our examination of firm behavior by focusing on the output supply decision and the relationship between quantity supplied and output price, *ceteris paribus*.

Price and Quantity Supplied: The Law of Supply

quantity supplied The amount of a particular product that a firm would be willing and able to offer for sale at a particular price during a given time period.

Quantity supplied is the amount of a particular product that firms would be willing and able to offer for sale at a particular price during a given time period. A **supply schedule** shows how much of a product firms will sell at alternative prices.

Let us look at an agricultural market as an example. Table 3.3 itemizes the quantities of soybeans that an individual representative farmer such as Clarence Brown might sell at various prices. If the market paid $1.50 or less for a bushel for soybeans, Brown would not supply any soybeans: When Farmer Brown looks at the costs of growing soybeans, including the opportunity cost of his time and land, $1.50 per bushel will not compensate him for those costs. At $1.75 per bushel, however, at least some soybean production takes place on Brown's farm, and a price increase from $1.75 to $2.25 per bushel causes the quantity supplied by Brown to increase from 10,000 to 20,000 bushels per year. The higher price may justify shifting land from wheat to soybean production or putting previously fallow land into soybeans, or it may lead to more intensive farming of land already in soybeans, using expensive fertilizer or equipment that was not cost-justified at the lower price.

supply schedule Shows how much of a product firms will sell at alternative prices.

Generalizing from Farmer Brown's experience, we can reasonably expect an increase in market price, ceteris paribus, to lead to an increase in quantity supplied for Brown and farmers like him. In other words, there is a positive relationship between the quantity of a good supplied and price. This statement sums up the **law of supply**: An increase in market price will lead to an increase in quantity supplied, and a decrease in market price will lead to a decrease in quantity supplied.

law of supply The positive relationship between price and quantity of a good supplied: An increase in market price, ceteris paribus, will lead to an increase in quantity supplied, and a decrease in market price will lead to a decrease in quantity supplied.

The information in a supply schedule may be presented graphically in a **supply curve**. Supply curves slope upward. The upward, or positive, slope of Brown's curve in Figure 3.6 reflects this positive relationship between price and quantity supplied.

Note in Brown's supply schedule, however, that when price rises from $4 to $5, quantity supplied no longer increases. Often an individual firm's ability to respond to an increase in price is constrained by its existing scale of operations, or capacity, in the short run. For example, Brown's ability to produce more soybeans depends on the size of his farm, the fertility of his soil, and the types of equipment he has. The fact that output stays constant at 45,000 bushels per year suggests that he is running up against the limits imposed by the size of his farm, the quality of his soil, and his existing technology.

supply curve A graph illustrating how much of a product a firm will sell at different prices.

Price (per Bushel)	Quantity Supplied (Bushels per Year)
$ 1.50	0
1.75	10,000
2.25	20,000
3.00	30,000
4.00	45,000
5.00	45,000

TABLE 3.3 Clarence Brown's Supply Schedule for Soybeans

Bushels of soybeans produced per year

In the longer run, however, Brown may acquire more land or technology may change, allowing for more soybean production. The terms *short run and long run* have precise meanings in economics; we will discuss them in detail later. Here it is important only to understand that time plays a critical role in supply decisions. When prices change, firms' immediate response may be different from what they are able to do after a month or a year. Short-run and long-run supply curves are often different.

Other Determinants of Supply

Of the factors we have listed that are likely to affect the quantity of output supplied by a given firm, we have thus far discussed only the price of output. Other factors that affect supply include the cost of producing the product and the prices of related products.

The Cost of Production   For a firm to make a profit, its revenue must exceed its costs. As an individual producer, like Farmer Brown, thinks about how much to supply at a particular price, the producer will be looking at his or her costs. Brown's supply decision is likely to change in response to changes in the cost of production. Cost of production depends on a number of factors, including the available technologies and the prices and quantities of the inputs needed by the firm (labor, land, capital, energy, and so on).

Technological change can have an enormous impact on the cost of production over time. The introduction of fertilizers, the development of complex farm machinery, and the use of bioengineering to increase the yield of individual crops have all powerfully affected the cost of producing agricultural products. Technology has similarly decreased the costs of producing flat screen televisions. When a technological advance lowers the cost of production, output is likely to increase. When yield per acre increases, individual farmers can and do produce more. The production of electronic calculators, and later personal computers and smartphones, boomed with the development of inexpensive techniques to produce microprocessors.

Cost of production is also directly affected by the price of the factors of production. In the spring of 2008, the world price of oil rose to more than $100 per barrel from below $20 in 2002. As a result, cab drivers faced higher gasoline prices, airlines faced higher fuel costs, and manufacturing firms faced higher heating bills. The result: Cab drivers probably spent less time driving around looking for customers, airlines cut a few low-profit routes, and some manufacturing plants stopped running extra shifts. The moral of this story: Increases in input prices raise costs of production and are likely to reduce supply. The reverse occurred in 2009–2010 when oil prices fell back to $75 per barrel and more recently in 2014-2015 when oil prices again fell.

The Prices of Related Products   Firms often react to changes in the prices of related products. For example, if land can be used for either corn or soybean production, an increase in soybean prices may cause individual farmers to shift acreage out of corn production into soybeans. Thus, an increase in soybean prices actually affects the amount of corn supplied.

Similarly, if beef prices rise, producers may respond by raising more cattle. However, leather comes from cowhide. Thus, an increase in beef prices may actually increase the supply of leather.

To summarize:

> Assuming that its objective is to maximize profits, a firm's decision about what quantity of output, or product, to supply depends on:
>
> 1. The price of the good or service.
> 2. The cost of producing the product, which in turn depends on:
>   - the price of required inputs (labor, capital, and land), and
>   - the technologies that can be used to produce the product.
> 3. The prices of related products.

Shift of Supply versus Movement along a Supply Curve

A supply curve shows the relationship between the quantity of a good or service supplied by a firm and the price that good or service brings in the market. Higher prices are likely to lead to an increase in quantity supplied, ceteris paribus. Remember: The supply curve is derived holding everything constant except price. When the price of a product changes ceteris paribus, a change in the quantity supplied follows—that is, a **movement along a supply curve** takes place. As you have seen, supply decisions are also influenced by factors other than price. New relationships between price and quantity supplied come about when factors other than price change, and the result is a **shift of a supply curve**. When factors other than price cause supply curves to shift, we say that there has been a *change in supply*.

Recall that the cost of production depends on the price of inputs and the technologies of production available. Now suppose that a major breakthrough in the production of soybeans has occurred: Genetic engineering has produced a superstrain of disease- and pest-resistant seed. Such a technological change would enable individual farmers to supply more soybeans at *any* market price. Table 3.4 and Figure 3.7 describe this change. At $3 a bushel, farmers would have produced 30,000 bushels from the old seed (schedule S_0 in Table 3.4); with the lower cost of production and higher yield resulting from the new seed, they produce 40,000 bushels (schedule S_1 in Table 3.4). At $1.75 per bushel, they would have produced 10,000 bushels from the old seed; but with the lower costs and higher yields, output rises to 23,000 bushels.

movement along a supply curve   The change in quantity supplied brought about by a change in price.

shift of a supply curve   The change that takes place in a supply curve corresponding to a new relationship between quantity supplied of a good and the price of that good. The shift is brought about by a change in the original conditions.

TABLE 3.4   Shift of Supply Schedule for Soybeans following Development of a New Disease-Resistant Seed Strain

Price (per Bushel)	Schedule S_0 Quantity Supplied (Bushels per Year Using Old Seed)	Schedule S_1 Quantity Supplied (Bushels per Year Using New Seed)
$ 1.50	0	5,000
1.75	10,000	23,000
2.25	20,000	33,000
3.00	30,000	40,000
4.00	45,000	54,000
5.00	45,000	54,000

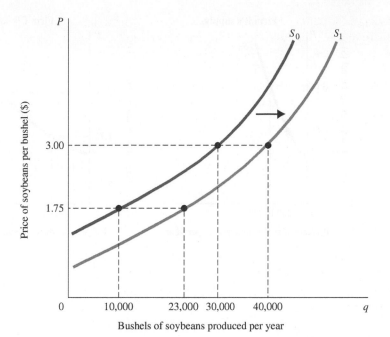

Bushels of soybeans produced per year

◀ FIGURE 3.7 **Shift of the Supply Curve for Soybeans Following Development of a New Seed Strain**
When the price of a product changes, we move *along* the supply curve for that product; the quantity supplied rises or falls. When any other factor affecting supply changes, the supply curve *shifts*.

Increases in input prices may also cause supply curves to shift. If Farmer Brown faces higher fuel costs, for example, his supply curve will shift to the left—that is, he will produce less at any given market price. As Brown's soybean supply curve shifts to the left, it intersects the price axis at a higher point, meaning that it would take a higher market price to induce Brown to produce any soybeans at all.

As with demand, it is important to distinguish between *movements along* supply curves (changes in quantity supplied) and *shifts in* supply curves (changes in supply):

Change in price of a good or service leads to
└──▶ change in *quantity supplied* (**movement along a supply curve**).
Change in costs, input prices, technology, or prices of related goods and services leads to
└──▶ change in *supply* (**shift of a supply curve**).

From Individual Supply to Market Supply

So far we have focused on the supply behavior of a single producer. For most markets many, many suppliers bring product to the consumer, and it is the behavior of all of those producers together that determines supply.

Market supply is determined in the same fashion as market demand. It is simply the sum of all that is supplied each period by all producers of a single product. Figure 3.8 derives a market supply curve from the supply curves of three individual firms. (In a market with more firms, total market supply would be the sum of the amounts produced by each of the firms in that market.) As the table in Figure 3.8 shows, at a price of $3, farm A supplies 30,000 bushels of soybeans, farm B supplies 10,000 bushels, and farm C supplies 25,000 bushels. At this price, the total amount supplied in the market is 30,000 + 10,000 + 25,000, or 65,000 bushels. At a price of $1.75, however, the total amount supplied is only 25,000 bushels (10,000 + 5,000 + 10,000). Thus, the market supply curve is the simple addition of the individual supply curves of all the firms in a particular market—that is, the sum of all the individual quantities supplied at each price.

The position and shape of the market supply curve depends on the positions and shapes of the individual firms' supply curves from which it is derived. The market supply curve also depends on the number of firms that produce in that market. If firms that produce for a particular market are earning high profits, other firms may be tempted to go into that line of business. The popularity and profitability of professional football has, three times, led to the formation of new leagues. When new firms enter an industry, the supply curve shifts to the right. When firms go out of business, or "exit" the market, the supply curve shifts to the left.

market supply The sum of all that is supplied each period by all producers of a single product.

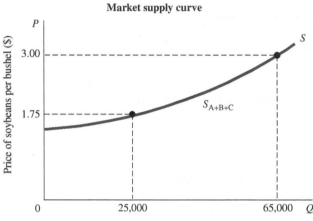

	Quantity (q) Supplied by			Total Quantity Supplied in
Price	A	B	C	the Market (Q)
$3.00	30,000 +	10,000 +	25,000	= 65,000
1.75	10,000 +	5,000 +	10,000	= 25,000

▲ **FIGURE 3.8** **Deriving Market Supply from Individual Firm Supply Curves**
Total supply in the marketplace is the sum of all the amounts supplied by all the firms selling in the market. It is the sum of all the individual quantities supplied at each price.

3.5 LEARNING OBJECTIVE

Be able to explain how a market that is not in equilibrium responds to restore an equilibrium.

Market Equilibrium

So far, we have identified a number of factors that influence the amount that households demand and the amount that firms supply in product (output) markets. The discussion has emphasized the role of market price as a determinant of both quantity demanded and quantity supplied. We are now ready to see how supply and demand in the market interact to determine the final market price.

In our discussions, we have separated household decisions about how much to demand from firm decisions about how much to supply. The operation of the market, however, clearly depends on the interaction between suppliers and demanders. At any moment, one of three conditions prevails in every market: (1) The quantity demanded exceeds the quantity supplied at the current price, a situation called *excess demand*; (2) the quantity supplied exceeds the quantity demanded at the current price, a situation called *excess supply*; or (3) the quantity supplied equals the quantity demanded at the current price, a situation called **equilibrium**. At equilibrium, no tendency for price to change exists.

equilibrium The condition that exists when quantity supplied and quantity demanded are equal. At equilibrium, there is no tendency for price to change.

excess demand or shortage The condition that exists when quantity demanded exceeds quantity supplied at the current price.

Excess Demand

Excess demand, or a shortage, exists when quantity demanded is greater than quantity supplied at the current price. Figure 3.9, which plots both a supply curve and a demand curve on the same graph, illustrates such a situation. As you can see, market demand at

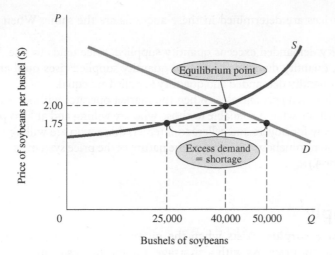

▲ FIGURE 3.9 Excess Demand, or Shortage

At a price of $1.75 per bushel, quantity demanded exceeds quantity supplied. When *excess demand* exists, there is a tendency for price to rise. When quantity demanded equals quantity supplied, excess demand is eliminated and the market is in equilibrium. Here the equilibrium price is $2.00 and the equilibrium quantity is 40,000 bushels.

$1.75 per bushel (50,000 bushels) exceeds the amount that farmers are currently supplying (25,000 bushels).

When excess demand occurs in an unregulated market, there is a tendency for price to rise as demanders compete against each other for the limited supply. The adjustment mechanisms may differ, but the outcome is always the same. For example, consider the mechanism of an auction. In an auction, items are sold directly to the highest bidder. When the auctioneer starts the bidding at a low price, many people bid for the item. At first, there is a shortage: Quantity demanded exceeds quantity supplied. As would-be buyers offer higher and higher prices, bidders drop out until the one who offers the most ends up with the item being auctioned. Price rises until quantity demanded and quantity supplied are equal.

At a price of $1.75 (see Figure 3.9 again), farmers produce soybeans at a rate of 25,000 bushels per year, but at that price, the demand is for 50,000 bushels. Most farm products are sold to local dealers who in turn sell large quantities in major market centers, where bidding would push prices up if quantity demanded exceeded quantity supplied. As price rises above $1.75, two things happen: (1) The quantity demanded falls as buyers drop out of the market and perhaps choose a substitute, and (2) the quantity supplied increases as farmers find themselves receiving a higher price for their product and shift additional acres into soybean production.[4]

This process continues until the shortage is eliminated. In Figure 3.9, this occurs at $2.00, where quantity demanded has fallen from 50,000 to 40,000 bushels per year and quantity supplied has increased from 25,000 to 40,000 bushels per year. When quantity demanded and quantity supplied are equal and there is no further bidding, the process has achieved an equilibrium, a situation in which *there is no natural tendency for further adjustment.* Graphically, the point of equilibrium is the point at which the supply curve and the demand curve intersect.

Increasingly, items are auctioned over the Internet. Companies such as eBay connect buyers and sellers of everything from automobiles to wine and from computers to airline tickets. Auctions are occurring simultaneously with participants located across the globe. The principles

---

[4] Once farmers have produced in any given season, they cannot change their minds and produce more, of course. When we derived Clarence Brown's supply schedule in Table 3.3, we imagined him reacting to prices that existed at the time he decided how much land to plant in soybeans. In Figure 3.9, the upward slope shows that higher prices justify shifting land from other crops. Final price may not be determined until final production figures are in. For our purposes here, however, we have ignored this timing problem. The best way to think about it is that demand and supply are *flows,* or *rates,* of production—that is, we are talking about the number of bushels produced *per production period.* Adjustments in the rate of production may take place over a number of production periods.

through which prices are determined in these auctions are the same: When excess demand exists, prices rise.

When quantity demanded exceeds quantity supplied, price tends to rise. When the price in a market rises, quantity demanded falls and quantity supplied rises until an equilibrium is reached at which quantity demanded and quantity supplied are equal.

This process is called *price rationing*. When the market operates without interference, price increases will distribute what is available to those who are willing and able to pay the most. As long as there is a way for buyers and sellers to interact, those who are willing to pay more will make that fact known somehow. (We discuss the nature of the price system as a rationing device in detail in Chapter 4.)

Excess Supply

excess supply *or* surplus
The condition that exists when quantity supplied exceeds quantity demanded at the current price.

Excess supply, *or* a surplus, exists when the quantity supplied exceeds the quantity demanded at the current price. As with a shortage, the mechanics of price adjustment in the face of a surplus can differ from market to market. For example, if automobile dealers find themselves with unsold cars in the fall when the new models are coming in, you can expect to see price cuts. Sometimes dealers offer discounts to encourage buyers; sometimes buyers themselves simply offer less than the price initially asked. After Christmas, most stores have big sales during which they lower the prices of overstocked items. Quantities supplied exceeded quantities demanded at the current prices, so stores cut prices. Many Web sites exist that do little more than sell at a discount clothing and other goods that failed to sell at full price during the past season.

Figure 3.10 illustrates another excess supply/surplus situation. At a price of $3 per bushel, suppose farmers are supplying soybeans at a rate of 65,000 bushels per year, but buyers are demanding only 25,000. With 40,000 bushels of soybeans going unsold, the market price falls. As price falls from $3.00 to $2.00, quantity supplied decreases from 65,000 bushels per year to 40,000. The lower price causes quantity demanded to rise from 25,000 to 40,000. At $2.00, quantity demanded and quantity supplied are equal. For the data shown here, $2.00 and 40,000 bushels are the equilibrium price and quantity, respectively.

Although the mechanism by which price is adjusted differs across markets, the outcome is the same:

> When quantity supplied exceeds quantity demanded at the current price, the price tends to fall. When price falls, quantity supplied is likely to decrease and quantity demanded is likely to increase until an equilibrium price is reached where quantity supplied and quantity demanded are equal.

▶ **FIGURE 3.10 Excess Supply or Surplus**
At a price of $3.00, quantity supplied exceeds quantity demanded by 40,000 bushels. This excess supply will cause the price to fall.

Changes in Equilibrium

When supply and demand curves shift, the equilibrium price and quantity change. The following example will help to illustrate this point and show us how equilibrium is restored in markets in which either demand or supply changes.

South America is a major producer of coffee beans. In the mid-1990s, a major freeze hit Brazil and Colombia and drove up the price of coffee on world markets to a record $2.40 per pound. Bad weather in Colombia in 2005 and more recently in 2012 caused similar shifts in supply.

Figure 3.11 illustrates how the freezes pushed up coffee prices. Initially, the market was in equilibrium at a price of $1.20. At that price, the quantity demanded was equal to quantity supplied (13.2 billion pounds). At a price of $1.20 and a quantity of 13.2 billion pounds, the demand curve (labeled D) intersected the initial supply curve (labeled S_0). (Remember that equilibrium exists when quantity demanded equals quantity supplied—the point at which the supply and demand curves intersect.)

The freeze caused a decrease in the supply of coffee beans. That is, the freeze caused the supply curve to shift to the left. In Figure 3.11, the new supply curve (the supply curve that shows the relationship between price and quantity supplied after the freeze) is labeled S_1.

At the initial equilibrium price, $1.20, there is now a shortage of coffee. If the price were to remain at $1.20, quantity demanded would not change; it would remain at 13.2 billion pounds. However, at that price, quantity supplied would drop to 6.6 billion pounds. At a price of $1.20, quantity demanded is greater than quantity supplied.

When excess demand exists in a market, price can be expected to rise, and rise it did. As the figure shows, price rose to a new equilibrium at $2.40. At $2.40, quantity demanded is again equal to quantity supplied, this time at 9.9 billion pounds—the point at which the new supply curve (S_1) intersects the demand curve.

Notice that as the price of coffee rose from $1.20 to $2.40, two things happened. First, the quantity demanded declined (a movement along the demand curve) as people shifted to substitutes such as tea and hot cocoa. Second, the quantity supplied began to rise, but within the limits imposed by the damage from the freeze. (It might also be that some countries or areas with high costs of production, previously unprofitable, came into production and shipped to

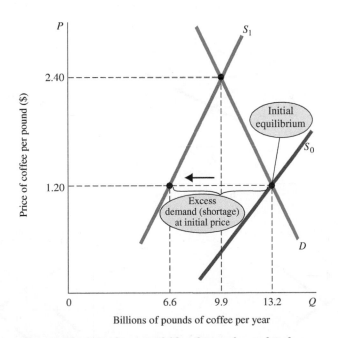

▲ **FIGURE 3.11** **The Coffee Market: A Shift of Supply and Subsequent Price Adjustment**

Before the freeze, the coffee market was in equilibrium at a price of $1.20 per pound. At that price, quantity demanded equaled quantity supplied. The freeze shifted the supply curve to the left (from S_0 to S_1), increasing the equilibrium price to $2.40.

the world market at the higher price.) That is, the quantity supplied increased in response to the higher price *along* the new supply curve, which lies to the left of the old supply curve. The final result was a higher price ($2.40), a smaller quantity finally exchanged in the market (9.9 billion pounds), and coffee bought only by those willing to pay $2.40 per pound.

Figure 3.12 summarizes the possible supply and demand shifts that have been discussed and the resulting changes in equilibrium price and quantity. Study the graphs carefully to ensure that you understand them.

a. Demand shifts

1. Increase in income: X is a normal good

2. Increase in income: X is an inferior good

3. Decrease in income: X is a normal good

4. Decrease in income: X is an inferior good

5. Increase in the price of a substitute for X

6. Increase in the price of a complement for X

7. Decrease in the price of a substitute for X

8. Decrease in the price of a complement for X

b. Supply shifts

9. Increase in the cost of production of X

10. Decrease in the cost of production of X

▲ **FIGURE 3.12** **Examples of Supply and Demand Shifts for Product X**

ECONOMICS IN PRACTICE

Quinoa

Those of you who follow a vegetarian diet, or even those of you who are foodies, likely have had quinoa sometime within the last few months. Once eaten mostly by people in Peru and Bolivia, and a reputed favorite of the Incas, quinoa, a high-protein grain, has found a large market among food aficionados. Growth in vegetarianism effectively shifted the demand curve for quinoa to the right.

With an upward sloping supply curve, this shift in demand resulted in increased prices. Farmers grew richer, whereas some local consumers found themselves facing higher prices for a staple product. Over time, these higher prices encouraged more farmers to enter the quinoa market. This shifted the supply curve to the right, helping to moderate the price increases. But quinoa growing turns out to be a tricky affair. Quinoa grows best in high altitudes with cold climates. It thrives on soil fertilized by the dung of herds of llama and sheep. Thus, while supply clearly shifted with new farmer entry, the particular nature of the production process limited that shift and in the end, despite the supply response, prices increased.

THINKING PRACTICALLY

1. Use a graph to show the movement in prices and quantities described in the quinoa market.

Demand and Supply in Product Markets: A Review

As you continue your study of economics, you will discover that it is a discipline full of controversy and debate. There is, however, little disagreement about the basic way that the forces of supply and demand operate in free markets. If you hear that a freeze in Florida has destroyed a good portion of the citrus crop, you can bet that the price of oranges will rise. If you read that the weather in the Midwest has been good and a record corn crop is expected, you can bet that corn prices will fall. When fishermen in Massachusetts go on strike and stop bringing in the daily catch, you can bet that the price of local fish will go up.

Here are some important points to remember about the mechanics of supply and demand in product markets:

1. A demand curve shows how much of a product a household would buy if it could buy all it wanted at the given price. A supply curve shows how much of a product a firm would supply if it could sell all it wanted at the given price.
2. Quantity demanded and quantity supplied are always per time period—that is, per day, per month, or per year.
3. The demand for a good is determined by price, household income and wealth, prices of other goods and services, tastes and preferences, and expectations.
4. The supply of a good is determined by price, costs of production, and prices of related products. Costs of production are determined by available technologies of production and input prices.
5. Be careful to distinguish between movements along supply and demand curves and shifts of these curves. When the price of a good changes, the quantity of that good demanded or supplied changes—that is, a movement occurs along the curve. When any other factor that affects supply or demand changes, the curve shifts, or changes position.
6. Market equilibrium exists only when quantity supplied equals quantity demanded at the current price.

ECONOMICS IN PRACTICE

Why Do the Prices of Newspapers Rise?

In 2006, the average price for a daily edition of a Baltimore newspaper was $0.50. In 2007, the average price had risen to $0.75. Three different analysts have three different explanations for the higher equilibrium price.

Analyst 1: The higher price for Baltimore newspapers is good news because it means the population is better informed about public issues. These data clearly show that the citizens of Baltimore have a new, increased regard for newspapers.

Analyst 2: The higher price for Baltimore newspapers is bad news for the citizens of Baltimore. The higher cost of paper, ink, and distribution reflected in these higher prices will further diminish the population's awareness of public issues.

Analyst 3: The higher price for Baltimore newspapers is an unfortunate result of newspapers trying to make money as many consumers have turned to the Internet to access news coverage for free.

As economists, we are faced with two tasks in looking at these explanations: Do they make sense based on what we know about economic principles? And if they do make sense, can we figure out which explanation applies to the case of rising newspaper prices in Baltimore?

What is Analyst 1 saying? Her observation about consumers' new increased regard for newspapers tells us something about the demand curve. Analyst 1 seems to be arguing that tastes have changed in favor of newspapers, which would mean a shift in the demand curve to the right. With upward-sloping supply, such a shift would produce a price increase. So Analyst 1's story is plausible.

Analyst 2 refers to an increased cost of newsprint. This would cause production costs of newspapers to rise, shifting the supply curve to the left. A downward-sloping demand curve also results in increased prices. So Analyst 2 also has a plausible story.

Since Analyst 1 and Analyst 2 have plausible stories based on economic principles, we can look at evidence to see who is in fact right. If you go back to the graphs in Figure 3.12 on p. 64, you will find a clue. When demand shifts to the right (as in Analyst 1's story) the price rises, but so does the quantity as shown in Figure (a). When supply shifts to the left (as in Analyst 2's story) the price rises, but the quantity falls as shown in Figure (b). So we would look at what happened to newspaper circulation during this period to see whether the price increase is from the demand side or the supply side. In fact, in most markets, including Baltimore, quantities of newspapers bought have been falling, so Analyst 2 is most likely correct.

But be careful. Both analysts may be correct. If demand shifts to the right and supply shifts to the left by a greater amount, the price will rise and the quantity sold will fall.

What about Analyst 3? Analyst 3 clearly never had an economics course! Free Internet access to news is a substitute for print media. A decrease in the price of this substitute should shift the demand for newspapers to the left. The result should be a lower price, not a price increase. The fact that the newspaper publishers are "trying to make money" faced with this new competition does not change the laws of supply and demand.

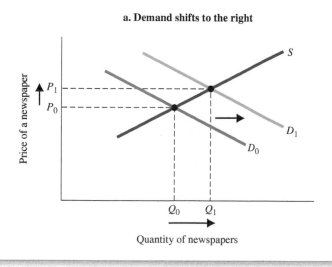

a. Demand shifts to the right

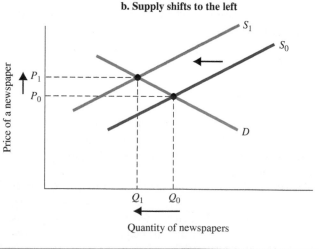

b. Supply shifts to the left

Looking Ahead: Markets and the Allocation of Resources

You can already begin to see how markets answer the basic economic questions of what is produced, how it is produced, and who gets what is produced. A firm will produce what is profitable to produce. If the firm can sell a product at a price that is sufficient to ensure a profit after production costs are paid, it will in all likelihood produce that product. Resources will flow in the direction of profit opportunities.

- Demand curves reflect what people are willing and able to pay for products; demand curves are influenced by incomes, wealth, preferences, prices of other goods, and expectations. Because product prices are determined by the interaction of supply and demand, prices reflect what people are willing to pay. If people's preferences or incomes change, resources will be allocated differently. Consider, for example, an increase in demand—a shift in the market demand curve. Beginning at an equilibrium, households simply begin buying more. At the equilibrium price, quantity demanded becomes greater than quantity supplied. When there is excess demand, prices will rise, and higher prices mean higher profits for firms in the industry. Higher profits, in turn, provide existing firms with an incentive to expand and new firms with an incentive to enter the industry. Thus, the decisions of independent private firms responding to prices and profit opportunities determine *what* will be *produced*. No central direction is necessary.

  Adam Smith saw this self-regulating feature of markets more than 200 years ago:

  > Every individual…by pursuing his own interest…promotes that of society. He is led…by an invisible hand to promote an end which was no part of his intention.[5]

  The term Smith coined, the *invisible hand*, has passed into common parlance and is still used by economists to refer to the self-regulation of markets.

- Firms in business to make a profit have a good reason to choose the best available technology—lower costs mean higher profits. Thus, individual firms determine *how* to produce their products, again with no central direction.

- So far, we have barely touched on the question of distribution—*who* gets what is produced? You can see part of the answer in the simple supply and demand diagrams. When a good is in short supply, price rises. As they do, those who are willing and able to continue buying do so; others stop buying.

The next chapter begins with a more detailed discussion of these topics. How, exactly, is the final allocation of resources (the mix of output and the distribution of output) determined in a market system?

---

[5] Adam Smith, *The Wealth of Nations*, Modern Library Edition (New York: Random House, 1937), p. 456 (1st ed., 1776).

SUMMARY

1. In societies with many people, production must satisfy wide-ranging tastes and preferences, and producers must therefore specialize.

3.1 FIRMS AND HOUSEHOLDS: THE BASIC DECISION-MAKING UNITS *p. 43*

2. A *firm* exists when a person or a group of people decides to produce a product or products by transforming resources, or *inputs*, into *outputs*—the products that are sold in the market. Firms are the primary producing units in a market economy. We assume that firms make decisions to try to maximize profits.

3. *Households* are the primary consuming units in an economy. All households' incomes are subject to constraints.

3.2 INPUT MARKETS AND OUTPUT MARKETS: THE CIRCULAR FLOW *p. 43*

4. Households and firms interact in two basic kinds of markets: *product or output markets* and *input or factor markets*. Goods and services intended for use by households are exchanged in output markets. In output markets, competing firms supply and competing households demand. In input markets, competing firms demand and competing households supply.

5. Ultimately, firms choose the quantities and character of outputs produced, the types and quantities of inputs demanded, and the technologies used in production. Households choose the types and quantities of products demanded and the types and quantities of inputs supplied.

3.3 DEMAND IN PRODUCT/OUTPUT MARKETS *p. 45*

6. The quantity demanded of an individual product by an individual household depends on (1) price, (2) income, (3) wealth, (4) prices of other products, (5) tastes and preferences, and (6) expectations about the future.

7. *Quantity demanded* is the amount of a product that an individual household would buy in a given period if it could buy all that it wanted at the current price.

8. A *demand schedule* shows the quantities of a product that a household would buy at different prices. The same information can be presented graphically in a *demand curve*.

9. The *law of demand* states that there is a negative relationship between price and quantity demanded *ceteris paribus*: As price rises, quantity demanded decreases and vice versa. Demand curves slope downward.

10. All demand curves eventually intersect the price axis because there is always a price above which a household cannot or will not pay. Also, all demand curves eventually intersect the quantity axis because demand for most goods is limited, if only by time, even at a zero price.

11. When an increase in income causes demand for a good to rise, that good is a *normal good*. When an increase in income causes demand for a good to fall, that good is an *inferior good*.

12. If a rise in the price of good X causes demand for good Y to increase, the goods are *substitutes*. If a rise in the price of X causes demand for Y to fall, the goods are *complements*.

13. *Market demand* is simply the sum of all the quantities of a good or service demanded per period by all the households buying in the market for that good or service. It is the sum of all the individual quantities demanded at each price.

3.4 SUPPLY IN PRODUCT/OUTPUT MARKETS *p. 55*

14. *Quantity supplied* by a firm depends on (1) the price of the good or service; (2) the cost of producing the product, which includes the prices of required inputs and the technologies that can be used to produce the product; and (3) the prices of related products.

15. *Market supply* is the sum of all that is supplied in each period by all producers of a single product. It is the sum of all the individual quantities supplied at each price.

16. It is important to distinguish between *movements* along demand and supply curves and *shifts* of demand and supply curves. The demand curve shows the relationship between price and quantity demanded. The supply curve shows the relationship between price and quantity supplied. A change in price is a movement along the curve. Changes in tastes, income, wealth, expectations, or prices of other goods and services cause demand curves to shift; changes in costs, input prices, technology, or prices of related goods and services cause supply curves to shift.

3.5 MARKET EQUILIBRIUM *p. 60*

17. When quantity demanded exceeds quantity supplied at the current price, *excess demand* (or a *shortage*) exists and the price tends to rise. When prices in a market rise, quantity demanded falls and quantity supplied rises until an equilibrium is reached at which quantity supplied and quantity demanded are equal. At *equilibrium*, there is no further tendency for price to change.

18. When quantity supplied exceeds quantity demanded at the current price, *excess supply* (or a *surplus*) exists and the price tends to fall. When price falls, quantity supplied decreases and quantity demanded increases until an equilibrium price is reached where quantity supplied and quantity demanded are equal.

—— REVIEW TERMS AND CONCEPTS ——

capital market, *p. 44*

complements, complementary goods, *p. 49*

demand curve, *p. 47*

demand schedule, *p. 46*

entrepreneur, *p. 43*

equilibrium, *p. 60*

excess demand *or* shortage, *p. 60*

excess supply *or* surplus, *p. 62*

factors of production, *p. 44*

firm, *p. 43*

households, *p. 43*

income, *p. 49*

inferior goods, *p. 49*

input *or* factor markets, *p. 44*

labor market, *p. 44*

land market, *p. 44*

law of demand, *p. 47*

law of supply, *p. 56*

market demand, *p. 53*

market supply, *p. 59*

movement along a demand curve, *p. 53*

movement along a supply curve, *p. 58*

normal goods, *p. 49*

perfect substitutes, *p. 49*

product *or* output markets, *p. 44*

profit, *p. 56*

quantity demanded, *p. 45*

quantity supplied, *p. 56*

shift of a demand curve, *p. 53*

shift of a supply curve, *p. 58*

substitutes, *p. 49*

supply curve, *p. 56*

supply schedule, *p. 56*

wealth *or* net worth, *p. 49*

MyEconLab Visit **www.myeconlab.com** to complete these exercises online and get instant feedback. Exercises that update with real time data are marked with art 🔟.

PROBLEMS

All problems are available on MyEconLab.

3.1 FIRMS AND HOUSEHOLDS: THE BASIC DECISION-MAKING UNITS

LEARNING OBJECTIVE: Understand the roles of firms, entrepreneurs, and households in the market.

1.1 List three examples of entrepreneurs in the tech industry and the firms they created. Explain how these people fit the definition of entrepreneur.

3.2 INPUT MARKETS AND OUTPUT MARKETS: THE CIRCULAR FLOW

LEARNING OBJECTIVE: Understand the role of households as both suppliers to firms and buyers of what firms produce.

2.1 Identify whether each of the following transactions will take place in an input market or in an output market, and whether firms or households are demanding the good or service or supplying the good or service.
  a. Anderson works 37 hours each week as a clerk at the county courthouse.
  b. Mei Lin purchases a 3-week Mediterranean cruise vacation for her parents.
  c. Caterpillar doubles employment at its Huntsville, Alabama factory.
  d. The Greyson family sells their 250-acre ranch to Marriott so it can build a new resort and golf course.

3.3 DEMAND IN PRODUCT/ OUTPUT MARKETS

LEARNING OBJECTIVE: Understand what determines the position and shape of the demand curve and what factors move you along a demand curve and what factors shift the demand curve.

3.1 [**Related to the *Economics in Practice* on p. 50**] Merchandise sales for professional sports leagues is a multibillion dollar business, and leagues such as the NBA, NFL, and MLB have strict licensing rules for official league merchandise. Suppose you are a huge NBA fan and wish to purchase an authentic NBA jersey in large. Go to the NBA Store's Website at store.nba.com and click on "Jerseys." Select a team and then click on "Authentic" and find the price of the jerseys. Do the same for two other teams. Would the jerseys you found be considered perfect substitutes or just substitutes? Why? Do you think there are other products available that would be considered substitute products for the authentic jerseys you looked up? Briefly explain.

3.2 Explain whether each of the following statements describes a change in demand or a change in quantity demanded, and specify whether each change represents an increase or a decrease.
  a. Julio believes the price of tires will rise next month, so he purchases a set of 4 for his pickup truck today.

  b. After an article is published asserting that eating kale causes hair loss, sales of kale drop by 75 percent.
  c. The Oink-N-Chew company experiences a significant decline in sales when it doubles the price of its bacon-flavored bubblegum.
  d. An increase in the federal minimum wage results in a decline in sales of fast food.
  e. An unexpected decrease in the price of peanut butter results in an increase in banana sales.

3.3 For each of the five statements (a–e) in the previous question, draw a demand graph representing the appropriate change in quantity demanded or change in demand.

3.4 [**Related to the *Economics in Practice* on p. 51**] In the town of Hurley, Wisconsin, an unseasonably warm summer saw temperatures rising into the mid-90s for a weeklong stretch in July. This was almost 20 degrees above the average high temperature of 77 degrees for this hottest month of the year. This unexpected heat wave resulted in a significant increase in household purchases of central air conditioning systems, which are uncommon in this part of the country. Which determinant or determinants of demand were most likely factors in the households' decisions to purchase these air conditioning systems, and how would these purchases affect the demand curve for central air conditioning systems?

3.4 SUPPLY IN PRODUCT/OUTPUT MARKETS

LEARNING OBJECTIVE: Be able to distinguish between forces that shift a supply curve and changes that cause a movement along a supply curve.

4.1 The market for fitness trackers is made up of five firms, and the data in the following table represents each firm's quantity supplied at various prices. Fill in the column for the quantity supplied in the market, and draw a supply graph showing the market data.

	Quantity supplied by:					
PRICE	FIRM A	FIRM B	FIRM C	FIRM D	FIRM E	MARKET
$25	5	3	2	0	5	
50	7	5	5	3	6	
75	9	7	8	6	7	
100	11	10	11	9	8	

4.2 The following sets of statements contain common errors. Identify and explain each error:
  a. Supply decreases, causing prices to rise. Higher prices cause supply to increase. Therefore, prices fall back to their original levels.

b. The supply of pineapples in Hawaii increases, causing pineapple prices to fall. Lower prices mean that the demand for pineapples in Hawaiian households will increase, which will reduce the supply of pineapples and increase their price.

3.5 MARKET EQUILIBRIUM

LEARNING OBJECTIVE: Be able to explain how a market that is not in equilibrium responds to restore an equilibrium.

5.1 Illustrate the following with supply and demand curves:

a. With increased access to wireless technology and lighter weight, the demand for tablet computers has increased substantially. Tablets have also become easier and cheaper to produce as new technology has come online. Despite the shift of demand, prices have fallen.

b. Cranberry production in Massachusetts totaled 1.85 million barrels in 2013, a 15 percent decrease from the 2.12 million barrels produced in 2012. Demand decreased by even more than supply, dropping 2013 prices to $32.30 per barrel from $47.90 in 2012.

c. During the high-tech boom in the late 1990s, San Jose office space was in high demand and rents were high. With the national recession that began in March 2001, however, the market for office space in San Jose (Silicon Valley) was hit hard, with rents per square foot falling. In 2005, the employment numbers from San Jose were rising slowly and rents began to rise again. Assume for simplicity that no new office space was built during the period.

d. Before economic reforms were implemented in the countries of Eastern Europe, regulation held the price of bread substantially below equilibrium. When reforms were implemented, prices were deregulated and the price of bread rose dramatically. As a result, the quantity of bread demanded fell and the quantity of bread supplied rose sharply.

e. The steel industry has been lobbying for high taxes on imported steel. Russia, Brazil, and Japan have been producing and selling steel on world markets at $610 per metric ton, well below what equilibrium would be in the United States with no imports. If no imported steel was permitted into the country, the equilibrium price would be $970 per metric ton. Show supply and demand curves for the United States, assuming no imports; then show what the graph would look like if U.S. buyers could purchase all the steel that they wanted from world markets at $610 per metric ton; label the portion of the graph that represents the quantity of imported steel.

5.2 On Saturday, September 13, the Los Angeles Dodgers and the San Francisco Giants played baseball at AT&T Park in San Francisco. Both teams were in pursuit of league championships. Tickets to the game were sold out, and many more fans would have attended if additional tickets had been available. On that same day, the Miami Marlins and the Philadelphia Phillies played each other and sold tickets to only 26,163 people in Philadelphia.

The Phillies stadium, Citizens Bank Park, holds 43,651. AT&T Park in San Francisco holds 41,915. Assume for simplicity that tickets to all regular-season games are priced at $40.

a. Draw supply and demand curves for the tickets to each of the two games. (*Hint:* Supply is fixed. It does not change with price.) Draw one graph for each game.

b. Is there a pricing policy that would have filled the ballpark for the Phillies game?

c. The price system was not allowed to work to ration the San Francisco tickets when they were initially sold to the public. How do you know? How do you suppose the tickets were rationed?

5.3 Do you agree or disagree with each of the following statements? Briefly explain your answers and illustrate each with supply and demand curves.

a. The price of a good rises, causing the demand for another good to fall. Therefore, the two goods are substitutes.

b. A shift in supply causes the price of a good to fall. The shift must have been an increase in supply.

c. During 2009, incomes fell sharply for many Americans. This change would likely lead to a decrease in the prices of both normal and inferior goods.

d. Two normal goods cannot be substitutes for each other.

e. If demand increases and supply increases at the same time, price will clearly rise.

f. The price of good A falls. This causes an increase in the price of good B. Therefore, goods A and B are complements.

5.4 Through October 2014, the U.S. government administered two programs that affected the market for cigarettes. Media campaigns and labeling requirements, which are still in place, aim at making the public aware of the health dangers of cigarettes, and until 2014 the Department of Agriculture also maintained price supports for tobacco. Under this program, the supported price was above the market equilibrium price and the government limited the amount of land that could be devoted to tobacco production. Were these two programs at odds with the goal of reducing cigarette consumption? As part of your answer, illustrate graphically the effects of both policies on the market for cigarettes.

5.5 During the period 2006 through 2010, housing production in the United States fell from a rate of more than 2.27 million housing starts per year to a rate of less than 500,000, a decrease of greater than 80 percent. At the same time, the number of new households slowed to a trickle. Students without a job moved in with their parents, fewer immigrants came to the United States, and more of those already here went home. If there are fewer households, it is a decline in demand. If fewer new units are built, it is a decline in supply.

a. Draw a standard supply and demand diagram, which shows the demand for new housing units that are purchased each month, and the supply of new units built and put on the market each month. Assume that the quantity supplied and quantity demanded are equal at 45,000 units and at a price of $200,000.

b. On the same diagram show a decline in demand. What would happen if this market behaved like most markets?

c. Now suppose that prices did not change immediately. Sellers decided not to adjust price even though demand is below supply. What would happen to the number of homes for sale (the inventory of unsold new homes) if prices stayed the same following the drop in demand?

d. Now suppose that the supply of new homes put on the market dropped, but price still stayed the same at $200,000. Can you tell a story that brings the market back to equilibrium without a drop in price?

e. Go to www.census.gov/newhomesales. Look at the current press release, which contains data for the most recent month and the past year. What trends can you observe?

5.6 For each of the following statements, draw a diagram that illustrates the likely effect on the market for eggs. Indicate in each case the impact on equilibrium price and equilibrium quantity.

    a. The surgeon general warns that high-cholesterol foods cause heart attacks.

    b. The price of bacon, a complementary product, decreases.

    c. The price of chicken feed increases.

    d. Caesar salads become trendy at dinner parties. (The dressing is made with raw eggs.)

    e. A technological innovation reduces egg breakage during packing.

*5.7 Suppose the demand and supply curves for eggs in the United States are given by the following equations:

$$Q_d = 100 - 20P$$
$$Q_s = 10 + 40P$$

where Q_d = millions of dozens of eggs Americans would like to buy each year; Q_s = millions of dozens of eggs U.S. farms would like to sell each year; and P = price per dozen eggs.

    a. Fill in the following table:

Price (Per Dozen)	Quantity Demanded (Q_d)	Quantity Supplied (Q_s)
$ .50	____	____
$ 1.00	____	____
$ 1.50	____	____
$ 2.00	____	____
$ 2.50	____	____

    b. Use the information in the table to find the equilibrium price and quantity.

    c. Graph the demand and supply curves and identify the equilibrium price and quantity.

5.8 Housing policy analysts debate the best way to increase the number of housing units available to low-income households. One strategy—the demand-side strategy—is to provide people with housing vouchers, paid for by the government, that can be used to rent housing supplied by the private market. Another—a supply-side strategy—is to have the government subsidize housing suppliers or to build public housing.

    a. Illustrate these supply- and demand-side strategies using supply and demand curves. Which results in higher rents?

    b. Critics of housing vouchers (the demand-side strategy) argue that because the supply of housing to low-income households is limited and does not respond to higher rents, demand vouchers will serve only to drive up rents

and make landlords better off. Illustrate their point with supply and demand curves.

*5.9 Suppose the market demand for pizza is given by

$Q_d = 300 - 20P$ and the market supply for pizza is given by

$Q_s = 20P - 100$, where P = price (per pizza).

    a. Graph the supply and demand schedules for pizza using $5 through $15 as the value of P.

    b. In equilibrium, how many pizzas would be sold and at what price?

    c. What would happen if suppliers set the price of pizza at $15? Explain the market adjustment process.

    d. Suppose the price of hamburgers, a substitute for pizza, doubles. This leads to a doubling of the demand for pizza. (At each price, consumers demand twice as much pizza as before.) Write the equation for the new market demand for pizza.

    e. Find the new equilibrium price and quantity of pizza.

5.10 [**Related to the *Economics in Practice* on p. 65**] The growing popularity of quinoa has had an impact on the market for brown rice. With its higher fiber, protein, and iron content, quinoa is replacing brown rice as a staple food for many health-conscious individuals. Draw a supply and demand graph that shows how this increase in demand for quinoa has affected the market for brown rice. Describe what has happened to the equilibrium price and quantity of brown rice. What could brown rice producers do to return the price or quantity to the initial equilibrium price or quantity? Briefly explain if it is possible for brown rice producers to return both the price and quantity to the initial equilibriums without a change in consumer behavior.

5.11 The following table represents the market for solar wireless keyboards. Plot this data on a supply and demand graph and identify the equilibrium price and quantity. Explain what would happen if the market price is set at $60, and show this on the graph. Explain what would happen if the market price is set at $30, and show this on the graph.

Price	Quantity Demanded	Quantity Supplied
$ 10.00	28	0
20.00	24	3
30.00	20	6
40.00	16	9
50.00	12	12
60.00	8	15
70.00	4	18

5.12 [**Related to the *Economics in Practice* on p. 66**] Analyst 1 suggested that the demand curve for newspapers in Baltimore might have shifted to the right because people were becoming more literate. Think of two other plausible stories that would result in this demand curve shifting to the right.

*Note: Problems with an asterisk are more challenging.

4

Demand and Supply Applications

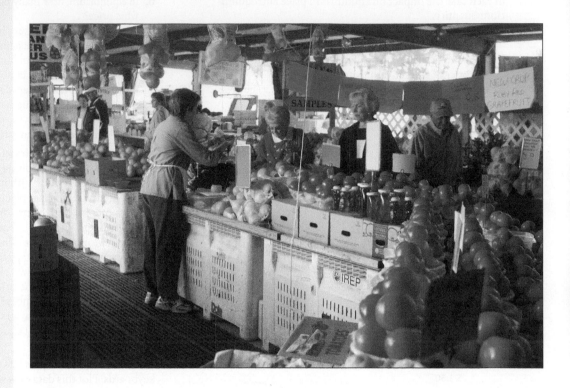

Every society has a system of institutions that determines what is produced, how it is produced, and who gets what is produced. In some societies, these decisions are made centrally, through planning agencies or by government directive. However, in every society, many decisions are made in a *decentralized* way, through the operation of markets.

Markets exist in all societies, and Chapter 3 provided a bare-bones description of how markets operate. In this chapter, we continue our examination of demand, supply, and the price system.

The Price System: Rationing and Allocating Resources

The market system, also called the *price system*, performs two important and closely related functions. First, it provides an automatic mechanism for distributing scarce goods and services. That is, it serves as a **price rationing** device for allocating goods and services to consumers when the quantity demanded exceeds the quantity supplied. Second, the price system ultimately determines both the allocation of resources among producers and the final mix of outputs.

4.1 LEARNING OBJECTIVE

Understand how price floors and price ceilings work in the market place.

price rationing The process by which the market system allocates goods and services to consumers when quantity demanded exceeds quantity supplied.

Price Rationing

Consider the simple process by which the price system eliminates a shortage. Figure 4.1 shows hypothetical supply and demand curves for wheat. Wheat is produced around the world, with large supplies coming from Russia and from the United States. Wheat is sold in a world market and used to produce a range of food products, from cereals and breads to processed foods, which line the kitchens of the average consumer. Wheat is thus demanded by large food companies as they produce breads, cereals, and cake for households.

As Figure 4.1 shows, the equilibrium price of wheat was $160 per metric ton in the spring of 2010. At this price, farmers from around the world were expected to bring 61.7 million metric tons to market. Supply and demand were equal. Market equilibrium existed at a price of $160 per metric ton because at that price, quantity demanded was equal to quantity supplied. (Remember that equilibrium occurs at the point where the supply and demand curves intersect. In Figure 4.1, this occurs at point C.)

In the summer of 2010, Russia experienced its warmest summer on record. Fires swept through Russia, destroying a substantial portion of the Russian wheat crop. With almost a third of the world wheat normally produced in Russia, the effect of this environmental disaster on world wheat supply was substantial. In the figure, the supply curve for wheat, which had been drawn in expectation of harvesting all the wheat planted in Russia along with the rest of the world, now shifted to the left, from $S_{\text{spring 2010}}$ to $S_{\text{fall 2010}}$. This shift in the supply curve created a situation of excess demand at the old price of $160. At that price, the quantity demanded is 61.7 million metric tons, but the burning of much of the Russia supply left the world with only 35 millions of metric tons expected to be supplied. Quantity demanded exceeded quantity supplied at the original price by 26.7 million metric tons.

The reduced supply caused the price of wheat to rise sharply. As the price rises, the available supply is "rationed." Those who are willing and able to pay the most get it. You can see the market's rationing function clearly in Figure 4.1. As the price rises from $160, the quantity

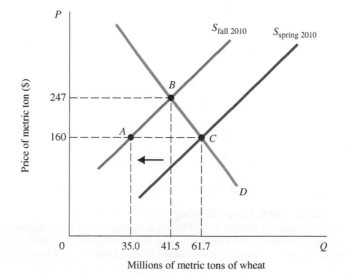

◀ **FIGURE 4.1 The Market for Wheat**
Fires in Russia in the summer of 2010 caused a shift in the world's supply of wheat to the left, causing the price to increase from $160 per metric ton to $247. The equilibrium moved from C to B.

demanded declines along the demand curve, moving from point C (61.7 million tons) toward point B (41.5 million tons). The higher prices mean that prices for products like Pepperidge Farm bread and Shredded Wheat cereal, which use wheat as an essential ingredient, also rise. People bake fewer cakes and begin to eat more rye bread and switch from Shredded Wheat to Corn Flakes in response to the price changes.

As prices rise, wheat farmers also change their behavior, though supply responsiveness is limited in the short term. Farmers outside of Russia, seeing the price rise, harvest their crops more carefully, getting more precious grains from each stalk. Perhaps some wheat is taken out of storage and brought to market. Quantity supplied increases from 35 million metric tons (point A) to 41.5 million tons (point B). The price increase has encouraged farmers who can to make up for part of the Russia wheat loss.

A new equilibrium is established at a price of $247 per metric ton, with 41.5 million tons transacted. The market has determined who gets the wheat: *The lower total supply is rationed to those who are willing and able to pay the higher price.*

This idea of "willingness to pay" is central to the distribution of available supply, and willingness depends on both desire (preferences) and income/wealth. Willingness to pay does not necessarily mean that only the rich will continue to buy wheat when the price increases. For anyone to continue to buy wheat at a higher price, his or her enjoyment comes at a higher cost in terms of other goods and services.

In sum:

> The adjustment of price is the rationing mechanism in free markets. Price rationing means that whenever there is a need to ration a good—that is, when a shortage exists—in a free market, the price of the good will rise until quantity supplied equals quantity demanded—that is, until the market clears.

There is some price that will clear any market you can think of. Consider the market for a famous painting such as Jackson Pollock's *No. 5, 1948*, illustrated in Figure 4.2. At a low price, there would be an enormous excess demand for such an important painting. The price would be bid up until there was only one remaining demander. Presumably, that price would be very high. In fact, the Pollock painting sold for a record $140 million in 2006. If the product is in strictly scarce supply, as a single painting is, its price is said to be *demand-determined*. That is, its price is determined solely and exclusively by the amount that the highest bidder or highest bidders are willing to pay.

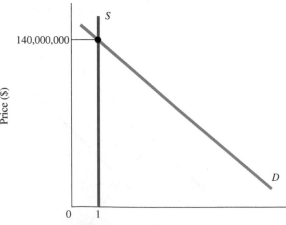

▲ **FIGURE 4.2 Market for a Rare Painting**
There is some price that will clear any market, even if supply is strictly limited. In an auction for a unique painting, the price (bid) will rise to eliminate excess demand until there is only one bidder willing to purchase the single available painting. Some estimate that the *Mona Lisa* would sell for $600 million if auctioned.

One might interpret the statement that "there is some price that will clear any market" to mean "everything has its price," but that is not exactly what it means. Suppose you own a small silver bracelet that has been in your family for generations. It is quite possible that you would not sell it for *any* amount of money. Does this mean that the market is not working, or that quantity supplied and quantity demanded are not equal? Not at all. It simply means that *you* are the highest bidder. By turning down all bids, you must be willing to forgo what anybody offers for it.

Constraints on the Market and Alternative Rationing Mechanisms

On occasion, both governments and private firms decide to use some mechanism other than the market system to ration an item for which there is excess demand at the current price. Policies designed to stop price rationing are commonly justified in a number of ways.

The rationale most often used is fairness. It is not "fair" to let landlords charge high rents, not fair for oil companies to run up the price of gasoline, not fair for insurance companies to charge enormous premiums, and so on. After all, the argument goes, we have no choice but to pay—housing and insurance are necessary, and one needs gasoline to get to work. The Economics in Practice box on page 76 describes complaints against price increases following Hurricane Sandy in 2012. Regardless of the rationale for controlling prices, the following examples will make it clear that trying to bypass the pricing system is often more difficult and more costly than it at first appears.

Oil, Gasoline, and OPEC   One of the most important prices in the world is the price of crude oil. Millions of barrels of oil are traded every day. It is a major input into virtually every product produced. It heats our homes, and it is used to produce the gasoline that runs our cars. Its production has led to massive environmental disasters as well as wars. Its price has fluctuated wildly, leading to major macroeconomic problems. But oil is like other commodities in that its price is determined by the basic forces of supply and demand. Oil provides a good example of how markets work and how markets sometimes fail.

The Organization of the Petroleum Exporting Countries (OPEC) is an organization of twelve countries (Algeria, Angola, Ecuador, Iran, Iraq, Kuwait, Libya, Nigeria, Qatar, Saudi Arabia, the United Arab Emirates, and Venezuela) that together had about one-third of the global market share of oil sales in 2015, although the supply of oil produced in the United States has been growing as a result of new developments in hydraulic fracturing (fracking). In 1973 and 1974, OPEC imposed an embargo on shipments of crude oil to the United States. What followed was a drastic reduction in the quantity of gasoline available at local gas pumps, given the large market share of OPEC at the time.

Had the market system been allowed to operate, refined gasoline prices would have increased dramatically until quantity supplied was equal to quantity demanded. However, the government decided that rationing gasoline only to those who were willing and able to pay the most was unfair, and Congress imposed a **price ceiling**, or maximum price, of $0.57 per gallon of leaded regular gasoline. That price ceiling was intended to keep gasoline "affordable," but it also perpetuated the shortage. At the restricted price, quantity demanded remained greater than quantity supplied, and the available gasoline had to be divided up somehow among all potential demanders.

> **price ceiling**   A maximum price that sellers may charge for a good, usually set by government.

You can see the effects of the price ceiling by looking carefully at Figure 4.3. If the price had been set by the interaction of supply and demand, it would have increased to approximately $1.50 per gallon. Instead, Congress made it illegal to sell gasoline for more than $0.57 per gallon. At that price, quantity demanded exceeded quantity supplied and a shortage existed. Because the price system was not allowed to function, an alternative rationing system had to be found to distribute the available supply of gasoline.

Several devices were tried. The most common of all nonprice rationing systems is **queuing**, a term that means waiting in line. During 1974, long lines formed daily at gas stations, starting

> **queuing**   Waiting in line as a means of distributing goods and services: a nonprice rationing mechanism.

▲ FIGURE 4.3   Excess Demand (Shortage) Created by a Price Ceiling
In 1974, a ceiling price of $0.57 cents per gallon of leaded regular gasoline was imposed. If the price had been set by the interaction of supply and demand instead, it would have increased to approximately $1.50 per gallon. At $0.57 per gallon, the quantity demanded exceeded the quantity supplied. Because the price system was not allowed to function, an alternative rationing system had to be found to distribute the available supply of gasoline.

as early as 5 AM. Under this system, gasoline went to those people who were willing to pay the most, but the sacrifice was measured in hours and aggravation instead of dollars.[1]

favored customers   Those who receive special treatment from dealers during situations of excess demand.

A second nonprice rationing device used during the gasoline crisis was that of **favored customers**. Many gas station owners decided not to sell gasoline to the general public, but to reserve their scarce supplies for friends and favored customers. Not surprisingly, many customers tried to become "favored" by offering side payments to gas station owners. Owners also charged high prices for service. By doing so, they increased the actual price of gasoline but hid it in service overcharges to get around the ceiling.

ration coupons   Tickets or coupons that entitle individuals to purchase a certain amount of a given product per month.

Yet another method of dividing up available supply is the use of **ration coupons**. It was suggested in both 1974 and 1979 that families be given ration tickets or coupons that would entitle them to purchase a certain number of gallons of gasoline each month. That way, everyone would get the same amount regardless of income. Such a system had been employed in the United States during the 1940s when wartime price ceilings on meat, sugar, butter, tires, nylon stockings, and many other items were imposed.

When ration coupons are used with no prohibition against trading them, however, the result is almost identical to a system of price rationing. Those who are willing and able to pay the most buy up the coupons and use them to purchase gasoline, chocolate, fresh eggs, or anything else that

---

[1] You can also show formally that the result is inefficient—that there is a resulting net loss of total value to society. First, there is the cost of waiting in line. Time has a value. With price rationing, no one has to wait in line and the value of that time is saved. Second, there may be additional lost value if the gasoline ends up in the hands of someone who places a lower value on it than someone else who gets no gas. Suppose, for example, that the market price of gasoline if unconstrained would rise to $2 but that the government has it fixed at $1. There will be long lines to get gas. Imagine that to motorist A, 10 gallons of gas is worth $35 but that she fails to get gas because her time is too valuable to wait in line. To motorist B, 10 gallons is worth only $15, but his time is worth much less, so he gets the gas. In the end, A could pay B for the gas and both would be better off. If A pays B $30 for the gas, A is $5 better off and B is $15 better off. In addition, A does not have to wait in line. Thus, the allocation that results from nonprice rationing involves a net loss of value. Such losses are called *deadweight losses*. See p. 84 of this chapter.

ECONOMICS IN PRACTICE

Why Is My Hotel Room So Expensive? A Tale of Hurricane Sandy

In October 2012 Hurricane Sandy hit the northeastern United States. In New York, New Jersey, and Connecticut flooding in particular caused disruption. In the aftermath of the storm, as individuals and public workers began to clean up, prices for a number of items began to rise. At this point, you should be able to predict which prices likely rose the most.

Before Sandy struck we would expect that most of the markets in these states, as in other areas, were more or less in equilibrium. The only merchants who actually *could* raise prices after the storm are ones who face either a large shift to the right of the demand curve facing them or a shift to the left of the supply curve in their market. Otherwise, if merchants post Sandy raised prices, they would simply end up with surplus goods on the shelf. So if we want to predict which prices rose after Sandy, all we need to do is to look at those businesses facing large shifts in either their demand or supply curves after the storm. With many people forced out of their homes, hotel rooms became scarce. With power out, generators became more valuable. With trees down, tree removal services heard from many more customers. In other words, all of these businesses saw a large shift out of demand curves in their markets and none would find it easy to quickly increase their output levels. One can't really build a Holiday Inn overnight! Higher prices were now possible.

As it turned out, gas prices at the pump also rose. Yet one might well have thought that following Sandy, people would drive less, given the conditions of roads and business closings. Here, the more likely problem was a shift in the supply curve, as delivery trucks found it hard to restock gas stations. A shift in the supply curve made higher prices possible, particularly given the fact that those people who did need to go to work really needed that gas!

As we suggest in the text, in some cases government policy controls how much prices *are allowed* to rise after an emergency. In the case of Hurricane Sandy, all three states lodged

complaints of price gouging against numerous businesses, virtually all in the hotel, tree removal, gas station, or generator sales business. In New Jersey, a law against gouging prohibits price increases of more than 10 percent in an emergency situation. Connecticut and New York are more graphic in their definitions, but less precise. In these states, price gouging involves price increases in emergencies which are "unconscionably excessive." Economics will not be much help in translating that definition into a number. But at this point we hope you can see that economics can very much help us predict what kinds of businesses are likely to be charged with the offense.

THINKING PRACTICALLY

1. Gas prices rose after Sandy as supply shifted to the left, or inward, given transport problems. Transport problems likely also affected the delivery of Cheerios. Do you expect the price of Cheerios to also rise substantially? Why or why not?

---

is sold at a restricted price.[2] This means that the price of the restricted good will effectively rise to the market-clearing price. For instance, suppose that you decide not to sell your ration coupon. You are then forgoing what you would have received by selling the coupon. Thus, the "effective" price of the good you purchase will be higher (if only in opportunity cost) than the restricted price. Even when trading coupons is declared illegal, it is virtually impossible to stop black markets from developing. In a **black market**, illegal trading takes place at market-determined prices.

black market   A market in which illegal trading takes place at market-determined prices.

Rationing Mechanisms for Concert and Sports Tickets   Tickets for sporting events such as the World Series, the Super Bowl, and the World Cup command huge prices in the open market. In many cases, the prices are substantially above the original issue price. One of the

---

[2] Of course, if you are assigned a number of tickets and you sell them, you are better off than you would be with price rationing. Ration coupons thus serve as a way of redistributing income.

hottest basketball tickets ever was one to the Boston Celtics and Los Angeles Lakers' NBA final series in 2010 that LA won in seven games. The online price for a courtside seat to one of the games in Los Angeles was $19,000.

You might ask why a profit-maximizing enterprise would not charge the highest price it could? The answer depends on the event. If the Chicago Cubs got into the World Series, the people of Chicago would buy all the tickets available for thousands of dollars each. But if the Cubs actually *charged* $2,000 a ticket, the hard-working fans would be furious: "Greedy Cubs Gouge Fans" the headlines would scream. Ordinary loyal fans earning reasonable salaries would not be able to afford those prices. Next season, perhaps some of those irate fans would change loyalties, supporting the White Sox over the Cubs. In part to keep from alienating loyal fans, prices for championship games are held down. It is interesting to look at this case to see how charging a ticket price lower than market plays out.

Let's consider a concert at the Staples Center, which has 20,000 seats. The supply of tickets is thus fixed at 20,000. Of course, there are good seats and bad seats, but to keep things simple, let's assume that all seats are the same and that the promoters charge $50 per ticket for all tickets. This is illustrated in Figure 4.4. Supply is represented by a vertical line at 20,000. Changing the price does not change the supply of seats. In the figure the quantity demanded at the price of $50 is 38,000, so at this price there is excess demand of 18,000.

Who would get to buy the $50 tickets? As in the case of gasoline, a variety of rationing mechanisms might be used. The most common is queuing, waiting in line. The tickets would go on sale at a particular time, and people would show up and wait. Now ticket sellers have virtual waiting rooms online. Tickets for the World Series go on sale at a particular time in September, and the people who log on to team Web sites at the right moment get into an electronic queue and can buy tickets. Often tickets are sold out in a matter of minutes.

There are also, of course, favored customers. Those who get tickets without queuing are local politicians, sponsors, and friends of the artist or friends of the players.

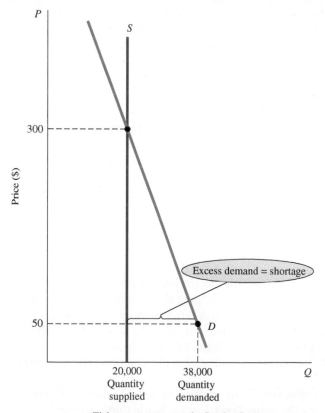

Tickets to a concert at the Staples Center

▲ **FIGURE 4.4** **Supply of and Demand for a Concert at the Staples Center**
At the face-value price of $50, there is excess demand for seats to the concert. At $50 the quantity demanded is greater than the quantity supplied, which is fixed at 20,000 seats. The diagram shows that the quantity demanded would equal the quantity supplied at a price of $300 per ticket.

But "once the dust settles," the power of technology and the concept of *opportunity cost* take over. Even if you get the ticket for the (relatively) low price of $50, that is not the true cost. The true cost is what you give up to sit in the seat. If people on eBay, StubHub, or Ticketmaster are willing to pay $300 for your ticket, that's what you must pay, or sacrifice, to go to the concert. Many people—even strong fans—will choose to sell that ticket. Once again, it is difficult to stop the market from rationing the tickets to those people who are willing and able to pay the most.

> No matter how good the intentions of private organizations and governments, it is difficult to prevent the price system from operating and to stop people's willingness to pay from asserting itself. Every time an alternative is tried, the price system seems to sneak in the back door. With favored customers and black markets, the final distribution may be even more unfair than what would result from simple price rationing.

Prices and the Allocation of Resources

Thinking of the market system as a mechanism for allocating scarce goods and services among competing demanders is revealing, but the market determines more than just the distribution of final outputs. It also determines what gets produced and how resources are allocated among competing uses.

Consider a change in consumer preferences that leads to an increase in demand for a specific good or service. During the 1980s, for example, people began going to restaurants more frequently than before. Researchers think that this trend, which continues today, is partially the result of social changes (such as a dramatic rise in the number of two-earner families) and partially the result of rising incomes. The market responded to this change in demand by shifting resources, both capital and labor, into more and better restaurants.

With the increase in demand for restaurant meals, the price of eating out rose and the restaurant business became more profitable. The higher profits attracted new businesses and provided old restaurants with an incentive to expand. As new capital, seeking profits, flowed into the restaurant business, so did labor. New restaurants need chefs. Chefs need training, and the higher wages that came with increased demand provided an incentive for them to get it. In response to the increase in demand for training, new cooking schools opened and existing schools began to offer courses in the culinary arts. This story could go on and on, but the point is clear:

> Price changes resulting from shifts of demand in output markets cause profits to rise or fall. Profits attract capital; losses lead to disinvestment. Higher wages attract labor and encourage workers to acquire skills. At the core of the system, supply, demand, and prices in input and output markets determine the allocation of resources and the ultimate combinations of goods and services produced.

Price Floor

As we have seen, price ceilings, often imposed because price rationing is viewed as unfair, result in alternative rationing mechanisms that are inefficient and may be equally unfair. Some of the same arguments can be made for price floors. A **price floor** is a minimum price below which exchange is not permitted. If a price floor is set above the equilibrium price, the result will be excess supply; quantity supplied will be greater than quantity demanded.

The most common example of a price floor is the **minimum wage**, which is a floor set for the price of labor. Employers (who demand labor) are not permitted under federal law to pay a wage less than $7.25 per hour (in 2015) to workers (who supply labor). Many states have much higher minimum wages; Washington, for example, had a minimum wage in 2015 of $9.47 per hour. Critics of the minimum wage argue that since it is above equilibrium, it may result in less labor hired.

price floor A minimum price below which exchange is not permitted.

minimum wage A price floor set for the price of labor.

Supply and Demand Analysis: An Oil Import Fee

The basic logic of supply and demand is a powerful tool of analysis. As an extended example of the power of this logic, we will consider a proposal to impose a tax on imported oil. The idea of taxing imported oil is hotly debated, and the tools we have learned thus far will show us the effects of such a tax.

In 2012 the United States imported 45 percent of its oil. Of the imports, 22 percent come from the Persian Gulf States. Given the political volatility of that area of the world, many politicians have advocated trying to reduce our dependence on foreign oil. One tool often suggested by both politicians and economists to accomplish this goal has been an import oil tax or tariff.

Supply and demand analysis makes the arguments of the import tax proponents easier to understand. Figure 4.5(a) shows the U.S. market for oil as of late 2012. The world price of oil is at slightly more than $80, and the United States is assumed to be able to buy *all the oil that it wants* at this price. This means that domestic producers cannot charge any more than $80 per barrel. The curve labeled *Supply* $_{US}$ shows the amount that domestic suppliers will produce at each price level. At a price of $80, domestic production is 7 million barrels per day. U.S. producers will produce at point A on the supply curve. The total quantity of oil demanded in the United States in 2012 was approximately 13 million barrels per day. At a price of $80, the quantity demanded in the United States is point B on the demand curve.

The difference between the total quantity demanded (13 million barrels per day) and domestic production (7 million barrels per day) is total imports (6 million barrels per day).

▶ **FIGURE 4.5 The U.S. Market for Crude Oil, 2012**

In 2012 the world market price for crude oil was approximately $80 per barrel. Domestic production in the United States that year averaged about 7 million barrels per day, whereas crude oil demand averaged just under 13 million barrels per day. The difference between production and consumption were made up of net imports of approximately 6 million barrels per day, as we see in panel (a).

If the government imposed a tax in this market of 33..33 percent, or $26.64, that would increase the world price to $106.64. That higher price causes quantity demanded to fall below its original level of 13 million barrels, while the price increase causes domestic production to rise above the original level. As we see in panel b, the effect is a reduction in import levels.

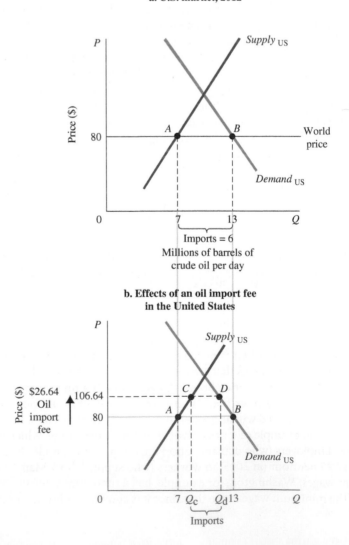

a. U.S. market, 2012

b. Effects of an oil import fee in the United States

ECONOMICS IN PRACTICE

The Price Mechanism at Work for Shakespeare

Every summer, New York City puts on free performances of Shakespeare in the Park. Tickets are distributed on a first-come-first-serve basis at the Delacorte Theatre in the park beginning at 1 PM on the day of the show. People usually begin lining up at 6 AM when the park opens; by 10 AM the line has typically reached a length sufficient to give away all available tickets.

When you examine the people standing in line for these tickets, most of them seem to be fairly young. Many carry book bags identifying them as students in one of New York's many colleges. Of course, all college students may be fervent Shakespeare fans, but can you think of another reason for the composition of the line? Further, when you attend one of the plays and look around, the audience appears much older and much sleeker than the people who were standing in line. What is going on?

Although the tickets are "free" in terms of financial costs, their true price includes the value of the time spent standing in line. Thus, the tickets are cheaper for people (for example, students) whose time value is lower than they are for high-wage earners, like an investment banker from Goldman Sachs. The true cost of a ticket is $0 plus the opportunity cost of the time spent in line. If the average person spends 4 hours in line, as is done in the Central Park case, for someone with a high wage, the true cost of the ticket might be very high. For example, a lawyer who earns $300 an hour would be giving up $1,200 to wait in line. It should not surprise you to see more people waiting in line for whom the tickets are inexpensive.

What about the people who are at the performance? Think about our discussion of the power of entrepreneurs. In this case, the students who stand in line as consumers of the tickets also can play a role as producers. In fact, the students can produce tickets relatively cheaply by waiting in line. They

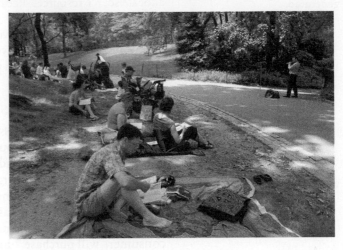

can then turn around and sell those tickets to the high-wage Shakespeare lovers. These days eBay is a great source of tickets to free events, sold by individuals with low opportunity costs of their time who queued up. Craigslist even provides listings for people who are willing to wait in line for you.

Of course, now and again we do encounter a busy business-person in one of the Central Park lines. Recently, one of the authors encountered one and asked him why he was waiting in line rather than using eBay, and he replied that it reminded him of when he was young, waiting in line for rock concerts.

THINKING PRACTICALLY

1. Many museums offer free admission one day a week, on a weekday. On that day we observe that museum-goers are more likely to be senior citizens than on a typical Saturday. Why?

Now suppose that the government levies a tax of $33\frac{1}{3}$ percent on imported oil. Because the import price is $80, this tax rate translates into a tax of $26.64, which increases the price per barrel paid by U.S. importers to $106.64 ($80 + $26.64). This new, higher price means that U.S. producers can also charge up to $106.64 for a barrel of crude. Note, however, that the tax is paid only on imported oil. Thus, the entire 106.64 paid for domestic crude goes to domestic producers.

Figure 4.5(b) shows the result of the tax. First, because of a higher price, the quantity demanded drops. This is a movement *along* the demand curve from point B to point D. At the same time, the quantity supplied by domestic producers increases. This is a movement *along* the supply curve from point A to point C. With an increase in domestic quantity supplied and a decrease in domestic quantity demanded, imports decrease, as we can see clearly as Q_d-Q_c is smaller than the original 6 billions barrels per day.

The tax also generates revenues for the federal government. The total tax revenue collected is equal to the tax per barrel ($26.64) times the number of imported barrels (Q_d-Q_c).

What does all of this mean? In the final analysis, an oil import fee would increase domestic production and reduce overall consumption. To the extent that one believes that Americans are consuming too much oil, the reduced consumption may be a good thing. We also see that the tax increases the price of oil in the United States.

Supply and Demand and Market Efficiency

Clearly, supply and demand curves help explain the way that markets and market prices work to allocate scarce resources. Recall that when we try to understand "how the system works," we are doing "positive economics."

Supply and demand curves can also be used to illustrate the idea of market efficiency, an important aspect of "normative economics." To understand the ideas, you first must understand the concepts of consumer and producer surplus.

Consumer Surplus

If we think hard about the lessons of supply and demand, we can see that the market forces us to reveal a great deal about our personal preferences. If you are free to choose within the constraints imposed by prices and your income and you decide to buy a hamburger for $2.50, you have "revealed" that a hamburger is worth at least $2.50 to you. Consumers reveal who they are by what they choose to buy and do.

This idea of purchases as preference revelation underlies a lot of the valuation economists do. Look at the demand curve in Figure 4.6(a). At the current market price of $2.50, consumers will purchase 7 million hamburgers per month. In this market, consumers who value a hamburger at $2.50 or more will buy it, and those who have lower values will do without.

consumer surplus The difference between the maximum amount a person is willing to pay for a good and its current market price.

As the figure shows, however, some people value hamburgers at more than $2.50. At a price of $5.00, for example, consumers would still buy 1 million hamburgers. These million hamburgers have a value to their buyers of $5.00 each. If consumers can buy these burgers for only $2.50, they would earn a **consumer surplus** of $2.50 per burger. Consumer surplus is the difference between the maximum amount a person is willing to pay for a good and its current market price. The consumer surplus earned by the people willing to pay $5.00 for a hamburger is approximately equal to the shaded area between point A and the price, $2.50.

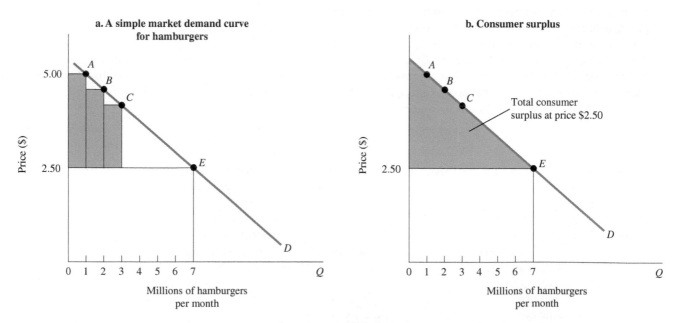

▲ **FIGURE 4.6 Market Demand and Consumer Surplus**
As illustrated in Figure 4.6(a), some consumers (see point A) are willing to pay as much as $5.00 each for hamburgers. Since the market price is just $2.50, they receive a consumer surplus of $2.50 for each hamburger that they consume. Others (see point B) are willing to pay something less than $5.00 and receive a slightly smaller surplus. Because the market price of hamburgers is just $2.50, the area of the shaded triangle in Figure 4.6(b) is equal to total consumer surplus.

The second million hamburgers in Figure 4.6(a) are valued at more than the market price as well, although the consumer surplus gained is slightly less. Point *B* on the market demand curve shows the maximum amount that consumers would be willing to pay for the second million hamburgers. The consumer surplus earned by these people is equal to the shaded area between *B* and the price, $2.50. Similarly, for the third million hamburgers, maximum willingness to pay is given by point *C*; consumer surplus is a bit lower than it is at points *A* and *B*, but it is still significant.

The total value of the consumer surplus suggested by the data in Figure 4.6(a) is roughly equal to the area of the shaded triangle in Figure 4.6(b). To understand why this is so, think about offering hamburgers to consumers at successively lower prices. If the good were actually sold for $2.50, those near point *A* on the demand curve would get a large surplus; those at point *B* would get a smaller surplus. Those at point *E* would get no surplus.

Producer Surplus

Similarly, the supply curve in a market shows the amount that firms willingly produce and supply to the market at various prices. Presumably it is because the price is sufficient to cover the costs or the opportunity costs of production and give producers enough profit to keep them in business. When speaking of cost of production, we include everything that a producer must give up to produce a good.

A simple market supply curve like the one in Figure 4.7(a) illustrates this point quite clearly. At the current market price of $2.50, producers will produce and sell 7 million hamburgers. There is only one price in the market, and the supply curve tells us the quantity supplied at each price.

Notice, however, that if the price were just $0.75 (75 cents), although production would be much lower—most producers would be out of business at that price—a few producers would actually be supplying burgers. In fact, producers would supply about 1 million burgers to the market. These firms must have lower costs: They are more efficient or they have access to raw beef at a lower price or perhaps they can hire low-wage labor.

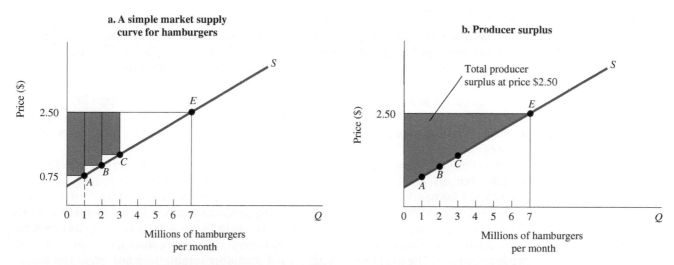

▲ **FIGURE 4.7 Market Supply and Producer Surplus**
As illustrated in Figure 4.7(a), some producers are willing to produce hamburgers for a price of $0.75 each. Because they are paid $2.50, they earn a producer surplus equal to $1.75. Other producers are willing to supply hamburgers at prices less than $2.50, and they also earn producers surplus. Because the market price of hamburgers is $2.50, the area of the shaded triangle in Figure 4.7(b) is equal to total producer surplus.

▶ **FIGURE 4.8** **Total Producer and Consumer Surplus**

Total producer and consumer surplus is greatest where supply and demand curves intersect at equilibrium.

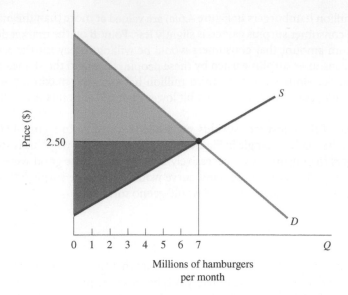

producer surplus The difference between the current market price and the cost of production for the firm.

If these efficient, low-cost producers are able to charge $2.50 for each hamburger, they are earning what is called a **producer surplus**. Producer surplus is the difference between the current market price and the cost of production for the firm. The first million hamburgers would generate a producer surplus of $2.50 minus $0.75, or $1.75 per hamburger: a total of $1.75 million. The second million hamburgers would also generate a producer surplus because the price of $2.50 exceeds the producers' total cost of producing these hamburgers, which is above $0.75 but much less than $2.50.

The total value of the producer surplus received by producers of hamburgers at a price of $2.50 per burger is roughly equal to the shaded triangle in Figure 4.7(b). Those producers just able to make a profit producing burgers will be near point E on the supply curve and will earn very little in the way of surplus.

Competitive Markets Maximize the Sum of Producer and Consumer Surplus

In the preceding example, the quantity of hamburgers supplied and the quantity of hamburgers demanded are equal at $2.50. Figure 4.8 shows the total net benefits to consumers and producers resulting from the production of 7 million hamburgers. Consumers receive benefits in excess of the price they pay and equal to the blue shaded area between the demand curve and the price line at $2.50; the area is equal to the amount of consumer surplus being earned. Producers receive compensation in excess of costs and equal to the red-shaded area between the supply curve and the price line at $2.50; the area is equal to the amount of producer surplus being earned.

Now consider the result to consumers and producers if production were to be reduced to 4 million burgers. Look carefully at Figure 4.9(a). At 4 million burgers, consumers are willing to pay $3.75 for hamburgers and there are firms whose costs make it worthwhile to supply at a price as low as $1.50, yet something is stopping production at 4 million. The result is a loss of both consumer and producer surplus. You can see in Figure 4.9(a) that if production were expanded from 4 million to 7 million, the market would yield more consumer surplus and more producer surplus. The total loss of producer and consumer surplus from *underproduction* and, as we will see shortly, from overproduction is referred to as a **deadweight loss**. In Figure 4.9(a) the deadweight loss is equal to the area of triangle ABC shaded in yellow.

deadweight loss The total loss of producer and consumer surplus from underproduction or overproduction.

Figure 4.9(b) illustrates how a deadweight loss of both producer and consumer surplus can result from *overproduction* as well. For every hamburger produced above 7 million, consumers are willing to pay less than the cost of production. The cost of the resources needed to produce

a. Deadweight loss from underproduction

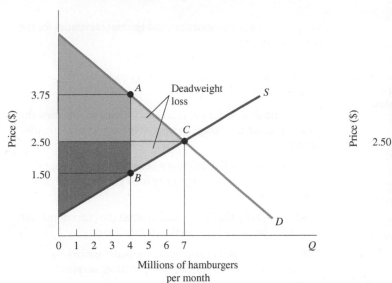

b. Deadweight loss from overproduction

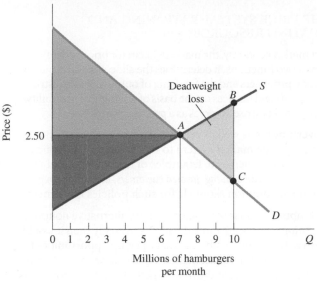

▲ **FIGURE 4.9 Deadweight Loss**

Figure 4.9(a) shows the consequences of producing 4 million hamburgers per month instead of 7 million hamburgers per month. Total producer and consumer surplus is reduced by the area of triangle *ABC* shaded in yellow. This is called the deadweight loss from underproduction. Figure 4.9(b) shows the consequences of producing 10 million hamburgers per month instead of 7 million hamburgers per month. As production increases from 7 million to 10 million hamburgers, the full cost of production rises above consumers' willingness to pay, resulting in a deadweight loss equal to the area of triangle *ABC*.

hamburgers above 7 million exceeds the benefits to consumers, resulting in a net loss of producer and consumer surplus equal to the yellow shaded area *ABC*.

Potential Causes of Deadweight Loss From Under- and Overproduction

Most of the next few chapters will discuss perfectly competitive markets in which prices are determined by the free interaction of supply and demand. As you will see, when supply and demand interact freely, competitive markets produce what people want at the least cost, that is, they are efficient. Beginning in Chapter 13, however, we will begin to relax assumptions and will discover a number of naturally occurring sources of market failure. Monopoly power gives firms the incentive to underproduce and overprice, taxes and subsidies may distort consumer choices, external costs such as pollution and congestion may lead to over- or underproduction of some goods, and artificial price floors and price ceilings may have the same effects.

Looking Ahead

We have now examined the basic forces of supply and demand and discussed the market/price system. These fundamental concepts will serve as building blocks for what comes next. Whether you are studying microeconomics or macroeconomics, you will be studying the functions of markets and the behavior of market participants in more detail in the following chapters.

Because the concepts presented in the first four chapters are so important to your understanding of what is to come, this might be a good time for you to review this material.

SUMMARY

4.1 THE PRICE SYSTEM: RATIONING AND ALLOCATING RESOURCES *p. 73*

1. In a market economy, the market system (or price system) serves two functions. It determines the allocation of resources among producers and the final mix of outputs. It also distributes goods and services on the basis of willingness and ability to pay. In this sense, it serves as a *price rationing* device.

2. Governments as well as private firms sometimes decide not to use the market system to ration an item for which there is excess demand. Examples of nonprice rationing systems include *queuing, favored customers, and ration coupons.* The most common rationale for such policies is "fairness."

3. Attempts to bypass the market and use alternative nonprice rationing devices are more difficult and costly than it would seem at first glance. Schemes that open up opportunities for favored customers, black markets, and side payments often end up less "fair" than the free market. A supply curve shows the relationship between the quantity producers are willing to supply to the market and the price of a good.

4.2 SUPPLY AND DEMAND ANALYSIS: AN OIL IMPORT FEE *p. 80*

4. The basic logic of supply and demand is a powerful tool for analysis. For example, supply and demand analysis shows that an oil import tax will reduce quantity of oil demanded, increase domestic production, and generate revenues for the government.

4.3 SUPPLY AND DEMAND AND MARKET EFFICIENCY *p. 82*

5. Supply and demand curves can also be used to illustrate the idea of market efficiency, an important aspect of normative economics.

6. *Consumer surplus* is the difference between the maximum amount a person is willing to pay for a good and the current market price.

7. *Producer surplus* is the difference between the current market price and the cost of production for the firm.

8. At free market equilibrium with competitive markets, the sum of consumer surplus and producer surplus is maximized.

9. The total loss of producer and consumer surplus from underproduction or overproduction is referred to as a *deadweight loss.*

REVIEW TERMS AND CONCEPTS

black market, *p. 77*

consumer surplus, *p. 82*

deadweight loss, *p. 84*

favored customers, *p. 76*

minimum wage, *p. 79*

price ceiling, *p. 75*

price floor, *p. 79*

price rationing, *p. 73*

producer surplus, *p. 84*

queuing, *p. 75*

ration coupons, *p. 76*

PROBLEMS

All problems are available on MyEconLab.

4.1 THE PRICE SYSTEM: RATIONING AND ALLOCATING RESOURCES

LEARNING OBJECTIVE: Understand how price floors and price ceilings work in the market place.

1.1 Illustrate the following with supply and demand curves:
   a. In November 2014, Andy Warhol's silkscreen artwork *Triple Elvis [Ferus Type]* was sold at Christie's Auction House in New York for $81.9 million.
   b. In March 2015, hogs in the United States were selling for 62 cents per pound, down from 98 cents per pound a year before. This was due primarily to the fact that supply had increased during the period.
   c. In 2015, the demand for organic produce continued to rise, and represented 11 percent of all produce purchased in U.S. supermarkets. At the same time, the number of farmers growing organic crops had increased by 119 percent since 2007. The overall result was a drop in the

average price of organic produce and an increase in the quantity of organic produce sold.

1.2 Every demand curve must eventually hit the quantity axis because with limited incomes, there is always a price so high that there is no demand for the good. Do you agree or disagree? Why?

1.3 When excess demand exists for tickets to a major sporting event or a concert, profit opportunities exist for scalpers. Explain briefly using supply and demand curves to illustrate. Some argue that scalpers work to the advantage of everyone and are "efficient." Do you agree or disagree? Explain briefly.

1.4 In an effort to "support" the price of some agricultural goods, the Department of Agriculture pays farmers a subsidy in cash for every acre that they leave *unplanted*. The Agriculture Department argues that the subsidy increases the "cost" of planting and that it will reduce supply and increase the price of competitively produced agricultural goods. Critics argue that because the subsidy is a payment to farmers, it will reduce costs and lead to lower prices. Which argument is correct? Explain.

1.5 The rent for 2-bedroom apartments in Detroit has fallen from an average of $796 in September 2014 to $717 in March 2015. Demand for 2-bedroom apartments in Detroit was falling during this period as well. This is hard to explain because the law of demand says that lower prices should lead to higher demand. Do you agree or disagree? Explain your answer.

1.6 Illustrate the following with supply or demand curves:
   a. In Joseph Heller's iconic novel, *Catch 22*, one of the characters was paid by the government to not grow alfalfa. According to the story's narrator, "The more alfalfa he did not grow, the more money the government gave him, and he spent every penny he didn't earn on new land to increase the amount of alfalfa he did not produce."
   b. In 2015, Chipotle suspended the sale of pork at one-third of its restaurants due to animal welfare concerns, and this had a significant impact on the amount of chicken entrees it sold to customers.
   c. From 2007 to 2014, median income in the United States fell by 8 percent, shifting the demand for gasoline. During that same time period, crude oil prices fell 35 percent, shifting the supply of gasoline. At the new equilibrium, the quantity of gasoline sold is less than it was before. (Crude oil is used to produce gasoline.)

1.7 Illustrate the following with supply or demand curves:
   a. A situation of excess labor demand caused by a salary cap in the National Basketball Association (NBA).
   b. The effect of a sharp decrease in gasoline prices on the demand for electric vehicles.

1.8 [**Related to the *Economics in Practice* on p. 77**] The feature states that in New Jersey, a law against price gouging prohibits price increases of more than 10 percent in an emergency situation. Assume that prior

to Sandy the equilibrium price for portable generators was $100 and the equilibrium quantity was 200 units per month. After Sandy, demand increased to 500 units per month and generator sellers raised prices to the maximum amount allowed by law. Do you think that the new higher price will be high enough to meet the increased demand? Use a supply and demand graph to explain your answer.

1.9 In April 2015, the U.S. Energy Information Administration projected that the average retail price for regular-grade gasoline would be $2.45 per gallon for the remainder of the year. Do some research on the price of gasoline. Has this projection been accurate? What is the price of regular-grade gasoline today in your city or town? If it is below $2.45 per gallon, what are the reasons? Similarly, if it is higher than $2.45, what has happened to drive up the price? Illustrate with supply and demand curves.

1.10 Many cruise lines offer 5-day trips. A disproportionate number of these trips leave port on Thursday and return late Monday. Why might this be true?

1.11 [**Related to the *Economics in Practice* on p. 81**] Lines for free tickets to see free Shakespeare in Central Park are often long. A local politician has suggested that it would be a great service if the park provided music to entertain those who are waiting in line. What do you think of this suggestion?

1.12 The following graph represents the market for wheat. The equilibrium price is $20 per bushel and the equilibrium quantity is 14 million bushels.

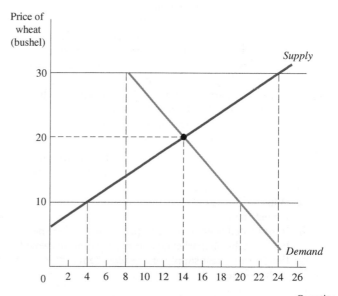

a. Explain what will happen if the government establishes a price ceiling of $10 per bushel of wheat in this market? What if the price ceiling was set at $30?

b. Explain what will happen if the government establishes a price floor of $30 per bushel of wheat in this market. What if the price floor was set at $10?

4.2 SUPPLY AND DEMAND ANALYSIS: AN OIL IMPORT FEE

LEARNING OBJECTIVE: Analyze the economic impact of an oil import tax.

2.1 Suppose that the world price of oil is $60 per barrel and that the United States can buy all the oil it wants at this price. Suppose also that the demand and supply schedules for oil in the United States are as follows:

Price ($ Per Barrel)	U.S. Quantity Demanded	U.S. Quantity Supplied
55	26	14
60	24	16
65	22	18
70	20	20
75	18	22

a. On graph paper, draw the supply and demand curves for the United States.

b. With free trade in oil, what price will Americans pay for their oil? What quantity will Americans buy? How much of this will be supplied by American producers? How much will be imported? Illustrate total imports on your graph of the U.S. oil market.

c. Suppose the United States imposes a tax of $5 per barrel on imported oil. What quantity would Americans buy? How much of this would be supplied by American producers? How much would be imported? How much tax would the government collect?

d. Briefly summarize the impact of an oil import tax by explaining who is helped and who is hurt among the following groups: domestic oil consumers, domestic oil producers, foreign oil producers, and the U.S. government.

2.2 Use the data in the preceding problem to answer the following questions. Now suppose that the United States allows no oil imports.

a. What are the equilibrium price and quantity for oil in the United States?

b. If the United States imposed a price ceiling of $65 per barrel on the oil market and prohibited imports, would there be an excess supply or an excess demand for oil? If so, how much?

c. Under the price ceiling, quantity supplied and quantity demanded differ. Which of the two will determine how much oil is purchased? Briefly explain why.

4.3 SUPPLY AND DEMAND AND MARKET EFFICIENCY

LEARNING OBJECTIVE: Explain how consumer and producer surplus are generated.

3.1 Use the following diagram to calculate total consumer surplus at a price of $12 and production of 500 thousand flu vaccinations per day. For the same equilibrium, calculate total producer surplus. Assuming price remained at $12 but production was cut to 200 thousand vaccinations per day, calculate producer surplus and consumer surplus. Calculate the deadweight loss from underproduction.

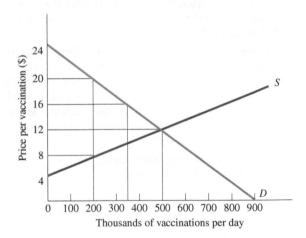

3.2 Suppose the market demand for a cup of cappuccino is given by $Q_D = 24 - 4P$ and the market supply for a cup of cappuccino is given by $Q_S = 8P - 12$, where P = price (per cup).

a. Graph the supply and demand schedules for cappuccino.

b. What is the equilibrium price and equilibrium quantity?

c. Calculate consumer surplus and producer surplus, and identify these on the graph.

3.3 On April 20, 2010, an oil-drilling platform owned by British Petroleum exploded in the Gulf of Mexico, causing oil to leak into the gulf at estimates of 1.5 to 2.5 million gallons per day for well more than 2 months. As a result of the oil spill, the government closed more than 25 percent of federal waters, which devastated the commercial fishing industry in the area. Explain how the reduction in supply from the reduced fishing waters either increased or decreased consumer surplus and producer surplus, and show these changes graphically.

3.4 The following graph represents the market for DVDs.

a. Find the values of consumer surplus and producer surplus when the market is in equilibrium, and identify these areas on the graph.

b. If underproduction occurs in this market, and only 9 million DVDs are produced, what happens to the amounts of consumer surplus and producer surplus? What is the value of the deadweight loss? Identify these areas on the graph.

c. If overproduction occurs in this market, and 27 million DVDs are produced, what happens to the amounts of consumer surplus and producer surplus? Is there a deadweight loss with overproduction? If so, what is its value? Identify these areas on the graph.

5

Introduction to Macroeconomics

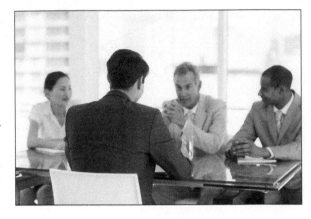

When the macroeconomy is doing well, jobs are easy to find, incomes are generally rising, and profits of corporations are high. On the other hand, if the macroeconomy is in a slump, new jobs are scarce, incomes are not growing well, and profits are low. Students who entered the job market in the boom of the late 1990s in the United States, on average, had an easier time finding a job than did those who entered in the recession of 2008–2009. The sluggish economy that continued into 2013 had negative effects on millions of people. Given the large effect that the macroeconomy can have on our lives, it is important that we understand how it works.

We begin by discussing the differences between microeconomics and macroeconomics that we glimpsed in Chapter 1. **Microeconomics** examines the functioning of individual industries and the behavior of individual decision-making units, typically firms and households. With a few assumptions about how these units behave (firms maximize profits; households maximize utility), we can derive useful conclusions about how markets work and how resources are allocated.

Instead of focusing on the factors that influence the production of particular products and the behavior of individual industries, **macroeconomics** focuses on the determinants of total national output. Macroeconomics studies not household income but *national* income, not individual prices but the *overall* price level. It does not analyze the demand for labor in the automobile industry but instead total employment in the economy.

Both microeconomics and macroeconomics are concerned with the decisions of households and firms. Microeconomics deals with individual decisions; macroeconomics deals with the sum of these individual decisions. *Aggregate* is used in macroeconomics to refer to sums. When we speak of **aggregate behavior**, we mean the behavior of all households as well as the behavior of all firms. We also speak of aggregate consumption and aggregate investment, which refer to total consumption and total investment in the economy, respectively.

Because microeconomists and macroeconomists look at the economy from different perspectives, you might expect that they would reach somewhat different conclusions about the way the economy behaves. This is true to some extent. Microeconomists generally conclude that markets work well. They see prices as flexible, adjusting to maintain equality between quantity supplied and quantity demanded. Macroeconomists, however, observe that important prices in the economy—for example, the wage rate (or price of labor)—often seem "sticky." **Sticky prices** are prices that do not always adjust rapidly to maintain equality between quantity supplied and quantity demanded. Microeconomists do not expect to see the quantity of apples supplied exceeding the quantity of apples demanded because the price of apples is not sticky. On the other hand, macroeconomists—who analyze aggregate behavior—examine periods of high unemployment, where the quantity of labor supplied appears to exceed the quantity of labor demanded. At such times, it appears that wage rates do not fall fast enough to equate the quantity of labor supplied and the quantity of labor demanded.

Macroeconomic Concerns

Three of the major concerns of macroeconomics are

- Output growth
- Unemployment
- Inflation and deflation

Government policy makers would like to have high output growth, low unemployment, and low inflation. We will see that these goals may conflict with one another and that an important point in understanding macroeconomics is understanding these conflicts.

Output Growth

Instead of growing at an even rate at all times, economies tend to experience short-term ups and downs in their performance. The technical name for these ups and downs is the **business cycle**. The main measure of how an economy is doing is **aggregate output**, the total quantity of goods and services produced in the economy in a given period. When less is produced (in other words, when aggregate output decreases), there are fewer goods and services to go around and the average standard of living declines. When firms cut back on production, they also lay off workers, increasing the rate of unemployment.

Recessions are periods during which aggregate output declines. It has become conventional to classify an economic downturn as a "recession" when aggregate output declines for two consecutive quarters. A prolonged and deep recession is called a **depression**, although economists do not agree on when a recession becomes a depression. Since the 1930s the United States has experienced one depression (during the 1930s) and eight recessions: 1946, 1954, 1958, 1974–1975, 1980–1982, 1990–1991, 2001, and 2008–2009. Other countries also experienced recessions in the twentieth century, some roughly coinciding with U.S. recessions and some not.

A typical business cycle is illustrated in Figure 5.1. Because most economies, on average, grow over time, the business cycle in Figure 5.1 shows a positive trend—the *peak* (the highest point) of a new business cycle is higher than the peak of the previous cycle. The period from a

microeconomics Examines the functioning of individual industries and the behavior of individual decision-making units—firms and households.

macroeconomics Deals with the economy as a whole. Macroeconomics focuses on the determinants of total national income, deals with aggregates such as aggregate consumption and investment, and looks at the overall level of prices instead of individual prices.

aggregate behavior The behavior of all households and firms together.

sticky prices Prices that do not always adjust rapidly to maintain equality between quantity supplied and quantity demanded.

business cycle The cycle of short-term ups and downs in the economy.

aggregate output The total quantity of goods and services produced in an economy in a given period.

recession A period during which aggregate output declines. Conventionally, a period in which aggregate output declines for two consecutive quarters.

depression A prolonged and deep recession.

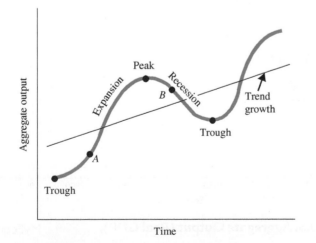

▲ **FIGURE 5.1 A Typical Business Cycle**
In this business cycle, the economy is expanding as it moves through point *A* from the trough to the peak. When the *economy* moves from a peak down to a trough, through point *B*, the economy is in recession.

expansion or boom The period in the business cycle from a trough up to a peak during which output and employment grow.

contraction, recession, *or* slump The period in the business cycle from a peak down to a trough during which output and employment fall.

trough, or bottom of the cycle, to a peak is called an **expansion or a boom**. During an expansion, output and employment grow. The period from a peak to a trough is called a **contraction, recession, *or* slump**, when output and employment fall.

In judging whether an economy is expanding or contracting, note the difference between the level of economic activity and its rate of change. If the economy has just left a trough (point A in Figure 5.1), it will be growing (rate of change is positive), but its level of output will still be low. If the economy has just started to decline from a peak (point B), it will be contracting (rate of change is negative), but its level of output will still be high. The business cycle drawn in Figure 5.1 is symmetrical, which means that the length of an expansion is the same as the length of a contraction. Most business cycles are not symmetrical, however. It is possible, for example, for the expansion phase to be longer than the contraction phase. When contraction comes, it may be fast and sharp, whereas expansion may be slow and gradual. Moreover, the economy is not nearly as regular as the business cycle in Figure 5.1 indicates. The ups and downs in the economy tend to be erratic.

Figure 5.2 shows the actual business cycles in the United States between 1900 and 2014. Although many business cycles have occurred in the last 115 years, each is unique. The economy is not so simple that it has regular cycles.

The periods of the Great Depression and World War I and II show the largest fluctuations in Figure 5.2, although other large contractions and expansions have taken place. Note the expansion in the 1960s and the five recessions since 1970. Some of the cycles have been long; some have been short. Note also that aggregate output actually increased between 1933 and 1937, even though it was still quite low in 1937. The economy did not come out of the Depression until the defense buildup prior to the start of World War II. Note also that business cycles were more extreme before World War II than they have been since then. Finally, note that the recovery from the 2008–2009 recession was unusually slow.

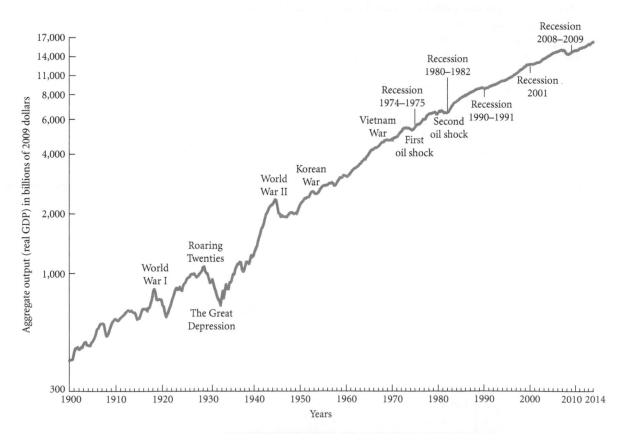

▲ FIGURE 5.2 **U.S. Aggregate Output (Real GDP),** MyEconLab Real-time data
1900–2014
The periods of the Great Depression and World War I and II show the largest fluctuations in aggregate output.

Unemployment

You cannot listen to the news or read a newspaper without noticing that data on the unemployment rate are released each month. The **unemployment rate**—the percentage of the labor force that is unemployed—is a key indicator of the economy's health. Because the unemployment rate is usually closely related to the economy's aggregate output, announcements of each month's new figure are followed with great interest by economists, politicians, and policy makers.

Although macroeconomists are interested in learning why the unemployment rate has risen or fallen in a given period, they also try to answer a more basic question: Why is there any unemployment at all? Part of the answer to this question is straightforward, coming from the fact that adjustments in labor markets generally take some time. At times people decide to quit their jobs and look for something better. Until they find a new job, they will be unemployed. At any time, some firms may go bankrupt because of competition from rivals, bad management, or bad luck. Employees of such firms typically are not able to find new jobs immediately, and while they are looking for work, they will be unemployed. Also, workers entering the labor market for the first time may require a few weeks or months to find a job. All of these factors tell us that some positive rate of unemployment is inevitable in a dynamic economy.

A key question in macroeconomics is how the economy adjusts when the unemployment rate rises beyond this base level. Supply and demand analysis leads us to expect a market response to the existence of unemployed workers. Specifically, when there is unemployment beyond some minimum amount, there is an excess supply of workers—at the going wage rates, there are people who want to work who cannot find work. Microeconomic theory tells us that excess supply causes a decrease in the price of the commodity in question. As prices fall, quantity demanded rises and the quantity supplied falls. In the end prices fall enough so that quantity supplied equals the quantity demanded, and equilibrium is restored as the market clears.

The existence of unemployment seems to imply that the aggregate labor market is not in equilibrium—that something prevents the quantity supplied and the quantity demanded from equating. Why do labor markets not clear when other markets do, or is it that labor markets are clearing and the unemployment data reflect something different? This is one of the ongoing debates in macroeconomics.

> **unemployment rate** The percentage of the labor force that is unemployed.

Inflation and Deflation

Inflation is an increase in the overall price level. Keeping inflation low has long been a goal of government policy. Especially problematic are **hyperinflations**, or periods of very rapid increases in the overall price level.

Most Americans are unaware of what life is like under high inflation. In some countries at some times, people were accustomed to prices rising by the day, by the hour, or even by the minute. During the hyperinflation in Bolivia in 1984 and 1985, the price of one egg rose from 3,000 pesos to 10,000 pesos in 1 week. In 1985, three bottles of aspirin sold for the same price as a luxury car had sold for in 1982. At the same time, the problem of handling money became a burden. Bolivia's currency, printed in West Germany and England, was the country's third biggest import in 1984, surpassed only by wheat and mining equipment. In December 2014 the inflation rate in Venezuela reached 68 percent, and the country experienced numerous street protests against the policies of the relatively new president, Nicolas Maduro. Very high inflation can destabilize economies and governments. Hyperinflations are rare. Nonetheless, economists have devoted much effort to identifying the costs and consequences of even moderate inflation. Does anyone gain from inflation? Who loses? What costs does inflation impose on society? How severe are they? What causes inflation? What is the best way to stop it? Here too we find debate. A decrease in the overall price level is called **deflation**. In some periods in U.S. history and recently in Japan, deflation has occurred over an extended period of time. In 2015 the European Union began to take steps to fight what was seen as the early stages of deflation in that region. The goal of policy makers is to avoid prolonged periods of deflation as well as inflation to pursue the macroeconomic goal of stability.

> **inflation** An increase in the overall price level.
>
> **hyperinflation** A period of very rapid increases in the overall price level.
>
> **deflation** A decrease in the overall price level.

5.2 LEARNING OBJECTIVE

Discuss the interaction among the four components of the macroeconomy.

The Components of the Macroeconomy

Understanding how the macroeconomy works can be challenging because a great deal is going on at one time. Everything seems to affect everything else. To see the big picture, it is helpful to divide the participants in the economy into four broad groups: (1) *households*, (2) *firms*, (3) the *government*, and (4) the *rest of the world*. Households and firms make up the private sector, the government is the public sector, and the rest of the world is the foreign sector. These four groups interact in the economy in a variety of ways, many involving either receiving or paying income.

The Circular Flow Diagram

circular flow A diagram showing the flows in and out of the sectors in the economy.

A useful way of seeing the economic interactions among the four groups in the economy is a **circular flow** diagram, which shows the income received and payments made by each group. A simple circular flow diagram is pictured in Figure 5.3.

Let us walk through the circular flow step by step. Households work for firms and the government, and they receive wages for their work. Our diagram shows a flow of wages *into* households as payment for those services. Households also receive interest on corporate and government bonds and dividends from firms. Many households receive other payments from the government, such as Social Security benefits, veterans' benefits, and welfare payments. Economists call these kinds of payments from the government (for which the recipients do not supply goods, services, or labor) **transfer payments**. Together, these receipts make up the total income received by the households.

transfer payments Cash payments made by the government to people who do not supply goods, services, or labor in exchange for these payments. They include Social Security benefits, veterans' benefits, and welfare payments.

Households buy goods and services from firms and pay taxes to the government. These items make up the total amount paid out by the households. The difference between the total receipts and the total payments of the households is the amount that the households save or dissave. If households receive more than they spend, they *save* during the period. If they receive

▶ **FIGURE 5.3** **The Circular Flow of Payments**

Households receive income from firms and the government, purchase goods and services from firms, and pay taxes to the government. They also purchase foreign-made goods and services (imports). Firms receive payments from households and the government for goods and services; they pay wages, dividends, interest, and rents to households and taxes to the government. The government receives taxes from firms and households, pays firms and households for goods and services—including wages to government workers—and pays interest and transfers to households. Finally, people in other countries purchase goods and services produced domestically (exports).

Note: Although not shown in this diagram, firms and governments also purchase imports.

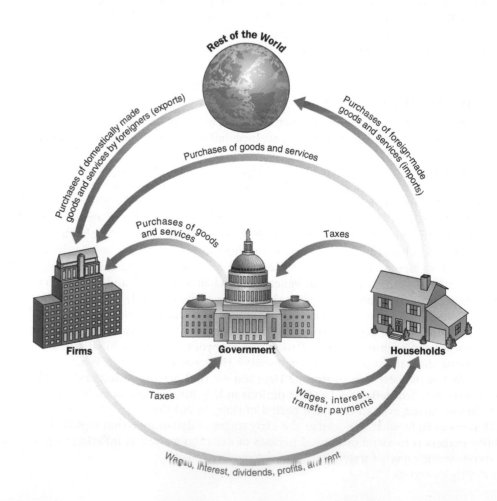

less than they spend, they *dissave*. A household can dissave by using up some of its previous savings or by borrowing. In the circular flow diagram, household spending is shown as a flow *out* of households. Saving by households is sometimes termed a "leakage" from the circular flow because it withdraws income, or current purchasing power, from the system.

Firms sell goods and services to households and the government earning revenue, which shows up in the circular flow diagram as a flow *into* the firm sector. Firms pay wages, interest, and dividends to households, and firms pay taxes to the government. These payments are shown flowing *out* of firms.

The government collects taxes from households and firms. The government also makes payments. It buys goods and services from firms, pays wages and interest to households, and makes transfer payments to households. If the government's revenue is less than its payments, the government is dissaving.

Finally, households spend some of their income on *imports*—goods and services produced in the rest of the world. Similarly, people in foreign countries purchase *exports*—goods and services produced by domestic firms and sold to other countries.

One lesson of the circular flow diagram is that everyone's expenditure is someone else's receipt. If you buy a personal computer from Dell, you make a payment to Dell, and Dell receives revenue. If Dell pays taxes to the government, it has made a payment and the government has received revenue. Everyone's expenditures go somewhere. It is impossible to sell something without there being a buyer, and it is impossible to make a payment without there being a recipient. Every transaction must have two sides.

The Three Market Arenas

Another way of looking at the ways households, firms, the government, and the rest of the world relate to one another is to consider the markets in which they interact. We divide the markets into three broad arenas: (1) the goods-and-services market, (2) the labor market, and (3) the money (financial) market.

Goods-and-Services Market Households and the government purchase goods and services from firms in the *goods-and-services market*. In this market, firms also purchase goods and services from each other. For example, Levi Strauss buys denim from other firms to make its blue jeans. In addition, firms buy capital goods from other firms. If General Motors needs new robots on its assembly lines, it may buy them from another firm instead of making them. The *Economics in Practice* in Chapter 1 describes how Apple, in constructing its iPod, buys parts from a number of other firms.

Firms *supply* to the goods-and-services market. Households, the government, and firms *demand* from this market. Finally, the rest of the world buys from and sells to the goods-and-services market. The United States imports hundreds of billions of dollars' worth of automobiles, DVDs, oil, and other goods. In the case of Apple's iPod, inputs come from other firms located in countries all over the world. At the same time, the United States exports hundreds of billions of dollars' worth of computers, airplanes, and agricultural goods.

Labor Market Interaction in the *labor market* takes place when firms and the government purchase labor from households. In this market, households *supply* labor and firms and the government *demand* labor. In the U.S. economy, firms are the largest demanders of labor, although the government is also a substantial employer. The total supply of labor in the economy depends on the sum of decisions made by households. Individuals must decide whether to enter the labor force (whether to look for a job at all) and how many hours to work.

Labor is also supplied to and demanded from the rest of the world. In recent years, the labor market has become an international market. For example, vegetable and fruit farmers in California would find it difficult to bring their product to market if it were not for the labor of migrant farm workers from Mexico. For years, Turkey has provided Germany with "guest workers" who are willing to take low-paying jobs that more prosperous German workers avoid. Call centers run by major U.S. corporations are sometimes staffed by labor in India and other developing countries.

Money Market In the *money market*—sometimes called the *financial market*—households purchase stocks and bonds from firms. Households *supply* funds to this market in the expectation of earning income in the form of dividends on stocks and interest on bonds. Households also *demand* (borrow) funds from this market to finance various purchases. Firms borrow to build new facilities in the hope of earning more in the future. The government borrows by issuing bonds to fund public programs. Much of the borrowing and lending of households, firms, the government, and the rest of the world are coordinated by financial institutions—commercial banks, savings and loan associations, insurance companies, and the like. These institutions take deposits from one group and lend them to others, often moving funds from one part of the world to another.

When a firm, a household, or the government borrows to finance a purchase, it has an obligation to pay that loan back, usually at some specified time in the future. Most loans also involve payment of interest as a fee for the use of the borrowed funds. When a loan is made, the borrower usually signs a "promise to repay," or *promissory note*, and gives it to the lender. When the federal government borrows, it issues "promises" called **Treasury bonds, notes, *or* bills** in exchange for money. Firms can borrow from banks, or in the case of corporations, they can issue **corporate bonds**.

Instead of issuing bonds to raise funds, corporations can also issue shares of stock. A **share of stock** is a financial instrument that gives the holder a share in the firm's ownership and therefore the right to share in the firm's profits. If the firm does well, the value of the stock increases and the stockholder receives a *capital gain*[1] on the initial purchase. In addition, the stock may pay **dividends**—that is, the firm may return some of its profits directly to its stockholders instead of retaining the profits to buy capital. If the firm does poorly, so does the stockholder. The capital value of the stock may fall, and dividends may not be paid. Stocks are traded in exchanges in many parts of the world, with the largest exchanges located in New York, London, and Tokyo.

Stocks and bonds are simply contracts, or agreements, between parties. I agree to loan you a certain amount, and you agree to repay me this amount plus something extra at some future date, or I agree to buy part ownership in your firm, and you agree to give me a share of the firm's future profits.

A critical variable in the money market is the *interest rate*. Although we sometimes talk as if there is only one interest rate, there is never just one interest rate at any time. Instead, the interest rate on a given loan reflects the length of the loan and the perceived risk to the lender. A business that is just getting started must pay a higher rate than General Motors pays. A 30-year mortgage has a different interest rate than a 90-day loan. Nevertheless, interest rates tend to move up and down together, and their movement reflects general conditions in the financial market.

The Role of the Government in the Macroeconomy

The government plays a major role in the macroeconomy, so a useful way of learning how the macroeconomy works is to consider how the government uses policy to affect the economy. The two main policy instruments of the government are (1) fiscal policy and (2) monetary policy. Much of the study of macroeconomics is learning how fiscal and monetary policies work.

Fiscal policy refers to the government's decisions about how much to tax and spend. The federal government collects taxes from households and firms and spends those funds on goods and services ranging from missiles to parks to social security payments to interstate highways. Taxes take the form of personal income taxes, social security taxes, and corporate profits taxes, among others. An *expansionary* fiscal policy is a policy in which taxes are cut or government spending increases. A *contractionary* fiscal policy is the reverse.

Monetary policy in the United States is conducted by the Federal Reserve, the nation's central bank. The Fed, as it is usually called, controls short-term interest rates in the economy. The Fed's decisions have important effects on the economy. In fact, the task of trying to smooth out business cycles in the United States has historically been left to the Fed (that is, to monetary

Treasury bonds, notes, *or* bills Promissory notes issued by the federal government when it borrows money.

corporate bonds Promissory notes issued by corporations when they borrow money.

shares of stock Financial instruments that give to the holder a share in the firm's ownership and therefore the right to share in the firm's profits.

dividends The portion of a firm's profits that the firm pays out each period to its shareholders.

fiscal policy Government policies concerning taxes and spending.

monetary policy The tools used by the Federal Reserve to control short term interest rates.

---

[1] A *capital gain* occurs whenever the value of an asset increases. If you bought a stock for $1,000 and it is now worth $1,500, you have earned a capital gain of $500. A capital gain is "realized" when you sell the asset. Until you sell, the capital gain is *accrued* but not *realized*.

policy). The chair of the Federal Reserve, currently Janet Yellen, is sometimes said to be the second-most powerful person in the United States after the president. As we will see later in the text, the Fed played a more active role in the 2008–2009 recession than it had in previous recessions. Fiscal policy, however, also played an active role in the 2008–2009 recession and its aftermath.

A Brief History of Macroeconomics

The severe economic contraction and high unemployment of the 1930s, the decade of the **Great Depression**, spurred a great deal of thinking about macroeconomic issues, especially unemployment. Figure 5.2 shows that this period had the largest and longest aggregate output contraction in the twentieth century in the United States. The 1920s had been prosperous years for the U.S. economy. Virtually everyone who wanted a job could get one, incomes rose substantially, and prices were stable. Beginning in late 1929, things took a sudden turn for the worse. In 1929, 1.5 million people were unemployed. By 1933, that had increased to 13 million out of a labor force of 51 million. In 1933, the United States produced about 27 percent fewer goods and services than it had in 1929. In October 1929, when stock prices collapsed on Wall Street, billions of dollars of personal wealth were lost. Unemployment remained above 14 percent of the labor force until 1940. (See the *Economics in Practice*, p. 98, "Macroeconomics in Literature," for Fitzgerald's and Steinbeck's take on the 1920s and 1930s.)

Before the Great Depression, economists applied microeconomic models, sometimes referred to as "classical" or "market clearing" models, to economy-wide problems. As we suggested, classical supply and demand analysis assumed that an excess supply of labor would drive down wages to a new equilibrium level. The decline in the wage rate would in turn raise the quantity of labor demanded by firms, erasing the unemployment. The prediction was clear: unemployment could not persist. But, during the Great Depression, unemployment levels remained high for nearly 10 years. In large measure, the failure of simple classical models to explain the prolonged existence of high unemployment provided the impetus for the development of macroeconomics. It is not surprising that what we now call macroeconomics was born in the 1930s.

One of the most important works in the history of economics, *The General Theory of Employment, Interest and Money*, by John Maynard Keynes, was published in 1936. Building on what was already understood about markets and their behavior, Keynes set out to construct a theory that would explain the confusing economic events of his time.

Much of macroeconomics has roots in Keynes's work. According to Keynes, it is not prices and wages alone that determine the level of employment, as classical models had suggested, but that the level of aggregate demand (sometimes called "total spending") for goods and services also plays a role. Moreover, Keynes believed that governments could intervene in the economy and affect the level of output and employment. When private demand is low, Keynes argued, governments could stimulate aggregate demand and, by so doing, lift the economy out of recession. (Keynes was a larger-than-life figure, one of the Bloomsbury group in England that included, among others, Virginia Woolf and Clive Bell.)

After World War II and especially in the 1950s, Keynes's views began to gain increasing influence over both professional economists and government policy makers. Governments came to believe that they could intervene in their economies to attain specific employment and output goals. They began to use their powers to tax and spend as well as their ability to affect interest rates and the money supply for the explicit purpose of controlling the economy's level of spending and therefore its ups and downs. This view of government policy became firmly established in the United States with the passage of the Employment Act of 1946. This act established the President's Council of Economic Advisers, a group of economists who advise the president on economic issues. The act also committed the federal government to intervening in the economy to prevent large declines in output and employment.

The notion that the government could and should act to stabilize the macroeconomy reached the height of its popularity in the 1960s. During these years, Walter Heller, the chairman of the Council of Economic Advisers under both President John Kennedy and President Lyndon B. Johnson, alluded to **fine-tuning** as the government's role in regulating inflation and

5.3 LEARNING OBJECTIVE

Summarize the macroeconomic history of the United States between 1929 and 1970.

Great Depression The period of severe economic contraction and high unemployment that began in 1929 and continued throughout the 1930s.

fine-tuning The phrase used by Walter Heller to refer to the government's role in regulating inflation and unemployment.

ECONOMICS IN PRACTICE

Macroeconomics in Literature

As you know, the language of economics includes a heavy dose of graphs and equations. But the underlying phenomena that economists study are the stuff of novels as well as graphs and equations. The following two passages, from *The Great Gatsby* by F. Scott Fitzgerald and *The Grapes of Wrath* by John Steinbeck, capture in graphic, although not graphical, form the economic growth and spending of the Roaring Twenties and the human side of the unemployment of the Great Depression. *The Great Gatsby*, written in 1925, is set in the 1920s, whereas *The Grapes of Wrath*, written in 1939, is set in the early 1930s. If you look at Figure 5.2 for these two periods, you will see the translation of Fitzgerald and Steinbeck into macroeconomics.

From *The Great Gatsby*

At least once a fortnight a corps of caterers came down with several hundred feet of canvas and enough colored lights to make a Christmas tree of Gatsby's enormous garden. On buffet tables, garnished with glistening hors d'œuvre, spiced baked hams crowded against salads of harlequin designs and pastry pigs and turkeys bewitched to a dark gold. In the main hall a bar with a real brass rail was set up, and stocked with gins and liquors and with cordials so long forgotten that most of his female guests were too young to know one from another.

By seven o'clock the orchestra has arrived—no thin five piece affair but a whole pit full of oboes and trombones and saxophones and viols and cornets and piccolos and low and high drums. The last swimmers have come in from the beach now and are dressing upstairs; the cars from New York are parked five deep in the drive, and already the halls and salons and verandas are gaudy with primary colors and hair shorn in strange new ways and shawls beyond the dreams of Castile.

From *The Grapes of Wrath*

The moving, questing people were migrants now. Those families who had lived on a little piece of land, who had lived and died on forty acres, had eaten or starved on the produce of forty acres, had now the whole West to rove in. And they scampered about, looking for work; and the highways were streams of people, and the ditch banks were lines of people. Behind them more were coming. The great highways streamed with moving people.

THINKING PRACTICALLY

1. As we indicate in the introduction to this chapter, macroeconomics focuses on three concerns. Which of these concerns is covered in *The Grapes of Wrath* excerpt?

2. What economics textbook is featured in *The Great Gatsby*?
   Hint: Go to fairmodel.econ.yale.edu/rayfair/pdf/2000c.pdf.

Source: From *The Grapes of Wrath* by John Steinbeck, copyright 1939, renewed © 1967 by John Steinbeck. Used by permission of Viking Penguin, a division of Penguin Group (USA) Inc. and Penguin Group (UK) Ltd.

unemployment. During the 1960s, many economists believed the government could use the tools available to manipulate unemployment and inflation levels fairly precisely.

The optimism about the government's ability to finely manage the economy was short-lived. In the 1970s and early 1980s, the U.S. economy had wide fluctuations in employment, output, and inflation. In 1974–1975 and again in 1980–1982, the United States experienced a severe recession. Although not as catastrophic as the Great Depression of the 1930s, these two recessions left millions without jobs and resulted in billions of dollars of lost output and income. In 1974–1975 and again in 1979–1981, the United States also saw high rates of inflation.

The 1970s was thus a period of stagnation and high inflation, which came to be called stagflation. **Stagflation** is defined as a situation in which there is high inflation at the same time

stagflation A situation of both high inflation and high unemployment.

there are slow or negative output growth and high unemployment. Until the 1970s, high inflation had been observed only in periods when the economy was prospering and unemployment was low. The problem of stagflation was vexing both for macroeconomic theorists and policy makers concerned with the health of the economy.

It was clear by 1975 that the macroeconomy was more difficult to control than Heller's words or textbook theory had led economists to believe. The events of the 1970s and early 1980s had an important influence on macroeconomic theory. Much of the faith in the simple Keynesian model and the "conventional wisdom" of the 1960s was lost. Although we are now 45 years past the 1970s, the discipline of macroeconomics is still in flux and there is no agreed-upon view of how the macroeconomy works. Many important issues have yet to be resolved. This makes macroeconomics hard to teach but exciting to study.

The U.S. Economy Since 1970

5.4 LEARNING OBJECTIVE

Describe the U.S. economy since 1970.

In the following chapters, it will be useful to have a picture of how the U.S. economy has performed recently. Since 1970, the U.S. economy has experienced five recessions and two periods of high inflation. The period since 1970 is illustrated in Figures 5.4, 5.5, and 5.6. These figures are based on quarterly data (that is, data for each quarter of the year). The first quarter consists of January, February, and March; the second quarter consists of April, May, and June; and so on. The Roman numerals I, II, III, and IV denote the four quarters. For example, 1972 III refers to the third quarter of 1972.

Figure 5.4 plots aggregate output for 1970 I–2014 IV. The five recessionary periods are 1974 I–1975 I, 1980 II–1982 IV, 1990 III–1991 I, 2001 I–2001 III, and 2008 I–2009 II.[2] These five periods are shaded in the figure. Figure 5.5 plots the unemployment rate for the same overall period with the same shading for the recessionary periods. Note that unemployment rose in all

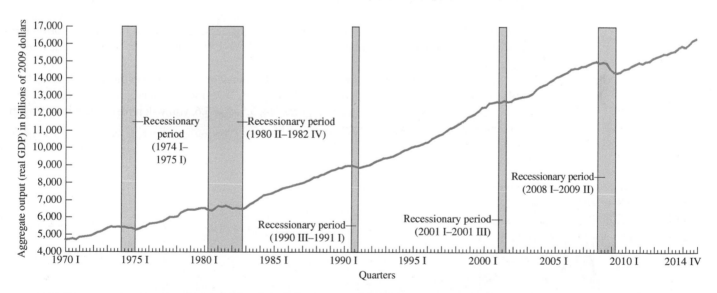

▲ **FIGURE 5.4 Aggregate Output (Real GDP), 1970 I–2014 IV** MyEconLab Real-time data
Aggregate output in the United States since 1970 has risen overall, but there have been five recessionary periods: 1974 I–1975 I, 1980 II–1982 IV, 1990 III–1991 I, 2001 I–2001 III, and 2008 I–2009 II.

---

[2] Regarding the 1980 II–1982 IV period, output rose in 1980 IV and 1981 I before falling again in 1981 II. Given this fact, one possibility would be to treat the 1980 II–1982 IV period as if it included two separate recessionary periods: 1980 II–1980 III and 1981 I–1982 IV. Because the expansion was so short-lived, however, we have chosen not to separate the period into two parts. These periods are close to but are not exactly the recessionary periods defined by the National Bureau of Economic Research (NBER). The NBER is considered the "official" decider of recessionary periods. One problem with the NBER definitions is that they are never revised, but the macro data are, sometimes by large amounts. This means that the NBER periods are not always those that would be chosen using the latest revised data. In November 2008 the NBER declared that a recession began in December 2007. In September 2010 it declared that the recession ended in June 2009.

▲ **FIGURE 5.5** **Unemployment Rate, 1970 I–2014 IV** MyEconLab Real-time data

The U.S. unemployment rate since 1970 shows wide variations. The five recessionary reference periods show increases in the unemployment rate.

five recessions. In the 1974–1975 recession, the unemployment rate reached a maximum of 8.8 percent in the second quarter of 1975. During the 1980–1982 recession, it reached a maximum of 10.7 percent in the fourth quarter of 1982. The unemployment rate continued to rise after the 1990–1991 recession and reached a peak of 7.6 percent in the third quarter of 1992. In the 2008-2009 recession it reached a peak of 9.9 percent in the fourth quarter of 2009. By 2015 the unemployment rate was 5.5 percent.

Figure 5.6 plots the inflation rate for 1970 I–2014 IV. The two high inflation periods are 1973 IV–1975 IV and 1979 I–1981 IV, which are shaded. In the first high inflation period, the inflation rate peaked at 11.1 percent in the first quarter of 1975. In the second high inflation period, inflation peaked at 10.2 percent in the first quarter of 1981. Since 1983, the inflation rate has been quite low by the standards of the 1970s. Since 1992, it has been between about 1 and 3 percent.

In the following chapters, we will explain the behavior of and the connections among variables such as output, unemployment, and inflation. When you understand the forces at work in creating the movements shown in Figures 5.4, 5.5, and 5.6, you will have come a long way in understanding how the macroeconomy works.

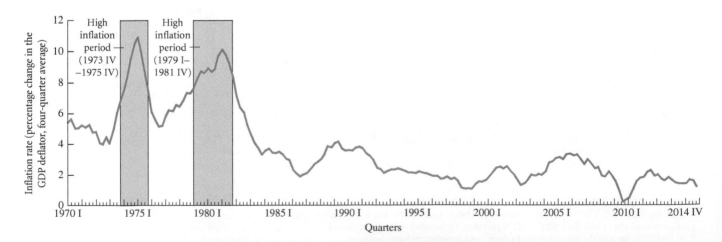

▲ **FIGURE 5.6** **Inflation Rate (Percentage Change** MyEconLab Real-time data
in the GDP Deflator, Four-Quarter Average), 1970 I–2014 IV

Since 1970, inflation has been high in two periods: 1973 IV–1975 IV and 1979 I–1981 IV. Inflation between 1983 and 1992 was moderate. Since 1992, it has been fairly low.

SUMMARY

1. *Microeconomics* examines the functioning of individual industries and the behavior of individual decision-making units. *Macroeconomics* is concerned with the sum, or aggregate, of these individual decisions—the consumption of *all* households in the economy, the amount of labor supplied and demanded by *all* individuals and firms, and the total amount of *all* goods and services produced.

5.1 MACROECONOMIC CONCERNS *p. 91*

2. The three topics of primary concern to macroeconomists are the growth rate of aggregate output, the level of unemployment, and increases in the overall price level, or *inflation*.

5.2 THE COMPONENTS OF THE MACROECONOMY *p. 94*

3. The *circular flow* diagram shows the flow of income received and payments made by the four groups in the economy—households, firms, the government, and the rest of the world. Everybody's expenditure is someone else's receipt—every transaction must have two sides.

4. Another way of looking at how households, firms, the government, and the rest of the world relate is to consider the markets in which they interact: the goods-and-services market, labor market, and money (financial) market.

5. Among the tools that the government has available for influencing the macroeconomy are *fiscal policy* (decisions on taxes and government spending) and *monetary policy* (control of short term interest rates).

5.3 A BRIEF HISTORY OF MACROECONOMICS *p. 97*

6. Macroeconomics was born out of the effort to explain the *Great Depression* of the 1930s. Since that time, the discipline has evolved, concerning itself with new issues as the problems facing the economy have changed. Through the late 1960s, it was believed that the government could fine-tune the economy to keep it running on an even keel at all times. The poor economic performance of the 1970s, however, showed that *fine-tuning* does not always work.

5.4 THE U.S. ECONOMY SINCE 1970 *p. 99*

7. Since 1970, the U.S. economy has seen five *recessions* and two periods of high inflation.

REVIEW TERMS AND CONCEPTS

aggregate behavior, *p. 90*
aggregate output, *p. 91*
business cycle, *p. 91*
circular flow, *p. 94*
contraction, recession, *or slump, p. 92*
corporate bonds, *p. 96*
deflation, *p. 93*
depression, *p. 91*
dividends, *p. 96*

expansion *or boom, p. 92*
fine-tuning, *p. 97*
fiscal policy, *p. 96*
Great Depression, *p. 97*
hyperinflation, *p. 93*
inflation, *p. 93*
macroeconomics, *p. 90*
microeconomics, *p. 90*
monetary policy, *p. 96*

recession, *p. 91*
shares of stock, *p. 96*
stagflation, *p. 98*
sticky prices, *p. 90*
transfer payments, *p. 94*
Treasury bonds, notes, *or bills, p. 96*
unemployment rate, *p. 93*

PROBLEMS

All problems are available on MyEconLab.

5.1 MACROECONOMIC CONCERNS

LEARNING OBJECTIVE: Describe the three primary concerns of macroeconomics.

1.1 Define inflation. Assume that you live in a simple economy in which only three goods are produced and traded: cashews, pecans, and almonds. Suppose that on January 1, 2015, cashews sold for $12.50 per pound, pecans were $4.00 per pound, and almonds were $5.50 per pound. At the end of the year, you discover that the cashew crop was lower than expected and that cashew prices had increased to $17.00 per pound, but pecan prices stayed at $4.00 and almond prices had actually fallen to $3.00. Can you say what happened to the overall "price level"? How might you construct a measure of the "change in the price level"? What additional information might you need to construct your measure?

1.2 Define *unemployment*. Should everyone who does not hold a job be considered "unemployed"? To help with your answer, draw a supply and demand diagram depicting the labor market. What is measured along the demand curve? What factors determine the quantity of labor demanded during a given period? What is measured along the labor supply curve? What factors determine the quantity of labor supplied by households during a given period? What is the opportunity cost of holding a job?

1.3 According to the National Bureau of Economic Research (NBER), what has been dubbed the Great Recession officially began in December, 2007 and ended in June, 2009. During this recession, national output of goods and services fell from the second quarter of 2008 until the end of the recession in the second quarter of 2009, and then slowly began to increase. When the recession was officially declared as being over, the unemployment rate continued to rise, reaching 10 percent in October, 2009 and remained close to that level until April, 2010 when it slowly started to decline. During that 10-month period, the net loss in jobs in the U.S. economy was close to 1.4 million. How is it possible that output can rise while at the same time employment falls?

1.4 Describe the economy of your state. What is the most recently reported unemployment rate? How has the number of payroll jobs changed over the last 3 months and over the last year? How does your state's performance compare to the U.S. economy's performance over the last year? What explanations have been offered in the press? How accurate are they?

1.5 Explain briefly how macroeconomics is different from microeconomics. How can macroeconomists use microeconomic theory to guide them in their work, and why might they want to do so?

1.6 In 1974, the price of a first-class postage stamp was 10 cents, a loaf of bread averaged 28 cents, gasoline was 53 cents per gallon, and the average price of a new car was $3,500. In 2014, the postage stamp cost 49 cents, a loaf of bread was $2.46, gasoline averaged $3.36 per gallon, and the average new car cost $32,531. From this statement, it follows that consumers today are worse off than consumers in 1975. Comment.

5.2 THE COMPONENTS OF THE MACROECONOMY

LEARNING OBJECTIVE: Discuss the interaction between the four components of the macroeconomy.

2.1 During 1993 when the economy was growing slowly, President Clinton recommended a series of spending cuts and tax increases designed to reduce the deficit. These were passed by Congress in the Omnibus Budget Reconciliation Act of 1993. Some who opposed the bill argued that the United States was pursuing a "contractionary fiscal policy" at precisely the wrong time. Explain their logic.

2.2 In which of the three market arenas is each of the following goods traded?
  a. The athletic skills of the Green Bay Packers' quarterback Aaron Rodgers
  b. Shares of Nike stock
  c. The hair-braiding abilities of a hair stylist in Akron, Ohio
  d. A Gibson Les Paul Custom guitar
  e. Corporate bonds issued by Verizon
  f. An Apple Watch

5.3 A BRIEF HISTORY OF MACROECONOMICS

LEARNING OBJECTIVE: Summarize the macroeconomic history of the United States between 1929 and 1970.

3.1 Many of the expansionary periods during the twentieth century occurred during wars. Why do you think this is true?

3.2 John Maynard Keynes was the first to show that government policy could be used to change aggregate output and prevent recession by stabilizing the economy. Describe the economy of the world at the time Keynes was writing. Describe the economy of the United States today. What measures are being proposed by potential presidential candidates for the election of 2016 to stimulate growth in the economy? Do any of these proposed policies follow the policies proposed by John Maynard Keynes? If so, which policies and from which candidates?

3.3 Assume that the demand for flight attendants increases significantly as a result of an increase in demand for air travel. Explain what will happen to unemployment using both classical and Keynesian reasoning.

3.4 Explain why the length and severity of the Great Depression necessitated a fundamental rethinking of the operations of the macroeconomy.

5.4 THE U.S. ECONOMY SINCE 1970

LEARNING OBJECTIVE: Describe the U.S. Economy Since 1970.

4.1 [**Related to the** *Economics in Practice* **on p. 98**] The *Economics in Practice* describes prosperity and recession as they are depicted in literature. In mid-2009, there was a debate about whether the U.S. economy had entered an economic expansion. Look at the data on real GDP growth and unemployment and describe the pattern since 2007. You can find raw data on employment and unemployment at www.bls.gov, and you can find raw data on real GDP growth at www.bea.gov. Summarize what happened in mid-2009. Did the United States enter an economic expansion? Explain.

Measuring National Output and National Income

6

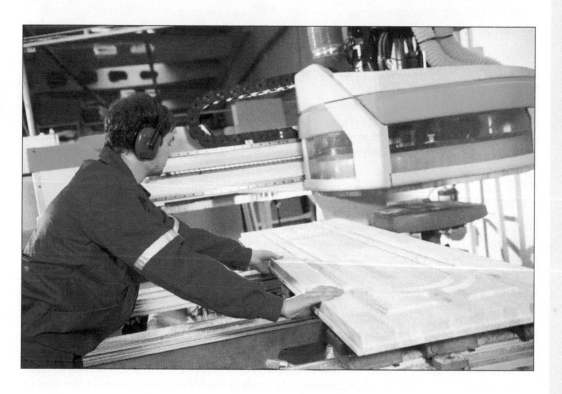

We saw in the last chapter that macroeconomics is concerned with aggregate output, unemployment, and inflation. In this chapter, we discuss the measurement of aggregate output and inflation. In the next chapter, we discuss the measurement of unemployment. Accurate measures of these variables are critical for understanding the economy. Without good measures, economists would have a hard time analyzing how the economy works and policy makers would have little to guide them on which policies are best for the economy.

Much of the macroeconomic data we use come from the **national income and product accounts**, which are compiled by the Bureau of Economic Analysis (BEA) of the U.S. Department of Commerce. It is hard to overestimate the importance of these accounts. They are, in fact, one of the great inventions of the twentieth century. (See the *Economics in Practice*, p. 112.) They not only convey data about the performance of the economy but also provide a conceptual framework that macroeconomists use to think about how the pieces of the economy fit together. When economists think about the macroeconomy, the categories and vocabulary they use come from the national income and product accounts.

The national income and product accounts can be compared with the mechanical or wiring diagrams for an automobile engine. The diagrams do not explain how an engine works, but they identify the key parts of an engine and show how they are connected. Trying to understand the macroeconomy without understanding national income accounting is like trying to fix an engine without a mechanical diagram and with no names for the engine parts.

103

national income and product accounts Data collected and published by the government describing the various components of national income and output in the economy.

There are literally thousands of variables in the national income and product accounts. In this chapter, we discuss only the most important. This chapter is meant to convey the way the national income and product accounts represent or organize the economy and the *sizes* of the various pieces of the economy.

6.1 LEARNING OBJECTIVE

Describe GDP fundamentals and differentiate between GDP and GNP.

Gross Domestic Product

The key concept in the national income and product accounts is **gross domestic product (GDP)**.

gross domestic product (GDP) The total market value of all final goods and services produced within a given period by factors of production located within a country.

> GDP is the total market value of a country's output. It is the market value of all final goods and services produced within a given period of time by factors of production located within a country.

U.S. GDP for 2014—the value of all output produced by factors of production in the United States in 2014—was $17,418.9 billion.

GDP is a critical concept. Just as an individual firm needs to evaluate the success or failure of its operations each year, so the economy as a whole needs to assess itself. GDP, as a measure of the total production of an economy, provides us with a country's economic report card. Because GDP is so important, we need to take time to explain exactly what its definition means.

Final Goods and Services

final goods and services Goods and services produced for final use.

intermediate goods Goods that are produced by one firm for use in further processing or for resale by another firm.

First, note that the definition refers to **final goods and services**. Many goods produced in the economy are not classified as *final* goods, but instead as intermediate goods. **Intermediate goods** are produced by one firm for use in further processing or for resale by another firm. For example, tires sold to automobile manufacturers are intermediate goods. The chips that go in Apple's iPhone are also intermediate goods. The value of intermediate goods is not counted in GDP.

Why are intermediate goods not counted in GDP? Suppose that in producing a car, General Motors (GM) pays $200 to Goodyear for tires. GM uses these tires (among other components) to assemble a car, which it sells for $24,000. The value of the car (including its tires) is $24,000, not $24,000 + $200. The final price of the car already reflects the value of all its components. To count in GDP both the value of the tires sold to the automobile manufacturers and the value of the automobiles sold to the consumers would result in double counting. It would also lead us to conclude that a decision by GM to produce its own tires rather than buy them from Goodyear leads to a reduction in the value of goods produced by the economy.

value added The difference between the value of goods as they leave a stage of production and the cost of the goods as they entered that stage.

Double counting can also be avoided by counting only the value added to a product by each firm in its production process. The **value added** during some stage of production is the difference between the value of goods as they leave that stage of production and the cost of the goods as they entered that stage. Value added is illustrated in Table 6.1. The four stages of the production of a gallon of gasoline are: (1) oil drilling, (2) refining, (3) shipping, and (4) retail sale. In the first stage, value added is the value of the crude oil. In the second stage, the refiner purchases the oil from the driller, refines it into gasoline, and sells it to the shipper. The refiner pays the driller $3.00 per gallon and charges the shipper $3.30. The value added by the refiner is thus

TABLE 6.1	Value Added in the Production of a Gallon of Gasoline (Hypothetical Numbers)	
Stage of Production	Value of Sales	Value Added
(1) Oil drilling	$3.00	$3.00
(2) Refining	3.30	0.30
(3) Shipping	3.60	0.30
(4) Retail sale	4.00	0.40
Total value added		$4.00

$0.30 per gallon. The shipper then sells the gasoline to retailers for $3.60. The value added in the third stage of production is $0.30. Finally, the retailer sells the gasoline to consumers for $4.00. The value added at the fourth stage is $0.40, and the total value added in the production process is $4.00, the same as the value of sales at the retail level. Adding the total values of sales at each stage of production ($3.00 + $3.30 + $3.60 + $4.00 = $13.90) would significantly overestimate the value of the gallon of gasoline.

> In calculating GDP, we can sum up the value added at each stage of production or we can take the value of final sales. We do not use the value of total sales in an economy to measure how much output has been produced.

Exclusion of Used Goods and Paper Transactions

GDP is concerned only with new, or current, production. Old output is not counted in current GDP because it was already counted when it was produced. It would be double counting to count sales of used goods in current GDP. If someone sells a used car to you, the transaction is not counted in GDP because no new production has taken place. Similarly, a house is counted in GDP only at the time it is built, not each time it is resold. In short:

> GDP does not count transactions in which money or goods changes hands and in which no new goods and services are produced.

Sales of stocks and bonds are not counted in GDP. These exchanges are transfers of ownership of assets, either electronically or through paper exchanges, and do not correspond to current production. What if you sell the stock or bond for more than you originally paid for it? Profits from the stock or bond market have nothing to do with current production, so they are not counted in GDP. However, if you pay a fee to a broker for selling a stock of yours to someone else, this fee is counted in GDP because the broker is performing a service for you. This service is part of current production. Be careful to distinguish between exchanges of stocks and bonds for money (or for other stocks and bonds), which do not involve current production, and fees for performing such exchanges, which do.

Exclusion of Output Produced Abroad by Domestically Owned Factors of Production

> GDP is the value of output produced by factors of production *located within a country*.

The three basic factors of production are land, labor, and capital. The output produced by U.S. citizens abroad—for example, U.S. citizens working for a foreign company—is *not* counted in U.S. GDP because the output is not produced within the United States. Likewise, profits earned abroad by U.S. companies are not counted in U.S. GDP. However, the output produced by foreigners working in the United States is counted in U.S. GDP because the output is produced within the United States. Also, profits earned in the United States by foreign-owned companies are counted in U.S. GDP.

It is sometimes useful to have a measure of the output produced by factors of production owned by a country's citizens regardless of where the output is produced. This measure is called **gross national product (GNP)**. For most countries, including the United States, the difference between GDP and GNP is small. In 2014, GNP for the United States was $17,630.6 billion, which is close to the $17,418.9 billion value for U.S. GDP.

The distinction between GDP and GNP can be tricky. Consider the Honda plant in Marysville, Ohio. The plant is owned by the Honda Corporation, a Japanese firm, but most

gross national product (GNP) The total market value of all final goods and services produced within a given period by factors of production owned by a country's citizens, regardless of where the output is produced.

of the workers employed at the plant are U.S. workers. Although all the output of the plant is included in U.S. GDP, only part of it is included in U.S. GNP. The wages paid to U.S. workers are part of U.S. GNP, whereas the profits from the plant are not. The profits from the plant are counted in Japanese GNP because this is output produced by Japanese-owned factors of production (Japanese capital in this case). The profits, however, are not counted in Japanese GDP because they were not earned in Japan.

Calculating GDP

6.2 LEARNING OBJECTIVE

Explain two methods for calculating GDP.

expenditure approach A method of computing GDP that measures the total amount spent on all final goods and services during a given period.

income approach A method of computing GDP that measures the income—wages, rents, interest, and profits—received by all factors of production in producing final goods and services.

GDP can be computed two ways. One way is to add up the total amount spent on all final goods and services during a given period. This is the **expenditure approach** to calculating GDP. The other way is to add up the income—wages, rents, interest, and profits—received by all factors of production in producing final goods and services. This is the **income approach** to calculating GDP. These two methods lead to the same value for GDP for the reason we discussed in the previous chapter: *Every payment (expenditure) by a buyer is at the same time a receipt (income) for the seller.* We can measure either income received or expenditures made, and we will end up with the same total output.

Suppose the economy is made up of just one firm and the firm's total output this year sells for $1 million. Because the total amount spent on output this year is $1 million, this year's GDP is $1 million. (Remember: The expenditure approach calculates GDP on the basis of the total amount spent on final goods and services in the economy.) However, *every one* of the million dollars of GDP either is paid to someone or remains with the owners of the firm as profit. Using the income approach, we add up the wages paid to employees of the firm, the interest paid to those who lent money to the firm, and the rents paid to those who leased land, buildings, or equipment to the firm. What is left over is profit, which is, of course, income to the owners of the firm. If we add up the incomes of all the factors of production, including profits to the owners, we get a GDP of $1 million.

The Expenditure Approach

Recall from the previous chapter the four main groups in the economy: households, firms, the government, and the rest of the world. There are also four main categories of expenditure:

- Personal consumption expenditures (*C*): household spending on consumer goods
- Gross private domestic investment (*I*): spending by firms and households on new capital, that is, plant, equipment, inventory, and new residential structures
- Government consumption and gross investment (*G*)
- Net exports (*EX* − *IM*): net spending by the rest of the world, or exports (*EX*) minus imports (*IM*)

The expenditure approach calculates GDP by adding together these four components of spending. It is shown here in equation form:

$$GDP = C + I + G + (EX - IM)$$

personal consumption expenditures (C) Expenditures by consumers on goods and services.

durable goods Goods that last a relatively long time, such as cars and household appliances.

nondurable goods Goods that are used up fairly quickly, such as food and clothing.

services The things we buy that do not involve the production of physical things, such as legal and medical services and education.

U.S. GDP was $17,418.9 billion in 2014. The four components of the expenditure approach are shown in Table 6.2, along with their various categories.

Personal Consumption Expenditures (C) The largest part of GDP consists of **personal consumption expenditures (C)**. Table 6.2 shows that in 2014, the amount of personal consumption expenditures accounted for 68.5 percent of GDP. These are expenditures by consumers on goods and services.

There are three main categories of consumer expenditures: durable goods, nondurable goods, and services. **Durable goods**, such as automobiles, furniture, and household appliances, last a relatively long time. **Nondurable goods**, such as food, clothing, gasoline, and cigarettes, are used up fairly quickly. Payments for **services**—those things we buy that do not involve the

ECONOMICS IN PRACTICE

Where Does eBay Get Counted?

eBay runs an online marketplace with more than 220 million registered users who buy and sell 2.4 billion items a year, ranging from children's toys to oil paintings. In December 2007, one eBay user auctioned off a 1933 Chicago World's Fair pennant. The winning bid was slightly more than $20.

eBay is traded on the New York Stock Exchange, employs hundreds of people, and has a market value of about $40 billion. With regard to eBay, what do you think gets counted as part of current GDP?

That 1933 pennant, for example, does not get counted. The production of that pennant was counted back in 1933. The many cartons of K'nex bricks sent from one home to another don't count either. Their value was counted when the bricks were first produced. What about a newly minted Scrabble game? One of the interesting features of eBay is that it has changed from being a market in which individuals market their hand-me-downs to a place that small and even large businesses use as a sales site. The value of the new Scrabble game would be counted as part of this year's GDP if it were produced this year.

So do any of eBay's services count as part of GDP? eBay's business is to provide a marketplace for exchange. In doing so, it uses labor and capital and creates value. In return for creating this value, eBay charges fees to the sellers that use its site. The value of these fees does enter into GDP. So although the old knickknacks that people sell on eBay do

not contribute to current GDP, the cost of finding an interested buyer for those old goods does indeed get counted.

THINKING PRACTICALLY

1. John has a 2009 Honda Civic. In 2013, he sells it to Mary for $10,000. Is that $10,000 counted in the GDP for 2013?

2. If John is an automobile dealer, does that change your answer to Question 1 at all?

production of physical items—include expenditures for doctors, lawyers, and educational institutions. As Table 6.2 shows, in 2014, durable goods expenditures accounted for 7.5 percent of GDP, nondurables for 15.3 percent, and services for 45.7 percent. Almost half of GDP is now service consumption.

TABLE 6.2   Components of U.S. GDP, 2014: The Expenditure Approach

	Billions of Dollars ($)		Percentage of GDP (%)	
Personal consumption expenditures (C)	11,930.3		68.5	
Durable goods		1,302.5		7.5
Nondurable goods		2,666.2		15.3
Services		7,961.7		45.7
Gross private domestic investment (I)	2,851.6		16.4	
Nonresidential		2,210.5		12.7
Residential		559.1		3.2
Change in business inventories		82.0		0.5
Government consumption and gross investment (G)	3,175.2		18.2	
Federal		1,219.2		7.0
State and local		1,956.1		11.2
Net exports (EX − IM)	−538.2		−3.1	
Exports (EX)		2,337.0		13.4
Imports (IM)		2,875.2		16.5
Gross domestic product	17,418.9		100.0	

Note: Numbers may not add exactly because of rounding.
Source: U.S. Bureau of Economic Analysis, March 27, 2015.

Gross Private Domestic Investment (I)   *Investment*, as we use the term in economics, refers to the purchase of new capital—housing, plants, equipment, and inventory. The economic use of the term is in contrast to its everyday use, where *investment* often refers to purchases of stocks, bonds, or mutual funds.

Total investment in capital by the private sector is called **gross private domestic investment (I)**. Expenditures by firms for machines, tools, plants, and so on make up **nonresidential investment.**[1] Because these are goods that firms buy for their own final use, they are part of "final sales" and counted in GDP. Expenditures for new houses and apartment buildings constitute **residential investment**. The third component of gross private domestic investment, the **change in business inventories**, is the amount by which firms' inventories change during a period. Business inventories can be looked at as the goods that firms produce now but intend to sell later. In 2014, gross private domestic investment accounted for 16.4 percent of GDP. Of that, 12.7 percent was nonresidential investment, 3.2 percent was residential investment, and 0.5 percent was change in business inventories.

Change in Business Inventories   Why is the change in business inventories considered a component of investment—the purchase of new capital? To run a business most firms hold inventories, in part because they cannot predict exactly how much will be sold each day and want to avoid losing sales by running out of a product. Inventories—goods produced for later sale—are counted as capital because they produce value in the future. An increase in inventories is an increase in capital.

Regarding GDP, remember that it is not the market value of total final *sales* during the period, but rather the market value of total final *production*. The relationship between total production and total sales is as follows:

$$GDP = \text{Final sales} + \text{Change in business inventories}$$

Total production (GDP) equals final sales of domestic goods plus the change in business inventories. In 2014, production in the United States was larger than sales by $82.0 billion. The stock of inventories at the end of 2014 was $82.0 billion *larger* than it was at the end of 2013—the change in business inventories was $82.0 billion.

Gross Investment versus Net Investment   During the process of production, capital (especially machinery and equipment) produced in previous periods gradually wears out. GDP includes newly produced capital goods but does not take account of capital goods "consumed" in the production process. As a result, GDP overstates the real production of an economy because it does not account for the part of that production that serves just to replace worn out capital.

The amount by which an asset's value falls each period is called its **depreciation.**[2] A personal computer purchased by a business today may be expected to have a useful life of 4 years before becoming worn out or obsolete. Over that period, the computer steadily depreciates.

What is the relationship between gross investment (I) and depreciation? **Gross investment** is the total value of all newly produced capital goods (plant, equipment, housing, and inventory) produced in a given period. It takes no account of the fact that some capital wears out and must be replaced. **Net investment** is equal to gross investment minus depreciation. Net investment is a measure of how much the stock of capital *changes* during a period. Positive net investment means that the amount of new capital produced exceeds the amount that wears out, and negative net investment means that the amount of new capital produced is less than the amount that wears out. Therefore, if net investment is positive, the capital stock has increased, and if net

gross private domestic investment (I)   Total investment in capital—that is, the purchase of new housing, plants, equipment, and inventory by the private (or nongovernment) sector.

nonresidential investment   Expenditures by firms for machines, tools, plants, and so on.

residential investment   Expenditures by households and firms on new houses and apartment buildings.

change in business inventories   The amount by which firms' inventories change during a period. Inventories are the goods that firms produce now but intend to sell later.

depreciation   The amount by which an asset's value falls in a given period.

gross investment   The total value of all newly produced capital goods (plant, equipment, housing, and inventory) produced in a given period.

net investment   Gross investment minus depreciation.

---

[1] The distinction between what is considered investment and what is considered consumption is sometimes fairly arbitrary. A firm's purchase of a car or a truck is counted as investment, but a household's purchase of a car or a truck is counted as consumption of durable goods. In general, expenditures by firms for items that last longer than a year are counted as investment expenditures. Expenditures for items that last less than a year are seen as purchases of intermediate goods.
[2] This is the formal definition of economic depreciation. Because depreciation is difficult to measure precisely, accounting rules allow firms to use shortcut methods to approximate the amount of depreciation that they incur each period. To complicate matters even more, the U.S. tax laws allow firms to deduct depreciation for tax purposes under a different set of rules.

investment is negative, the capital stock has decreased. Put another way, the capital stock at the end of a period is equal to the capital stock that existed at the beginning of the period plus net investment:

$$\text{capital}_{\text{end of period}} = \text{capital}_{\text{beginning of period}} + \text{net investment}$$

Government Consumption and Gross Investment (G) **Government consumption and gross investment (G)** include expenditures by federal, state, and local governments for final goods (bombs, pencils, school buildings) and services (military salaries, congressional salaries, school teachers' salaries). Some of these expenditures are counted as government consumption, and some are counted as government gross investment. Government transfer payments (Social Security benefits, veterans' disability stipends, and so on) are not included in G because these transfers are not purchases of anything currently produced. The payments are not made in exchange for any goods or services. Because interest payments on the government debt are also counted as transfers, they are excluded from GDP on the grounds that they are not payments for current goods or services.

As Table 6.2 shows, government consumption and gross investment accounted for $3,175.2 billion, or 18.2 percent of U.S. GDP, in 2014. Federal government consumption and gross investment accounted for 7.0 percent of GDP, and state and local government consumption and gross investment accounted for 11.2 percent.

Net Exports (EX − IM) The value of **net exports (EX − IM)** is the difference between *exports* (sales to foreigners of U.S.-produced goods and services) and *imports* (U.S. purchases of goods and services from abroad). This figure can be positive or negative. In 2014, the United States exported less than it imported, so the level of net exports was negative (−$538.2 billion). Before 1976, the United States was generally a net exporter—exports exceeded imports, so the net export figure was positive.

The reason for including net exports in the definition of GDP is simple. Consumption, investment, and government spending (*C*, *I*, and *G*, respectively) include expenditures on goods produced at home and abroad. Therefore, *C* + *I* + *G* overstates domestic production because it contains expenditures on foreign-produced goods—that is, imports (*IM*), which have to be subtracted from GDP to obtain the correct figure. At the same time, *C* + *I* + *G* understates domestic production because some of what a nation produces is sold abroad and therefore is not included in *C*, *I*, or *G*—exports (*EX*) have to be added in. If a U.S. firm produces computers and sells them in Germany, the computers are part of U.S. production and should be counted as part of U.S. GDP.

The Income Approach

We now turn to calculating GDP using the income approach, which looks at GDP in terms of who receives it as income rather than as who purchases it.

We begin with the concept of **national income**, which is defined in Table 6.3. National income is the sum of eight income items. **Compensation of employees**, the largest of the eight items by far, includes wages and salaries paid to households by firms and by the government, as well as various supplements to wages and salaries such as contributions that employers make to social insurance and private pension funds. **Proprietors' income** is the income of unincorporated businesses. **Rental income**, a minor item, is the income received by property owners in the form of rent. **Corporate profits**, the second-largest item of the eight, is the income of corporations. **Net interest** is the interest paid by business. (Interest paid by households and the government is not counted in GDP because it is not assumed to flow from the production of goods and services.)

The sixth item, **indirect taxes minus subsidies**, includes taxes such as sales taxes, customs duties, and license fees less subsidies that the government pays for which it receives no goods or services in return. (Subsidies are like negative taxes.) The value of indirect taxes minus subsidies is thus net revenue received by the government. **Net business transfer payments** are net transfer

government consumption and gross investment (G) Expenditures by federal, state, and local governments for final goods and services.

net exports (EX − IM) The difference between exports (sales to foreigners of U.S.-produced goods and services) and imports (U.S. purchases of goods and services from abroad). The figure can be positive or negative.

national income The total income earned by the factors of production owned by a country's citizens.

compensation of employees Includes wages, salaries, and various supplements—employer contributions to social insurance and pension funds, for example—paid to households by firms and by the government.

proprietors' income The income of unincorporated businesses.

rental income The income received by property owners in the form of rent.

corporate profits The income of corporations.

net interest The interest paid by business.

indirect taxes minus subsidies Taxes such as sales taxes, customs duties, and license fees less subsidies that the government pays for which it receives no goods or services in return. Is net revenue received by the government.

net business transfer payments Net transfer payments by businesses to others.

TABLE 6.3   National Income, 2014

	Billions of Dollars ($)	Percentage of National Income (%)
National income	15,070.4	100.0
Compensation of employees	9,221.6	61.2
Proprietors' income	1,380.2	9.2
Rental income	640.2	4.2
Corporate profits	2,089.8	13.9
Net interest	486.3	3.2
Indirect taxes minus subsidies	1,145.8	7.6
Net business transfer payments	140.6	0.9
Surplus of government enterprises	−34.2	−0.2

Source: U.S. Bureau of Economic Analysis, March 27, 2015.

surplus of government enterprises Income of government enterprises.

payments by businesses to others and are thus income of others. The final item is the **surplus of government enterprises**, which is the income of government enterprises. Table 6.3 shows that this item was negative in 2014: government enterprises on net ran at a loss.

National income is the total income of the country, but it is not quite GDP. Table 6.4 shows what is involved in going from national income to GDP. Table 6.4 first shows that in moving from GDP to GNP, we need to add receipts of factor income from the rest of the world and subtract payments of factor income to the rest of the world. National income is income of the country's citizens, not the income of the residents of the country. So we first need to move from GDP to GNP. This, as discussed previously, is a minor adjustment.

net national product (NNP) Gross national product minus depreciation; a nation's total product minus what is required to maintain the value of its capital stock.

We then need to subtract depreciation from GNP, which is a large adjustment. GNP less depreciation is called **net national product (NNP)**. Why is depreciation subtracted? To see why, go back to the example previously in this chapter in which the economy is made up of just one firm and total output (GDP) for the year is $1 million. Assume that after the firm pays wages, interest, and rent, it has $100,000 left. Assume also that its capital stock depreciated by $40,000 during the year. National income includes corporate profits (see Table 6.3), and in calculating corporate profits, the $40,000 depreciation is subtracted from the $100,000, leaving profits of $60,000. So national income does not include the $40,000. When we calculate GDP using the expenditure approach, however, depreciation is not subtracted. We simply add consumption, investment, government spending, and net exports. In our simple example, this is just $1 million. We thus must subtract depreciation from GDP (actually GNP when there is a rest-of-the-world sector) to get national income.

statistical discrepancy Data measurement error.

Table 6.4 shows that net national product and national income are the same except for a **statistical discrepancy**, a data measurement error. If the government were completely accurate in its data collection, the statistical discrepancy would be zero. The data collection, however, is not perfect, and the statistical discrepancy is the measurement error in each period. Table 6.4 shows that in 2014, this error was $176.0 billion, which is small compared to national income of $15,070.4 billion.

TABLE 6.4   GDP, GNP, NNP, and National Income, 2014

	Dollars ($, Billions)
GDP	17,418.9
Plus: Receipts of factor income from the rest of the world	+827.7
Less: Payments of factor income to the rest of the world	−616.0
Equals: **GNP**	17,630.6
Less: Depreciation	−2,736.2
Equals: **Net national product (NNP)**	14,894.4
Less: Statistical discrepancy	−176.0
Equals: National income	15,070.4

Source: U.S. Bureau of Economic Analysis, March 27, 2015.

TABLE 6.5	National Income, Personal Income, Disposable Personal Income, and Personal Saving, 2014	
		Dollar (Billions, $)
National income		15,070.4
Less: Amount of national income not going to households		−341.8
Equals: **Personal income**		14,728.6
Less: Personal income taxes		−1,742.9
Equals: **Disposable personal income**		12,985.8
Less: Personal consumption expenditures		−11,930.3
Personal interest payments		−256.8
Transfer payments made by households		−170.3
Equals: **Personal saving**		628.3
Personal saving as a percentage of disposable personal income:		4.8%

Source: U.S. Bureau of Economic Analysis, March 27, 2015.

We have so far seen from Table 6.3 the various income items that make up total national income, and we have seen from Table 6.4 how GDP and national income are related. A useful way to think about national income is to consider how much of it goes to households. The total income of households is called **personal income**, and it turns out that almost all of national income is personal income. Table 6.5 shows that of the $15,070.4 billion in national income in 2014, $14,728.6 billion was personal income. The second line in Table 6.5, the amount of national income not going to households, includes the profits of corporations not paid to households in the form of dividends, called the *retained earnings* of corporations. This is income that stays inside corporations for some period rather than going to households, and so it is part of national income but not personal income.

Personal income is the income received by households before they pay personal income taxes. The amount of income that households have to spend or save is called **disposable personal income, *or* after-tax income**. It is equal to personal income minus personal income taxes, as shown in Table 6.5.

Because disposable personal income is the amount of income that households can spend or save, it is an important income concept. Table 6.5 shows there are three categories of spending: (1) personal consumption expenditures, (2) personal interest payments, and (3) transfer payments made by households. The amount of disposable personal income left after total personal spending is **personal saving.** If your monthly disposable income is $500 and you spend $450, you have $50 left at the end of the month. Your personal saving is $50 for the month. Your personal saving level can be negative: If you earn $500 and spend $600 during the month, you have *dissaved* $100. To spend $100 more than you earn, you will have to borrow the $100 from someone, take the $100 from your savings account, or sell an asset you own.

The **personal saving rate** is the percentage of disposable personal income saved, an important indicator of household behavior. A low saving rate means households are spending a large fraction of their income. As Table 6.5 shows, the U.S. personal saving rate in 2014 was 4.8 percent. Saving rates tend to rise during recessionary periods, when consumers become anxious about their future, and fall during boom times, as pent-up spending demand gets released. In 2005 the saving rate got down to 2.5 percent.

Nominal versus Real GDP

We have thus far looked at GDP measured in **current dollars**, or the current prices we pay for goods and services. When we measure something in current dollars, we refer to it as a *nominal* value. **Nominal GDP** is GDP measured in current dollars—all components of GDP valued at their current prices.

In most applications in macroeconomics, however, nominal GDP is not what we are after. It is not a good measure of aggregate output over time. Why? Assume that there is only one

personal income The total income of households.

disposable personal income *or* after-tax income Personal income minus personal income taxes. The amount that households have to spend or save.

personal saving The amount of disposable income that is left after total personal spending in a given period.

personal saving rate The percentage of disposable personal income that is saved. If the personal saving rate is low, households are spending a large amount relative to their incomes; if it is high, households are spending cautiously.

current dollars The current prices that we pay for goods and services.

Discuss the difference between real GDP and nominal GDP.

nominal GDP Gross domestic product measured in current dollars.

ECONOMICS IN PRACTICE

GDP: One of the Great Inventions of the 20th Century

As the 20th century drew to a close, the U.S. Department of Commerce embarked on a review of its achievements. At the conclusion of this review, the Department named the development of the national income and product accounts as "its achievement of the century."

J. Steven Landefeld *Director, Bureau of Economic Analysis*

While the GDP and the rest of the national income accounts may seem to be arcane concepts, they are truly among the great inventions of the twentieth century.

Paul A. Samuelson and William D. Nordhaus

GDP! The right concept of economy-wide output, accurately measured. The U.S. and the world rely on it to tell where we are in the business cycle and to estimate long-run growth. It is the centerpiece of an elaborate and indispensable system of social accounting, the national income and product accounts. This is surely the single most innovative achievement of the Commerce Department in the 20th century. I was fortunate to become an economist in the 1930's when Kuznets, Nathan, Gilbert, and Jaszi were creating this most important set of economic time series. In economic theory, macroeconomics was just beginning at the same time. Complementary, these two innovations deserve much credit for the improved performance of the economy in the second half of the century.

James Tobin

FROM THE *SURVEY OF CURRENT BUSINESS*

Prior to the development of the NIPAs [national income and product accounts], policy makers had to guide the economy using limited and fragmentary information about the state of the economy. The Great Depression underlined the problems of incomplete data and led to the development of the national accounts:

One reads with dismay of Presidents Hoover and then Roosevelt designing policies to combat the Great Depression of the 1930s on the basis of such sketchy data as stock price indices, freight car loadings, and incomplete indices of industrial production. The fact was that comprehensive measures of national income and output did not exist at the time. The Depression, and with it the growing role of government in the economy, emphasized the need for such measures and led to the development of a comprehensive set of national income accounts.

Richard T. Froyen

In response to this need in the 1930s, the Department of Commerce commissioned Nobel laureate Simon Kuznets of the National Bureau of Economic Research to develop a set of national economic accounts.... Professor Kuznets coordinated the work of researchers at the National Bureau of Economic Research in New York and his staff at Commerce. The original set of accounts was presented in a report to Congress in 1937 and in a research report, *National Income, 1929–35....*

The national accounts have become the mainstay of modern macroeconomic analysis, allowing policy makers, economists, and the business community to analyze the impact of different tax and spending plans, the impact of oil and other price shocks, and the impact of monetary policy on the economy as a whole and on specific components of final demand, incomes, industries, and regions.

THINKING PRACTICALLY

1. The articles emphasize the importance of being able to measure an economy's output to improve government policy. Looking at recent news, can you identify one economic policy debate or action that referenced GDP?

Source: U.S. Department of Commerce, Bureau of Economics, "GDP: One of the Great Inventions of the 20th Century," Survey of Current Business, January 2000, pp. 6–9.

good—say, pizza, which is the same quality year after year. In each year 1 and 2, one hundred units (slices) of pizza were produced. Production thus remained the same for year 1 and year 2. Suppose the price of pizza increased from $1.00 per slice in year 1 to $1.10 per slice in year 2. Nominal GDP in year 1 is $100 (100 units $\times$ $1.00 per unit), and nominal GDP in year 2 is $110 (100 units $\times$ $1.10 per unit). Nominal GDP has increased by $10 even though no more slices of pizza were produced and the quality of the pizza did not improve. If we use nominal GDP to measure growth, we can be misled into thinking production has grown when all that has really happened is a rise in the price level (inflation).

If there were only one good in the economy—for example, pizza—it would be easy to measure production and compare one year's value to another's. We would add up all the pizza slices produced each year. In the example, production is 100 in both years. If the number of slices had increased to 105 in year 2, we would say production increased by 5 slices between year 1 and year 2, which is a 5 percent increase. Alas, however, there is more than one good in the economy which makes adjusting for price changes more complex.

The following is a discussion of how the BEA adjusts nominal GDP for price changes. As you read the discussion, you will see that this adjustment is not easy. Even in an economy of just apples and oranges, it would not be obvious how to add up apples and oranges to get an overall measure of output. The BEA's task is to add up thousands of goods, each of whose price is changing over time.

In the following discussion, we will use the concept of a **weight**, either price weights or quantity weights. What is a weight? It is easiest to define the term by an example. Suppose in your economics course there is a final exam and two other tests. If the final exam counts for one-half of the grade and the other two tests for one-fourth each, the "weights" are one-half, one-fourth, and one-fourth. If instead the final exam counts for 80 percent of the grade and the other two tests for 10 percent each, the weights are 0.8, 0.1, and 0.1. The more important an item is in a group, the larger its weight.

weight   The importance attached to an item within a group of items.

Calculating Real GDP

Nominal GDP adjusted for price changes is called *real GDP*. All the main issues involved in computing real GDP can be discussed using a simple three-good economy and 2 years. Table 6.6 presents all the data that we will need. The table presents price and quantity data for 2 years and three goods. The goods are labeled A, B, and C, and the years are labeled 1 and 2. P denotes price, and Q denotes quantity. Keep in mind that everything in the following discussion, including the discussion of the GDP deflation, is based on the numbers in Table 6.6. Nothing has been brought in from the outside. The table is the entire economy.

The first thing to note from Table 6.6 is that *nominal output*—in current dollars—in year 1 for good A is the number of units of good A produced in year 1 (6) times the price of good A in year 1 ($0.50), which is $3.00. Similarly, nominal output in year 1 is 7 $\times$ $0.30 = $2.10 for good B and 10 $\times$ $0.70 = $7.00 for good C. The sum of these three amounts, $12.10 in column 5, is nominal GDP in year 1 in this simple economy. Nominal GDP in year 2—calculated by

TABLE 6.6 A Three-Good Economy								
	(1)	(2)	(3)	(4)	(5)	(6)	(7)	(8)
	Production		Price per Unit		GDP in Year 1 in Year 1 Prices	GDP in Year 2 in Year 1 Prices	GDP in Year 1 in Year 2 Prices	GDP in Year 2 in Year 2 Prices
	Year 1 Q_1	Year 2 Q_2	Year 1 P_1	Year 2 P_2	$P_1 \times Q_1$	$P_1 \times Q_2$	$P_2 \times Q_1$	$P_2 \times Q_2$
Good A	6	11	$0.50	$0.40	$ 3.00	$ 5.50	$ 2.40	$ 4.40
Good B	7	4	0.30	1.00	2.10	1.20	7.00	4.00
Good C	10	12	0.70	0.90	7.00	8.40	9.00	10.80
Total					$12.10 Nominal GDP in year 1	$15.10	$18.40	$19.20 Nominal GDP in year 2

using the year 2 quantities and the year 2 prices—is $19.20 (column 8). Nominal GDP has risen from $12.10 in year 1 to $19.20 in year 2, an increase of 58.7 percent.[3]

You can see that the price of each good changed between year 1 and year 2—the price of good A fell (from $0.50 to $0.40) and the prices of goods B and C rose (B from $0.30 to $1.00; C from $0.70 to $0.90). Some of the change in nominal GDP between years 1 and 2 is as a result of price changes and not production changes. How much can we attribute to price changes and how much to production changes? Here things get tricky. The procedure that the BEA used before 1996 was to pick a **base year** and to use the prices in that base year as weights to calculate real GDP. This is a **fixed-weight procedure** because the weights used, which are the prices, are the same for all years—namely, the prices that prevailed in the base year.

Let us use the fixed-weight procedure and year 1 as the base year, which means using year 1 prices as the weights. Then in Table 6.6, real GDP in year 1 is $12.10 (column 5) and real GDP in year 2 is $15.10 (column 6). Note that both columns use year 1 prices and that nominal and real GDP are the same in year 1 because year 1 is the base year. Real GDP has increased from $12.10 to $15.10, an increase of 24.8 percent.

Let us now use the fixed-weight procedure and year 2 as the base year, which means using year 2 prices as the weights. In Table 6.6, real GDP in year 1 is $18.40 (column 7) and real GDP in year 2 is $19.20 (column 8). Note that both columns use year 2 prices and that nominal and real GDP are the same in year 2, because year 2 is the base year. Real GDP has increased from $18.40 to $19.20, an increase of 4.3 percent.

This example shows that growth rates can be sensitive to the choice of the base year—24.8 percent using year 1 prices as weights and 4.3 percent using year 2 prices as weights. For many policy decisions, the growth rates play a role so that large differences coming from a seemingly arbitrary choice of base year is troubling. The old BEA procedure simply picked one year as the base year and did all the calculations using the prices in that year as weights. The new BEA procedure makes two important changes. The first (using the current example) is to take the average of the two years' price changes, in other words, to "split the difference" between 24.8 percent and 4.3 percent. What does "splitting the difference" mean? One way is to take the average of the two numbers, which is 14.55 percent. What the BEA does is to take the *geometric* average, which for the current example is 14.09 percent.[4] These two averages (14.55 percent and 14.09 percent) are quite close, and the use of either would give similar results. The point here is not that the geometric average is used, but that the first change is to split the difference using some average. When prices are going up, this procedure will lower the estimates of real growth rates relative to the use of year 1 as a base year, and conversely when prices are falling. Note that this new procedure requires two "base" years because 24.8 percent was computed using year 1 prices as weights and 4.3 percent was computed using year 2 prices as weights.

The second BEA change is to use years 1 and 2 as the base years when computing the percentage change between years 1 and 2, then use years 2 and 3 as the base years when computing the percentage change between years 2 and 3, and so on. The two base years change as the calculations move through time. The series of percentage changes computed this way is taken to be the series of growth rates of real GDP. So in this way, nominal GDP is adjusted for price changes. To make sure you understand this, review the calculations in Table 6.6, which provides all the data you need to see what is going on.

Calculating the GDP Deflator

We now switch gears from real GDP, a quantity measure, to the GDP deflator, a price measure. One of economic policy makers' goals is to keep changes in the overall price level small. For this reason, policy makers not only need good measures of how real output is changing but also good measures of how the overall price level is changing. The GDP deflator is one measure of the overall price level. We can use the data in Table 6.6 to show how the BEA computes the GDP deflator.

In Table 6.6, the price of good A fell from $0.50 in year 1 to $0.40 in year 2, the price of good B rose from $0.30 to $1.00, and the price of good C rose from $0.70 to $0.90. If we are interested

---

base year The year chosen for the weights in a fixed-weight procedure.

fixed-weight procedure A procedure that uses weights from a given base year.

---

[3] The percentage change is calculated as $[(19.20 - 12.10)/12.10] \times 100 = .587 \times 100 = 58.7$ percent.
[4] The geometric average is computed as the square root of 124.8×104.3, which is 114.09.

only in how individual prices change, this is all the information we need. However, if we are interested in how the overall price *level* changes, we need to weight the individual prices in some way. Is it getting more expensive to live in this economy or less expensive? In this example that clearly depends on how people spend their incomes. So, the obvious weights to use are the quantities produced, but which quantities—those of year 1 or year 2? The same issues arise here for the quantity weights as for the price weights in computing real GDP.

Let us first use the fixed-weight procedure and year 1 as the base year, which means using year 1 quantities as the weights. Then in Table 6.6, the "bundle" price in year 1 is $12.10 (column 5) and the bundle price in year 2 is $18.40 (column 7). Both columns use year 1 quantities. The bundle price has increased from $12.10 to $18.40, an increase of 52.1 percent.

Next, use the fixed-weight procedure and year 2 as the base year, which means using year 2 quantities as the weights. Then the bundle price in year 1 is $15.10 (column 6), and the bundle price in year 2 is $19.20 (column 8). Both columns use year 2 quantities. The bundle price has increased from $15.10 to $19.20, an increase of 27.2 percent.

This example shows that overall price increases can be sensitive to the choice of the base year: 52.1 percent using year 1 quantities as weights and 27.2 percent using year 2 quantities as weights. Again, the old BEA procedure simply picked one year as the base year and did all the calculations using the quantities in the base year as weights. First, the new procedure splits the difference between 52.1 percent and 27.2 percent by taking the geometric average, which is 39.1 percent. Second, it uses years 1 and 2 as the base years when computing the percentage change between years 1 and 2, years 2 and 3 as the base years when computing the percentage change between years 2 and 3, and so on. The series of percentage changes computed this way is taken to be the series of percentage changes in the GDP deflator, that is, a series of inflation rates.

The Problems of Fixed Weights

To see why the BEA switched to the new procedure, let us consider a number of problems using fixed-price weights to compute real GDP. First, 1987 price weights, the last price weights the BEA used before it changed procedures, are not likely to be accurate for, say, 2014. Many structural changes took place in the U.S. economy between 1987 and 2014, and it seems unlikely that 1987 prices are good weights to use for this much later period.

Another problem is that the use of fixed-price weights does not account for the responses in the economy to supply shifts. Perhaps bad weather leads to a lower production of oranges in year 2. In a simple supply-and-demand diagram for oranges, this corresponds to a shift of the supply curve to the left, which leads to an increase in the price of oranges and a decrease in the quantity demanded. As consumers move up the demand curve, they are substituting away from oranges. If technical advances in year 2 result in cheaper ways of producing computers, the result is a shift of the computer supply curve to the right, which leads to a decrease in the price of computers and an increase in the quantity demanded. Consumers are substituting toward computers. (You should be able to draw supply-and-demand diagrams for both cases.) Table 6.6 shows this tendency. The quantity of good *A* rose between years 1 and 2 and the price decreased (the computer case), whereas the quantity of good *B* fell and the price increased (the orange case). The computer supply curve has been shifting to the right over time, primarily because of technical advances. The result has been large decreases in the price of computers and large increases in the quantity demanded.

To see why these responses pose a problem for the use of fixed-price weights, consider the data in Table 6.6. Because the price of good *A* was higher in year 1, the increase in production of good *A* is weighted more if we use year 1 as the base year than if we used year 2 as the base year. Also, because the price of good *B* was lower in year 1, the decrease in production of good *B* is weighted less if we use year 1 as the base year. These effects make the overall change in real GDP larger if we use year 1 price weights than if we use year 2 price weights. Using year 1 price weights ignores the kinds of substitution responses discussed in the previous paragraph and leads to what many believe are too-large estimates of real GDP changes. In the past, the BEA tended to move the base year forward about every 5 years, resulting in the past estimates of real GDP growth being revised downward. It is undesirable to have past growth estimates change simply because of the change to a new base year. The new BEA procedure avoids many of these fixed-weight problems.

Similar problems arise when using fixed-quantity weights to compute price indexes. For example, the fixed-weight procedure ignores the substitution away from goods whose prices are increasing and toward goods whose prices are decreasing or increasing less rapidly. The procedure tends to overestimate the increase in the overall price level. As discussed in the next chapter, there are still a number of price indexes that are computed using fixed weights. The GDP deflator differs because it does not use fixed weights. It is also a price index for all the goods and services produced in the economy. Other price indexes cover fewer domestically produced goods and services but also include some imported (foreign-produced) goods and services.

It should finally be stressed that there is no "right" way of computing real GDP. The economy consists of many goods, each with its own price, and there is no exact way of adding together the production of the different goods. We can say that the BEA's new procedure for computing real GDP avoids the problems associated with the use of fixed weights, and it seems to be an improvement over the old procedure. We will see in the next chapter, however, that the consumer price index (CPI)—a widely used price index—is still computed using fixed weights.

6.4 LEARNING OBJECTIVE

Discuss the limitations of using GDP to measure well-being.

Limitations of the GDP Concept

We generally think of increases in GDP as good. Increasing GDP (or preventing its decrease) is usually considered one of the chief goals of the government's macroeconomic policy. But there are some limitations to the use of GDP as a measure of welfare.

GDP and Social Welfare

If crime levels went down, society would be better off, but a decrease in crime is not an increase in output and is not reflected in GDP. Neither is an increase in leisure time. Yet to the extent that households want extra leisure time (instead of having it forced on them by a lack of jobs in the economy), an increase in leisure is also an increase in social welfare. Furthermore, some increases in social welfare are associated with a *decrease* in GDP. An increase in leisure during a time of full employment, for example, leads to a decrease in GDP because less time is spent on producing output.

Most nonmarket and domestic activities, such as housework and child care, are not counted in GDP even though they amount to real production. However, if I decide to send my children to day care or hire someone to clean my house or drive my car for me, GDP increases. The salaries of day care staff, cleaning people, and chauffeurs are counted in GDP, but the time I spend doing the same things is not counted. A mere change of institutional arrangements, even though no more output is being produced, can show up as a change in GDP.

Furthermore, GDP seldom reflects losses or social ills. GDP accounting rules do not adjust for production that pollutes the environment. The more production there is, the larger the GDP, regardless of how much pollution results in the process. The *Economics in Practice* box on the next page 117 discusses how counting for pollution affects GDP measures. GDP also has nothing to say about the distribution of output among individuals in a society. It does not distinguish, for example, between the case in which most output goes to a few people and the case in which output is evenly divided among all people.

The Informal Economy

informal economy The part of the economy in which transactions take place and in which income is generated that is unreported and therefore not counted in GDP.

Many transactions are missed in the calculation of GDP even though, in principle, they should be counted. Most illegal transactions are missed unless they are "laundered" into legitimate business. Income that is earned but not reported as income for tax purposes is usually missed, although some adjustments are made in the GDP calculations to take misreported income into account. The part of the economy that should be counted in GDP but is not is sometimes called the **informal economy**.

ECONOMICS IN PRACTICE

Green Accounting

The national income and product accounts include all market activities. So purchased child care is included, but child care provided by parents is not. Recently many economists and policy makers have become concerned about the exclusion of one particularly large and important non-market activity from the national income accounts: the environment.

Many industries when they produce goods also produce air pollution as a by-product. The market goods these firms produce go into the national income and product accounts, but the environmental costs of air pollution are not subtracted. How much difference does not counting of this by-product make? Recent work by Nick Muller, Robert Mendelsohn, and Bill Nordhaus estimates that for some industries in the United States, like stone mining and coal-powered electricity generation, including properly valued air pollution in the national income and product accounts as an offset to the value of the marketed goods produced by these industries would make the contribution of these industries to our nation's GDP negative![1]

THINKING PRACTICALLY

1. Why do you think we have not counted pollution in GDP measures in the past?

[1] Nicholas Muller, Robert Mendelsohn and William Nordhaus, "Environmental Accounting for Pollution in the United States Economy," *American Economics Review* August 2011, 1649–1675.

Tax evasion is usually thought to be one of the major incentives for people in developed countries to participate in the informal economy. Studies estimate the size of the U.S. informal economy at about 10 percent, whereas Europe is closer to 20 percent. In the developing world, for a range of reasons, the informal economy is much larger, particularly for women workers. In Latin America and Africa, it is estimated that the informal economy comprises well more than a third of GDP in many nations.[5]

Why should we care about the informal economy? To the extent that GDP reflects only a part of economic activity instead of a complete measure of what the economy produces, it is misleading. Unemployment rates, for example, may be lower than officially measured if people work in the informal economy without reporting this fact to the government. Also, if the size of the informal economy varies among countries—as it does—we can be misled when we compare GDP among countries. For example, Italy's GDP would be much higher if we considered its informal sector as part of the economy, and Switzerland's GDP would change very little.

Gross National Income per Capita

Making comparisons across countries is difficult because such comparisons need to be made in a single currency, generally U.S. dollars. Converting GNP numbers for Japan into dollars requires converting from yen into dollars. Because exchange rates can change quite dramatically in short periods of time, such conversions are tricky. Recently, the World Bank adopted a new measuring system for international comparisons. The concept of **gross national income (GNI)** is GNP converted into dollars using an average of currency exchange rates over several years adjusted

gross national income (GNI)   GNP converted into dollars using an average of currency exchange rates over several years adjusted for rates of inflation.

---

[5] Jacques Chermes, "The Informal Economy," *Journal of Applied Economic Research*, 2012.

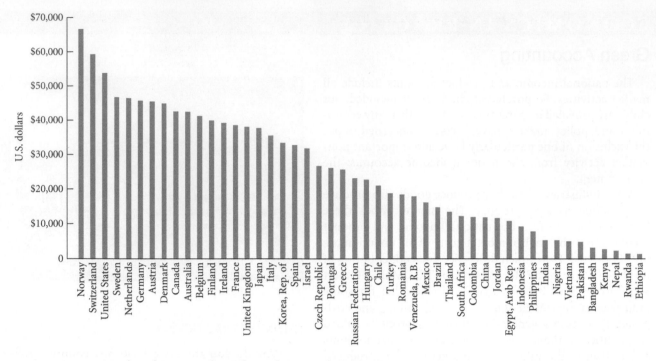

▲ **FIGURE 6.1** **National Income for Selected Countries, 2013**

Source: Data from GNI per capita, PPP (current international $), The World Bank Group, Retrieved from http://data.worldbank.org/indicator/NY.GNP.PCAP .PP.CD/countries/1W?display=default

for rates of inflation. Figure 6.1 lists the gross national income per capita (GNI divided by population) for various countries in 2013. Of the countries in the figure, Norway had the highest per capita GNI, followed by Switzerland, the United States, and the Netherlands. Ethiopia was estimated to have per capita GNI of only $1,380 in 2013. This compares to $66,520 for Norway.

Looking Ahead

This chapter has introduced many key variables in which macroeconomists are interested, including GDP and its components. There is much more to be learned about the data that macroeconomists use. In the next chapter, we will discuss the data on employment, unemployment, and the labor force. In Chapter 10, we will discuss the data on money and interest rates. Finally, in Chapter 19, we will discuss in more detail the data on the relationship between the United States and the rest of the world.

SUMMARY

1. One source of data on the key variables in the macroeconomy is the *national income and product accounts*. These accounts provide a conceptual framework that macroeconomists use to think about how the pieces of the economy fit together.

6.1 GROSS DOMESTIC PRODUCT *p. 104*

2. *Gross domestic product (GDP)* is the key concept in national income accounting. GDP is the total market value of all final goods and services produced within a given period by factors of production located within a country. GDP

excludes *intermediate goods*. To include goods when they are purchased as inputs and when they are sold as final products would be double counting and would result in an overstatement of the value of production.

3. GDP excludes all transactions in which money or goods change hands but in which no new goods and services are produced. GDP includes the income of foreigners working in the United States and the profits that foreign companies earn in the United States. GDP excludes the income of U.S. citizens working abroad and profits earned by U.S. companies in foreign countries.

4. *Gross national product* (GNP) is the market value of all final goods and services produced during a given period by factors of production owned by a country's citizens.

6.2 CALCULATING GDP *p. 106*

5. The *expenditure approach* to GDP adds up the amount spent on all final goods and services during a given period. The four main categories of expenditures are *personal consumption expenditures* (C), *gross private domestic investment* (I), *government consumption and gross investment* (G), and *net exports* (EX − IM). The sum of these categories equals GDP.

6. The three main components of *personal consumption expenditures* (C) are *durable goods*, *nondurable goods*, and *services*.

7. *Gross private domestic investment* (I) is the total investment made by the private sector in a given period. There are three kinds of investment: *nonresidential investment, residential investment,* and *changes in business inventories*. Gross investment does not take *depreciation*—the decrease in the value of assets—into account. *Net investment* is equal to gross investment minus depreciation.

8. *Government consumption and gross investment* (G) include expenditures by state, federal, and local governments for final goods and services. The value of *net exports* (EX − IM) equals the differences between exports (sales to foreigners of U.S.-produced goods and services) and imports (U.S. purchases of goods and services from abroad).

9. Because every payment (expenditure) by a buyer is a receipt (income) for the seller, GDP can be computed in terms of who receives it as income—the *income approach* to calculating gross domestic product.

10. GNP minus depreciation is *net national product* (NNP). *National income* is the total amount earned by the factors of production in the economy. It is equal to NNP except for a statistical discrepancy. *Personal income* is the total income of households. *Disposable personal income* is what households have to spend or save after paying their taxes. The *personal saving rate* is the percentage of disposable personal income saved instead of spent.

6.3 NOMINAL VERSUS REAL GDP *p. 111*

11. GDP measured in current dollars (the current prices that one pays for goods) is *nominal GDP*. If we use nominal GDP to measure growth, we can be misled into thinking that production has grown when all that has happened is a rise in the price level, or inflation. A better measure of production is *real GDP*, which is nominal GDP adjusted for price changes.

12. The GDP deflator is a measure of the overall price level.

6.4 LIMITATIONS OF THE GDP CONCEPT *p. 116*

13. We generally think of increases in GDP as good, but some problems arise when we try to use GDP as a measure of happiness or well-being. The peculiarities of GDP accounting mean that institutional changes can change the value of GDP even if real production has not changed. GDP ignores most social ills, such as pollution. Furthermore, GDP tells us nothing about what kinds of goods are being produced or how income is distributed across the population. GDP also ignores many transactions of the *informal economy*.

14. The concept of *gross national income* (GNI) is GNP converted into dollars using an average of currency exchange rates over several years adjusted for rates of inflation.

REVIEW TERMS AND CONCEPTS

base year, *p. 114*

change in business inventories, *p. 108*

compensation of employees, *p. 109*

corporate profits, *p. 109*

current dollars, *p. 111*

depreciation, *p. 108*

disposable personal income, *or* after-tax income, *p. 111*

durable goods, *p. 106*

expenditure approach, *p. 106*

final goods and services, *p. 104*

fixed-weight procedure, *p. 114*

government consumption and gross investment (G), *p. 109*

gross domestic product (GDP), *p. 104*

gross investment, *p. 108*

gross national income (GNI), *p. 117*

gross national product (GNP), *p. 105*

gross private domestic investment (I), *p. 108*

income approach, *p. 106*

indirect taxes minus subsidies, *p. 109*

informal economy, *p. 116*

intermediate goods, *p. 104*

national income, *p. 109*

national income and product accounts, *p. 103*

net business transfer payments, *p. 109*

net exports (EX − IM), *p. 109*

net interest, *p. 109*

net investment, *p. 108*

net national product (NNP), *p. 110*

nominal GDP, *p. 111*

nondurable goods, *p. 106*

nonresidential investment, *p. 108*

personal consumption expenditures (C), *p. 106*

personal income, *p. 111*

personal saving, *p. 111*

personal saving rate, *p. 111*

proprietors' income, *p. 109*

rental income, *p. 109*

residential investment, *p. 108*

services, *p. 106*

statistical discrepancy, *p. 110*

surplus of government enterprises, *p. 110*

value added, *p. 104*

weight, *p. 113*

Equations:
Expenditure approach to GDP:
$GDP = C + I + G + (EX - IM)$, *p. 106*

$GDP = $ Final sales + Change in business inventories, *p. 108*

$capital_{\text{end of period}} = capital_{\text{beginning of period}}$ + net investment, *p. 109*

PROBLEMS

All problems are available on MyEconLab.

6.1 GROSS DOMESTIC PRODUCT

LEARNING OBJECTIVE: Describe GDP fundamentals and differentiate between GDP and GNP.

1.1 Explain what double counting is and discuss why GDP is not equal to total sales.

1.2 [**Related to the *Economics in Practice* on p. 107**] Which of the following transactions would not be counted in GDP? Explain your answers.
   a. You buy a new pair of Lucchese Cowboy boots at the Lucchese factory in El Paso, Texas.
   b. You buy a vintage pair of Lucchese cowboy boots from a used clothing store in Jackson Hole, Wyoming.
   c. You take a day of vacation to work in your yard.
   d. A cat burglar sells $50,000 of stolen jewelry to an unscrupulous pawn shop.
   e. Amazon.com, Inc. issues new shares of stock to finance a new distribution warehouse.
   f. Amazon.com, Inc. builds a new distribution warehouse.
   g. Oralia buys 200 ostrich feathers that she uses to embellish the custom hats that she makes and sells.
   h. A private company builds a toll road to connect Nashville and Memphis.
   i. The government pays out unemployment benefits.
   j. AT&T purchases all the assets of DirecTV and takes over the company.
   k. You win $100,000 playing a slot machine at a casino in Reno, Nevada.

1.3 Tobias, a classic car enthusiast in Phoenix, occasionally offers for sale one of his classic automobiles at the Barrett-Jackson collector car auction in neighboring Scottsdale. In January 2016, Tobias put a 1929 Cadillac 341B in the auction, and it sold to a buyer in Riyadh, Saudi Arabia for $167,500. What part, if any, of this transaction will be included as a part of U.S. GDP in 2016?

1.4 Anissa makes custom bird houses in her garage and she buys all her supplies from a local lumber yard. Last year she purchased $3,500 worth of supplies and produced 250 bird houses. She sold all 250 bird houses to a local craft store for $25 each. The craft store sold all the bird houses to customers for $55 each. For the total bird house production, calculate the value added of Anissa and of the craft store.

6.2 CALCULATING GDP

LEARNING OBJECTIVE: Explain two methods for calculating GDP.

2.1 [**Related to the *Economics in Practice* on p. 112**] In a simple economy, suppose that all income is either compensation of employees or profits. Suppose also that there are no indirect taxes. Calculate gross domestic product from the following set of numbers. Show that the expenditure approach and the income approach add up to the same figure.

Consumption	$9,500
Investment	3,000
Depreciation	1,750
Profits	2,400
Exports	850
Compensation of employees	11,500
Government purchases	3,200
Direct taxes	1,200
Saving	1,600
Imports	900

2.2 How do we know that calculating GDP by the expenditure approach yields the same answer as calculating GDP by the income approach?

2.3 During 2002, real GDP in Japan rose about 1.3 percent. During the same period, retail sales in Japan fell 1.8 percent in real terms. What are some possible explanations for retail sales to consumers falling when GDP rises? (*Hint:* Think of the composition of GDP using the expenditure approach.)

2.4 If you buy a new car, the entire purchase is counted as consumption in the year in which you make the transaction. Explain briefly why this is in one sense an "error" in national income accounting. (*Hint:* How is the purchase of a car different from the purchase of a pizza?) How might you correct this error? How is housing treated in the National Income and Product Accounts? Specifically how does owner-occupied housing enter into the accounts? (Hint: Do some Web searching on "imputed rent on owner-occupied housing.")

2.5 Explain why imports are subtracted in the expenditure approach to calculating GDP.

2.6 Beginning in 2005, the housing market, which had been booming for years, turned. Housing construction dropped sharply in 2006. Go to www.bea.gov. Look at the GDP release and at past releases from 2005 to 2015. In real dollars, how much private residential fixed investment (houses, apartments, condominiums, and cooperatives) took place in each quarter from 2005 to 2015? What portion of GDP did housing construction represent? After 2006, residential fixed investment was declining sharply, yet GDP was growing until the end of 2007. What categories of aggregate spending kept things moving between 2006 and the end of 2007?

6.3 NOMINAL VERSUS REAL GDP

LEARNING OBJECTIVE: Discuss the difference between real GDP and nominal GDP.

3.1 As the following table indicates, GNP and real GNP were almost the same in 1972, but there was a $300 billion difference by mid-1975. Explain why. Describe what the numbers here suggest about conditions in the economy at the time. How do the conditions compare with conditions today?

Date (Year and Quarter)	GNP (Billions, $)	Real GNP (Billions, $)	Real GNP (% Change)	GNP Deflator (% Change)
72:2	1,172	1,179	7.62	2.93
72:3	1,196	1,193	5.11	3.24
72:4	1,233	1,214	7.41	5.30
73:1	1,284	1,247	10.93	5.71
73:2	1,307	1,248	.49	7.20
73:3	1,338	1,256	2.44	6.92
73:4	1,377	1,266	3.31	8.58
74:1	1,388	1,253	−4.00	7.50
74:2	1,424	1,255	.45	10.32
74:3	1,452	1,247	−2.47	10.78
74:4	1,473	1,230	−5.51	12.03
75:1	1,480	1,204	−8.27	10.86
75:2	1,517	1,219	5.00	5.07

3.2 What are some of the problems in using fixed weights to compute real GDP and the GDP deflator? How does the BEA's approach attempt to solve these problems?

3.3 The following table gives some figures from forecasts of real GDP (in 2005 dollars) and population done in mid-2014. According to the forecasts, approximately how much real growth will there be between 2018 and 2019? What is the per-capita real GDP projected to be in 2018 and in 2019? Compute the forecast rate of change in real GDP and per-capita real GDP between 2018 and 2019.

Real GDP 2018 (billions)	$18,121
Real GDP 2019 (billions)	$18,375
Population 2018 (millions)	329.3
Population 2019 (millions)	331.9

3.4 Look at a recent edition of *The Economist*. Go to the section on economic indicators. Go down the list of countries and make a list of the ones with the fastest and slowest GDP growth. Look also at the forecast rates of GDP growth. Go back to the table of contents at the beginning of the journal to see if there are articles about any of these countries. Write a paragraph or two describing the events or the economic conditions in one of the countries. Explain why they are growing or not growing rapidly.

3.5 By mid-2009, many economists believed that the recession had ended and the U.S. economy had entered an economic expansion. Define *recession* and *expansion*. Go to www.bea.gov and look at the growth of GDP during 2009. In addition, go to www.bls.gov and look at payroll employment and the unemployment rate. Had the recession ended and had the U.S. economy entered an expansion? What do you see in the data? Can you tell by reading newspapers or watching cable news whether the country had entered an expansion? Explain.

3.6 Gorgonzola is a small island nation with a simple economy that produces only six goods: sugar cane, yo-yos, rum, peanuts, harmonicas, and peanut butter. Assume that one-quarter of all the sugar cane is used to produce rum and one-half of all the peanuts are used to produce peanut butter.
   a. Use the production and price information in the table to calculate nominal GDP for 2015.
   b. Use the production and price information in the table to calculate real GDP for 2013, 2014, and 2015 using 2013 as the base year. What is the growth rate of real GDP from 2013 to 2014 and from 2014 to 2015?
   c. Use the production and price information in the table to calculate real GDP for 2013, 2014, and 2015 using 2014 as the base year. What is the growth rate of real GDP from 2013 to 2014 and from 2014 to 2015?

Product	2013 Quantity	2013 Price	2014 Quantity	2014 Price	2015 Quantity	2015 Price
Sugar cane	240	$0.80	240	$1.00	300	$1.15
Yo-yos	600	2.50	700	3.00	750	4.00
Rum	150	10.00	160	12.00	180	15.00
Peanuts	500	2.00	450	2.50	450	2.50
Harmonicas	75	25.00	75	30.00	85	30.00
Peanut butter	100	4.50	85	4.50	85	5.00

3.7 The following table contains nominal and real GDP data, in billions of dollars, from the U.S. Bureau of Economic Analysis for 2013 and 2014. The data is listed per quarter, and the real GDP data was calculated using 2009 as the base year. Fill in the columns for the GDP deflator and for the percent increase in price level.

Quarter	Nominal GDP	Real GDP	GDP Deflator	Percent Increase in Price Level
2013_q1	16,502.4	15,538.4		
2013_q2	16,619.2	15,606.6		
2013_q3	16,872.3	15,779.9		
2013_q4	17,078.3	15,916.2		
2014_q1	17,044.0	15,831.7		
2014_q2	17,328.2	16,010.4		
2014_q3	17,599.8	16,205.6		
2014_q4	17,703.7	16,294.7		

3.8 Evaluate the following statement: Even if the prices of a large number of goods and services in the economy increase dramatically, the real GDP for the economy can still fall, but if the prices of a large number of goods and services in the economy decrease dramatically, the real GDP for the economy cannot rise.

6.4 LIMITATIONS OF THE GDP CONCEPT

LEARNING OBJECTIVE: Discuss the limitations of using GDP to measure well-being.

4.1 GDP calculations do not directly include the economic costs of environmental damage—for example, global warming and acid rain. Do you think these costs should be included in GDP? Why or why not? How could GDP be amended to include environmental damage costs?

4.2 [**Related to the *Economics in Practice* on p. 117**] A World Bank brief entitled *Natural Capital Accounting* contains the following statement: "(A) major limitation of GDP is the limited representation of natural capital. The full contribution of natural capital like forests, wetlands, and agricultural land does not show up." Identify some additional examples of natural capital and explain how limited representation of these types of natural capital could affect the measurement of gross domestic product.

Source: *Natural Capital Accounting*, World Bank brief, May 20, 2015.

Unemployment, Inflation, and Long-Run Growth

7

Each month the U.S. Bureau of Labor Statistics (BLS) announces the value of the unemployment rate for the previous month. For example, on April 3, 2015, it announced that the unemployment rate for March 2015 was 5.5 percent. The unemployment rate is a key measure of how the economy is doing. This announcement is widely watched, and if the announced unemployment rate is different from what the financial markets expect, there can be large movements in those markets. It is thus important to know how the BLS computes the unemployment rate. The first part of this chapter describes how the unemployment rate is computed and discusses its various components.

Inflation is another key macroeconomic variable. The previous chapter discussed how the GDP deflator, the price deflator for the entire economy, is computed. The percentage change in the GDP deflator is a measure of inflation. There are, however, other measures of inflation, each pertaining to some part of the economy. The most widely followed price index is the consumer price index (CPI), and its measurement is discussed in this chapter. The CPI is also announced monthly by the BLS, and this announcement is widely followed by the financial markets as well. For example, on March 24, 2015, the BLS announced that the percentage change in the CPI for February 2015 was 0.2 percent for the month. After discussing the measurement of the CPI, this chapter discusses various costs of inflation as well as the concerns policy makers might have when there is deflation (a fall in the price level).

The last topic considered in this chapter is long-run growth. Although much of macroeconomics is concerned with explaining business cycles, long-run growth is also a major concern. The average yearly growth rate of U.S. real GDP depicted in Figure 5.2 in Chapter 5 is 3.3 percent. Although there were many ups and downs during the 115 years depicted in Figure 5.2, on average, the economy was growing at an annual 3.3 percent rate. In the last part of this chapter, we discuss the sources of this growth.

Keep in mind that this chapter is still descriptive. We begin our analysis of how the economy works in the next chapter.

Explain how unemployment is measured.

Unemployment

We begin our discussion of unemployment with its measurement.

Measuring Unemployment

The unemployment data released each month by the BLS are based on a survey of 60,000 households. Each interviewed household answers questions concerning the work activity of household members 16 years of age or older during the calendar week that contains the 12th of the month. (The survey is conducted in the week that contains the 19th of the month.)

If a household member 16 years of age or older worked 1 hour or more as a paid employee, either for someone else or in his or her own business or farm, the person is classified as **employed**. A household member is also considered employed if he or she worked 15 hours or more without pay in a family enterprise. Finally, a household member is counted as employed if the person held a job from which he or she was temporarily absent because of illness, bad weather, vacation, labor-management disputes, or personal reasons, regardless of whether he or she was paid.

Those who are not employed fall into one of two categories: (1) unemployed or (2) not in the labor force. To be considered **unemployed**, a person must be 16 years old or older, available for work, and have made specific efforts to find work during the previous 4 weeks. A person not looking for work because he or she does not want a job or has given up looking is classified as **not in the labor force**. People not in the labor force include full-time students, retirees, individuals in institutions, those staying home to take care of children, and discouraged job seekers.

The total **labor force** in the economy is the number of people employed plus the number of unemployed:

$$\text{labor force} = \text{employed} + \text{unemployed}$$

The total population 16 years of age or older is equal to the number of people in the labor force plus the number not in the labor force:

$$\text{population} = \text{labor force} + \text{not in labor force}$$

With these numbers, several ratios can be calculated. The **unemployment rate** is the ratio of the number of people unemployed to the total number of people in the labor force:

$$\text{unemployment rate} = \frac{\text{unemployed}}{\text{employed} + \text{unemployed}}$$

In March 2015, the labor force contained 156.906 million people, 148.331 million of whom were employed and 8.575 million of whom were unemployed and looking for work. The unemployment rate was 5.5 percent:

$$\frac{8.575}{148.331 + 8.575} = 5.5\%$$

The ratio of the labor force to the population 16 years old or over is called the **labor force participation rate**:

$$\text{labor force participation rate} = \frac{\text{labor force}}{\text{population}}$$

employed Any person 16 years old or older (1) who works for pay, either for someone else or in his or her own business for 1 or more hours per week, (2) who works without pay for 15 or more hours per week in a family enterprise, or (3) who has a job but has been temporarily absent with or without pay.

unemployed A person 16 years old or older who is not working, is available for work, and has made specific efforts to find work during the previous 4 weeks.

not in the labor force A person who is not looking for work because he or she does not want a job or has given up looking.

labor force The number of people employed plus the number of unemployed.

unemployment rate The ratio of the number of people unemployed to the total number of people in the labor force.

labor force participation rate The ratio of the labor force to the total population 16 years old or older.

ECONOMICS IN PRACTICE

Time Use for the Unemployed in a Recession

During the recession of 2008—2009, aggregate market work hours in the United States decreased substantially. A recent paper uses interesting new survey data to explore what the unemployed population did with these hours lost to the formal market.[1]

What would an economist expect to see in time use change for someone newly unemployed in a recession? First, we might expect people to spend some time looking for new jobs. Aguiar and his co-authors find that between 2 percent and 6 percent of the lost market hours go to job search. But clearly there are diminishing returns to job search, especially in a recession when new job opportunities are limited. What else did the survey reveal about time allocation? Twelve percent of the newly opened time went to activities tied to longer-run job placement, increased education, civic involvement, and health care. Other time, 35 percent of the hours lost, went to nonmarket work, cleaning, home maintenance, and child care. Clearly here the unemployed were substituting their own work for services they used to buy in the marketplace. For the unemployed worker, the opportunity cost of producing one's own home services is lower, so this change makes good economic sense. The remaining time, just under half the hours lost to the market, went to leisure activities, including sleeping.

THINKING PRACTICALLY

1. How would you expect the time use of the unemployed to differ in a boom time?

[1] Mark Aguiar, Erik Hurst, Louokas Karabarbounis,""Time Use During the Great Recession," *American Economic Review* 2013, 1664–1696

In March 2015, the population of 16 years old or older was 250.080 million. So the labor force participation rate was .63 (= 156.906/250.080).

Table 7.1 shows values of these variables for selected years since 1950. Although the unemployment rate has gone up and down over this period, the labor force participation rate grew steadily. Much of this increase was the result of the growth in the participation rate of women between the ages of 25 and 54. Column 3 in Table 7.1 shows how many new workers the U.S. economy has absorbed since 1950. The number of employed workers increased by 40.4 million between 1950 and 1980 and by 47.0 million between 1980 and 2014.

TABLE 7.1	Employed, Unemployed, and the Labor Force, 1950–2014					
	(1) Population 16 Years Old or Over (Millions)	(2) Labor Force (Millions)	(3) Employed (Millions)	(4) Unemployed (Millions)	(5) Labor Force Participation Rate (Percentage Points)	(6) Unemployment Rate (Percentage Points)
1950	105.0	62.2	58.9	3.3	59.2	5.3
1960	117.2	69.6	65.8	3.9	59.4	5.5
1970	137.1	82.8	78.7	4.1	60.4	4.9
1980	167.7	106.9	99.3	7.6	63.8	7.1
1990	189.2	125.8	118.8	7.0	66.5	5.6
2000	212.6	142.6	136.9	5.7	67.1	4.0
2010	232.8	153.9	139.1	14.8	64.7	9.6
2014	247.9	155.9	146.3	9.6	62.9	6.2

Note: Figures are civilian only (military excluded).

Source: Economic Report of the President, 2015 and U.S. Bureau of Labor Statistics.

Components of the Unemployment Rate

To get a better picture of unemployment in the United States, it is useful to look at unemployment rates across groups of people.

Unemployment Rates for Different Demographic Groups   There are large differences in rates of unemployment across demographic groups. Table 7.2 shows the unemployment rate for November 1982—the worst month of the recession in 1982—and for March 2015—a month of fairly low unemployment—broken down by race, sex, and age. In March 2015, when the overall unemployment rate was 5.5 percent, the rate for whites was 4.7 percent, whereas the rate for African Americans was more than twice that—10.1 percent.

During the recession of 1982, men fared worse than women. For African Americans, 19.3 percent of men 20 years and older and 16.5 percent of women 20 years and older were unemployed. Teenagers between 16 and 19 years of age fared worst. African Americans between 16 and 19 experienced an unemployment rate of 49.5 percent in November 1982. For whites between 16 and 19, the unemployment rate was 21.3 percent. The unemployment rate for teenagers was also high in March 2015, and African American men and women continue to have unemployment rates higher than their white counterparts.

Discouraged-Worker Effects   Many people believe that the unemployment rate underestimates the fraction of people who are involuntarily out of work. People who stop looking for work are classified as having dropped out of the labor force instead of being unemployed. During recessions, people may become discouraged about finding a job and stop looking. This lowers the unemployment rate as calculated by the BLS because those no longer looking for work are no longer counted as unemployed.

discouraged-worker effect
The decline in the measured unemployment rate that results when people who want to work but cannot find jobs grow discouraged and stop looking, thus dropping out of the ranks of the unemployed and the labor force.

To demonstrate how this **discouraged-worker effect** lowers the unemployment rate, suppose there are 10 million unemployed out of a labor force of 100 million. This means an unemployment rate of 10/100 = .10, or 10 percent. If 1 million of these 10 million unemployed people stopped looking for work and dropped out of the labor force, 9 million would be unemployed out of a labor force of 99 million. The unemployment rate would then drop to 9/99 = .091, or 9.1 percent.

The BLS survey provides some evidence on the size of the discouraged-worker effect. Respondents who indicate that they have stopped searching for work are asked why they stopped. If the respondent cites inability to find employment as the sole reason for not searching, that person might be classified as a discouraged worker.

The number of discouraged workers seems to hover around 1 percent of the size of the labor force in normal times. During the 1980–1982 recession, the number of discouraged workers increased steadily to a peak of 1.5 percent. In March 2015 discouraged workers were estimated to comprise about 0.5 percent of the size of the labor force. Some economists argue that adding the number of discouraged workers to the number who are now classified as unemployed gives a better picture of the unemployment situation.

The Duration of Unemployment   The unemployment rate measures unemployment at a given point in time. It tells us nothing about how long the average unemployed worker is out

TABLE 7.2   Unemployment Rates by Demographic Group, 1982 and 2015

	Years	November 1982	March 2015
Total		10.8	5.5
White		9.6	4.7
Men	20+	9.0	4.4
Women	20+	8.1	4.2
Both sexes	16–19	21.3	15.7
African American		20.2	10.1
Men	20+	19.3	10.0
Women	20+	16.5	9.2
Both sexes	16–19	49.5	25.0

Source: U.S. Bureau of Labor Statistics. Data are seasonally adjusted.

A Quiet Revolution: Women Join the Labor Force

Table 7.1 shows that the labor force participation rate in the United States increased from 59.2 percent in 1950 to 62.9 percent in 2014. Much of this increase was as a result of the increased participation of women in the labor force. In 1955, the labor force participation rate of women was 36 percent. For married women, the rate was even lower at 29 percent. By the 1990s, these numbers shifted considerably. In 1996, the labor force participation rate was 60 percent for all women and 62 percent for married women. The reasons for these changes are complex. Certainly, in the 1960s, there was a change in society's attitude toward women and paid work. In addition, the baby boom became the baby bust as greater availability of birth control led to fewer births.

By comparison, the participation rate for men declined over this period—from 85 percent in 1955 to 75 percent in 1996. Why the labor force participation rate for men fell is less clear than why the women's rate rose. No doubt, some men dropped out to assume more traditional women's roles, such as child care. Whatever the causes, the economy grew in a way that absorbed virtually all the new entrants during the period in question.

As women began joining the labor force in greater numbers in the 1970s and 1980s, their wages relative to men's wages actually fell. Most economists attribute this decline to the fact that less experienced women were entering the labor force, pointing out the importance of correcting for factors such as experience and education when we analyze labor markets.

At least some of the women entering the labor force at this time hired housecleaners and child care workers to perform tasks they had once done themselves. As we learned in

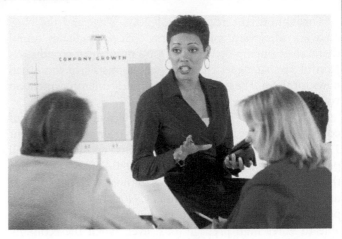

Chapter 6, the salaries of daycare staff and cleaning people are counted in GDP, whereas the value of these tasks when done by a husband or wife in a household is not part of GDP.

If you are interested in learning more about the economic history of American women, read the book *Understanding the Gender Gap: An Economic History of American Women* by Harvard University economist Claudia Goldin.

THINKING PRACTICALLY

1. When a household decides to hire someone else to clean their house and uses their extra time to watch television, the wages paid to that household worker increase GDP. Is economic output in fact larger?

of work. With a labor force of 1,000 people and an annual unemployment rate of 10 percent, we know that at any moment 100 people are unemployed. But a different picture emerges if it turns out that the same 100 people are unemployed all year, as opposed to a situation in which each of the 1,000 people has a brief spell of unemployment of a few weeks during the year. The duration statistics give us information on this feature of unemployment. Table 7.3 shows that during recessionary periods, the average duration of unemployment rises. Between 1979 and 1983, the average duration of unemployment rose from 10.8 weeks to 20.0 weeks. The slow growth following the 1990–1991 recession resulted in an increase in duration of unemployment to 17.7 weeks in 1992 and to 18.8 weeks in 1994. In 2000, average duration was down to 12.7 weeks, which then rose to 19.6 weeks in 2004. Between 2007 and 2009 average duration rose sharply from 16.9 weeks to 24.3 weeks. Following the recession it rose even more—to 39.5 weeks in 2012. Average duration was still high in 2014, at 33.7 weeks. This reflects the slow overall recovery from the recession.

The Costs of Unemployment

In the Employment Act of 1946, Congress declared that it was the continuing policy and responsibility of the federal government to use all practicable means . . . to promote maximum employment, production, and purchasing power.

In the years since, full employment has remained an important target of federal policy. Why should full employment be a policy objective of the federal government? What costs does unemployment impose on society?

ECONOMICS IN PRACTICE

The Consequences of Unemployment Persist

Throughout the recession of 2008–2009 and the slow recovery afterward many young college graduates found themselves unemployed, many for a number of months. As painful as that experience was, economists had more bad news for them. The negative effect of early unemployment on your career lasts for many years!

Lisa Kahn, a Yale economist, followed graduates of colleges from the period 1979–1989 over the subsequent 17 years.[1] You know from Chapter 5 that within this overall period there was one recession in 1980–1982. Kahn finds that even 15 years later, wage rates of those with post-college unemployment lagged substantially. Not only did low wages persist, but fewer graduates in recessionary periods were able to enter high prestige jobs, even when the economy recovered.

THINKING PRACTICALLY

1. Describe a mechanism that might help explain the persistence of wage-effects from a recession.

[1]Lisa Kahn, "The Long-Term Labor Consequences of Graduating from College in a Bad Economy," *Labour Economics*, April 2010.

Frictional, Structural, and Cyclical Unemployment　When we consider the various costs of unemployment, it is useful to categorize unemployment into three types:

- Frictional unemployment
- Structural unemployment
- Cyclical unemployment

In thinking about the social costs of unemployment, all unemployment is not created equal! When the BLS does its survey about work activity for the week containing the 12th of each month, it interviews many people who are involved in the normal search for work. Some are either newly entering the labor force, whereas others are switching jobs. This unemployment is both natural and beneficial for the economy. The portion of unemployment resulting from the

TABLE 7.3	Average Duration of Unemployment, 1970–2014				
	Weeks		Weeks		Weeks
1970	8.6	1985	15.6	2000	12.7
1971	11.3	1986	15.0	2001	13.1
1972	12.0	1987	14.5	2002	16.7
1973	10.0	1988	13.5	2003	19.2
1974	9.8	1989	11.9	2004	19.6
1975	14.2	1990	12.0	2005	18.4
1976	15.8	1991	13.7	2006	16.8
1977	14.3	1992	17.7	2007	16.9
1978	11.9	1993	18.0	2008	17.8
1979	10.8	1994	18.8	2009	24.3
1980	11.9	1995	16.6	2010	33.1
1981	13.7	1996	16.7	2011	39.4
1982	15.6	1997	15.8	2012	39.5
1983	20.0	1998	14.5	2013	36.6
1984	18.2	1999	13.4	2014	33.7

Source: U.S. Bureau of Labor Statistics.

normal turnover in the labor market is called **frictional unemployment**. As long as job search takes some time, the frictional unemployment rate will not be zero.

The industrial structure of the U.S. economy is continually changing. Manufacturing, for instance, has yielded part of its share of total employment to services and to finance, insurance, and real estate. Within the manufacturing sector, the steel and textile industries have contracted sharply, whereas high-technology sectors have expanded. The unemployment that arises from such structural shifts is usually called **structural unemployment**. Thus, the term *frictional unemployment* is used to denote short-run job/skill-matching problems, problems that last a few weeks, and *structural unemployment* denotes longer-run adjustment problems—those that tend to last for years. Although structural unemployment is an indication of a dynamic economy, it also brings with it cost to those who lose their jobs because their skills are obsolete.

Economists sometimes use the term **natural rate of unemployment** to refer to the unemployment rate that occurs in a normal functioning economy, subject to some frictional and structural unemployment. Estimates of the natural rate vary from 4 percent to 6 percent.

Between 2007 and 2009 the actual unemployment rate rose from 4.6 percent to 9.3 percent, and it seems unlikely that all of this rise was simply because of a rise in frictional and structural unemployment. Any unemployment that is above frictional plus structural is called **cyclical unemployment**. It seems likely that much of the unemployment in 2009, during the 2008–2009 recession, and during earlier recessions, was cyclical unemployment.

Social Consequences The costs of unemployment are neither evenly distributed across the population nor easily quantified. The social consequences of the Depression of the 1930s are perhaps the hardest to comprehend. Few emerged from this period unscathed. At the bottom were the poor and the fully unemployed, about 25 percent of the labor force. Even those who kept their jobs found themselves working part-time. Many people lost all or part of their savings as the stock market crashed and thousands of banks failed. Re-reading the excerpt from John Steinbeck's *The Grapes of Wrath* in Chapter 5 will give you a flavor for the social costs of the unemployment of that period. Many of you may also have seen friends or families lose valued jobs in the more recent recession of 2008–2009.

frictional unemployment The portion of unemployment that is as a result of the normal turnover in the labor market; used to denote short-run job/skill-matching problems.

structural unemployment The portion of unemployment that is as a result of changes in the structure of the economy that result in a significant loss of jobs in certain industries.

natural rate of unemployment The unemployment rate that occurs as a normal part of the functioning of the economy. Sometimes taken as the sum of the frictional unemployment rate and the structural unemployment rate.

cyclical unemployment Unemployment that is above frictional plus structural unemployment.

Inflation and Deflation

Describe the tools used to measure inflation and discuss the costs and effects of inflation.

In a market economy like the U.S. economy, prices of individual goods continually change as supply and demand shift. Indeed, a major concern of microeconomics is understanding the way in which relative prices change—why, for example, have computers become less expensive over time and dental services more expensive? In macroeconomics, we are concerned not with relative price changes, but with changes in the *overall* price level of goods and services. Inflation is defined as an increase in the overall price level, whereas deflation is a decrease in the overall price level.

The fact that all prices for the multitude of goods and services in our economy do not rise and fall together at the same rate makes measurement of inflation difficult. We have already explored measurement issues in Chapter 6 in defining the GDP deflator, which measures the price level for all goods and services in an economy. We turn now to look at a second, commonly used measure of the price level, the consumer price index.

The Consumer Price Index

The **consumer price index (CPI)** is the most widely followed price index. Unlike the GDP deflator, it is a fixed-weight index. It was first constructed during World War I as a basis for adjusting shipbuilders' wages, which the government controlled during the war. Currently, the CPI is computed by the BLS each month using a bundle of goods meant to represent the "market basket" purchased monthly by the typical urban consumer. The quantities of each good in the bundle that are used for the weights are based on extensive surveys of consumers. In fact, the BLS collects prices each month for about 71,000 goods and services from about 22,000 outlets in 44 geographic areas. For example, the cost of housing is included in the data

consumer price index (CPI) A price index computed each month by the Bureau of Labor Statistics using a bundle that is meant to represent the "market basket" purchased monthly by the typical urban consumer.

collection by surveying about 5,000 renters and 1,000 homeowners each month. Figure 7.1 shows the CPI market basket for December 2007.

Table 7.4 shows values of the CPI since 1950. The base period for this index is 1982–1984, which means that the index is constructed to have a value of 100.0 when averaged across these three years. The percentage change for a given year in the table is a measure of inflation in that year. For example, from 1970 to 1971, the CPI increased from 38.8 to 40.5, a percentage change of 4.4 percent. [The percentage change is (40.5 − 38.8) / 38.8 times 100.] The table shows the high inflation rates in the 1970s and early 1980s and the fairly low inflation rates since 1992.

Because the CPI is a fixed-weight price index (with the current base period 1982–1984), it suffers from the substitution problem discussed in the last chapter. With fixed weights, it does not account for consumers' substitution away from high-priced goods. The CPI thus has a tendency to overestimate the rate of inflation. This problem has important policy implications because government transfers such as Social Security payments are tied to the CPI. If inflation as measured by percentage changes in the CPI is biased upward, Social Security payments will grow more rapidly than they would with a better measure: The government is spending more than it otherwise would.

In response to the fixed-weight problem, in August 2002, the BLS began publishing a version of the CPI called the Chained Consumer Price Index, which uses changing weights. Although this version is not yet the main version, it may be that within a few years the BLS completely moves away from the fixed-weight version of the CPI. Remember, however, that even if this happens, the CPI will still differ in important ways from the GDP deflator, discussed in the last chapter. The CPI covers only consumer goods and services—those listed in Figure 7.1—whereas the GDP deflator covers all goods and services produced in the economy. Also, the CPI includes prices of imported goods, which the GDP deflator does not.

producer price indexes (PPIs) Measures of prices that producers receive for products at various stages in the production process.

Other popular price indexes are **producer price indexes (PPIs)**, once called *wholesale price indexes*. These are indexes of prices that producers receive for products at various stages in the production process, not just the final stage. The indexes are calculated separately for various stages in the production process. The three main categories are *finished goods*, *intermediate materials*, and *crude materials*, although there are subcategories within each of these categories.

One advantage of some of the PPIs is that they detect price increases early in the production process. Because their movements sometimes foreshadow future changes in consumer prices, they are considered to be leading indicators of future consumer prices.

▶ **FIGURE 7.1** **The CPI Market Basket**
The CPI market basket shows how a typical consumer divides his or her money among various goods and services. Most of a consumer's money goes toward housing, transportation, and food and beverages.

Source: The Bureau of Labor Statistics

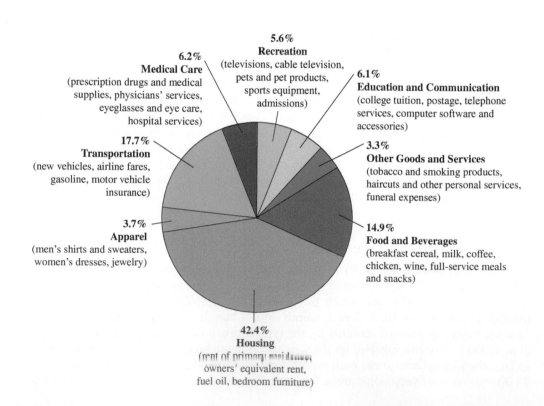

TABLE 7.4 The CPI, 1950–2014

	Percentage Change in CPI	CPI		Percentage Change in CPI	CPI
1950	1.3	24.1	1982	6.2	96.5
1951	7.9	26.0	1983	3.2	99.6
1952	1.9	26.5	1984	4.3	103.9
1953	0.8	26.7	1985	3.6	107.6
1954	0.7	26.9	1986	1.9	109.6
1955	−0.4	26.8	1987	3.6	113.6
1956	1.5	27.2	1988	4.1	118.3
1957	3.3	28.1	1989	4.8	124.0
1958	2.8	28.9	1990	5.4	130.7
1959	0.7	29.1	1991	4.2	136.2
1960	1.7	29.6	1992	3.0	140.3
1961	1.0	29.9	1993	3.0	144.5
1962	1.0	30.2	1994	2.6	148.2
1963	1.3	30.6	1995	2.8	152.4
1964	1.3	31.0	1996	3.0	156.9
1965	1.6	31.5	1997	2.3	160.5
1966	2.9	32.4	1998	1.6	163.0
1967	3.1	33.4	1999	2.2	166.6
1968	4.2	34.8	2000	3.4	172.2
1969	5.5	36.7	2001	2.8	177.1
1970	5.7	38.8	2002	1.6	179.9
1971	4.4	40.5	2003	2.3	184.0
1972	3.2	41.8	2004	2.7	188.9
1973	6.2	44.4	2005	3.4	195.3
1974	11.0	49.3	2006	3.2	201.6
1975	9.1	53.8	2007	2.8	207.3
1976	5.8	56.9	2008	3.9	215.3
1977	6.5	60.6	2009	−0.4	214.5
1978	7.6	65.2	2010	1.7	218.1
1979	11.3	72.6	2011	3.1	224.9
1980	13.5	82.4	2012	2.1	229.6
1981	10.3	90.9	2013	1.5	233.0
			2014	1.6	236.7

Sources: U.S. Bureau of Labor Statistics.

The Costs of Inflation

If you asked most people why inflation is bad, they would tell you that it lowers the overall standard of living by making goods and services more expensive. That is, it cuts into people's purchasing power. People are fond of recalling the days when a bottle of Coca-Cola cost a dime and a hamburger cost a quarter. Just think what we could buy today if prices had not changed. What people usually do not think about is what their incomes were in the "good old days." The fact that the cost of a Coke has increased from 10 cents to a dollar does not mean anything in real terms if people who once earned $5,000 now earn $50,000. During inflations, most prices—including input prices like wages—tend to rise together, and input prices determine both the incomes of workers and the incomes of owners of capital and land. So inflation by itself does not *necessarily* reduce one's purchasing power.

Inflation May Change the Distribution of Income Whether you gain or lose during a period of inflation depends on whether your income rises faster or slower than the prices of the things you buy. The group most often mentioned when the impact of inflation is discussed is people living on fixed incomes. If your income is fixed and prices rise, your ability to purchase goods and services falls proportionately.

Although the elderly are often thought of as living on fixed incomes, many pension plans pay benefits that are *indexed* to inflation, as we describe in the *Economics in Practice* on the next page. The benefits these plans provide automatically increase when the general price level rises. If prices rise 10 percent, benefits also rise 10 percent. The biggest source of income for many elderly people is Social Security. These benefits are fully indexed; when prices rise—that is, when the CPI rises—by 5 percent, Social Security benefits also increase by 5 percent.

Wages are also sometimes indexed to inflation through cost-of-living adjustments (COLAs) written into labor contracts. These contracts usually stipulate that future wage increases will be larger the larger is the rate of inflation. If wages are fully indexed, workers do not suffer a fall in real income when inflation rises, although wages are not always fully indexed.

One way of thinking about the effects of inflation on the distribution of income is to distinguish between *anticipated* and *unanticipated* inflation. If inflation is anticipated and contracts are made and agreements written with the anticipated value of inflation in mind, there need not be any effects of inflation on income distribution. Consider an individual who is thinking about retiring and has a pension that is not indexed to the CPI. If she knew what inflation was going to be for the next 20 or 30 years of her retirement, there would be no problem. She would just wait to retire until she had enough money to pay for her anticipated growing expenses. The problem occurs if, after she has retired, inflation is higher than she expected. At that point, she may face the prospect of having to return to work. Similarly, if I as a landlord expect inflation to be 2 percent per year over the next 3 years and offer my tenants a 3-year lease with a 2 percent rent increase each year, I will be in bad shape if inflation turns out to be 10 percent per year and causes all my costs to rise by 10 percent per year.

For another example, consider debtors versus creditors. It is commonly believed that debtors benefit at the expense of creditors during an inflation because with inflation they pay back less in the future in real terms than they borrowed. But this is not the case if the inflation is anticipated and the loan contract is written with this in mind.

Suppose that you want to borrow $100 from me to be paid back in a year and that we both agree that if there is no inflation the appropriate interest rate is 5 percent. Suppose also that we both anticipate that the inflation rate will be 10 percent. In this case we will agree on a 15 percent interest rate—you will pay me back $115 at the end of the year. By charging you 15 percent I have taken into account the fact that you will be paying me back with dollars worth 10 percent less in real terms than when you borrowed them. I am then not hurt by inflation and you are not helped if the actual inflation rate turns out to equal our anticipated rate. I am earning a 5 percent **real interest rate**—the difference between the interest rate on a loan and the inflation rate.

real interest rate The difference between the interest rate on a loan and the inflation rate.

Unanticipated inflation, on the other hand, is a different story. If the actual inflation rate during the year turns out to be 20 percent, I as a creditor will be hurt. I charged you 15 percent interest, expecting to get a 5 percent real rate of return, when I needed to charge you 25 percent to get the same 5 percent real rate of return. Because inflation was higher than anticipated, I got a negative real return of 5 percent. Inflation that is higher than anticipated benefits debtors; inflation that is lower than anticipated benefits creditors.

To summarize, the effects of anticipated inflation on the distribution of income are likely to be fairly small because people and institutions will adjust to the anticipated inflation. Unanticipated inflation, on the other hand, may have large effects, depending, among other things, on how much indexing to inflation there is. If many contracts are not indexed and are based on anticipated inflation rates that turn out to be wrong, there can be big winners and losers. In general, there is more uncertainty and risk when inflation is unanticipated. This uncertainty may prevent people from signing long-run contracts that would otherwise be beneficial for both parties.

Administrative Costs and Inefficiencies There may be costs associated even with anticipated inflation. One is the administrative cost associated with simply keeping up. During the rapid inflation in Israel in the early 1980s, a telephone hotline was set up to give the hourly price index. In Zimbabwe, where the inflation rate in June 2008 was estimated by some to be more than 1 million percent at an annual rate, the government was forced to print ever-increasing denominations of money. In 2009 Zimbabwe abandoned its currency and started using the U.S. dollar and the South African Rand to conduct business.

ECONOMICS IN PRACTICE

Chain-Linked Consumer Price Index in the News

The calculations described in Chapter 6 on how to construct a chain-linked price index may seem complicated and a bit arcane to you. But throughout the last months of 2012 and into early 2013, as Republicans and Democrats argued over the federal budget, chain linking became a hot topic.

As we know from the discussion of fixed weights in Chapter 6, chain linking a price index accounts for product substitution that people make in response to relative price changes. Fixed-weight price indices, which do not take into account this substitution, tend to overestimate inflation. There are two versions of the consumer price index (CPI), one using fixed weights and one using chain linking. The fixed-weight version is the one that is used to adjust social security benefits and veteran benefits to price changes. If, say, the CPI increases by 2 percent in a year, benefits are increased by 2 percent. If the chain-linked CPI were used instead, benefits would tend to increase more slowly because in general the chain-linked CPI increases less than does the fixed-weight CPI (because of product substitution). You may see where this is going. One way to decrease expenditures on social security and veteran benefits in the future would be to use the chain-linked CPI rather than the fixed-weight CPI. The nonpartisan Congressional Budget Office estimated that if the chain-linked CPI were adopted, it would save

the federal government about $145 billion over a 10-year period from the lower benefits.

THINKING PRACTICALLY

1. Tax brackets are also tied to the fixed-weight CPI. How would tax revenue be affected if the chain-linked CPI were used instead?

What about Deflation?

In 2015 most of the developed world experienced very little inflation. Indeed, the United States has not seen high inflation since the 1970s. Instead, governments in a number of countries have begun to worry about deflation hitting their economies. Why might we worry about price declines?

Part of the answer, of course, parallels the discussion of price increases. If prices fall and the fall is unanticipated, borrowers will gain at the expense of lenders, whereas those on fixed pensions will gain at the expense of the governments and firms paying those pensions. But deflation also brings with it another worry. It may be a signal that aggregate demand is too low to support full employment. We will have much to say about aggregate demand in future chapters.

Long-Run Growth

7.3 LEARNING OBJECTIVE

Discuss the components and implications of long-run growth.

In discussing long-run growth, it will be useful to begin with a few definitions. **Output growth** is the growth rate of the output of the entire economy. **Per-capita output growth** is the growth rate of output per person in the economy. If the population of a country is growing at the same rate as output, then per-capita output is not growing: Output growth is simply keeping up with population growth. Not everyone in a country works, and so output per worker is not the same as output per person. Output per worker is larger than output per person, and it is called productivity. **Productivity growth** is thus the growth rate of *output per worker*.

One measure of the economic welfare of a country is its per-capita output. Per-capita output can increase because productivity increases, as each worker now produces more than he or she did previously, or because there are more workers relative to nonworkers in the population. In the United States, both forces have been at work in increasing per-capita output.

output growth The growth rate of the output of the entire economy.

per-capita output growth The growth rate of output per person in the economy.

productivity growth The growth rate of output per worker.

Output and Productivity Growth

We have pointed out that aggregate output in the United States has grown at an annual rate of 3.3 percent since 1900, with year-to-year fluctuations. An area of economics called *growth theory* is concerned with the question of what determines this rate. Why 3.3 percent and not 2 percent or 4 percent? We take up this question in Chapter 16, but a few points are useful to make now.

In a simplified economy, machines (capital) and workers (labor) are needed to produce output. How can output increase in this economy? There are a number of ways. One way is to add more workers. With more workers, more output can be produced per machine per hour. Another way is to add more machines, so that each worker has more capital to work with. A third way is to increase the length of the work week. With workers and machines working more hours, more output can be produced. Output can thus increase if labor or capital increases or if the amount of time that labor and capital are working per week increases.

Another way for output to increase in our economy is for the quality of the workers to increase, perhaps through education, experience, or even better health. If workers become more physically fit by exercising more and eating less fat and more whole grains and fresh fruits and vegetables, their greater fitness may increase their output on the machines. People are sometimes said to be adding to their *human capital* when they increase their mental or physical skills.

The quality of the machines used in the workplace may also increase. In particular, new machines that replace old machines may allow more output to be produced per hour with the same number of workers. An obvious example is the replacement of an old computer with a new, faster one that allows more to be done per minute of work on the computer.

To summarize, output can increase when there are more workers, more skills per worker, more machines, better machines, or a longer workweek.

Output per worker hour is called *labor productivity* or sometimes just *productivity*. Output per worker hour is plotted in Figure 7.2 for the 1952 I–2014 IV period. Two features are immediately clear from the figure. First, there is an upward trend. Second, there are fairly sizable short-run fluctuations around the trend. Chapter 16 will discuss these short-run fluctuations, linking them to underutilization of an employed work force. For now, however, our main interest is the long-run trend.

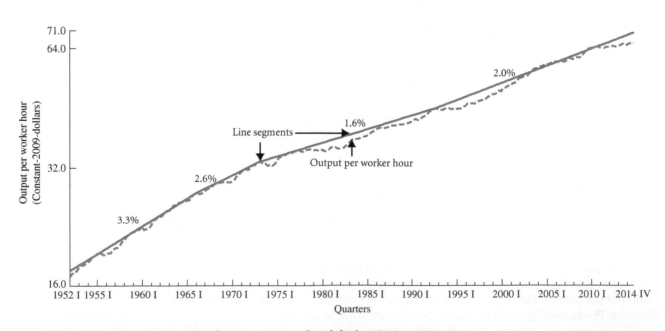

▲ **FIGURE 7.2** **Output per Worker Hour (Productivity), 1952 I–2014 IV**
Productivity grew much faster in the 1950s and 1960s than since.

▲ **FIGURE 7.3   Capital per Worker, 1952 I–2014 IV**
Capital per worker grew until about 1980 and then leveled off somewhat.

To smooth out the short-run fluctuations in Figure 7.2, we have added straight-line segments to the figure, where the segments roughly go through the high values. The slope of each line segment is the growth rate of productivity along the segment. The growth rates are listed in the figure. The different productivity growth rates in the figure tell an interesting story. From the 1950s through the mid-1960s, the growth rate was 3.3 percent. The rate then fell to 2.6 percent in the last half of the 1960s and early 1970s. Between the early 1970s and the early 1990s, the growth rate was much lower at 1.6 percent. Since the early 1990s, it has been 2.0 percent.

Why are the growth rates positive in Figure 7.2? Why has the amount of output that a worker can produce per hour risen in the last half-century? Part of the answer is that the amount of capital per worker has increased. In Figure 7.3 capital per worker is plotted for the same 1952 I–2014 IV period. It is clear from the figure that the amount of capital per worker has generally been rising. Therefore, with more capital per worker, more output can be produced per worker. The other part of the answer is that the quality of labor and capital has been increasing. Both the average skill of workers and the average quality of capital have been increasing. This means that more output can be produced per worker for a given quantity of capital because both workers and capital are getting better.

A harder question to answer concerning Figure 7.2 is why the growth rate of productivity was much higher in the 1950s and 1960s than it has been since the early 1970s. Again, part of the answer is that the amount of capital per worker rose more rapidly in the 1950s and 1960s than it has since then. This can be seen in Figure 7.3. The other part of the answer is, of course, that the quality of labor and capital must have increased more in the 1950s and 1960s than later, although this is difficult to explain or to get direct evidence on. Interestingly, it has been difficult to find big productivity gains from recent technological innovations in the communications area.

Looking Ahead

This ends our introduction to the basic concepts and problems of macroeconomics. The first chapter of this part introduced the field; the second chapter discussed the measurement of national product and national income; and this chapter discussed unemployment, inflation, and long-run growth. We are now ready to begin the analysis of how the macroeconomy works.

SUMMARY

7.1 UNEMPLOYMENT *p. 124*

1. The *unemployment rate* is the ratio of the number of *unemployed* people to the number of people in the *labor force*. To be considered unemployed and in the labor force, a person must be looking for work.

2. Big differences in rates of unemployment exist across demographic groups, regions, and industries. African Americans, for example, experience much higher unemployment rates than whites.

3. A person who decides to stop looking for work is considered to have dropped out of the labor force and is no longer classified as unemployed. People who stop looking because they are discouraged about finding a job are sometimes called *discouraged workers*.

4. Some unemployment is inevitable. Because new workers are continually entering the labor force, because industries and firms are continuously expanding and contracting, and because people switch jobs, there is a constant process of job search as workers and firms try to match the best people to the available jobs. This unemployment is both natural and beneficial for the economy.

5. The unemployment that occurs because of short-run job/skill-matching problems is called *frictional unemployment*. The unemployment that occurs because of longer-run structural changes in the economy is called *structural unemployment*. The *natural rate of unemployment* is the sum of the frictional rate and the structural rate. The increase in unemployment that

occurs during recessions and depressions is called *cyclical unemployment*.

7.2 INFLATION AND DEFLATION *p. 129*

6. The *consumer price index (CPI)* is a fixed-weight price index. It represents the "market basket" purchased by the typical urban consumer.

7. Whether people gain or lose during a period of inflation depends on whether their income rises faster or slower than the prices of the things they buy. The elderly are more insulated from inflation than most people think because Social Security benefits and many pensions are indexed to inflation.

8. Inflation is likely to have a larger effect on the distribution of income when it is unanticipated than when it is anticipated.

7.3 LONG-RUN GROWTH *p. 133*

9. Output growth depends on: (1) the growth rate of the capital stock, (2) the growth rate of output per unit of the capital stock, (3) the growth rate of labor, and (4) the growth rate of output per unit of labor.

10. Output per worker hour (labor productivity) rose faster in the 1950s and 1960s than it rose from the 1970s to 2014. An interesting question is whether labor productivity will rise faster in the future because of the Internet.

REVIEW TERMS AND CONCEPTS

consumer price index (CPI), *p. 129*
cyclical unemployment, *p. 129*
discouraged-worker effect, *p. 126*
employed, *p. 124*
frictional unemployment, *p. 129*
labor force, *p. 124*
labor force participation rate, *p. 124*
natural rate of unemployment, *p. 129*
not in the labor force, *p. 124*

output growth, *p. 133*
per-capita output growth, *p. 133*
producer price indexes (PPIs), *p. 130*
productivity growth, *p. 133*
real interest rate, *p. 132*
structural unemployment, *p. 129*
unemployed, *p. 124*
unemployment rate, *p. 124*

Equations:
labor force = employed + unemployed, *p. 124*
population = labor force + not in labor force, *p. 124*

$$\text{unemployment rate} = \frac{\text{unemployed}}{\text{employed} + \text{unemployed}},$$
p. 124

$$\text{labor force participation rate} = \frac{\text{labor force}}{\text{population}}, \text{ *p. 124*}$$

PROBLEMS

All problems are available on MyEconLab.

7.1 UNEMPLOYMENT

LEARNING OBJECTIVE: Explain how unemployment is measured.

1.1 In late 2010 economists were debating whether the U.S. economy was in a recession. GDP seemed to be rising, yet the unemployment rate was stuck at close to 10 percent.

In thinking about the economic distress experienced during a recession, which is the most important: high unemployment or falling GDP? Defend your answer.

1.2 When an inefficient firm or a firm producing a product that people no longer want goes out of business, people are unemployed, but that is part of the normal process of economic growth and development. The unemployment is part of the natural rate and need not concern policy makers. Discuss that statement and its relevance to the economy today.

1.3 What is the unemployment rate in your state today? What was it in 1970, 1975, 1982, and 2008? How has your state done relative to the national average? Do you know or can you determine why?

1.4 **[Related to the *Economics in Practice* on p. 127]** For each of the following events, explain what is likely to happen to the labor force participation rate:
   a. The federal minimum wage is abolished.
   b. The minimum legal working age is lowered from 16 to 14.
   c. The economy is in the midst of a prolonged period of economic growth.
   d. The federal government decreases the duration of unemployment benefits from a high of 99 weeks back to a maximum of 26 weeks.
   e. The federal government lowers the minimum age requirement for collecting Social Security benefits.

1.5 **[Related to the *Economics in Practice* on p. 128]** According to the National Bureau of Economic Research (NBER), the United States experienced five recessions from 1980 to 2010. Following is the NBER's list of the start and end dates for each of these recessions:
   January 1980 – July 1980
   July 1981 – November 1982
   July 1990 – March 1991
   March 2001 – November 2001
   December 2007 – June 2009

   Go to the Bureau of Labor Statistics Web site (www.bls .gov) and look up the monthly unemployment data since 1980. (Find BLS series number LNS14000000 and choose 1980 as the "from" date.) What were the unemployment rates for the starting and ending months for each of the five recessions? How long after each recession ended did it take for the unemployment rate to start to decrease, and how long did it take for the unemployment rate to return to the pre-recession level?

1.6 Go to www.bls.gov and click on the links for state and area employment and unemployment. Look at your home state and describe what changes have taken place in the workforce. Has the labor force participation rate gone up or down? Provide an explanation for the rate change. Are your state's experiences the same as the rest of the country? Provide an explanation of why your state's experiences are the same as or different from the rest of the country.

1.7 Consider the following statements:
   a. Fewer people are employed in Freedonia now than at any time in the past 75 years.
   b. The unemployment rate in Freedonia is lower now than it has been in 75 years.
   Can both of those statements be true at the same time? Explain.

1.8 Suppose the number of employed people in an economy is 312,545,372. The unemployment rate in this economy is 7.4 percent, or .074, and the labor force participation rate is 80 percent, or .80.
   a. What is the size of the labor force?
   b. How many people are unemployed?
   c. What is the size of the working-age population?

1.9 On average, nations in Europe pay higher unemployment benefits for longer periods of time than does the United States. How do you suppose this would impact the unemployment rates in these nations? Explain which type of unemployment you think is most directly affected by the size and duration of unemployment benefits.

1.10 In each of the following cases, classify the person as cyclically unemployed, structurally unemployed, frictionally unemployed, or not in the labor force. Explain your answers.
   a. Samuel quit his job as a bank teller to work full-time on his master's degree.
   b. Charmaine lost her job as a customer service representative when her employer outsourced the work to India.
   c. Lucy just graduated from law school and is deciding which job offer she will accept.
   d. Carlos got laid off from his job as a limo driver six months ago and gave up looking for a new job two months later.
   e. Byron quit his teaching job in Atlanta six weeks ago to look for a higher-paying job in Miami. He is still looking for a job.
   f. Arlisha lost her job as a restaurant manager due to a recession.

7.2 INFLATION AND DEFLATION

LEARNING OBJECTIVE: Describe the tools to measure inflation and discuss the costs and effects of inflation.

2.1 Suppose all wages, salaries, welfare benefits, and other sources of income were indexed to inflation. Would inflation still be considered a problem? Why or why not?

2.2 What do the CPI and PPIs measure? Why do we need both of these types of price indexes? (Think about what purpose you would use each one for.)

2.3 The CPI is a fixed-weight index. It compares the price of a fixed bundle of goods in one year with the price of the same bundle of goods in some base year. Calculate the price of a bundle containing 50 units of good X, 125 units of good Y, and 100 units of good Z in 2013, 2014, and 2015. Convert the results into an index by dividing each bundle price figure by the bundle price in 2013 and multiplying by 100. Calculate the percentage change in your index between 2013 and 2014 and again between 2014 and 2015. Was there inflation between 2014 and 2015?

Good	Quantity Consumed	2013 Prices	2014 Prices	2015 Prices
X	50	$2.00	$1.50	$2.00
Y	125	3.00	3.00	2.50
Z	100	0.75	1.25	1.50

2.4 **[Related to the *Economics in Practice* on p. 133]** In his 2015 State of the Union speech, President Barack Obama urged Congress to raise the federal minimum wage from $7.25 to $10.10 per hour, and stated that future minimum wage increases should be tied to the cost of living. Explain how tying the minimum wage to an index like the CPI could impact the economy? Do you suppose the impact would be different if the minimum wage was tied to the chain-linked CPI as opposed to the fixed-weight CPI? Explain.

2.5 Consider the following five situations. In which situation would a borrower be best off and in which situation would a lender be best off?

   a. The nominal interest rate is 6 percent and the inflation rate is 3 percent.

   b. The nominal interest rate is 13 percent and the inflation rate is 11 percent.

   c. The nominal interest rate is 3 percent and the inflation rate is −1 percent.

   d. The real interest rate is 8 percent and the inflation rate is 7 percent.

   e. The real interest rate is 5 percent and the inflation rate is 9 percent.

2.6 The CPI is 120 in year 1 and 150 in year 2. All inflation is anticipated. If the Gringotts Bank charges an interest rate of 30 percent in year 2, what is the bank's real interest rate?

7.3 LONG-RUN GROWTH

LEARNING OBJECTIVE: Discuss the components and implications of long-run growth.

3.1 Policy makers talk about the "capacity" of the economy to grow. What specifically is meant by the "capacity" of the economy? How might capacity be measured? In what ways is capacity limited by labor constraints and by capital constraints? What are the consequences if demand in the economy exceeds capacity? What signs would you look for?

3.2 What was the rate of growth in real GDP during the most recent quarter? You can find the answer in publications such as the *Survey of Current Business, The Economist, and Business Week*. Has growth been increasing or decreasing? What policies might you suggest for increasing the economy's potential long-run rate of growth?

3.3 An article in the *Gotham Times* states that the stock of capital and the workforce in Gotham are both increasing at an annual rate of 7 percent. The same article states that real output is growing by 11 percent. Explain if this is possible in the short run and in the long run.

PART III

The Core of Macroeconomic Theory

We now begin our discussion of the theory of how the macroeconomy works. We know how to calculate gross domestic product (GDP), but what factors *determine* it? We know how to define and measure inflation and unemployment, but what circumstances *cause* inflation and unemployment? What, if anything, can government do to reduce unemployment and inflation?

Analyzing the various components of the macroeconomy is a complex undertaking. The level of GDP, the overall price level, and the level of employment—three chief concerns of macroeconomists—are influenced by events in three broadly defined "markets":

■ Goods-and-services market

■ Financial (money) market

■ Labor market

We will explore each market, as well as the links between them, in our discussion of macroeconomic theory. Figure III.1 presents the plan of the next seven chapters, which form the core

CHAPTERS 8–9

The Goods-and-Services Market

- Planned aggregate expenditure
  Consumption *(C)*
  Planned investment *(I)*
  Government *(G)*
- Aggregate output (income) *(Y)*

CHAPTER 11

Full Equilibrium: *AS/AD* Model

- Aggregate supply curve
- Fed rule
- Aggregate demand curve

  Equilibrium interest rate *(r*)*
  Equilibrium output (income) *(Y*)*
  Equilibrium price level *(P*)*

CHAPTER 13

The Labor Market

- The supply of labor
- The demand for labor
- Employment and unemployment

CHAPTERS 10

The Money Market

- The supply of money
- The demand for money
- Interest rate *(r)*

CHAPTER 12

Policy and Cost Effects in the *AS/AD* model

▲ FIGURE III.1   **The Core of Macroeconomic Theory**

We build up the macroeconomy slowly. In Chapters 8 and 9, we examine the market for goods and services. In Chapter 10, we examine the money market. Chapter 11 introduces the aggregate supply (AS) curve and the Fed rule and derives the aggregate demand (AD) curve. Chapter 12 uses the AS/AD model to examine policy and cost effects, and Chapter 13 discusses the labor market.

of macroeconomic theory. In Chapters 8 and 9, we describe the market for goods and services, often called the *goods market*. In Chapter 8, we explain several basic concepts and show how the equilibrium level of output is determined in a simple economy with no government and no imports or exports. In Chapter 9, we add the government to the economy. In Chapter 10 we introduce the *money market* and discuss the way the U.S. central bank (the Federal Reserve) controls the interest rate.

Chapter 11 introduces the aggregate supply (*AS*) curve. It also discusses the behavior of the Federal Reserve regarding its interest rate decision, which is approximated by a "Fed rule." The Fed rule is then added to the analysis of the goods market to derive the aggregate demand (*AD*) curve. The resulting model, the "*AS/AD*" model, determines the equilibrium values of the interest rate (r), aggregate output (income) (Y), and the price level (P). Chapter 12 uses the *AS/AD* model to analyze policy and cost effects. Finally, Chapter 13 discusses the supply of and demand for labor and the functioning of the labor market in the macroeconomy. This material is essential to understanding how modern, developed economies function.

Aggregate Expenditure and Equilibrium Output

In the last several chapters we described a number of features of the U.S. economy, including real GDP, inflation, and unemployment, and we talked about how they are measured. Now we begin the analytical part of macroeconomics: How do the different parts of the economy interact to produce the time-profile of the U.S. economy that we described in the last few chapters?

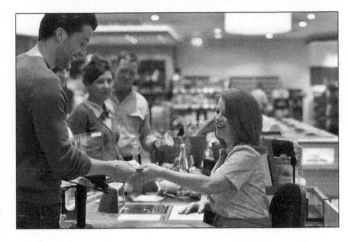

We begin with the simplest case, focusing on households and firms, asking what happens to the economy as a whole when investment increases. If suddenly all the managers of firms in the economy decided to expand their plants, how would that affect households and aggregate output? Once we understand how households and firms interact at the aggregate level, we will introduce government in Chapter 9. In subsequent chapters, we will make our simple economic model both more realistic, and as a result more complex, but the basic intuitions of these early chapters will remain. As we work through our model of the economy, we will focus, at least initially, on understanding movements in real gross domestic product (GDP), one of the central measures of macroeconomic activity. Because we are interested in tracking real changes in the level of economic activity, we focus on real, rather than nominal, output. So, although we will typically use dollars to measure GDP, you should think about this as dollars corrected for price level changes.

We saw previously that GDP can be calculated in terms of either income or expenditures. We will use the variable Y to refer to both **aggregate output** and **aggregate income**.

> In any given period, there is an exact equality between aggregate output (production) and aggregate income. You should be reminded of this fact whenever you encounter the combined term **aggregate output (income) (Y)**.

Aggregate output can also be considered the aggregate quantity supplied because it is the amount that firms are supplying (producing) during a period. In the discussions that follow, we use the term *aggregate output (income)* instead of *aggregate quantity supplied*, but keep in mind that the two are equivalent. Also remember that *aggregate output* means "real GDP." For ease of discussion we will sometimes refer to aggregate output (income) as simply "output" or "income."

From the outset, you must think in "real terms." For example, when we talk about output (Y), we mean real output, not nominal output. In the current chapter and the next, we will take as fixed the overall price level (P), so that nominal and real output are the same. Nevertheless, because eventually we will introduce the possibility of a changing price level, it is useful now to begin thinking of output (Y) as being in real terms.

Explain the principles of the Keynesian theory of consumption.

aggregate output   The total quantity of goods and services produced (or supplied) in an economy in a given period.

aggregate income   The total income received by all factors of production in a given period.

aggregate output (income) (Y)   A combined term used to remind you of the exact equality between aggregate output and aggregate income.

consumption function   The relationship between consumption and income.

The Keynesian Theory of Consumption

In 2012, the average U.S. family spent about $1,700 on clothing. For high-income families earning more than $150,000, the amount spent on clothing was higher, at about $5,500. We all recognize that for consumption as a whole, as well as for consumption of most specific categories of goods and services, consumption rises with income. This relationship between consumption and income is central to Keynes's model of the economy. Although Keynes recognized that many factors, including wealth and interest rates, play a role in determining consumption levels in the economy, in his classic *The General Theory of Employment, Interest, and Money*, current income played the key role:

> The fundamental psychological law, upon which we are entitled to depend with great confidence both *a priori* from our knowledge of human nature and from the detailed facts of experience, is that men [and women, too] are disposed, as a rule and on average, to increase their consumption as their incomes increase, but not by as much as the increase in their income.[1]

Keynes is telling us two things in this quote. First, if you find your income going up, you will spend more than you did before. But Keynes is also saying something about how much more you will spend: He predicts—based on his looking at the data and his understanding of people—that the rise in consumption will be less than the full rise in income. This simple observation plays a large role in helping us understand the workings of the aggregate economy.

The relationship between consumption and income is called a **consumption function**. Figure 8.1 shows a hypothetical consumption function for an individual household. The curve is labeled *c(y)*, which is read "*c* is a function of *y*," or "consumption is a function of income." Note that we have drawn the line with an upward slope, showing that consumption increases with income. To reflect Keynes's view that consumption increases less than one for one with income, we have drawn the consumption function with a slope of less than 1. The consumption function in Figure 8.1 is a straight line, telling us that an increase in income of $1 leads to the same increase in consumption regardless of the initial value of income. In practice, the consumption function may be curved, with the slope decreasing as income increases. This would tell us that the typical consumer spends less of the incremental income received as his or her income rises.

The consumption function in Figure 8.1 represents an individual household. In macroeconomics, however, we are interested in the behavior of the economy as a whole, the aggregate

▶ **FIGURE 8.1**

A Consumption Function for a Household

A consumption function for an individual household shows the level of consumption at each level of household income.

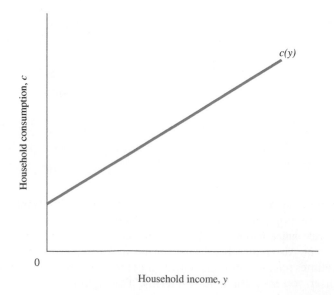

---

[1] John Maynard Keynes, *The General Theory of Employment, Interest, and Money* (1936), First Harbinger Ed. (New York: Harcourt Brace Jovanovich, 1964), p. 96.

The aggregate consumption function shows the level of aggregate consumption at each level of aggregate income. The upward slope indicates that higher levels of income lead to higher levels of consumption spending.

consumption of all households in the economy in relation to aggregate income. Figure 8.2 shows this aggregate consumption function, again using a straight line, or constant slope, for simplicity. With a straight-line consumption curve, we can use the following equation to describe the curve:

$$C = a + bY$$

Y is aggregate output (income), C is aggregate consumption, and a is the point at which the consumption function intersects the vertical axis—a constant. The letter b is the slope of the line, in this case $\Delta C / \Delta Y$ [because consumption (C) is measured on the vertical axis and income (Y) is measured on the horizontal axis].[2] Every time income increases (say by ΔY), consumption increases by b times ΔY. Thus, $\Delta C = b \times \Delta Y$ and $\Delta C / \Delta Y = b$. Suppose, for example, that the slope of the line in Figure 8.2 is 0.75 (that is, $b = .75$). An increase in income (ΔY) of $1,000 would then increase consumption by $b\Delta Y = 0.75 \times \$1,000$, or 750.

The **marginal propensity to consume (MPC)** is the fraction of a change in income that is consumed. In the consumption function here, b is the MPC. An MPC of .75 means consumption changes by .75 of the change in income. The slope of the consumption function is the MPC. An MPC less than 1 tells us that individuals spend less than 100 percent of their additional income, just as Keynes suggested.

marginal propensity to consume (MPC)   That fraction of a change in income that is consumed, or spent.

marginal propensity to consume ≡ slope of consumption function ≡ $\dfrac{\Delta C}{\Delta Y}$

Aggregate saving (S) in the economy, denoted S, is the difference between aggregate income and aggregate consumption:

aggregate saving (S)   The part of aggregate income that is not consumed.

$$S \equiv Y - C$$

The triple equal sign means that this equation is an **identity**, or something that is always true by definition. This equation simply says that income that is not consumed must be saved. If $0.75 of a $1.00 increase in income goes to consumption, $0.25 must go to saving. If income decreases by $1.00, consumption will decrease by $0.75 and saving will decrease by $0.25. The **marginal propensity to save (MPS)** is the fraction of a change in income that is saved: $\Delta S / \Delta Y$,

identity   Something that is always true by definition.

marginal propensity to save (MPS)   That fraction of a change in income that is saved.

---

[2] The Greek letter Δ (delta) means "change in." For example, ΔY (read "delta Y") means the "change in income." If income (Y) in 2012 is $100 and income in 2013 is $110, then ΔY for this period is $110 − $100 = $10. For a review of the concept of slope, see Appendix, Chapter 1.

where ΔS is the change in saving. Because everything not consumed is saved, the MPC and the MPS must add up to 1.

$$MPC + MPS \equiv 1$$

Because the MPC and the MPS are important concepts, it may help to review their definitions. The marginal propensity to consume (MPC) is the fraction of an increase in income that is consumed (or the fraction of a decrease in income that comes out of consumption).

The marginal propensity to save (MPS) is the fraction of an increase in income that is saved (or the fraction of a decrease in income that comes out of saving).

The numerical examples used in the rest of this chapter are based on the following consumption function:

$$C = \underbrace{100}_{a} + \underbrace{0.75\,Y}_{b}$$

This equation is simply an extension of the generic $C = a + bY$ consumption function we have been discussing, where a is 100 and b is 0.75. This function is graphed in Figure 8.3.

Because saving and consumption by definition add up to income, we can use the consumption curve to tell us about both consumption and saving. We do this in Figure 8.4. In this figure, we have drawn a 45-degree line from the origin. Everywhere along this line aggregate consumption is equal to aggregate income. Therefore, saving is zero. Where the consumption curve is *above* the 45-degree line, consumption exceeds income and saving is negative, that is, people borrow. Where the consumption function *crosses* the 45-degree line, consumption is equal to income and saving is zero. Where the consumption function is *below* the 45-degree line, consumption is less than income and saving is positive. Note that the slope of the saving function is $\Delta S/\Delta Y$, which is equal to the marginal propensity to save (MPS). The consumption function and the saving function are mirror images of each other. No information appears in one that

▶ **FIGURE 8.3 The Aggregate Consumption Function Derived from the Equation** $C = 100 + 0.75Y$
In this simple consumption function, consumption is 100 at an income of zero. As income rises, so does consumption. For every 100 increase in income, consumption rises by 75. The slope of the line is 0.75.

Aggregate Income, Y	Aggregate Consumption, C
0	100
80	160
100	175
200	250
400	400
600	550
800	700
1,000	850

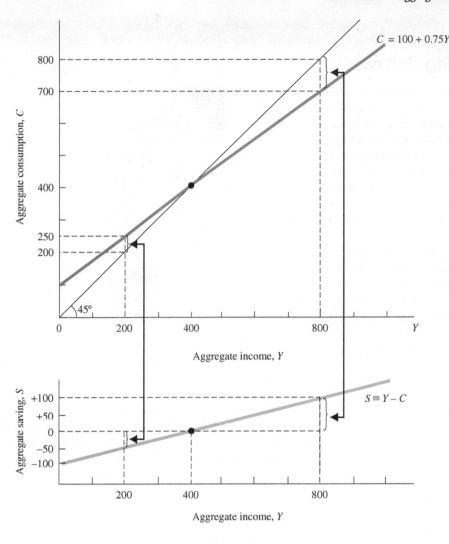

◀ **FIGURE 8.4**
Deriving the Saving Function from the Consumption Function in Figure 8.3
Because $S \equiv Y - C$, it is easy to derive the saving function from the consumption function. A 45-degree line drawn from the origin can be used as a convenient tool to compare consumption and income graphically. At $Y = 200$, consumption is 250. The 45-degree line shows us that consumption is larger than income by 50. Thus $S \equiv Y - C = -50$. At $Y = 800$, consumption is less than income by 100. Thus $S = 100$ when $Y = 800$.

Y	−	C	=	S
Aggregate Income		Aggregate Consumption		Aggregate Saving
0		100		−100
80		160		−80
100		175		−75
200		250		−50
400		400		0
600		550		50
800		700		100
1,000		850		150

does not appear in the other. These functions tell us how households in the aggregate will divide income between consumption spending and saving at every possible income level. In other words, they embody aggregate household behavior.

Other Determinants of Consumption

The assumption that consumption depends only on income is obviously a simplification. In practice, the decisions of households on how much to consume in a given period are also affected by their wealth, by the interest rate, and by their expectations of the future. Households with higher wealth are likely to spend more, other things being equal, than households with less wealth, even at the same income level. As we will see, these other factors shift the consumption function.

ECONOMICS IN PRACTICE

Behavioral Biases in Saving Behavior

This chapter has described how saving is related to income. Economists have generally assumed that people make their saving decisions rationally, just as they make other decisions about choices in consumption and the labor market. Saving decisions involve thinking about trade-offs between present and future consumption. Recent work in behavioral economics has highlighted the role of psychological biases in saving behavior and has demonstrated that seemingly small changes in the way saving programs are designed can result in big behavioral changes.

Many retirement plans are designed with an opt-in feature. That is, you need to take some action to enroll. Typically, when you begin a job, you need to check "yes" on the retirement plan enrollment form. Recent work in economics by James Choi of Yale University, Brigitte Madrian of Harvard and Dennis Shea, head of executive compensation at Aetna, suggests that simply changing the enrollment process from the opt-in structure just described to an opt-out system in which people are automatically enrolled unless they check the "no" box dramatically increases enrollment in retirement pension plans. In one study, the change from an opt-in to an opt-out system increased pension plan enrollment after 3 months of work from 65 percent to 98 percent of workers.

Behavioral economists have administered a number of surveys suggesting that people, on average, think they save too little of their income for retirement. Shlomo Benartzi, from the University of California, Los Angeles, and Richard Thaler, from the University of Chicago, devised a retirement program to try to increase saving rates. Under this plan, called Save More Tomorrow, employees are offered a program that allows them to precommit to save more whenever they get a pay raise. Behavioral economists argue that people find this option attractive because it is easier for them to

commit to making sacrifices tomorrow than it is for them to make those sacrifices today. (This is why many people resolve to diet some time in the future but continue to overeat today.) The Save More Tomorrow retirement plans have been put in place in a number of companies, including Vanguard, T. Rowe Price, and TIAA-CREF. Early results suggest dramatic increases in the saving rates of those enrolled, with saving rates quadrupling after 4 years and four pay raises.

THINKING PRACTICALLY

1. The Save More Tomorrow Plans encourage people to save more by committing themselves to future action. Can you think of examples in your own life of similar commitment devices you use?

The boom in the U.S. stock market in the last half of the 1990s and the boom in housing prices between 2003 and 2005, both of which increased household wealth substantially, led households to consume more than they otherwise would have in these periods. In 2009–2010, after a fall in housing prices and the stock market, consumption was less than it otherwise would have been.

For many households, interest rates also figure in to consumption and saving decisions. Lower interest rates reduce the cost of borrowing, so lower interest rates are likely to stimulate spending. (Conversely, higher interest rates increase the cost of borrowing and are likely to decrease spending.) Finally, as households think about what fraction of incremental income to consume versus save, their expectations about the future may also play a role. If households are optimistic and expect to do better in the future, they may spend more at present than if they think the future will be bleak.

Household expectations are also important regarding households' responses to changes in their income. If, for example, the government announces a tax cut, which increases after-tax income, households' responses to the tax cut will likely depend on whether the tax cut is expected to be temporary or permanent. If households expect that the tax cut will be in effect for only two years, their responses are likely to be smaller than if they expect the tax cut to be permanent.

We examine these issues in Chapter 15, where we take a closer look at household behavior regarding both consumption and labor supply. But for now, we will focus only on income, given that it is the most important determinant of consumption.

Planned Investment (*I*) versus Actual Investment

8.2 LEARNING OBJECTIVE

Explain the difference between planned investment and actual investment.

The output of an economy consists not only of goods consumed by households, but investments made by firms. Some firms' investments are in the form of plants and equipment. These investments in many ways look like some consumption expenditures of households. In a given period, a firm might buy $500,000 of new machinery, which would be part of aggregate output for the period, as would the purchase of automobiles by households. In Chapter 6, you learned that firms' investments also include inventories. Understanding how firms invest in inventories is a little more complicated, but it is important for understanding the way the macroeconomy works.

A firm's inventory is the stock of goods that it has awaiting sale. For many reasons, most firms want to hold some inventory. It is hard to predict exactly when consumers will want to purchase a new refrigerator, and most customers are not patient. Sometimes it is cheaper to produce goods in larger volumes than current demand requires, which leads firms to want to have inventory. From a macroeconomic perspective, however, inventory differs from other capital investments in one important way: Although purchases by firms of machinery and equipment are *always* deliberate, *sometimes* inventories build up (or decline) without any deliberate plan by firms. For this reason, there can be a difference between **planned investment**, which consists of the investments firms *plan* to make, and **actual investment**, which consists of all of firms' investments, including their unplanned changes in inventories.

planned investment (*I*) Those additions to capital stock and inventory that are planned by firms.

actual investment The actual amount of investment that takes place; it includes items such as unplanned changes in inventories.

Why are inventories sometimes different from what was planned? Recall that firms hold planned inventories in anticipation of sales, recognizing that the exact timing of sales may be uncertain. If a firm overestimates how much it will sell in a period, it will end up with more in inventory than it planned to have. On other occasions, inventories may be lower than planned when sales are stronger than expected. We will use *I* to refer to planned investment, not necessarily actual investment. As we will see shortly, the economy is in equilibrium only when planned investment and actual investment are equal.

Planned Investment and the Interest Rate (*r*)

8.3 LEARNING OBJECTIVE

Understand how planned investment is affected by the interest rate.

We have seen that there is an important difference between planned investment and actual investment, and this distinction will play a key role in the discussion of equilibrium in this chapter. But another important question is what determines planned investment in the first place? In practice planned investment depends on many factors, as you would expect, but here we focus on just one: the interest rate. Recall that investment includes a firm's purchase of new capital—new machines and plants. Whether a firm decides to invest in new capital depends on whether the expected profits from that machinery and those plants justify its costs. And one cost of an investment project is the interest cost. When a manufacturing firm builds a new plant, the contractor must be paid at the time the plant is built. The money needed to carry out such projects is generally borrowed and paid back over an extended period. The real cost of an investment project thus depends in part on the interest rate—the cost of borrowing. When the interest rate rises, it becomes more expensive to borrow and fewer projects are likely to be undertaken; increasing the interest rate, *ceteris paribus*, is likely to reduce the level of planned investment spending. When the interest rate falls, it becomes less costly to borrow and more investment projects are likely to be undertaken; reducing the interest rate, *ceteris paribus*, is likely to increase the level of planned investment spending.

The relationship between the interest rate and planned investment is illustrated by the downward-sloping demand curve in Figure 8.5. The higher the interest rate, the lower the level

▶ **FIGURE 8.5**
Planned Investment Schedule
Planned investment spending is a negative function of the interest rate. An increase in the interest rate from 3 percent to 6 percent reduces planned investment from I_0 to I_1.

of planned investment. At an interest rate of 3 percent, planned investment is I_0. When the interest rate rises from 3 to 6 percent, planned investment falls from I_0 to I_1. As the interest rate falls, however, more projects become profitable, so more investment is undertaken. The curve in Figure 8.5 is sometimes called the "marginal efficiency of investment" curve.

Other Determinants of Planned Investment

The assumption that planned investment depends only on the interest rate is obviously a simplification, just as is the assumption that consumption depends only on income. In practice, the decision of a firm on how much to invest depends on, among other things, its expectation of future sales. If a firm expects that its sales will increase in the future, it may begin to build up its capital stock—that is, to invest—now so that it will be able to produce more in the future to meet the increased level of sales. The optimism or pessimism of entrepreneurs about the future course of the economy can have an important effect on current planned investment. Keynes used the phrase *animal spirits* to describe the feelings of entrepreneurs, and he argued that these feelings affect investment decisions significantly.

We will come back to this issue in Chapter 15, where we will take a closer look at firm behavior (and household behavior), but until then to complete our simple model we will assume that planned investment depends only on the interest rate.

Explain how equilibrium output is determined.

equilibrium   Occurs when there is no tendency for change. In the macroeconomic goods market, equilibrium occurs when planned aggregate expenditure is equal to aggregate output.

The Determination of Equilibrium Output (Income)

Thus far, we have described the behavior of firms and households. In this simple setting, how does the economy achieve equilibrium and what does that equilibrium look like?

A number of definitions of **equilibrium** are used in economics but all use the idea that at equilibrium, there is no tendency for change. In microeconomics, equilibrium is said to exist in a particular market (for example, the market for bananas) at the price for which the quantity demanded is equal to the quantity supplied. At this point, both suppliers and demanders are satisfied. The equilibrium price of a good is the price at which suppliers want to furnish the amount that demanders want to buy. In the macroeconomic goods market, we will use a similar definition of equilibrium focused on a match between what is planned and what actually happens.

To define equilibrium for the macroeconomy, we start with a new variable, **planned aggregate expenditure (AE)**. Planned aggregate expenditure is, by definition, consumption plus planned investment:

$$AE \equiv C + I$$

Note that I is planned investment spending only. It does not include any unplanned increases or decreases in inventory. Note also that this is a definition. Aggregate expenditure is always equal to $C + I$, and we write it with the triple equal sign.

The economy is defined to be in equilibrium when aggregate output (Y) is equal to planned aggregate expenditure (AE).

$$\text{Equilibrium: } Y = AE$$

Because AE is, by definition, $C + I$, equilibrium can also be written:

$$\text{Equilibrium: } Y = C + I$$

It will help in understanding the equilibrium concept to consider what happens if the economy is out of equilibrium. First, suppose aggregate output is greater than planned aggregate expenditure:

$$Y > C + I$$

aggregate output > planned aggregate expenditure

When output is greater than planned spending, there is unplanned inventory investment. Firms planned to sell more of their goods than they sold, and the difference shows up as an unplanned increase in inventories. Next, suppose planned aggregate expenditure is greater than aggregate output:

$$C + I > Y$$

planned aggregate expenditure > aggregate output

When planned spending exceeds output, firms have sold more than they planned to. Inventory investment is smaller than planned. Planned and actual investment are not equal. Only when output is exactly matched by planned spending will there be no unplanned inventory investment. If there is unplanned inventory investment, this will be a state of disequilibrium. The mechanism by which the economy returns to equilibrium will be discussed later. Equilibrium in the goods market is achieved only when aggregate output (Y) and planned aggregate expenditure ($C + I$) are equal, or when actual and planned investment are equal.

Table 8.1 derives a planned aggregate expenditure schedule and shows the point of equilibrium for our numerical example. I is assumed to be fixed and equal to 25 for

planned aggregate expenditure (AE) The total amount the economy plans to spend in a given period. Equal to consumption plus planned investment: $AE \equiv C + I$

TABLE 8.1 Deriving the Planned Aggregate Expenditure Schedule and Finding Equilibrium.*

(1) Aggregate Output (Income) (Y)	(2) Aggregate Consumption (C)	(3) Planned Investment (I)	(4) Planned Aggregate Expenditure (AE) C + I	(5) Unplanned Inventory Change Y − (C + I)	(6) Equilibrium? (Y = AE?)
100	175	25	200	−100	No
200	250	25	275	−75	No
400	400	25	425	−25	No
500	475	25	500	0	Yes
600	550	25	575	+25	No
800	700	25	725	+75	No
1,000	850	25	875	+125	No

*The figures in column 2 are based on the equation $C = 100 + 0.75Y$.

these calculations. Remember that I depends on the interest rate, but the interest rate is fixed for purposes of this chapter. Remember also that all our calculations are based on $C = 100 + 0.75Y$. To determine planned aggregate expenditure, we add consumption spending (C) to planned investment spending (I) at every level of income. Glancing down columns 1 and 4, we see one and only one level at which aggregate output and planned aggregate expenditure are equal: $Y = 500$.

Figure 8.6 illustrates the same equilibrium graphically. Figure 8.6a adds planned investment, fixed at 25, to consumption at every level of income. Because planned investment is a constant, the planned aggregate expenditure function is simply the consumption function displaced vertically by that constant amount. Figure 8.6b shows the planned aggregate expenditure function with the 45-degree line. The 45-degree line represents all points on the graph where the variables on the horizontal and vertical axes are equal. Any point on the 45-degree line is a potential equilibrium point. The planned aggregate expenditure function crosses the 45-degree line at a single point, where $Y = 500$. (The point at which the two lines cross is sometimes called the *Keynesian cross*.) At that point, $Y = C + I$.

Now let us look at some other levels of aggregate output (income). First, consider $Y = 800$. Is this an equilibrium output? Clearly, it is not. At $Y = 800$, planned aggregate expenditure is 725 (see Table 8.1). This amount is less than aggregate output, which is 800. Because output is greater than planned spending, the difference ends up in inventory as unplanned inventory

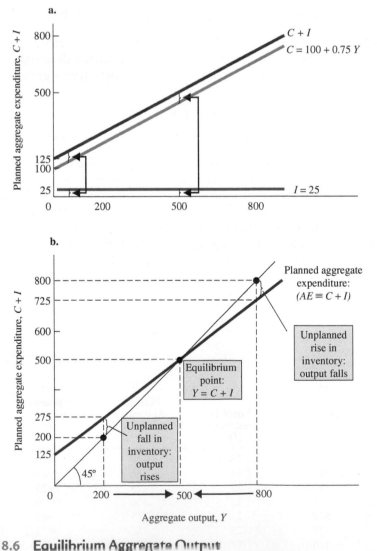

▲ FIGURE 8.6   **Equilibrium Aggregate Output**
Equilibrium occurs when planned aggregate expenditure and aggregate output are equal. Planned aggregate expenditure is the sum of consumption spending and planned investment spending.

investment. In this case, unplanned inventory investment is 75. In the aggregate, firms have more inventory than desired. As a result, firms have an incentive to change their production plans going forward. In this sense, the economy will not be in equilibrium.

Next, consider $Y = 200$. Is this an equilibrium output? No. At $Y = 200$, planned aggregate expenditure is 275. Planned spending (AE) is greater than output (Y), and there is an unplanned fall in inventory investment of 75. Again, firms in the aggregate will experience a different result from what they expected.

At $Y = 200$ and $Y = 800$, planned investment and actual investment are unequal. There is unplanned investment, and the system is out of balance. Only at $Y = 500$, where planned aggregate expenditure and aggregate output are equal, will planned investment equal actual investment.

Finally, let us find the equilibrium level of output (income) algebraically. Recall that we know the following:

$$Y = C + I \qquad \text{(equilbrium)}$$
$$C = 100 + 0.75Y \quad \text{(consumption function)}$$
$$I = 25 \qquad \text{(planned investment)}$$

By substituting the second and third equations into the first, we get:

$$Y = \underbrace{100 + 0.75\,Y}_{C} + \underbrace{25.}_{I}$$

There is only one value of Y for which this statement is true, and we can find it by rearranging terms:

$$Y - 0.75Y = 100 + 25$$
$$0.25Y = 125$$
$$Y = \frac{125}{0.25} = 500$$

The equilibrium level of output is 500, as shown in Table 8.1 and Figure 8.6.

The Saving/Investment Approach to Equilibrium

Because aggregate income must be saved or spent, by definition, $Y \equiv C + S$, which is an identity. The equilibrium condition is $Y = C + I$, but this is not an identity because it does not hold when we are out of equilibrium.[3] By substituting $C + S$ for Y in the equilibrium condition, we can write:

$$C + S = C + I$$

Because we can subtract C from both sides of this equation, we are left with:

$$S = I$$

Thus, only when planned investment equals saving will there be equilibrium.

Figure 8.7 reproduces the saving schedule derived in Figure 8.4 and the horizontal investment function from Figure 8.6. Notice that $S = I$ at one and only one level of aggregate output, $Y = 500$. At $Y = 500$, $C = 475$ and $I = 25$. At this level of Y, saving equals 25 and so $S = I$ and we are at an equilibrium.

---

[3] It would be an identity if I included unplanned inventory accumulations—in other words, if I were actual investment instead of planned investment.

▶ FIGURE 8.7 **The S = I Approach to Equilibrium**
Aggregate output is equal to planned aggregate expenditure only when saving equals planned investment (S = I). Saving and planned investment are equal at Y = 500.

Adjustment to Equilibrium

We have defined equilibrium and learned how to find it, but we have said nothing about how firms might react to *disequilibrium*. Let us consider the actions firms might take when planned aggregate expenditure exceeds aggregate output (income).

We already know the only way firms can sell more than they produce is by selling some inventory. This means that when planned aggregate expenditure exceeds aggregate output, unplanned inventory reductions have occurred. Firms have sold more than they planned. It seems reasonable to assume that firms will respond to unplanned inventory reductions by increasing output. If firms increase output, income must also increase. (Output and income are two ways of measuring the same thing.) As GM builds more cars, it hires more workers (or pays its existing workforce for working more hours), buys more steel, uses more electricity, and so on. These purchases by GM represent income for the producers of labor, steel, electricity, and so on. When firms try to keep their inventories stable by increasing production, this will generate more income in the economy as a whole. This will lead to more consumption. Remember, when income rises, so does consumption. The adjustment process will continue as long as output (income) is below planned aggregate expenditure. If firms react to unplanned inventory reductions by increasing output, an economy with planned spending greater than output will adjust to equilibrium, with Y higher than before.

If planned spending is less than output, there will be unplanned increases in inventories. In this case, firms will respond by reducing output. As output falls, income falls, consumption falls, and so on, until equilibrium is restored, with Y lower than before.

As Figure 8.6 shows, at any level of output above Y = 500, such as Y = 800, output will fall until it reaches equilibrium at Y = 500, and at any level of output below Y = 500, such as Y = 200, output will rise until it reaches equilibrium at Y = 500.[4]

8.5 LEARNING OBJECTIVE

Describe the multiplier process and use the multiplier equation to calculate changes in equilibrium.

The Multiplier

We are now ready to answer the question posed at the beginning of this chapter: What happens to the level of real output if all of the managers in the economy suddenly decide to increase planned investment from, say, 25 to 50? It may surprise you to learn that the change in equilibrium output will be *greater* than the initial change in planned investment. In fact, output will change by a multiple of the change in planned investment.

---

[4] In discussing simple supply and demand equilibrium in Chapters 3 and 4, we saw that when quantity supplied exceeds quantity demanded, the price falls and the quantity supplied declines. Similarly, when quantity demanded exceeds quantity supplied, the price rises and the quantity supplied increases. In the analysis here, we are ignoring potential changes in prices or in the price level and focusing on changes in the level of real output (income). Later, after we have introduced money and the price level into the analysis, prices will be important. At this stage, however, only aggregate output (income) (Y) adjusts when aggregate expenditure exceeds aggregate output (with inventory falling) or when aggregate output exceeds aggregate expenditure (with inventory rising).

ECONOMICS IN PRACTICE

General Motors' Silverado

We have indicated in the text that a change in inventories is a component of firm investment. For an automobile firm, the size of its inventory of cars and trucks is large. For example, for General Motors the ratio of sales to inventory (also called the Inventory Turnover ratio) in normal times is between 9 and 10. Contrast this with Google, which had an Inventory Turnover ratio of 75! To run its business, Google needs little inventory. This should not surprise you because Google is a software company. In the case of cars, we have a physical product, produced in large volumes for cost efficiencies and distributed through a massive dealership network located all over the world. If Google gets a new customer, it can serve that client instantly. For GM, a large stock of inventories is needed to make sure the right car or truck is in the right place when customers call.

Given how important inventories are in the auto industry, it is an interesting place to look at what happens when we have unplanned inventories. As we know from the data we have looked at, the United States was hit by a large recession in late 2008. This recession hit the auto makers hard; indeed GM entered bankruptcy shortly thereafter. By 2011, many business people expected a recovery and the lead executives at the then- reorganized GM were among them. In anticipation of new business, GM increased its production of its most profitable pickup truck, the Silverado. As we have seen previously, however, 2011 did not bring a strong recovery. The consequence for GM? By mid-2011 there were more than 280,000 Silverados at dealerships throughout the country, an inventory level equivalent to 122 days of sales. The normal inventory levels for trucks are about 90 days of sales. In short, GM experienced a large unplanned increase in inventories.

What did GM do? It should not surprise you to learn that in the next Christmas period, plants producing the Silverado were shuttered for three weeks rather than the usual two, as GM cut its production levels. Unplanned inventories created disequilbrium to which the GM executives responded by production cutbacks.

THINKING PRACTICALLY

1. Do you expect inventory turns for the average firm in the economy to increase or decrease as we enter a recession?

The **multiplier** is defined as the ratio of the change in the equilibrium level of output to a change in some exogenous variable. An **exogenous variable** is a variable that does not depend on the state of the economy—that is, a variable is exogenous if it does not change in response to changes in the economy. In this chapter, we treat planned investment as exogenous. This simplifies our analysis and provides a foundation for later discussions.

With planned investment exogenous, we can ask how much the equilibrium level of output changes when planned investment changes. Remember that we are not trying to explain *why* planned investment changes; we are simply asking how much the equilibrium level of output changes when (for whatever reason) planned investment changes. (Beginning in Chapter 11, we will no longer take planned investment as given and will explain how planned investment is determined.)

Consider a sustained increase in planned investment of 25—that is, suppose I increases from 25 to 50 and stays at 50. If equilibrium existed at $I = 25$, an increase in planned investment of 25 will cause a disequilibrium, with planned aggregate expenditure greater than aggregate output by 25. Firms immediately see unplanned reductions in their inventories. As a result, firms begin to increase output.

Let us say the increase in planned investment comes from an anticipated increase in world travel that comes, for example, from a decision by a major world power to lift restrictions on its citizen's ability to travel. This increase in expected travel demand leads airlines to purchase more

multiplier The ratio of the change in the equilibrium level of output to a change in some exogenous variable.

exogenous variable A variable that is assumed not to depend on the state of the economy—that is, it does not change when the economy changes.

airplanes, car rental companies to increase purchases of automobiles, and bus companies to purchase more buses (all capital goods). The firms experiencing unplanned inventory declines will be automobile manufacturers, bus producers, and aircraft producers—GM, Ford, Boeing, and so on. In response to declining inventories of planes, buses, and cars, these firms will increase output.

Now suppose these firms raise output by the full 25 increase in planned investment. Does this restore equilibrium? No, it does not because when output goes up, people earn more income and a part of that income will be spent. This increases planned aggregate expenditure even further. In other words, an increase in I also leads indirectly to an increase in C. To produce more airplanes, Boeing has to hire more workers or ask its existing employees to work more hours. It also must buy more engines from General Electric, more tires from Goodyear, and so on. Owners of these firms will earn more profits, produce more, hire more workers, and pay out more in wages and salaries. This added income does not vanish into thin air. It is paid to households that spend some of it and save the rest. The added production leads to added income, which leads to added consumption spending.

If planned investment (I) goes up by 25 initially *and is sustained at this higher level*, an increase of output of 25 will *not* restore equilibrium because it generates even more consumption spending (C). People buy more consumer goods. There are unplanned reductions of inventories of basic consumption items—washing machines, food, clothing, and so on—and this prompts other firms to increase output. The cycle starts all over again.

Output and income can rise significantly more than the initial increase in planned investment, but how much and how large is the multiplier? This is answered graphically in Figure 8.8. Assume that the economy is in equilibrium at point A, where equilibrium output is 500. The increase in I of 25 shifts the $AE \equiv C + I$ curve up by 25 because I is higher by 25 at every level of income. The new equilibrium occurs at point B, where the equilibrium level of output is 600. Like point A, point B is on the 45-degree line and is an equilibrium value. Output (Y) has increased by 100 (600–500), or four times the initial increase in planned investment of 25, between point A and point B. The multiplier in this example is 4. At point B, aggregate spending is also higher by 100. If 25 of this additional 100 is investment (I), as we know it is, the remaining 75 is added consumption (C). From point A to point B then, $\Delta Y = 100$, $\Delta I = 25$, and $\Delta C = 75$.

Why doesn't the multiplier process go on forever? The answer is that only a fraction of the increase in income is consumed in each round. Successive increases in income become smaller

▶ **FIGURE 8.8** **The Multiplier as Seen in the Planned Aggregate Expenditure Diagram**
At point A, the economy is in equilibrium at $Y = 500$. When I increases by 25, planned aggregate expenditure is initially greater than aggregate output. As output rises in response, additional consumption is generated, pushing equilibrium output up by a multiple of the initial increase in I. The new equilibrium is found at point B, where $Y = 600$. Equilibrium output has increased by 100 (600 − 500), or *four times* the amount of the increase in planned investment.

and smaller in each round of the multiplier process because of leakage as saving, until equilibrium is restored.

The size of the multiplier depends on the slope of the planned aggregate expenditure line. The steeper the slope of this line, the greater the change in output for a given change in investment. When planned investment is fixed, as in our example, the slope of the $AE \equiv C + I$ line is just the marginal propensity to consume ($\Delta C / \Delta Y$). The greater the MPC, the greater the multiplier. This should not be surprising. A large MPC means that consumption increases a great deal when income increases.

The Multiplier Equation

Is there a way to determine the size of the multiplier without using graphic analysis? Yes, there is.

Assume that the market is in equilibrium at an income level of $Y = 500$. Now suppose planned investment (*I*)—thus, planned aggregate expenditure (*AE*)—increases and remains higher by 25. Planned aggregate expenditure is greater than output, there is an unplanned inventory reduction, and firms respond by increasing output (income) (*Y*). This leads to a second round of increases, and so on.

What will restore equilibrium? Look at Figure 8.7 and recall: Planned aggregate expenditure ($AE \equiv C + I$) is not equal to aggregate output (*Y*) unless $S = I$; the leakage of saving must exactly match the injection of planned investment spending for the economy to be in equilibrium. Recall also that we assumed that planned investment jumps to a new, higher level and stays there; it is a *sustained* increase of 25 in planned investment spending. As income rises, consumption rises and so does saving. Our $S = I$ approach to equilibrium leads us to conclude that equilibrium will be restored only when saving has increased by exactly the amount of the initial increase in *I*. Otherwise, *I* will continue to be greater than *S* and $C + I$ will continue to be greater than *Y*. (The $S = I$ approach to equilibrium leads to an interesting paradox in the macro-economy. See the *Economics in Practice*, "The Paradox of Thrift" on the next page.)

It is possible to figure how much *Y* must increase in response to the additional planned investment before equilibrium will be restored. *Y* will rise, pulling *S* up with it until the change in saving is exactly equal to the change in planned investment—that is, until *S* is again equal to *I* at its new higher level. Because added saving is a *fraction* of added income (the MPS), the increase in *income* required to restore equilibrium must be a *multiple* of the increase in planned investment.

Recall that the marginal propensity to save (MPS) is the fraction of a change in income that is saved. It is defined as the change in S (ΔS) over the change in income (ΔY):

$$MPS = \frac{\Delta S}{\Delta Y}$$

Because ΔS must be equal to ΔI for equilibrium to be restored, we can substitute ΔI for ΔS and solve:

$$MPS = \frac{\Delta I}{\Delta Y}$$

Therefore,

$$\Delta Y = \Delta I \times \frac{1}{MPS}$$

As you can see, the change in equilibrium income (ΔY) is equal to the initial change in planned investment (ΔI) times $1/MPS$. The multiplier is $1/MPS$:

$$\text{multiplier} \equiv \frac{1}{MPS}$$

ECONOMICS IN PRACTICE

The Paradox of Thrift

An interesting paradox can arise when households attempt to increase their saving. What happens if households become concerned about the future and want to save more today to be prepared for hard times tomorrow? If households increase their planned saving, the saving schedule in the graph below shifts upward from S_0 to S_1. The plan to save more is a plan to consume less, and the resulting drop in spending leads to a drop in income. Income drops by a multiple of the initial shift in the saving schedule. Before the increase in saving, equilibrium exists at point A, where $S_0 = I$ and $Y = 500$. Increased saving shifts the equilibrium to point B, the point at which $S_1 = I$. New equilibrium output is 300—a decrease of 200 (ΔY) from the initial equilibrium.

By consuming less, households have actually *caused* the hard times about which they were apprehensive. Worse, the new equilibrium finds saving at the same level as it was before consumption dropped (25). In their attempt to save more, households have caused a contraction in output, and thus in income. They end up consuming less, but they have not saved any more.

It should be clear why saving at the new equilibrium is equal to saving at the old equilibrium. Equilibrium requires that saving equals planned investment, and because planned investment is unchanged, saving must remain unchanged for equilibrium to exist. This paradox shows that the interactions among sectors in the economy can be of crucial importance.

The paradox of thrift is "paradoxical" because it contradicts the widely held belief that "a penny saved is a penny earned." This may be true for an individual, but when society as a whole saves more, the result is a drop in income but no increased saving.

Does the paradox of thrift always hold? Recall our assumption that the interest rate is fixed. If the extra saving that the households want to do to ward off hard times leads to a fall in the interest rate, this will increase planned investment and thus shift up the I schedule in the figure. The paradox might then be avoided. Planned investment could increase enough so that the new equilibrium occurs at a higher level of income (and saving).

THINKING PRACTICALLY

1. Draw a consumption function corresponding to S_0 and S_1 and describe what is happening.

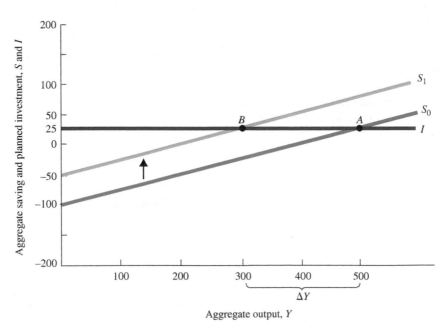

The Paradox of Thrift

An increase in planned saving from S_0 to S_1 causes equilibrium output to decrease from 500 to 300. The decreased consumption that accompanies increased saving leads to a contraction of the economy and to a reduction of income. But at the new equilibrium, saving is the same as it was at the initial equilibrium. Increased efforts to save have caused a drop in income but no overall change in saving.

Because $MPS + MPC \equiv 1$, $MPS \equiv 1 - MPC$. It follows that the multiplier is also equal to

$$\text{multiplier} \equiv \frac{1}{1 - MPC}$$

In our example, the MPC is .75; so the MPS must equal $1 - 0.75$, or 0.25. Thus, the multiplier is 1 divided by .25, or 4. The change in the equilibrium level of Y is 4 $\times$ 25, or 100.[5] Also note that the same analysis holds when planned investment falls. If planned investment falls by a certain amount and is sustained at this lower level, output will fall by a multiple of the reduction in I. As the initial shock is felt and firms cut output, they lay people off. The result: Income, and subsequently consumption, falls.

The Size of the Multiplier in the Real World

In considering the size of the multiplier, it is important to realize that the multiplier we derived in this chapter is based on a *very* simplified picture of the economy. First, we have assumed that planned investment is exogenous and does not respond to changes in the economy. Second, we have thus far ignored the role of government, financial markets, and the rest of the world in the macroeconomy. For these reasons, it would be a mistake to move on from this chapter thinking that national income can be increased by $100 billion simply by increasing planned investment spending by $25 billion. Nevertheless, even this simple model should give you some intuition as to why and how national income responds to increases in planned investment.

As we relax these assumptions in the following chapters, you will see that most of what we add to make our analysis more realistic has the effect of *reducing* the size of the multiplier. For example:

1. The Appendix to Chapter 9 shows that when tax payments depend on income (as they do in the real world), the size of the multiplier is reduced. As the economy expands, tax payments increase and act as a drag on the economy. The multiplier effect is smaller.
2. We will see in Chapter 11 that adding Fed behavior regarding the interest rate has the effect of reducing the size of the multiplier.
3. We will also see in Chapter 11 that adding the price level to the analysis reduces the size of the multiplier. We will see that part of an expansion of the economy is likely to take the form of an increase in the price level instead of an increase in real output. When this happens, the size of the multiplier is reduced.
4. The multiplier is also reduced when imports are introduced (in Chapter 19) because some domestic spending leaks into foreign markets.

These juicy tidbits give you something to look forward to as you proceed through the rest of this book. For now, however, it is enough to point out that in reality the size of the multiplier is probably about 2. This is much lower than the value of 4 that we used in this chapter but still tells us that an increase in planned investment has more of an effect than you might have expected before beginning this chapter!

Looking Ahead

In this chapter, we took the first step toward understanding how the economy works. We assumed that consumption depends on income, that planned investment is fixed, and that there is equilibrium. We discussed how the economy might adjust back to equilibrium when it is out of equilibrium. We also discussed the effects on equilibrium output from a change in planned investment and derived the multiplier. In the next chapter, we retain these assumptions and add the government to the economy.

---

[5] The multiplier can also be derived algebraically, as the Appendix to this chapter demonstrates.

SUMMARY

8.1 THE KEYNESIAN THEORY OF CONSUMPTION *p. 142*

1. Aggregate consumption is assumed to be a function of aggregate income.

2. The *marginal propensity to consume (MPC)* is the fraction of a change in income that is consumed, or spent. The *marginal propensity to save (MPS)* is the fraction of a change in income that is saved. Because all income must be saved or spent, $MPS + MPC \equiv 1$.

8.2 PLANNED INVESTMENT (*I*) VERSUS ACTUAL INVESTMENT *p. 147*

3. Planned investment may differ from actual investment because of unanticipated changes in inventories.

8.3 PLANNED INVESTMENT AND THE INTEREST RATE (*r*) *p. 147*

4. Planned investment depends on the interest rate, which is taken to be fixed for this chapter.

8.4 THE DETERMINATION OF EQUILIBRIUM OUTPUT (INCOME) *p. 148*

5. *Planned aggregate expenditure (AE)* equals consumption plus planned investment: $AE \equiv C + I$. *Equilibrium* in the goods market is achieved when planned aggregate expenditure equals aggregate output: $C + I = Y$. This holds if and only if planned investment and actual investment are equal.

6. Because aggregate income must be saved or spent, the equilibrium condition $Y = C + I$ can be rewritten as $C + S = C + I$, or $S = I$. Only when planned investment equals saving will there be equilibrium. This approach to equilibrium is the *saving/investment approach* to equilibrium.

7. When planned aggregate expenditure exceeds aggregate output (*income*), there is an unplanned fall in inventories. Firms will increase output. This increased output leads to increased income and even more consumption. This process will continue as long as output (income) is below planned aggregate expenditure. If firms react to unplanned inventory reductions by increasing output, an economy with planned spending greater than output will adjust to a new equilibrium, with Y higher than before.

THE MULTIPLIER *p. 152*

8. Equilibrium output changes by a multiple of the change in planned investment or any other *exogenous variable*. The *multiplier* is equal to $1/MPS$.

9. When households increase their planned saving, income decreases and saving does not change. Saving does not increase because in equilibrium, saving must equal planned investment and planned investment is fixed. If planned investment also increased, this *paradox of thrift* could be averted and a new equilibrium could be achieved at a higher level of saving and income. This result depends on the existence of a channel through which additional household saving finances additional investment.

REVIEW TERMS AND CONCEPTS

actual investment, *p. 147*

aggregate income, *p. 141*

aggregate output, *p. 141*

aggregate output (income) (*Y*), *p. 141*

aggregate saving (*S*), *p. 143*

consumption function, *p. 142*

equilibrium, *p. 148*

exogenous variable, *p. 153*

identity, *p. 143*

marginal propensity to consume (MPC), *p. 143*

marginal propensity to save (MPS), *p. 143*

multiplier, *p. 153*

planned aggregate expenditure (AE), *p. 149*

planned investment (*I*), *p. 147*

Equations: $S \equiv Y - C$, *p. 143*

$MPC \equiv$ slope of consumption

function $\equiv \dfrac{\Delta C}{\Delta Y}$, *p. 143*

$MPC + MPS \equiv 1$, *p. 144*

$AE \equiv C + I$, *p. 149*

Equilibrium condition: $Y = AE$ or $Y = C + I$, *p. 149*

Saving/investment approach to equilibrium: $S = I$, *p. 151*

Multiplier $\equiv \dfrac{1}{MPS} \equiv \dfrac{1}{1 - MPC}$, *p. 155*

PROBLEMS

All problems are available on MyEconLab.

8.1 THE KEYNESIAN THEORY OF CONSUMPTION

LEARNING OBJECTIVE: Explain the principles of the Keynesian theory of consumption.

1.1 Briefly define the following terms and explain the relationship between MPC and MPS and the relationship between aggregate output and aggregate income.
   a. MPC
   b. MPS
   c. Aggregate output
   d. Aggregate income

1.2 Fill in the aggregate saving column in the following table. Use the data in the table to calculate the consumption function and the saving function, and plot these functions as well as the 45-degree line on a graph. What are the values for the MPC and the MPS?

Aggregate Income, Y	Aggregate Consumption, C	Aggregate Saving, S
$ 0	$200	
100	250	
200	300	
300	350	
400	400	
500	450	
600	500	

1.3 [**Related to the *Economics in Practice* on p. 146**] The *Economics in Practice* describes some of the difficulties that households have with regard to decisions involving trade-offs between the present and the future. Explain briefly how the problem of global warming and the problem of adequate household saving are similar. Describe ways in which the concept of opportunity cost can be used to frame these two problems. What barriers might prevent households or societies from achieving satisfactory outcomes?

1.4 Assume in a simple economy that the level of saving is −800 when aggregate output equals zero and that the marginal propensity to save is 0.25. Derive the saving function and the consumption function, and draw a graph showing these functions. At what level of aggregate output does the consumption curve cross the 45-degree line? Explain your answer and show this on the graph.

8.2 PLANNED INVESTMENT (I) VERSUS ACTUAL INVESTMENT

LEARNING OBJECTIVE: Explain the difference between planned investment and actual investment.

2.1 Explain the difference between actual investment and planned investment. When are actual investment and planned investment equal? When is actual investment greater than planned investment? When is actual investment less than planned investment?

2.2 Suppose that in the year 2015, Oceanaire, Inc. planned to produce 500,000 units of its lightweight scuba tanks. Of the 500,000 it planned to produce, a total of 50,000 units would be added to the inventory at its new plant in Arizona. Also assume that these units have been selling at a price of $250 each and that the price has been constant over time. Suppose further that this year the firm built a new plant for $20 million and acquired $5 million worth of equipment. It had no other investment projects, and to avoid complications, assume no depreciation.

   Now suppose that at the end of the year, Oceanaire had produced 500,000 units but had only sold 400,000 units and that inventories now contained 100,000 units more than they had at the beginning of the year. At $250 each, that means that the firm added $25,000,000 in new inventory.
   a. How much did Oceanaire actually invest this year?
   b. How much did it plan to invest?
   c. Would Oceanaire produce more or fewer units next year? Why?

8.3 PLANNED INVESTMENT AND THE INTEREST RATE (r)

LEARNING OBJECTIVE: Understand how planned investment is affected by the interest rate.

3.1 Explain whether you agree or disagree with the following statement: "All else equal, businesses will generally plan more investment projects when interest rates rise, because higher interest rates mean businesses will earn more on those investments."

8.4 THE DETERMINATION OF EQUILIBRIUM OUTPUT (INCOME)

LEARNING OBJECTIVE: Explain how equilibrium output is determined.

4.1 The following data are estimates for the small island nation of Kaboom

Real GNP (Y...................... 800 million Kaboomian dollars
Planned investment spending) .... 200 million Kaboomian dollars

Kaboom is a simple economy with no government, no taxes, and no imports or exports. Kaboomers (citizens of Kaboom) are creatures of habit. They have a rule that everyone saves exactly 40 percent of income. Assume that planned investment is fixed and remains at 200 million Kaboomian dollars.

You are asked by the business editor of the *Explosive Times*, the local newspaper, to predict the economic events of the next few months. By using the data given, can you make a forecast? What is likely to happen to inventories? What is likely to happen to the level of real GDP? Is the economy at an equilibrium? When will things stop changing?

4.2 Go to www.commerce.gov. Click on "Bureau of Economic Analysis." Click next on "National" and then on the latest GDP release. Look through the report. Which of the components of aggregate expenditure appear to be growing or falling the fastest? What story can you tell about the current economic events from the data?

4.3 The following questions refer to this table:

Aggregate Output/Income	Consumption	Planned Investment
1,000	1,500	250
1,500	1,875	250
2,000	2,250	250
2,500	2,625	250
3,000	3,000	250
3,500	3,375	250
4,000	3,750	250
4,500	4,125	250

a. At each level of output, calculate saving. At each level of output, calculate unplanned investment (inventory change). What is likely to happen to aggregate output if the economy produces at each of the levels indicated? What is the equilibrium level of output?

b. Over each range of income (1,000 to 1,500, 1,500 to 2,000, and so on), calculate the marginal propensity to consume. Calculate the marginal propensity to save. What is the multiplier?

c. By assuming there is no change in the level of the *MPC* and the *MPS* and planned investment jumps by 125 and is sustained at that higher level, recompute the table. What is the new equilibrium level of *Y*? Is this consistent with what you compute using the multiplier?

4.4 This chapter argues that saving and spending behavior depend in part on wealth (accumulated savings and inheritance), but our simple model does not incorporate this effect. Consider the following model of a simple economy: $C = 50 + 0.8Y + 0.1W$

$$I = 200$$
$$W = 500$$
$$Y = C + I$$
$$S = Y - C$$

If you assume that wealth (*W*) and investment (*I*) remain constant (we are ignoring the fact that saving adds to the stock of wealth), what are the equilibrium levels of GDP (*Y*), consumption (*C*), and saving (*S*)? Now suppose that wealth increases by 100 percent to 1,000. Recalculate

the equilibrium levels of *Y*, *C*, and *S*. What impact does wealth accumulation have on GDP? Many were concerned with the large increase in stock values in the late 1990s. Does this present a problem for the economy? Explain.

4.5 You are given the following data concerning Freedonia, a legendary country:
(1) Consumption function: $C = 200 + 0.8Y$
(2) Investment function: $I = 100$
(3) $AE \equiv C + I$
(4) $AE = Y$
a. What is the marginal propensity to consume in Freedonia, and what is the marginal propensity to save?
b. Graph equations (3) and (4) and solve for equilibrium income.
c. Suppose equation (2) is changed to (2′) $I = 110$. What is the new equilibrium level of income? By how much does the $10 increase in planned investment change equilibrium income? What is the value of the multiplier?
d. Calculate the saving function for Freedonia. Plot this saving function on a graph with equation (2). Explain why the equilibrium income in this graph must be the same as in part b.

8.5 THE MULTIPLIER

LEARNING OBJECTIVE: Describe the multiplier process and use the multiplier equation to calculate changes in equilibrium.

5.1 Explain the multiplier intuitively. Why is it that an increase in planned investment of $100 raises equilibrium output by more than $100? Why is the effect on equilibrium output finite? How do we know that the multiplier is 1/*MPS*?

5.2 [**Related to the *Economics in Practice* on p. 156**] If households decide to save more, saving in the aggregate may fall. Explain this in words.

5.3 Use the graph to answer the questions that follow.

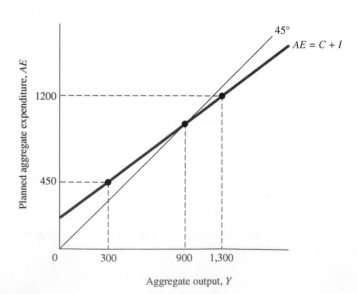

a. What is the value of the MPC?
b. What is the value of the MPS?
c. What is the value of the multiplier?
d. What is the amount of unplanned investment at aggregate output of 300, 900, and 1,300?

5.4 According to the Bureau of Economic Analysis, during the recession of 2008–2009, household saving as a fraction of disposable personal income increased from a low of just over 1 percent in the first quarter of 2008 to 5 percent in the second quarter of 2009. All else equal, what impact would this change in saving have on the MPC, MPS, and multiplier? How would this change affect equilibrium output when planned investment changes?

CHAPTER 8 APPENDIX

Deriving the Multiplier Algebraically

LEARNING OBJECTIVE

Show that the multiplier is 1 divided by 1 minus the MPC.

In addition to deriving the multiplier using the simple substitution we used in the chapter, we can also derive the formula for the multiplier by using simple algebra.

Recall that our consumption function is:

$$C = a + bY$$

where b is the marginal propensity to consume. In equilibrium:

$$Y = C + I$$

Now we solve these two equations for Y in terms of I. By substituting the first equation into the second, we get:

$$Y = \underbrace{a + bY}_{C} + I$$

This equation can be rearranged to yield:

$$Y - bY = a + I$$
$$Y(1 - b) = a + I$$

We can then solve for Y in terms of I by dividing through by $(I - b)$:

$$Y = (a + I)\left(\frac{1}{1 - b}\right)$$

Now look carefully at this expression and think about increasing I by some amount, ΔI, with a held constant. If I increases by ΔI, income will increase by

$$\Delta Y = \Delta I \times \frac{1}{1 - b}$$

Because $b \equiv MPC$, the expression becomes

$$\Delta Y = \Delta I \times \frac{1}{1 - MPC}$$

The multiplier is

$$\frac{1}{1 - MPC}$$

Finally, because $MPS + MPC = 1$, MPS is equal to $1 - MPC$, making the alternative expression for the multiplier $1/MPS$, just as we saw in this chapter.

9

The Government and Fiscal Policy

There is considerable debate over what the government can and should do in managing the macroeconomy. At one end of the spectrum are the Keynesians and their intellectual descendants who believe that the macroeconomy is likely to fluctuate too much if left on its own and that the government should smooth out fluctuations in the business cycle. These ideas can be traced to Keynes's analysis in *The General Theory*, which suggests that governments can use their taxing and spending powers to increase aggregate expenditure (and thereby stimulate aggregate output) in recessions or depressions. At the other end of the spectrum are those who claim that government spending is incapable of stabilizing the economy, or worse, is destabilizing and harmful. In this chapter, we turn to this set of questions.

The government has a variety of powers—including regulating firms' entry into and exit from an industry, setting standards for product quality, setting minimum wage levels, and regulating the disclosure of information—but in macroeconomics, we focus on two policy instruments: fiscal policy and monetary policy. **Fiscal policy**, the focus of this chapter, refers to the government's spending and taxing behavior—in other words, its budget policy. (The word *fiscal* comes from the root *fisc*, which refers to the "treasury" of a government.) Fiscal policy is generally divided into three categories: (1) policies concerning government purchases of goods and services, (2) policies concerning taxes, and (3) policies concerning transfer payments (such as unemployment compensation, Social Security benefits, welfare payments, and veterans' benefits) to households. **Monetary policy**, which we consider in the next chapter, refers to the behavior of the nation's central bank, the Federal Reserve, with respect to the interest rate.

Government in the Economy

Local, state, and federal governments have in some areas considerable control. In many cases, however, the *effect* of government decisions on the economy depends not only on the decision itself but also on the state of the economy. It is important to understand the limits of government control as well as its power. Taxes provide a good example. Tax rates are controlled by the government. By law, Congress has the authority to decide who and what should be taxed and at what rate. Tax *revenue*, on the other hand, is not subject to complete control by the government. Revenue from the personal income tax system depends on personal tax rates (which Congress sets) *and* on the income of the household sector (which depends on many factors not under direct government control, such as how much households decide to work). Revenue from the corporate profits tax depends on both corporate profits tax rates and the size of corporate profits. The government controls corporate tax rates but not the size of corporate profits.

Some government spending also depends on government decisions and on the state of the economy. In the United States, the unemployment insurance program pays benefits to unemployed people. When the economy goes into a recession, the number of unemployed workers increases and so does the level of government unemployment insurance payments. This occurs not because of a change in government decisions but because of the interaction between existing policies and the economy itself.

Because taxes and spending often go up or down in response to changes in the economy instead of as the result of deliberate decisions by policy makers, we will occasionally use **discretionary fiscal policy** to refer to changes in taxes or spending that are the result of deliberate changes in government policy.

9.1 LEARNING OBJECTIVE

Discuss the influence of fiscal policies on the economy.

fiscal policy   The government's spending and taxing policies.

monetary policy   The behavior of the Federal Reserve concerning interest rates.

discretionary fiscal policy   Changes in taxes or spending that are the result of deliberate changes in government policy.

Government Purchases (G), Net Taxes (T), and Disposable Income (Y_d)

We now add the government to the simple economy in Chapter 8. To keep things simple, we will combine two government activities—the collection of taxes and the payment of transfer payments—into a category we call **net taxes (T)**. Specifically, net taxes are equal to the tax payments made to the government by firms and households minus transfer payments made to households by the government. The other variable we will consider is government purchases of goods and services (G).

Our previous discussions of household consumption did not take taxes into account. We assumed that all the income generated in the economy was spent or saved by households. When we take into account the role of government, as Figure 9.1 does, we see that as income (Y) flows toward households, the government takes income from households in the form of net taxes (T). The income that ultimately gets to households is called **disposable, *or* after-tax, income (Y_d)**:

net taxes (T)   Taxes paid by firms and households to the government minus transfer payments made to households by the government.

disposable, *or* after-tax, income (Y_d)   Total income minus net taxes: $Y - T$.

$$\text{disposable income} \equiv \text{total income} - \text{net taxes}$$
$$Y_d \equiv Y - T$$

Y_d excludes taxes paid by households and includes transfer payments made to households by the government. For now, we are assuming that T does not depend on Y—that is, net taxes do not depend on income. This assumption is relaxed in Appendix B to this chapter. Taxes that do not depend on income are sometimes called *lump-sum taxes.*

As Figure 9.1 shows, the disposable income (Y_d) of households must end up as either consumption (C) or saving (S). Thus,

$$Y_d \equiv C + S$$

This equation is an identity—something that is always true.

▶ FIGURE 9.1 **Adding Net Taxes (*T*) and Government Purchases (*G*) to the Circular Flow of Income**

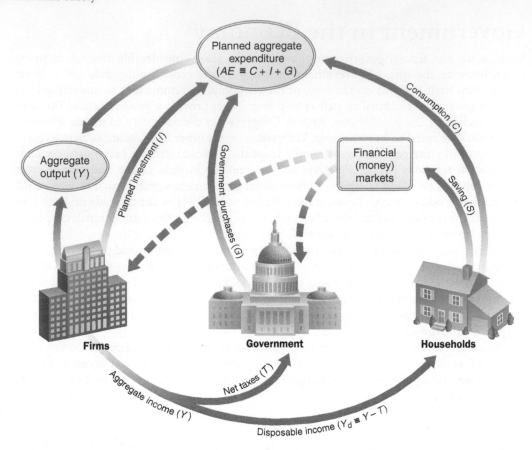

Because disposable income is aggregate income (*Y*) minus net taxes (*T*), we can write another identity:

$$Y - T \equiv C + S$$

By adding *T* to both sides:

$$Y \equiv C + S + T$$

This identity says that aggregate income gets cut into three pieces. Government takes a slice (net taxes, *T*), and then households divide the rest between consumption (*C*) and saving (*S*).

Because governments spend money on goods and services, we need to expand our definition of planned aggregate expenditure. Planned aggregate expenditure (*AE*) is the sum of consumption spending by households (*C*), planned investment by business firms (*I*), *and* government purchases of goods and services (*G*).

$$AE \equiv C + I + G$$

budget deficit The difference between what a government spends and what it collects in taxes in a given period: *G − T*.

A government's **budget deficit** is the difference between what it spends (*G*) and what it collects in taxes (*T*) in a given period:

$$\text{budget deficit} \equiv G - T$$

If *G* exceeds *T*, the government must borrow from the public to finance the deficit. It does so by selling Treasury bonds and bills (more on this later). In this case, a part of household saving (*S*) goes to the government. The dashed lines in Figure 9.1 mean that some household saving goes to firms to finance investment projects and some goes to the government to finance its deficit. If *G* is less than *T*, which means that the government is spending less than it is collecting in taxes, the government is running a *surplus*.

Adding Taxes to the Consumption Function   In Chapter 8, we assumed that aggregate consumption (C) depends on aggregate income (Y), and for the sake of illustration, we used a specific linear consumption function:

$$C = a + bY$$

where b is the marginal propensity to consume. We need to modify this consumption function because we have added government to the economy. With taxes a part of the picture, it makes sense to assume that disposable income (Y_d), instead of before-tax income (Y), determines consumption behavior. If you earn a million dollars but have to pay \$950,000 in taxes, you have no more disposable income than someone who earns only \$50,000 but pays no taxes. What you have available for spending on current consumption is your disposable income, not your before-tax income.

To modify our aggregate consumption function to incorporate disposable income instead of before-tax income, instead of $C = a + bY$, we write

$$C = a + bY_d$$

or

$$C = a + b(Y - T)$$

Our consumption function now has consumption depending on disposable income instead of before-tax income.

Planned Investment   What about planned investment? The government can affect investment behavior through its tax treatment of depreciation and other tax policies. Also, planned investment depends on the interest rate, as discussed in the previous chapter. For purposes of this chapter, we continue to assume that the interest rate is fixed. We will ignore any tax effects on planned investment and thus continue to assume that it is fixed (because the interest rate is fixed).

The Determination of Equilibrium Output (Income)

We know from Chapter 8 that equilibrium occurs where $Y = AE$—that is, where aggregate output equals planned aggregate expenditure. Remember that planned aggregate expenditure in an economy with a government is $AE \equiv C + I + G$, so equilibrium is

$$Y = C + I + G$$

The equilibrium analysis in Chapter 8 applies here also. If output (Y) exceeds planned aggregate expenditure ($C + I + G$), there will be an unplanned increase in inventories—actual investment will exceed planned investment. Conversely, if $C + I + G$ exceeds Y, there will be an unplanned decrease in inventories.

An example will illustrate the government's effect on the macroeconomy and the equilibrium condition. First, our consumption function, $C = 100 + 0.75Y$ before we introduced the government sector, now becomes

$$C = 100 + 0.75Y_d$$

or

$$C = 100 + 0.75(Y - T)$$

Second, we assume that G is 100 and T is 100.[1] In other words, the government is running a balanced budget, financing all of its spending with taxes. Third, we assume that planned investment (I) is 100.

---

[1] As we pointed out previously, the government does not have complete control over tax revenues and transfer payments. We ignore this problem here, however, and set T, tax revenues minus transfers, at a fixed amount. Things will become more realistic later in this chapter and in Appendix B.

TABLE 9.1	Finding Equilibrium for $I = 100$, $G = 100$, and $T = 100$								
(1)	(2)	(3)	(4)	(5)	(6)	(7)	(8)	(9)	(10)
Output (Income) Y	Net Taxes T	Disposable Income $Y_d \equiv Y - T$	Consumption Spending $C = 100 + 0.75Y_d$	Saving S $Y_d - C$	Planned Investment Spending I	Government Purchases G	Planned Aggregate Expenditure $C + I + G$	Unplanned Inventory Change $Y - (C + I + G)$	Adjustment to Disequilibrium
300	100	200	250	−50	100	100	450	−150	Output ↑
500	100	400	400	0	100	100	600	−100	Output ↑
700	100	600	550	50	100	100	750	−50	Output ↑
900	100	800	700	100	100	100	900	0	Equilibrium
1,100	100	1,000	850	150	100	100	1,050	−50	Output ↓
1,300	100	1,200	1,000	200	100	100	1,200	−100	Output ↓
1,500	100	1,400	1,150	250	100	100	1,350	−150	Output ↓

Table 9.1 calculates planned aggregate expenditure at several levels of disposable income. For example, at $Y = 500$, disposable income is $Y - T$, or 400. Therefore, $C = 100 + 0.75(400) = 400$. Assuming that I is fixed at 100 and assuming that G is fixed at 100, planned aggregate expenditure is 600 ($C + I + G = 400 + 100 + 100$). Because output ($Y$) is only 500, planned spending is greater than output by 100. As a result, there is an unplanned inventory decrease of 100, giving firms an incentive to raise output. Thus, output of 500 is below equilibrium.

If $Y = 1,300$, then $Y_d = 1,200$, $C = 1,000$, and planned aggregate expenditure is 1,200. Here planned spending is *less* than output, there will be an unplanned inventory increase of 100, and firms have an incentive to cut back output. Thus, output of 1,300 is above equilibrium. Only when output is 900 are output and planned aggregate expenditure equal, and only at $Y = 900$ does equilibrium exist.

In Figure 9.2, we derive the same equilibrium level of output graphically. First, the consumption function is drawn, taking into account net taxes of 100. The old function was $C = 100 + 0.75Y$. The new function is $C = 100 + 0.75(Y - T)$ or $C = 100 + 0.75(Y - 100)$, rewritten as $C = 100 + 0.75Y - 75$, or $C = 25 + 0.75Y$. For example, consumption at an income of zero is 25 ($C = 25 + 0.75Y = 25 + 0.75(0) = 25$). The marginal propensity to consume has not changed—we assume that it remains 0.75. Note that the consumption function in Figure 9.2 plots the points in columns 1 and 4 of Table 9.1.

Planned aggregate expenditure, recall, adds planned investment to consumption. Now in addition to 100 in investment, we have government purchases of 100. Because I and G are constant at 100 each at all levels of income, we add $I + G = 200$ to consumption at every level of income. The result is the new AE curve. This curve is just a plot of the points in columns 1 and 8 of Table 9.1. The 45-degree line helps us find the equilibrium level of real output, which we already know, is 900. If you examine any level of output above or below 900, you will find disequilibrium. At $Y = 500$, for example, people want to consume 400, which with planned investment of 100 and government purchases of 100, gives planned aggregate expenditure of 600. Output is, however, only 500. Inventories will fall below what was planned, and firms will have an incentive to increase output.

The Saving/Investment Approach to Equilibrium

As in the last chapter, we can also examine equilibrium using the saving/investment approach. Look at the circular flow of income in Figure 9.1. The government takes out net taxes (T) from the flow of income—a leakage—and households save (S) some of their income—also a leakage from the flow of income. The planned spending injections are government purchases (G) and planned investment (I). If leakages ($S + T$) equal planned injections ($I + G$), there is equilibrium:

saving/investment approach to equilibrium: $S + T = I + G$

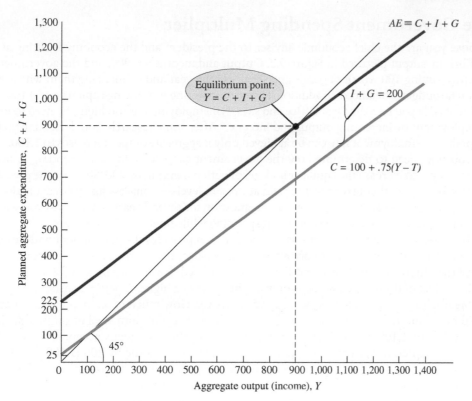

◀ **FIGURE 9.2 Finding Equilibrium Output/ Income Graphically**
Because G and I are both fixed at 100, the aggregate expenditure function is the new consumption function displaced upward by $I + G = 200$. Equilibrium occurs at $Y = C + I + G = 900$.

To derive this, we know that in equilibrium, aggregate output (income) (Y) equals planned aggregate expenditure (AE). By definition, AE equals $C + I + G$, and by definition, Y equals $C + S + T$. Therefore, at equilibrium

$$C + S + T = C + I + G$$

Subtracting C from both sides leaves:

$$S + T = I + G$$

Note that equilibrium does *not* require that $G = T$ (a balanced government budget) or that $S = I$. It is only necessary that the sum of S and T equals the sum of I and G.

Column 5 of Table 9.1 calculates aggregate saving by subtracting consumption from disposal income at every level of disposable income ($S \equiv Y_d - C$). Because I and G are fixed, $I + G$ equals 200 at every level of income. Using the table to add saving and taxes ($S + T$), we see that $S + T$ equals 200 only at $Y = 900$. Thus, the equilibrium level of output (income) is 900, the same answer we arrived at through numerical and graphic analysis.

Fiscal Policy at Work: Multiplier Effects

9.2 LEARNING OBJECTIVE

Describe the effects of three fiscal policy multipliers.

You can see from Figure 9.2 that if the government were able to change the levels of either G or T, it would be able to change the equilibrium level of output (income). At this point, we are assuming that the government controls G and T. In this section, we will review three multipliers:

- Government spending multiplier
- Tax multiplier
- Balanced-budget multiplier

The Government Spending Multiplier

Suppose you are the chief economic adviser to the president and the economy is sitting at the equilibrium output pictured in Figure 9.2. Output and income are 900, and the government is currently buying 100 worth of goods and services each year and is financing them with 100 in taxes. The budget is balanced. In addition, firms are investing (producing capital goods) 100. The president calls you into the Oval Office and says, "Unemployment is too high. We need to lower unemployment by increasing output and income." After some research, you determine that an acceptable unemployment rate can be achieved only if aggregate output increases to 1,100.

You now need to determine how the government can use taxing and spending policy—fiscal policy—to increase the equilibrium level of national output by 200. Suppose the president has let it be known that taxes must remain at present levels—Congress just passed a major tax reform package—so adjusting T is out of the question for several years. That leaves you with G. Your only option is to increase government spending while holding taxes constant.

To increase spending without raising taxes (which provides the government with revenue to spend), the government must borrow. When G is bigger than T, the government runs a deficit and the difference between G and T must be borrowed. For the moment, we will ignore the possible effect of the deficit and focus only on the effect of a higher G with T constant.

Meanwhile, the president is awaiting your answer. How much of an increase in spending would be required to generate an increase of 200 in the equilibrium level of output, pushing it from 900 to 1,100 and reducing unemployment to the president's acceptable level? You might be tempted to say that because we need to increase income by 200 (1,100 − 900), we should increase government spending by the same amount. But what will happen if we raise G by 200? The increased government spending will throw the economy out of equilibrium. Because G is a component of aggregate spending, planned aggregate expenditure will increase by 200. Planned spending will be greater than output, inventories will be lower than planned, and firms will have an incentive to increase output. Suppose output rises by the desired 200. You might think, "We increased spending by 200 and output by 200, so equilibrium is restored."

There is more to the story than this. The moment output rises, the economy is generating more income. This was the desired effect: the creation of more employment. The newly employed workers are also consumers, and some of their income gets spent. With higher consumption spending, planned spending will be greater than output, inventories will be lower than planned, and firms will raise output (and thus raise income) again. This time firms are responding to the new consumption spending. Already, total income is over 1,100.

This story should sound familiar. It is the multiplier in action. Although this time it is government spending (G) that is changed rather than planned investment (I), the effect is the same as the multiplier effect we described in Chapter 8. An increase in government spending has the same impact on the equilibrium level of output and income as an increase in planned investment. A dollar of extra spending from either G or I is identical with respect to its impact on equilibrium output. The equation for the government spending multiplier is the same as the equation for the multiplier for a change in planned investment.

$$\text{government spending multiplier} \equiv \frac{1}{MPS} \equiv \frac{1}{1 - MPC}$$

We derive the government spending multiplier algebraically in Appendix A to this chapter.

Formally, the **government spending multiplier** is defined as the ratio of the change in the equilibrium level of output to a change in government spending. This is the same definition we used in the previous chapter, but now the exogenous variable is government spending instead of planned investment.

Remember that we were thinking of increasing government spending (G) by 200. We can use the multiplier analysis to see what the new equilibrium level of Y would be for an increase in G of 200. The multiplier in our example is 4. (Because b—the MPC—is .75, the MPS must be 1 − 0.75 = 0.25; and 1/(0.25 = 4.) Thus, Y will increase by 800 (4 × 200). Because the initial level of Y was 900, the new equilibrium level of Y is 900 + 800 = 1,700 when G is increased by 200.

government spending multiplier The ratio of the change in the equilibrium level of output to a change in government spending.

TABLE 9.2 Finding Equilibrium after a Government Spending Increase of 50*

(1)	(2)	(3)	(4)	(5)	(6)	(7)	(8)	(9)	(10)
Output (Income) Y	Net Taxes T	Disposable Income $Y_d \equiv Y - T$	Consumption Spending $C = 100 + .75Y_d$	Saving S $Y_d - C$	Planned Investment Spending I	Government Purchases G	Planned Aggregate Expenditure $C + I + G$	Unplanned Inventory Change $Y - (C + I + G)$	Adjustment to Disequilibrium
300	100	200	250	−50	100	150	500	−200	Output ↑
500	100	400	400	0	100	150	650	−150	Output ↑
700	100	600	550	50	100	150	800	−100	Output ↑
900	100	800	700	100	100	150	950	−50	Output ↑
1,100	100	1,000	850	150	100	150	1,100	0	Equilibrium
1,300	100	1,200	1,000	200	100	150	1,250	+50	Output ↓

*G has increased from 100 in Table 9.1 to 150 here.

The level of 1,700 is much larger than the level of 1,100 that we calculated as being necessary to lower unemployment to the desired level. Let us back up then. If we want Y to increase by 200 and if the multiplier is 4, we need G to increase by only $200/4 = 50$. If G increases by 50, the equilibrium level of Y will change by 200 and the new value of Y will be 1,100 (900 + 200), as desired.

Looking at Table 9.2, we can check our answer to make sure it is an equilibrium. Look first at the old equilibrium of 900. When government purchases (G) were 100, aggregate output (income) was equal to planned aggregate expenditure ($AE \equiv C + I + G$) at $Y = 900$. Now G has increased to 150. At $Y = 900$, ($C + I + G$) is greater than Y, there is an unplanned fall in inventories, and output will rise, but by how much? The multiplier told us that equilibrium income would rise by four times the 50 change in G. Y should rise by $4 \times 50 = 200$, from 900 to 1,100, before equilibrium is restored. Let us check. If $Y = 1,100$, consumption is $C = 100 + 0.75Y_d = 100 + 0.75(1,000) = 850$. Because I equals 100 and G now equals 100 (the original level of G) + 50 (the additional G brought about by the fiscal policy change) =150, $C + I + G = 850 + 100 + 150 = 1,100$. $Y = AE$, and the economy is in equilibrium.

The graphic solution to the president's problem is presented in Figure 9.3. An increase of 50 in G shifts the planned aggregate expenditure function up by 50. The new equilibrium income occurs where the new AE line (AE_2) crosses the 45-degree line, at $Y = 1,100$.

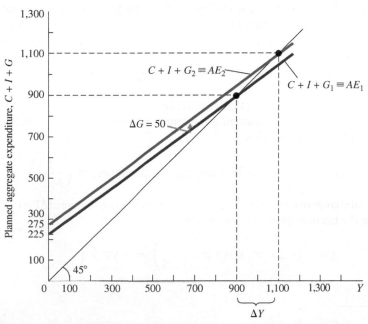

◀ FIGURE 9.3 **The Government Spending Multiplier**

Increasing government spending by 50 shifts the AE function up by 50. As Y rises in response, additional consumption is generated. Overall, the equilibrium level of Y increases by 200, from 900 to 1,100.

The Tax Multiplier

Remember that fiscal policy includes policies concerning government spending *and* policies concerning taxation. To see what effect a change in tax policy has on the economy, imagine the following. You are still chief economic adviser to the president, but now you are instructed to devise a plan to reduce unemployment to an acceptable level *without* increasing the level of government spending. In your plan, instead of increasing government spending (G), you decide to cut taxes and maintain the current level of spending. A tax cut increases disposable income, which is likely to lead to added consumption spending. (Remember our general rule that increased income leads to increased consumption.) Would the decrease in taxes affect aggregate output (income) the same as an increase in G?

A decrease in taxes would certainly increase aggregate output. The government spends no less than it did before the tax cut, and households find that they have a larger after-tax (or disposable) income than they had before. This leads to an increase in consumption. Planned aggregate expenditure will increase, which will lead to inventories being lower than planned, which will lead to more workers being hired to increase output. With more workers employed, more income will be generated, causing a second-round increase in consumption, and so on. Thus, income will increase by a multiple of the decrease in taxes, but there is a "wrinkle." The multiplier for a change in taxes is *not the same* as the multiplier for a change in government spending. Why does the **tax multiplier**—the ratio of change in the equilibrium level of output to a change in taxes—differ from the spending multiplier? To answer that question, we need to compare the ways in which a tax cut and a spending increase work their way through the economy.

tax multiplier The ratio of change in the equilibrium level of output to a change in taxes.

Look at Figure 9.1. When the government increases spending, there is an immediate and direct impact on the economy's *total* spending. Because G is a component of planned aggregate expenditure, an increase in G leads to a dollar-for-dollar increase in planned aggregate expenditure. When taxes are cut, there is no direct impact on spending. Taxes enter the picture only because they have an effect on the household's disposable income, which influences household's consumption (which is part of total spending). As Figure 9.1 shows, the tax cut flows through households before affecting aggregate expenditure.

Let us assume that the government decides to cut taxes by $1. By how much would spending increase? We already know the answer. The marginal propensity to consume (MPC) tells us how much consumption spending changes when disposable income changes. In the example running through this chapter, the marginal propensity to consume out of disposable income is 0.75. This means that if households' after-tax incomes rise by $1.00, they will increase their consumption not by the full $1.00, but by only $0.75.[2]

In summary, when government spending increases by $1, planned aggregate expenditure increases initially by the full amount of the rise in G, or $1. When taxes are cut, however, the initial increase in planned aggregate expenditure is only the MPC times the change in taxes. Because the initial increase in planned aggregate expenditure is smaller for a tax cut than for a government spending increase, the final effect on the equilibrium level of income will also be smaller.

The size of the tax multiplier is calculated in the same way we derived the multiplier for an increase in investment and an increase in government purchases. The final change in the equilibrium level of output (income) (Y) is

$$\Delta Y = \text{(initial increase in aggregate expenditure)} \times \left(\frac{1}{MPS} \right)$$

Because the initial change in aggregate expenditure caused by a tax change of ΔT is $(-\Delta T \times MPC)$, we can solve for the tax multiplier by substitution:

$$\Delta Y = (-\Delta T \times MPC) \times \left(\frac{1}{MPS} \right) = -\Delta T \times \left(\frac{MPC}{MPS} \right)$$

---

[2] What happens to the other $0.25? Remember that whatever households do not consume is, by definition, saved. The other $0.25 thus gets allocated to saving.

Because a tax cut will cause an *increase* in consumption expenditures and output and a tax increase will cause a *reduction* in consumption expenditures and output, the tax multiplier is a negative multiplier:

$$\text{tax multiplier} \equiv -\left(\frac{MPC}{MPS}\right)$$

We derive the tax multiplier algebraically in Appendix A to this chapter.

If the *MPC* is .75, as in our example, the multiplier is $-0.75/0.25 = -3$. A tax cut of 100 will increase the equilibrium level of output by $-100 \times -3 = 300$. This is different from the effect of our government spending multiplier of 4. Under those same conditions, a 50 increase in *G* will increase the equilibrium level of output by 200 (50×4). If we wanted to increase output by 200, we would need a tax cut of 200/3 or 66.67.

The Balanced-Budget Multiplier

We have now discussed (1) changing government spending with no change in taxes and (2) changing taxes with no change in government spending. What if government spending and taxes are increased by the same amount? That is, what if the government decides to pay for its extra spending by increasing taxes by the same amount? The government's budget deficit would not change because the increase in expenditures would be matched by an increase in tax income.

You might think in this case that equal increases in government spending and taxes have no effect on equilibrium income. After all, the extra government spending equals the extra amount of tax revenues collected by the government. This is not so. Take, for example, a government spending increase of $40 billion. We know from the preceding analysis that an increase in *G* of 40, with taxes (*T*) held constant, should increase the equilibrium level of income by $40 \times$ the government spending multiplier. The multiplier is 1/*MPS* or $1/0.25 = 4$. The equilibrium level of income should rise by 160 (40×4).

Now suppose that instead of keeping tax revenues constant, we finance the 40 increase in government spending with an equal increase in taxes so as to maintain a balanced budget. What happens to aggregate spending as a result of the rise in *G* and the rise in *T*? There are two initial effects. First, government spending rises by 40. This effect is direct, immediate, and positive. Now the government also collects 40 more in taxes. The tax increase has a *negative* impact on overall spending in the economy, but it does not fully offset the increase in government spending.

The final impact of a tax increase on aggregate expenditure depends on how households respond to it. The only thing we know about household behavior so far is that households spend 75 percent of their added income and save 25 percent. We know that when disposable income falls, both consumption and saving are reduced. A tax *increase* of 40 reduces disposable income by 40, and that means consumption falls by $40 \times MPC$. Because $MPC = 0.75$, consumption falls by 30 (40×0.75). The net result in the beginning is that government spending rises by 40 and consumption spending falls by 30. Aggregate expenditure increases by 10 right after the simultaneous balanced-budget increases in *G* and *T*.

So a balanced-budget increase in *G* and *T* will raise output, but by how much? How large is this **balanced-budget multiplier?** The answer may surprise you:

$$\text{balanced-budget multiplier} \equiv 1$$

Let us combine what we know about the tax multiplier and the government spending multiplier to explain this. To find the final effect of a simultaneous increase in government spending and increase in net taxes, we need to add the multiplier effects of the two. The government spending multiplier is 1/*MPS*. The tax multiplier is $-MPC/MPS$. Their sum is $(1/MPS) + (-MPC/MPS) \equiv (1 - MPC)/MPS$. Because $MPC + MPS \equiv 1, 1 - MPC \equiv MPS$. This means that $(1 - MPC)/MPS \equiv MPS/MPS \equiv 1$. (We also derive the balanced-budget multiplier in Appendix A to this chapter.)

balanced-budget multiplier
The ratio of change in the equilibrium level of output to a change in government spending where the change in government spending is balanced by a change in taxes so as not to create any deficit. The balanced-budget multiplier is equal to 1: The change in *Y* resulting from the change in *G* and the equal change in *T* is exactly the same size as the initial change in *G* or *T*.

TABLE 9.3 Finding Equilibrium after a Balanced-Budget Increase in G and T of 200 Each*

(1) Output (Income) Y	(2) Net Taxes T	(3) Disposable Income $Y_d = Y - T$	(4) Consumption Spending $C = 100 + 0.75Y_d$	(5) Planned Investment Spending I	(6) Government Purchases G	(7) Planned Aggregate Expenditure $C + I + G$	(8) Unplanned Inventory Change $Y - (C + I + G)$	(9) Adjustment to Disequilibrium
500	300	200	250	100	300	650	−150	Output ↑
700	300	400	400	100	300	800	−100	Output ↑
900	300	600	550	100	300	950	−50	Output ↑
1,100	300	800	700	100	300	1,100	0	Equilibrium
1,300	300	1,000	850	100	300	1,250	+50	Output ↓
1,500	300	1,200	1,000	100	300	1,400	+100	Output ↓

*Both G and T have increased from 100 in Table 9.1 to 300 here.

Returning to our example, recall that by using the government spending multiplier, a 40 increase in G would *raise* output at equilibrium by 160 (40× the government spending multiplier of 4). By using the tax multiplier, we know that a tax hike of 40 will *reduce* the equilibrium level of output by 120 (40 × the tax multiplier, −3). The net effect is 160 minus 120, or 40. It should be clear then that the effect on equilibrium Y is equal to the balanced increase in G and T. In other words, the net increase in the equilibrium level of Y resulting from the change in G and the change in T are exactly the size of the initial change in G or T.

If the president wanted to raise Y by 200 without increasing the deficit, a simultaneous increase in G and T of 200 would do it. To see why, look at the numbers in Table 9.3. In Table 9.1, we saw an equilibrium level of output at 900. With both G and T up by 200, the new equilibrium is 1,100—higher by 200. At no other level of Y do we find (C + I + G) = Y. An increase in government spending has a direct initial effect on planned aggregate expenditure; a tax increase does not. The initial effect of the tax increase is that households cut consumption by the MPC times the change in taxes. This change in consumption is less than the change in taxes because the MPC is less than 1. The positive stimulus from the government spending increase is thus greater than the negative stimulus from the tax increase. The net effect is that the balanced-budget multiplier is 1.

Table 9.4 summarizes everything we have said about fiscal policy multipliers.

A Warning Although we have added government, the story told about the multiplier is still incomplete and oversimplified. For example, we have been treating net taxes (T) as a lump-sum, fixed amount, whereas in practice, taxes depend on income. Appendix B to this chapter shows that the size of the multiplier is reduced when we make the more realistic assumption that taxes depend on income. We continue to add more realism and difficulty to our analysis in the chapters that follow.

TABLE 9.4 Summary of Fiscal Policy Multipliers

	Policy Stimulus	Multiplier	Final Impact on Equilibrium Y
Government spending multiplier	Increase or decrease in the level of government purchases: ΔG	$\dfrac{1}{MPS}$	$\Delta G \times \dfrac{1}{MPS}$
Tax multiplier	Increase or decrease in the level of net taxes: ΔT	$\dfrac{-MPC}{MPS}$	$\Delta T \times \dfrac{-MPC}{MPS}$
Balanced-budget multiplier	Simultaneous balanced-budget increase or decrease in the level of government purchases and net taxes: $\Delta G = \Delta T$	1	ΔG

The Federal Budget

The **federal budget** lists in detail all the things the government plans to spend money on and all the sources of government revenues for the coming year. It therefore describes the government's fiscal policy in granular detail. Of course, the budget is not simply an economic document but is the product of a complex interplay of social, political, and economic forces.

The Budget in 2014

A highly aggregated version of the federal budget is shown in Table 9.5. In 2014, the government had total receipts of $3,300.8 billion, largely from personal income taxes ($1,374.2 billion) and contributions for social insurance ($1,149.4 billion). (Contributions for social insurance are employer and employee Social Security taxes.) Receipts from corporate income taxes accounted for $497.3 billion, or only 15.1 percent of total receipts. Not everyone is aware of the fact that corporate income taxes as a percentage of government receipts are quite small relative to personal income taxes and Social Security taxes.

The federal government also spent $3,883.1 billion in expenditures in 2014. Of this, $1,863.4 billion represented transfer payments to persons (Social Security benefits, military retirement benefits, and unemployment compensation).[3] Consumption ($965.2 billion) was the next-largest component, followed by grants-in-aid given to state and local governments by the federal government ($500.9 billion), and interest payments on the federal debt ($441.3 billion).

The difference between the federal government's receipts and its expenditures is the federal **surplus (+) *or* deficit (−)** , which is federal government saving. Table 9.5 shows that the federal government spent much more than it took in during 2014, resulting in a deficit of $582.3 billion.

9.3 LEARNING OBJECTIVE

Compare and contrast the federal budgets of three U.S. government administrations.

federal budget   The budget of the federal government.

federal surplus (+) *or* (−) deficit   Federal government receipts minus expenditures.

TABLE 9.5   Federal Government Receipts and Expenditures, 2014

	Amount (Billions, $)	Percentage of Total (%)
Current receipts		
Personal income taxes	1,374.2	41.6
Excise taxes and customs duties	134.1	4.1
Corporate income taxes	497.3	15.1
Taxes from the rest of the world	18.9	0.6
Contributions for social insurance	1,149.4	34.8
Interest receipts and rents and royalties	78.1	2.4
Current transfer receipts from business and persons	68.5	2.1
Current surplus of government enterprises	−19.7	−0.6
Total	3,300.8	100.0
Current expenditures		
Consumption expenditures	965.2	9.9
Transfer payments to persons	1,863.4	48.0
Transfer payments to the rest of the world	55.3	1.4
Grants-in-aid to state and local governments	500.9	12.9
Interest payments	441.3	11.4
Subsidies	56.9	1.5
Total	3,883.1	100.0
Net federal government saving–surplus (+) or deficit (−)		
(Total current receipts – Total current expenditures)	−582.3	

Source: Government Receipts and Expenditures First Quarter of 2015 , U.S. Bureau of Economic Analysis, March 27, 2015

MyEconLab Real-time data

---

[3] Remember that there is an important difference between transfer payments and government purchases of goods and services (consumption expenditures). Much of the government budget goes for things that an economist would classify as transfers (payments that are grants or gifts) instead of purchases of goods and services. Only the latter are included in our variable G. Transfers are counted as part of net taxes.

Fiscal Policy since 1993: The Clinton, Bush, and Obama Administrations

Between 1993 and the current edition of this text, the United States has had three different presidents, two Democrats and a Republican. The fiscal policy implemented by each president reflects both the political philosophy of the administration and the differing economic conditions each faced. Figures 9.4, 9.5, and 9.6 trace the fiscal policies of the Clinton (1993–2000), Bush (2001–2008), and first and half of the second Obama administrations (2009–2014).

Figure 9.4 plots total federal personal income taxes as a percentage of total taxable income. This is a graph of the average personal income tax rate. As the figure shows, the average tax rate increased substantially during the Clinton administrations. Much of this increase was the result of a tax bill that was passed in 1993 during the first Clinton administration. The figure then shows the dramatic effects of the tax cuts during the first Bush administration. The large fall in the average tax rate in 2001 III was because of a tax rebate passed after the 9/11 terrorist attacks. Although the average tax rate went back up in 2001 IV, it then fell substantially as the Bush tax cuts began to be felt. The average tax rate remained low during the beginning of the first Obama administration. This was in part due to the large ($787 billion) stimulus bill that was passed in February 2009. The bill consisted of tax cuts and government spending increases, mostly for the 2009–2010 period enacted in response to the recession. In 2011–2012 the average tax rate was somewhat higher than it was in 2009–2010 because of the winding down of the stimulus bill. The average tax rate has continued to rise after 2010, reflecting various tax increases that were passed in this period. The overall tax policy of the federal government is thus clear from Figure 9.4. The average tax rate rose sharply under President Clinton, fell sharply under President Bush, and remained low initially under President Obama before beginning to rise.

Table 9.5 shows that the three most important spending variables of the federal government are consumption expenditures, transfer payments to persons, and grants-in-aid to state and local governments. Consumption expenditures, which are government expenditures on goods and services, are part of GDP. Transfer payments and grants-in-aid are not spending on current output (GDP), but just transfers from the federal government to people and state and local governments. Figure 9.5 plots two spending ratios. One is federal government consumption expenditures as a percentage of GDP, and the other is transfer payments to persons plus grants-in-aid to state and local governments as a percentage of GDP. The figure shows that consumption expenditures as a percentage of GDP generally fell during the Clinton administrations, generally rose during the Bush administrations, and remained high during the first Obama administration. The increase during the Bush administrations reflects primarily the spending on the Iraq war. The initial increase during the Obama administration reflects the effects of the stimulus bill

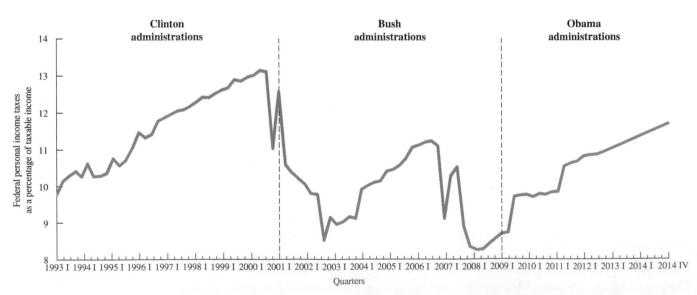

▲ **FIGURE 9.4**   **Federal Personal Income Taxes as a Percentage of Taxable Income, 1993 I–2014 IV**

MyEconLab Real-time data

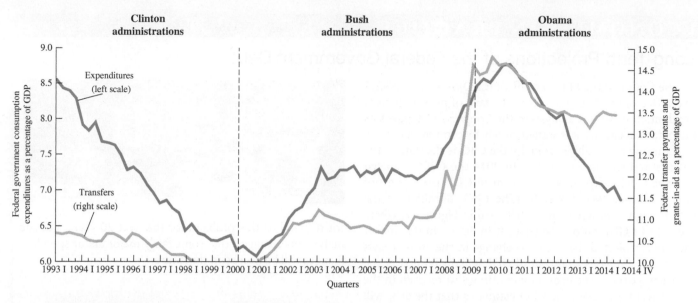

▲ **FIGURE 9.5** **Federal Government Consumption Expenditures as a Percentage of GDP and Federal Transfer Payments and Grants-in-Aid as a Percentage of GDP, 1993 I–2014 IV**

MyEconLab Real-time data

and increased spending for the Afghanistan war. Expenditures as a fraction of GDP have been falling during the second Obama administration.

Figure 9.5 also shows that transfer payments as a percentage of GDP generally rose during the Bush administrations especially near the end, and remained high in the Obama administration. The percent was flat or slightly falling during the Clinton administrations. Some of the fall between 1996 and 2000 was because of President Clinton's welfare reform legislation. Some of the rise from 2001 on is as a result of increased Medicare payments. The high initial values in the Obama administration again reflect the effects of the stimulus bill and various extensions.

Figure 9.6 plots the federal government surplus (+) or deficit (−1) as a percentage of GDP. The figure shows that during the Clinton administrations the federal budget moved from

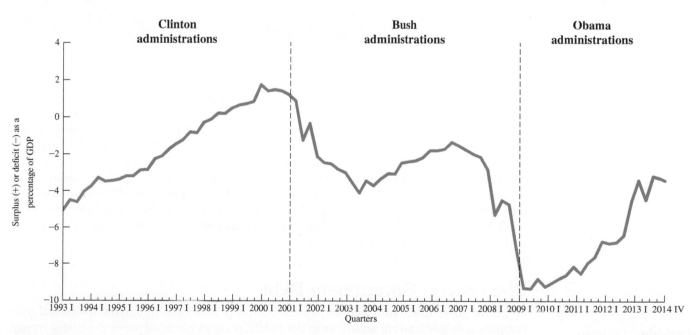

▲ **FIGURE 9.6** **The Federal Government Surplus (+) or Deficit (−) as a Percentage of GDP, 1993 I–2014 IV**

MyEconLab Real-time data

Long-Term Projections of the Federal Government Debt

The Congressional Budget Office (CBO) is an administrative office of the Congress, given the task of providing independent, nonpartisan analysis to the Congress as it makes its budgetary decisions. It is staffed largely by economists.

Among the analyses done by the CBO is the state of the deficits and the national debt.[1] In 2014 the CBO estimated that the federal debt was 74 percent of GDP, the highest of any year since World War II. (The CBO definition of the debt is slightly different from that used in Figure 9.7, where the debt to GDP ratio is 64 percent in 2014.) In this report the CBO projected that with no change in the current laws in place, the debt as a percent of GDP will decrease over the next few years as the economy continues to recover. In the longer term, however, the CBO estimates that the debt will increase substantially, reaching more that 100 percent of GDP by 2039, largely because of the costs associated with the aging of the U.S. population. Of course, it is not expected by anyone—including the CBO—that laws and policies will

not respond to this problem for the next 20 years. But the analysis does suggest that some fairly major tax or spending changes will be needed in the future.

THINKING PRACTICALLY

1. Why does the aging of the population increase the debt?

[1] CBO, "Long Term Budget Outlook, "July 15, 2014.

substantial deficit to noticeable surplus. This, of course, should not be surprising because the average tax rate generally rose during this period and spending as a percentage of GDP generally fell. Figure 9.6 then shows that the surplus turned into a substantial deficit during the first Bush administration. This also should not be surprising since the average tax rate generally fell during this period and spending as a percentage of GDP generally rose. The deficit rose sharply in the beginning of the Obama administration—to 9.3 percent of GDP by the second quarter of 2009. Again, this is not a surprise. The average tax rate remained low and spending increased substantially. The deficit-to-GDP ratio has been improving during the second Obama administration, reflecting the increase in taxes in Figure 9.4 and the fall in spending in Figure 9.5. To summarize, Figures 9.4, 9.5, and 9.6 show clearly the large differences in the fiscal policies of the three administrations. Tax rates generally rose and spending as a percentage of GDP generally fell during the Clinton administrations, and the opposite generally happened during the Bush and first Obama administrations.

As you look at these differences, you should remember that the decisions that governments make about levels of spending and taxes reflect not only macroeconomic concerns but also microeconomic issues and political philosophy. President Clinton's welfare reform program resulted in a decrease in government transfer payments but was motivated in part by interest in improving market incentives. President Bush's early tax cuts were based less on macroeconomic concerns than on political philosophy, while the increased spending came from international relations. President Obama's fiscal policy, on the other hand, was motivated by macroeconomic concerns. The stimulus bill was designed to mitigate the effects of the recession that began in 2008. Whether tax and spending policies are motivated by macroeconomic concerns or not, they have macroeconomic consequences.

The Federal Government Debt

federal debt The total amount owed by the federal government.

When the government runs a deficit, it must borrow to finance it. To borrow, the federal government sells government securities to the public. It issues pieces of paper promising to pay a certain amount, with interest, in the future. In return, it receives funds from the buyers of the paper and uses these funds to pay its bills. This borrowing increases the **federal debt**, the

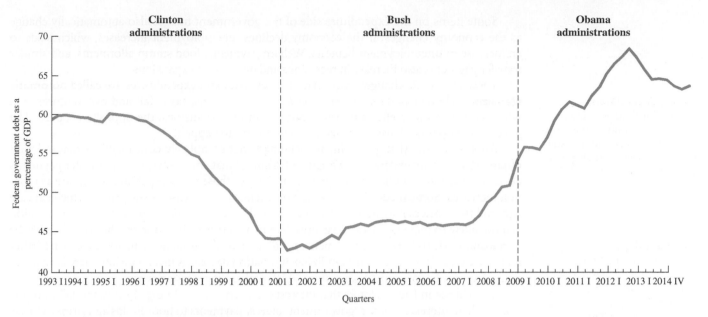

▲ **FIGURE 9.7 The Federal Government Debt as a Percentage of GDP, 1993 I–2014 IV**

MyEconLab Real-time data

total amount owed by the federal government. The federal debt is the total of all accumulated deficits minus surpluses over time. Conversely, if the government runs a surplus, the federal debt falls.

Some of the securities that the government issues end up being held by the federal government at the Federal Reserve or in government trust funds, the largest of which is Social Security. The term **privately held federal debt** refers only to the *privately held* debt of the U.S. government.

The privately held federal government debt as a percentage of GDP is plotted in Figure 9.7 for the 1993 I–2014 IV period. The percentage fell during the second Clinton administration, when the budget was in surplus, and it mostly rose during the Bush administrations, when the budget was in deficit. The rise during the first Obama administration was dramatic. During the second Obama administration the debt to GDP ratio has leveled off.

privately held federal debt The privately held (non-government-owned) debt of the U.S. government.

The Economy's Influence on the Government Budget

9.4 LEARNING OBJECTIVE

Explain the influence of the economy on the federal government budget.

We have just seen that an administration's fiscal policy is sometimes affected by the state of the economy. The Obama administration, for example, increased government spending and lowered taxes in response to the recession of 2008–2009. It is also the case, however, that the economy affects the federal government budget even if there are no explicit fiscal policy changes. There are effects that the government has no direct control over. They can be lumped under the general heading of "automatic stabilizers and destabilizers."

Automatic Stabilizers and Destabilizers

Most of the tax revenues of the government result from applying a tax rate decided by the government to a base that reflects the underlying activity of the economy. The corporate profits tax, for example, comes from applying a rate (say 35 percent) to the profits earned by firms. Income taxes come from applying rates shown in tax tables to income earned by individuals. Tax revenues thus depend on the state of the economy even when the government does not change tax rates. When the economy goes into a recession, tax revenues will fall, even if rates remain constant, and when the economy picks up, so will tax revenues. As a result, deficits fall in expansions and rise in recessions, other things being equal.

Some items on the expenditure side of the government budget also automatically change as the economy changes. If the economy declines, unemployment increases, which leads to an increase in unemployment benefits. Welfare payments, food stamp allotments, and similar transfer payments also increase in recessions and decrease in expansions.

These automatic changes in government revenues and expenditures are called **automatic stabilizers**. They help stabilize the economy. In recessions, taxes fall and expenditures rise, which creates positive effects on the economy, and in expansions, the opposite happens. The government does not have to change any laws for this to happen.

Another reason that government spending is not completely controllable is that inflation often picks up in an expansion. We saw in Chapter 7 that some government transfer payments are tied to the rate of inflation (changes in the CPI); so these transfer payments increase as inflation increases. Some medical care transfer payments also increase as the prices of medical care rise, and these prices may be affected by the overall rate of inflation. To the extent that inflation is more likely to increase in an expansion than in a recession, inflation can be considered to be an **automatic destabilizer**. Government spending increases as inflation increases, which further fuels the expansion, which is destabilizing. If inflation decreases in a recession, there is an automatic decrease in government spending, which makes the recession worse.

We will see in later chapters that interest rates tend to rise in expansions and fall in recessions. When interest rates rise, government interest payments to households and firms increase (because households and firms hold much of the government debt), which is interest income to the households and firms. Government spending on interest payments thus tends to rise in expansions and fall in contractions, which, other things being equal, is destabilizing. We will see in later chapters, however, that interest rates also have negative effects on the economy, and these negative effects are generally larger than the positive effects from the increase in government interest payments. The net effect of an increase in interest rates on the economy is thus generally negative. But this is getting ahead of our story.

Since 1982 personal income tax brackets have been tied to the overall price level. Prior to this they were not, which led to what was called **fiscal drag**. If tax brackets are not tied to the price level, then as the price level rises and thus people's nominal incomes rise, people move into higher brackets; so the average tax rates that they pay increase. This is a "drag" on the economy, hence the name fiscal drag. In 1982, the United States instituted an alternative Minimum Tax (AMT), directed at higher income individuals who had a number of special tax deductions. These individuals were subject to an alternative calculation of their income taxes, which essentially eliminated some deductions and imposed a (lower) flat tax. In contrast to the standard tax tables, the income level at which the AMT would kick in remained constant over the subsequent 30 years until finally indexed to inflation in 2013. For this period, the AMT tax created fiscal drag. It is interesting to note that fiscal drag is actually an automatic stabilizer in that the number of people moving into higher tax brackets increases in expansions and falls in contractions. By indexing the tax brackets to the overall price level, the legislation in 1982 eliminated the fiscal drag caused by inflation from taxes other than the AMT. If incomes rise only because of inflation, there is no change in average tax rates because the brackets are changed each year. The inflation part of the automatic stabilizer has been eliminated.

automatic stabilizers
Revenue and expenditure items in the federal budget that automatically change with the state of the economy in such a way as to stabilize GDP.

automatic destabilizers
Revenue and expenditure items in the federal budget that automatically change with the state of the economy in such a way as to destabilize GDP.

fiscal drag The negative effect on the economy that occurs when average tax rates increase because taxpayers have moved into higher income brackets during an expansion.

Full-Employment Budget

We have seen that the state of the economy has a big effect on the budget deficit. When the economy turns down, automatic stabilizers act to increase the deficit; the government may also take further actions intended to pull the economy out of a slump. Under these conditions, running a deficit may seem like a good idea. When the economy is thriving, however, deficits may be more problematic. In particular, if the government runs deficits in good times as well as bad, the overall debt is surely going to rise, which may be unsustainable in the long run. Instead of looking simply at the size of the surplus or deficit, economists have developed an alternative way to calibrate deficits. By examining what the budget would be like if the economy were producing at the full-employment level of output—the so-called **full-employment budget**—we can establish a benchmark for evaluating fiscal policy.

full-employment budget
What the federal budget would be if the economy were producing at the full employment level of output.

The distinction between the actual and full-employment budget is important. Suppose the economy is in a slump and the deficit is $250 billion. Also suppose that if there were full employment, the deficit would fall to $75 billion. The $75 billion deficit that would remain even with full employment would be because of the structure of tax and spending programs instead of the state of the economy. This deficit—the deficit that remains at full employment—is sometimes called the **structural deficit**. The $175 billion ($250 billion − $75 billion) part of the deficit caused by the fact the economy is in a slump is known as the **cyclical deficit**. The existence of the cyclical deficit depends on where the economy is in the business cycle, and it ceases to exist when full employment is reached. By definition, the cyclical deficit of the full-employment budget is zero.

Table 9.5 shows that the federal government deficit in 2014 was $582.3 billion. How much of this was cyclical and how much was structural? The U.S. economy was still not quite at full employment in 2014, and so some of the deficit was cyclical.

structural deficit The deficit that remains at full employment.

cyclical deficit The deficit that occurs because of a downturn in the business cycle.

Looking Ahead

We have now seen how households, firms, and the government interact in the goods market, how equilibrium output (income) is determined, and how the government uses fiscal policy to influence the economy. In the next chapter we analyze the money market and monetary policy—the government's other major tool for influencing the economy.

SUMMARY

1. The government can affect the macroeconomy through two specific policy channels. *Fiscal policy* refers to the government's taxing and spending behavior. *Discretionary fiscal policy* refers to changes in taxes or spending that are the result of deliberate changes in government policy. *Monetary policy* refers to the behavior of the Federal Reserve concerning the interest rate.

9.1 GOVERNMENT IN THE ECONOMY *p. 163*

2. The government does not have complete control over tax revenues and certain expenditures, which are partially dictated by the state of the economy.

3. As a participant in the economy, the government makes purchases of goods and services (*G*), collects taxes, and makes transfer payments to households. *Net taxes* (*T*) is equal to the tax payments made to the government by firms and households minus transfer payments made to households by the government.

4. *Disposable*, or *after-tax, income* (Y_d) is equal to the amount of income received by households after taxes: $Y_d \equiv Y - T$. After-tax income determines households' consumption behavior.

5. The *budget deficit* is equal to the difference between what the government spends and what it collects in taxes: $G - T$. When *G* exceeds *T*, the government must borrow from the public to finance its deficit.

6. In an economy in which government is a participant, planned aggregate expenditure equals consumption spending by households (*C*) plus planned investment spending by firms (*I*) plus government spending on goods and services (*G*): $AE \equiv C + I + G$. Because the condition $Y = AE$ is necessary for the economy to be in equilibrium, it follows that $Y = C + I + G$ is the macroeconomic equilibrium condition. The economy is also in equilibrium when leakages out of the system equal injections into the system. This occurs when saving and net taxes (the leakages) equal planned investment and government purchases (the injections): $S + T = I + G$.

9.2 FISCAL POLICY AT WORK: MULTIPLIER EFFECTS *p. 167*

7. Fiscal policy has a multiplier effect on the economy. A change in government spending gives rise to a multiplier equal to 1/MPS. A change in taxation brings about a multiplier equal to −MPC/MPS. A simultaneous equal increase or decrease in government spending and taxes has a multiplier effect of 1.

9.3 THE FEDERAL BUDGET *p. 173*

8. During the two Clinton administrations, the federal budget went from being in deficit to being in surplus. This was reversed during the two Bush administrations, driven by tax rate decreases and government spending increases. The deficit increased further during the beginning of the first Obama administration and then began to improve.

9.4 THE ECONOMY'S INFLUENCE ON THE GOVERNMENT BUDGET *p. 177*

9. *Automatic stabilizers* are revenue and expenditure items in the federal budget that automatically change with the state of the economy and that tend to stabilize GDP. For example, during expansions, the government automatically takes in more revenue because people are making more money that is taxed.

10. The *full-employment budget* is an economist's construction of what the federal budget would be if the economy were producing at a full-employment level of output. The *structural deficit* is the federal deficit that remains even at full employment. The *cyclical deficit* is that part of the total deficit caused by the economy operating at less than full employment.

REVIEW TERMS AND CONCEPTS

automatic destabilizer, *p. 178*

automatic stabilizers, *p. 178*

balanced-budget multiplier, *p. 171*

budget deficit, *p. 164*

cyclical deficit, *p. 179*

discretionary fiscal policy, *p. 163*

disposable, *or after-tax, income* (Y_d), *p. 163*

federal budget, *p. 173*

federal debt, *p. 176*

federal surplus (+) *or deficit* (−), *p. 173*

fiscal drag, *p. 178*

fiscal policy, *p. 162*

full-employment budget, *p. 178*

government spending multiplier, *p. 168*

monetary policy, *p. 162*

net taxes (*T*), *p. 163*

privately held federal debt, *p. 177*

structural deficit, *p. 179*

tax multiplier, *p. 170*

Equations:

Disposable income: $Y_d \equiv Y - T$, *p. 163*

$AE \equiv C + I + G$, *p. 164*

Government budget deficit $\equiv G - T$, *p. 164*

Equilibrium in an economy with a government: $Y \equiv C + I + G$, *p. 165*

Saving/investment approach to equilibrium in an economy with a government: $S + T = I + G$, *p. 166*

Government spending multiplier

$$\equiv \frac{1}{MPS} \equiv \frac{1}{1 - MPC}, \text{ } p. \text{ } 168$$

Tax multiplier $\equiv -\left(\dfrac{MPC}{MPS}\right)$, *p. 171*

Balanced-budget multiplier $\equiv 1$, *p. 171*

PROBLEMS

All problems are available on MyEconLab.

9.1   GOVERNMENT IN THE ECONOMY

LEARNING OBJECTIVE: Discuss the influence of fiscal policies on the economy.

1.1 Define *saving* and *investment*. Data for the simple economy of Newt show that in 2015, saving exceeded investment and the government is running a balanced budget. What is likely to happen? What would happen if the government were running a deficit and saving were equal to investment?

1.2 Expert economists in the economy of Bongo estimate the following:

	Billion Bongos
Real output/income	1,200
Government purchases	300
Total net taxes	300
Investment spending (planned)	200

Assume that Bongoliers consume 80 percent of their disposable incomes and save 20 percent.

a. You are asked by the business editor of the *Bongo Tribune* to predict the events of the next few months. By using the data given, make a forecast. (Assume that investment is constant.)

b. If no changes were made, at what level of GDP (*Y*) would the economy of Bongo settle?

c. Some local conservatives blame Bongo's problems on the size of the government sector. They suggest cutting government purchases by 25 billion Bongos. What effect would such cuts have on the economy? (Be specific.)

1.3 Assume that in 2015, the following prevails in the Republic of Nurd:

$Y = \$200$	$G = \$0$
$C = \$160$	$T = \$0$
$S = \$40$	
$I \text{ (planned)} = \$30$	

Assume that households consume 80 percent of their income, they save 20 percent of their income, $MPC = 0.8$, and $MPS = 0.2$. That is, $C = 0.8Y_d$ and $S = 0.2Y_d$.

a. Is the economy of Nurd in equilibrium? What is Nurd's equilibrium level of income? What is likely to happen in the coming months if the government takes no action?

b. If $200 is the "full-employment" level of *Y*, what fiscal policy might the government follow if its goal is full employment?

c. If the full-employment level of *Y* is $250, what fiscal policy might the government follow?

d. Suppose $Y = \$200, C = \$160, S = \$40$, and $I = \$40$. Is Nurd's economy in equilibrium?

e. Starting with the situation in part d, suppose the government starts spending $30 each year with no taxation and continues to spend $30 every period. If *I* remains constant, what will happen to the equilibrium level of Nurd's domestic product (Y)? What will the new levels of C and S be?

f. Starting with the situation in part d, suppose the government starts taxing the population $30 each year without spending anything and continues to tax at that rate every period. If *I* remains constant, what will happen to the equilibrium level of Nurd's domestic product (Y)? What will be the new levels of C and S? How does your answer to part f differ from your answer to part e? Why?

1.4 Some economists claim World War II ended the Great Depression of the 1930s. The war effort was financed by borrowing massive sums of money from the public. Explain how a war could end a recession. Look at recent and back issues of the *Economic Report of the President* or the *Statistical Abstract of the United States*. How large was the federal government's debt as a percentage of GDP in 1946? How large is it today?

1.5 Evaluate the following statement: For an economy to be in equilibrium, planned investment spending plus government purchases must equal saving plus net taxes.

1.6 For the data in the following table, the consumption function is $C = 800 + 0.6(Y - T)$. Fill in the columns in the table and identify the equilibrium output.

Output	Net Taxes	Disposable Income	Consumption Spending	Saving	Planned Investment Spending	Government Purchases	Planned Aggregate Expenditure	Unplanned Inventory Change
2,100	100				300	400		
2,600	100				300	400		
3,100	100				300	400		
3,600	100				300	400		
4,100	100				300	400		
4,600	100				300	400		
5,100	100				300	400		

1.7 For each of the following sets of data, determine if output will need to increase, decrease, or remain the same to move the economy to equilibrium:

a. $Y = 1,000$; $C = 100 + 0.75(Y - T)$; $I = 200$; $G = 150$; $T = 100$
b. $Y = 5,000$; $C = 200 + 0.9(Y - T)$; $I = 500$; $G = 400$; $T = 300$
c. $Y = 2,000$; $C = 150 + 0.5(Y - T)$; $I = 150$; $G = 150$; $T = 50$
d. $Y = 1,600$; $C = 300 + 0.6(Y - T)$; $I = 250$; $G = 150$; $T = 100$

9.2 FISCAL POLICY AT WORK: MULTIPLIER EFFECTS

LEARNING OBJECTIVE: Describe the effects of three fiscal policy multipliers.

2.1 Use your answer to Problem 1.6 to calculate the *MPC*, *MPS*, government spending multiplier, and tax multiplier. Draw a graph showing the data for consumption spending, planned aggregate expenditures, and aggregate output. Be sure to identify the equilibrium point on your graph.

2.2 Suppose that the government of Ansonia is experiencing a large budget deficit with fixed government expenditures of $G = 250$ and fixed taxes of $T = 150$. Assume that consumers of Ansonia behave as described in the following consumption function:

$$C = 300 + 0.8(Y - T)$$

Suppose further that investment spending is fixed at 200. Calculate the equilibrium level of GDP in Ansonia. Solve for equilibrium levels of *Y*, *C*, and *S*. Next, assume that the Republican Congress in Ansonia succeeds in reducing taxes by 30 to a new fixed level of 120. Recalculate the equilibrium level of GDP using the tax multiplier. Solve for equilibrium levels of *Y*, *C*, and *S* after the tax cut and check to ensure that the multiplier worked. What arguments are likely to be used in support of such a tax cut? What arguments might be used to oppose such a tax cut?

2.3 A $1 increase in government spending will raise equilibrium income more than a $1 tax cut will, yet both have the same impact on the budget deficit. So if we care about the budget deficit, the best way to stimulate the economy is through increases in spending, not cuts in taxes. Comment.

2.4 Answer the following:
a. $MPS = 0.1$. What is the government spending multiplier?
b. $MPC = 0.6$. What is the government spending multiplier?
c. $MPS = 0.25$. What is the government spending multiplier?
d. $MPC = 0.5$. What is the tax multiplier?
e. $MPS = 0.2$. What is the tax multiplier?
f. If the government spending multiplier is 8, what is the tax multiplier?
g. If the tax multiplier is −5, what is the government spending multiplier?
h. If government purchases and taxes are increased by $500 billion simultaneously, what will the effect be on equilibrium output (income)?

2.5 What is the balanced-budget multiplier? Explain why the balanced-budget multiplier is equal to 1.

9.3 THE FEDERAL BUDGET

LEARNING OBJECTIVE: Compare and contrast the federal budgets of three U.S. government administrations.

3.1 You are appointed secretary of the treasury of a recently independent country called Rugaria. The currency of Rugaria is the lav. The new nation began fiscal operations this year, and the budget situation is that the government will spend 10 million lavs and taxes will be 9 million lavs. The 1-million-lav difference will be borrowed from the public by selling 10-year government bonds paying 5 percent interest. The interest on the outstanding bonds must be added to spending each year, and we assume that additional taxes are raised to cover that interest. Assuming that the budget stays the same except for the interest on the debt for 10 years, what will be the accumulated debt? What will the size of the budget be after 10 years?

3.2 [**Related to the *Economics in Practice* on p. 176**] Federal government expenditures and receipts for the simple economy of the nation of Topanga are listed in the table in the next column. The government of Topanga would like to reduce the debt-to-GDP ratio, and the Finance Minister of Topanga has proposed the following: "The best way to reduce the debt-to-GDP ratio is to increase GDP, because with a larger GDP, the ratio will have to get smaller. I therefore propose that government expenditures be increased by 25 percent, personal income taxes be reduced by 25 percent, corporate income taxes be reduced by 25 percent, and contributions for social insurance be reduced by 25 percent. All of these moves will increase GDP by 10 percent by increasing consumer spending, business spending, and government spending by the exact amounts of the increased spending and reduced taxes." Assuming that GDP will, indeed, increase by 10 percent and the only changes to the data in the table are those proposed by the Finance Minister, answer the following questions:

a. What is the current debt-to-GDP ratio?
b. What is the amount of the current budget deficit or surplus?

c. With the proposals made by the Finance Minister, what will be the amount of the new budget deficit or surplus and what will be the new debt-to-GDP ratio?
d. Based on your answer to part (c), will the Finance Minister's proposals work to reduce the debt-to-GDP ratio? Explain.

Debt	$20 million
GDP	$40 million
Government expenditures	$5 million
Government transfer payments	$5 million
Interest payment	$1 million
Personal income tax receipts	$6 million
Corporate income tax receipts	$1 million
Contributions for social insurance	$4 million

9.4 THE ECONOMY'S INFLUENCE ON THE GOVERNMENT BUDGET

LEARNING OBJECTIVE: Explain the influence of the economy on the federal government budget.

4.1 Suppose all tax collections are fixed (instead of dependent on income) and all spending and transfer programs are fixed (in the sense that they do not depend on the state of the economy, as, for example, unemployment benefits now do). In this case, would there be any automatic stabilizers in the government budget? Would there be any distinction between the full-employment deficit and the actual budget deficit? Explain.

CHAPTER 9 APPENDIX A

LEARNING OBJECTIVE

Show that the government spending multiplier is 1 divided by 1 minus the *MPC*.

Deriving the Fiscal Policy Multipliers

The Government Spending and Tax Multipliers

In the chapter, we noted that the government spending multiplier is 1/*MPS*. (This is the same as the investment multiplier.) We can also derive the multiplier algebraically using our hypothetical consumption function:

$$C = a + b(Y - T)$$

where *b* is the marginal propensity to consume. As you know, the equilibrium condition is

$$Y = C + I + G$$

By substituting for *C*, we get

$$Y = a + b(Y - T) + I + G$$
$$Y = a + bY - bT + I + G$$

This equation can be rearranged to yield

$$Y - bY = a + I + G - bT$$
$$Y(1 - b) = a + I + G - bT$$

Now solve for Y by dividing through by $(1 - b)$:

$$Y = \frac{1}{(1 - b)}(a + I + G - bT)$$

We see from this last equation that if G increases by 1 with the other determinants of Y (a, I, and T) remaining constant, Y increases by $1/(1 - b)$. The multiplier is, as before, simply $1/(1 - b)$, where b is the marginal propensity to consume. Of course, $1 - b$ equals the marginal propensity to save, so the government spending multiplier is $1/MPS$.

We can also derive the tax multiplier. The last equation says that when T increases by \$1, holding a, I, and G constant, income decreases by $b/(1 - b)$ dollars. The tax multiplier is $-b/(1 - b)$, or $-MPC/(1 - MPC) = -MPC/MPS$. (Remember, the negative sign in the resulting tax multiplier shows that it is a *negative* multiplier.)

The Balanced-Budget Multiplier

It is easy to show formally that the balanced-budget multiplier equals 1. When taxes and government spending are simultaneously increased by the same amount, there are two effects on planned aggregate expenditure: one positive and one negative. The initial impact of a balanced-budget increase in government spending and taxes on aggregate expenditure would be the *increase* in government purchases (ΔG) minus the *decrease* in consumption (ΔC) caused by the tax increase. The decrease in consumption brought about by the tax increase is equal to $\Delta C = \Delta T(MPC)$.

initial increase in spending:	ΔG
− initial decrease in spending:	$\Delta C = \Delta T(MPC)$
= net initial increase in spending	$\Delta G - \Delta T(MPC)$

In a balanced-budget increase, $\Delta G = \Delta T$; so in the above equation for the net initial increase in spending we can substitute ΔG for ΔT.

$$\Delta G - \Delta G(MPC) = \Delta G(1 - MPC)$$

Because $MPS = (1 - MPC)$, the net initial increase in spending is:

$$\Delta G(MPS)$$

We can now apply the expenditure multiplier $\left(\dfrac{1}{MPS}\right)$ to this net initial increase in spending:

$$\Delta Y = \Delta G(MPS)\left(\frac{1}{MPS}\right) = \Delta G$$

Thus, the final total increase in the equilibrium level of Y is just equal to the initial balanced increase in G and T. That means the balanced-budget multiplier equals 1, so the final increase in real output is of the same magnitude as the initial change in spending.

CHAPTER 9 APPENDIX B

The Case in Which Tax Revenues Depend on Income

LEARNING OBJECTIVE

Explain why the multiplier falls when taxes depend on income.

In this chapter, we used the simplifying assumption that the government collects taxes in a lump sum. This made our discussion of the multiplier effects somewhat easier to follow. Now suppose that the government collects taxes not solely as a lump sum that is paid regardless of income but also partly in the form of a proportional levy against income. This is a more realistic assumption. Typically, tax collections either are based on income (as with the personal income tax) or follow the ups and downs in the economy (as with sales taxes). Instead of setting taxes equal to some fixed amount, let us say that tax revenues depend on income. If we call the amount of net taxes collected T, we can write $T = T_0 + tY$.

This equation contains two parts. First, we note that net taxes (T) will be equal to an amount T_0 if income (Y) is zero. Second, the tax rate (t) indicates how much net taxes change as income changes. Suppose T_0 is equal to -200 and t is $1/3$. The resulting tax function is $T = -200 + 1/3Y$, which is graphed in Figure 9B.1. Note that when income is zero, the government collects "negative net taxes," which simply means that it makes transfer payments of 200. As income rises, tax collections increase because every extra dollar of income generates $0.33 in extra revenues for the government.

How do we incorporate this new tax function into our discussion? All we do is replace the old value of T (in the example in the chapter, T was set equal to 100) with the new value, $-200 + 1/3Y$. Look first at the consumption equation. Consumption (C) still depends on disposable income, as it did before. Also, disposable income is still $Y - T$, or income minus taxes. Instead of disposable income equaling $Y - 100$, however, the new equation for disposable income is

$$Y_d = Y - T$$
$$Y_d = Y - (-200 + 1/3Y)$$
$$Y_d = Y + 200 - 1/3Y$$

Because consumption still depends on after-tax income, exactly as it did before, we have

$$C = 100 + 0.75Y_d$$
$$C = 100 + 0.75(Y + 200 - 1/3Y)$$

Nothing else needs to be changed. We solve for equilibrium income exactly as before, by setting planned aggregate expenditure equal to aggregate output. Recall that planned aggregate expenditure is $C + I + G$ and aggregate output is Y. If we assume, as before, that $I = 100$ and $G = 100$, the equilibrium is

$$Y = C + I + G$$
$$Y = \underbrace{100 + 0.75(Y + 200 - 1/3Y)}_{C} + \underbrace{100}_{I} + \underbrace{100}_{G}$$

▶ FIGURE 9B.1 **The Tax Function**
This graph shows net taxes (taxes minus transfer payments) as a function of aggregate income.

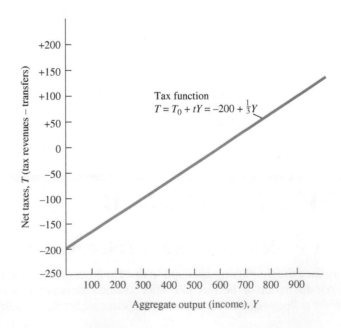

This equation may look difficult to solve, but it is not. It simplifies to

$$Y = 100 + 0.75Y + 150 - 25Y + 100 + 100$$
$$Y = 450 + 0.5Y$$
$$0.5Y = 450$$

This means that $Y = 450/0.5 = 900$, the new equilibrium level of income.

Consider the graphic analysis of this equation as shown in Figure 9B.2, where you should note that when we make taxes a function of income (instead of a lump-sum amount), the AE function becomes *flatter* than it was before. Why? When tax collections do not depend on income, an increase in income of $1 means disposable income also increases by a dollar. Because taxes are a constant amount, adding more income does not raise the amount of taxes paid. Disposable income therefore changes dollar for dollar with any change in income.

When taxes depend on income, a $1 increase in income does not increase disposable income by a full dollar because some of the additional dollar goes to pay extra taxes. Under the modified tax function of Figure 9B.2, an extra dollar of income will increase disposable income by only $0.67 because $0.33 of the extra dollar goes to the government in the form of taxes.

No matter how taxes are calculated, the marginal propensity to consume out of disposable (or after-tax) income is the same—each extra dollar of disposable income will increase consumption spending by $0.75. However, a $1 change in before-tax income does not have the same effect on disposable income in each case. Suppose we were to increase income by $1. With the lump-sum tax function, disposable income would rise by $1.00, and consumption would increase by the MPC times the change in Y_d, or $0.75. When taxes depend on income, disposable income would rise by only $0.67 from the $1.00 increase in income and consumption would rise by only the MPC times the change in disposable income, or $0.75 \times 0.67 = \$0.50$.

If a $1.00 increase in income raises expenditure by $0.75 in one case and by only $0.50 in the other, the second aggregate expenditure function must be flatter than the first.

The Government Spending and Tax Multipliers Algebraically

All this means that if taxes are a function of income, the three multipliers (investment, government spending, and tax) are less than they would be if taxes were a lump-sum amount. By using the same linear consumption function we used in Chapters 7 and 8, we can derive the multiplier:

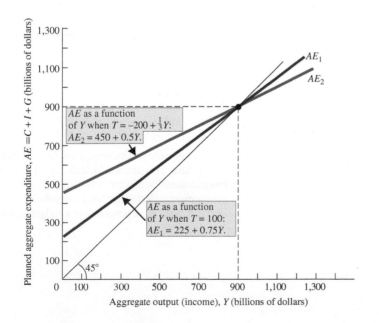

◄ **FIGURE 9B.2**
Different Tax Systems
When taxes are strictly lump-sum ($T = 100$) and do not depend on income, the aggregate expenditure function is steeper than when taxes depend on income.

$$C = a + b(Y - T)$$
$$C = a + b(Y - T_0 - tY)$$
$$C = a + bY - bT_0 - btY$$

We know that $Y = C + I + G$. Through substitution we get

$$Y = \underbrace{a + bY - bT_0 - btY}_{C} + I + G$$

Solving for Y:

$$Y = \frac{1}{1 - b + bt}(a + I + G - bT_0)$$

This means that a \$1 increase in G or I (holding a and T_0 constant) will increase the equilibrium level of Y by

$$\frac{1}{1 - b + bt}$$

If $b = MPC = 0.75$ and $t = 0.20$, the spending multiplier is 2.5. (Compare this to 4, which would be the value of the spending multiplier if taxes were a lump sum, that is, if $t = 0$.)

Holding a, I, and G constant, a fixed or lump-sum tax cut (a cut in T_0) will increase the equilibrium level of income by

$$\frac{b}{1 - b + bt}$$

Thus, if $b = MPC = 0.75$ and $t = 0.20$, the tax multiplier is -1.875. (Compare this to -3, which would be the value of the tax multiplier if taxes were a lump sum.)

─────────────── **APPENDIX SUMMARY** ───────────────

1. When taxes depend on income, a \$1 increase in income does not increase disposable income by a full dollar because some of the additional dollar must go to pay extra taxes.

This means that if taxes are a function of income, the three multipliers (investment, government spending, and tax) are less than they would be if taxes were a lump-sum amount.

─────────────── **APPENDIX PROBLEMS** ───────────────

All problems are available on MyEconLab.

APPENDIX B: THE CASE IN WHICH TAX REVENUES DEPEND ON INCOME

LEARNING OBJECTIVE: Explain why the multiplier falls when taxes depend on income.

1A.1 Assume the following for the economy of a country:

    a. Consumption function: $C = 60 + 0.75Y_d$
    b. Investment: $I = 75$
    c. Government spending: $G = 45$
    d. Net taxes: $T = -25 + 0.2Y$
    e. Disposable income: $Y_d \equiv Y - T$
    f. Equilibrium: $Y = C + I + G$

Solve for equilibrium income. (*Hint:* Be very careful in doing the calculations. They are not difficult, but it is easy to make careless mistakes that produce wrong results.) How much does the government collect in net taxes when the economy is in equilibrium? What is the government's budget deficit or surplus?

Money, the Federal Reserve, and the Interest Rate

In the last two chapters, we explored how consumers, firms, and the government interact in the goods market. In this chapter, we show how the money market works in the macroeconomy. We begin by defining money and describing its role in the U.S. economy. Microeconomics has little to say about money. Microeconomic theories and models are concerned primarily with *real* quantities (apples, oranges, hours of labor) and *relative* prices (the price of apples relative to the price of oranges or the price of labor relative to the prices of other goods). By contrast, as we will now see, money is an important part of the macroeconomy.

An Overview of Money

You often hear people say things like, "He makes a lot of money" (in other words, "He has a high income") or "She's worth a lot of money" (meaning "She is very wealthy"). It is true that your employer uses money to pay you your income, and your wealth may be accumulated in the form of money. However, "money" is defined differently in macroeconomics.

What Is Money?

Most people take the ability to obtain and use money for granted. When the whole monetary system works well, as it generally does in the United States, the basic mechanics of the system are virtually invisible. People take for granted that they can walk into any store, restaurant, boutique, or gas station and buy whatever they want as long as they have enough green pieces of paper or a debit card with a large enough balance in their checking account.

The idea that you can buy things with money is so natural and obvious that it seems absurd to mention it, but stop and ask yourself: "How is it that a store owner is willing to part with a steak and a loaf of bread that I can eat in exchange for access to some pieces of paper that are intrinsically worthless?" Why, on the other hand, are there times and places where it takes a shopping cart full of money to purchase a dozen eggs? The answers to these questions lie in what money is—a means of payment, a store of value, and a unit of account.

A Means of Payment, or Medium of Exchange   Money is vital to the working of a market economy. Imagine what life would be like without it. The alternative to a monetary economy is **barter**, people exchanging goods and services for other goods and services directly instead of exchanging via the medium of money.

> **barter**   The direct exchange of goods and services for other goods and services.

How does a barter system work? Suppose you want bacon, eggs, and orange juice for breakfast. Instead of going to the store and buying these things with money, you would have to find someone who has the items and is willing to trade them. You would also have to have something the bacon seller, the orange juice purveyor, and the egg vendor want. Having pencils to trade will do you no good if the bacon, orange juice, and egg sellers do not want pencils.

A barter system requires a *double coincidence of wants* for trade to take place. That is, to effect a trade, you have to find someone who has what you want and that person must also want what you have. Where the range of goods traded is small, as it is in relatively unsophisticated economies, it is not difficult to find someone to trade with and barter is often used. In a complex society with many goods, barter exchanges involve an intolerable amount of effort. Imagine trying to find people who offer for sale all the things you buy in a typical trip to the supermarket and who are willing to accept goods that you have to offer in exchange for their goods.

> **medium of exchange, or means of payment**   What sellers generally accept and buyers generally use to pay for goods and services.

Some agreed-to **medium of exchange (*or* means of payment)** neatly eliminates the double-coincidence-of-wants problem. Under a monetary system, money is exchanged for goods or services when people buy things; goods or services are exchanged for money when people sell things. No one ever has to trade goods for other goods directly. Money is a lubricant in the functioning of a market economy.

A Store of Value   Economists have identified other roles for money aside from its primary function as a medium of exchange. Money also serves as a **store of value**—an asset that can be used to transport purchasing power from one time period to another. If you raise chickens and at the end of the month sell them for more than you want to spend and consume immediately, you may keep some of your earnings in the form of money until the time you want to spend it.

> **store of value**   An asset that can be used to transport purchasing power from one time period to another.

There are many other stores of value besides money. You could have decided to hold your "surplus" earnings by buying such things as antique paintings, or diamonds, which you could sell later when you want to spend your earnings. Money has several advantages over these other stores of value. First, it comes in convenient denominations and is easily portable. Debit cards and phones that provide access to the money in your checking account make money even more convenient. You do not have to worry about making change for a Renoir painting to buy a gallon

ECONOMICS IN PRACTICE

Don't Kill the Birds!

In most countries commodity monies were abandoned many years ago. At one point, sea shells and other artifacts from nature were commonly used. One of the more interesting examples of a commodity money is described by David Houston, an ethno-ornithologist.[1]

In the nineteenth century, elaborate rolls of red feathers harvested from the Scarlet Honeyeater bird were used as currency between the island of Santa Cruz and nearby Pacific Islands. Feathers were made into rolls of more than 10 meters in length and were never worn, displayed, or used. Their sole role was to serve as currency in a complex valuation system. Houston tells us that more than 20,000 of these birds were killed each year to create this "money," adding considerably to bird mortality. Running the printing presses is much easier.

Today, one of the few remaining uses of commodity monies is the use of dolphin teeth in the Solomon Islands. Apparently there is even a problem with counterfeiting as people try to pass off fruit bat teeth as dolphin teeth![2]

THINKING PRACTICALLY

1. Why do red feather rolls and dolphin teeth make good commodity monies, whereas coconut shells would not?

[1]*David Houston,* "The Impact of the Red Feather Currency on the Population of the Scarlet Honeyeater on Santa Cruz," in Sonia Tidemann and Andrew Gosler, eds., *Ethno-Ornithology: Birds, Indigenous Peoples, Culture and Society* (London, Earthscan Publishers, 2010), pp. 55–66.

[2]*The Wall Street Journal,* excerpted from "Shrinking Dollar Meets Its Match in Dolphin Teeth" by Yaroslav Trofimov. Copyright 2008 by *Dow Jones & Company, Inc.* Reproduced with permission of *Dow Jones & Company, Inc.* via Copyright Clearance Center.

---

of gasoline. Second, because money is also a means of payment, it is easily exchanged for goods at all times. These two factors compose the **liquidity property of money**. Money is easily spent, flowing out of your hands like liquid.

The main disadvantage of money as a store of value is that the value of money falls when the prices of goods and services rise. If the price of potato chips rises from $1 per bag to $2 per bag, the value of a dollar bill in terms of potato chips falls from one bag to half a bag. When this happens, it may be better to use potato chips (or antiques or real estate) as a store of value. Indeed, there have been times of rising prices when people hoard goods rather than storing money to support their future needs.

liquidity property of money The property of money that makes it a good medium of exchange as well as a store of value: It is portable and readily accepted and thus easily exchanged for goods.

A Unit of Account Money also serves as a **unit of account**—a consistent way of quoting prices. All prices are quoted in monetary units. A textbook is quoted as costing $90, not 150 bananas or 5 pizzas. Obviously, a standard unit of account is extremely useful when quoting prices. This function of money may have escaped your notice—what else would people quote prices in except money?

unit of account A standard unit that provides a consistent way of quoting prices.

Commodity and Fiat Monies

Introductory economics textbooks are full of stories about the various items that have been used as money by various cultures—candy bars, cigarettes (in World War II prisoner-of-war camps), huge wheels of carved stone (on the island of Yap in the South Pacific, beads (among North American Indians), cattle (in southern Africa), and small green scraps of paper (in contemporary North America). The *Economics in Practice* box on the preceding page describes the use of bird feathers as money. These various kinds of money are generally divided into two groups, commodity monies and fiat money.

commodity monies Items used as money that also have intrinsic value in some other use.

Commodity monies are those items used as money that also have an intrinsic value in some other use. For example, prisoners of war made purchases with cigarettes, quoted prices in terms of cigarettes, and held their wealth in the form of accumulated cigarettes. Of course, cigarettes could also be smoked—they had an alternative use apart from serving as money. In fact, one of the problems with commodity monies, like cigarettes, is that their value may change when demand for them as items of use falls. If no one in prison smoked, the value of the cigarettes would likely fall, perhaps even to zero. Gold represents another form of commodity money. For hundreds of years gold could be used directly to buy things, but it also had other uses, ranging from jewelry to dental fillings.

fiat, or token, money Items designated as money that are intrinsically worthless.

By contrast, money in the United States today is mostly fiat money. **Fiat money**, sometimes called **token money**, is money that is intrinsically worthless. The actual value of a 1-, 10-, or 50-dollar bill is basically zero; what other uses are there for a small piece of paper with some green ink on it?

Why would anyone accept worthless scraps of paper as money instead of something that has some value, such as gold, cigarettes, or cattle? If your answer is "because the paper money is backed by gold or silver," you are wrong. There was a time when dollar bills were convertible directly into gold. The government backed each dollar bill in circulation by holding a certain amount of gold in its vaults. If the price of gold were $35 per ounce, for example, the government agreed to sell 1 ounce of gold for 35 dollar bills. However, dollar bills are no longer backed by any commodity—gold, silver, or anything else. They are exchangeable only for dimes, nickels, pennies, other dollars, and so on. The good news here is that the value of this money does not depend on the value of money in another use, as in the case of cigarettes. The harder question is why it has any value at all!

legal tender Money that a government has required to be accepted in settlement of debts.

The public accepts paper money as a means of payment and a store of value because the government has taken steps to ensure that its money is accepted. The government declares its paper money to be **legal tender**. That is, the government declares that its money must be accepted in settlement of debts. It does this by fiat (hence *fiat money*). It passes laws defining certain pieces of paper printed in certain inks on certain plates to be legal tender, and that is that. Printed on every Federal Reserve note in the United States is "This note is legal tender for all debts, public and private." Often the government can get a start on gaining acceptance for its paper money by requiring that it be used to pay taxes.

currency debasement The decrease in the value of money that occurs when its supply is increased rapidly.

Aside from declaring its currency legal tender, the government usually does one other thing to ensure that paper money will be accepted: It promises the public that it will not print paper money so fast that it loses its value. Expanding the supply of currency so rapidly that it loses much of its value has been a problem throughout history and is known as **currency debasement.** Debasement of the currency has been a special problem of governments that lack the strength to take the politically unpopular step of raising taxes. Printing money to be used on government expenditures of goods and services can serve as a substitute for tax increases, and weak governments have often relied on the printing press to finance their expenditures. An interesting example is Zimbabwe. In 2007, faced with a need to improve the public water system, Zimbabwe's president, Robert Mugabe, said, "Where money for projects cannot be found, we will print it" (reported in the *Washington Post*, July 29, 2007). In later chapters we will see the way in which this strategy for funding public projects can lead to serious inflation.

Measuring the Supply of Money in the United States

We now turn to the various kinds of money in the United States. Recall that money is used to buy things (a means of payment), to hold wealth (a store of value), and to quote prices (a unit of account). Unfortunately, these characteristics apply to a broad range of assets in the U.S. economy in addition to dollar bills. As we will see, it is not at all clear where we should draw the line and say, "Up to this is money, beyond this is something else."

To solve the problem of multiple monies, economists have given different names to different measures of money. The two most common measures of money are transactions money, also called M1, and broad money, also called M2.

M1: Transactions Money What should be counted as money? Coins and dollar bills, as well as higher denominations of currency, must be counted as money—they fit all the requirements. What about checking accounts? Checks, too, can be used to buy things and can serve as a store of value. Debit cards provide even easier access to funds in checking accounts, as do smartphones linked to checking accounts. In fact, bankers call checking accounts *demand deposits* because depositors have the right to cash in (demand) their entire checking account balance at any time. That makes your checking account balance virtually equivalent to bills in your wallet, and it should be included as part of the amount of money you hold, as we have done thus far in our discussion.

If we take the value of all currency (including coins) held outside of bank vaults and add to it the value of all demand deposits, traveler's checks, and other checkable deposits, we have defined **M1, *or* transactions money.** As its name suggests, this is the money that can be directly used for transactions—to buy things.

M1, *or* transactions money Money that can be directly used for transactions.

$$M1 \equiv \text{currency held outside banks} + \text{demand deposits} + \text{traveler's checks} + \text{other checkable deposits}$$

M1 at the end of February 2015 was $2,988.2 billion. M1 is a stock measure—it is measured at a point in time. It is the total amount of coins and currency outside of banks and the total dollar amount in checking accounts.

M2: Broad Money Although M1 is the most widely used measure of the money supply, there are other measures as well. Although many savings accounts cannot be used for transactions directly, it is easy to convert them into cash or to transfer funds from them into a checking account. What about money market accounts (which allow only a few checks per month but pay market-determined interest rates) and money market mutual funds (which sell shares and use the proceeds to purchase short-term securities)? These can be used to write checks and make purchases, although only over a certain amount.

near monies Close substitutes for transactions money, such as savings accounts and money market accounts.

If we add **near monies**, close substitutes for transactions money, to M1, we get **M2**, called **broad money** because it includes not-quite-money monies such as savings accounts, money market accounts, and other near monies.

M2, *or* broad money M1 plus savings accounts, money market accounts, and other near monies.

$$M2 \equiv M1 + \text{Savings accounts} + \text{Money market accounts} + \text{Other near monies}$$

M2 at the end of February 2015 was $11,820.3 billion, considerably larger than the total M1 of $2,988.2 billion. The main advantage of looking at M2 instead of M1 is that M2 is sometimes more stable. For instance, when banks introduced new forms of interest-bearing checking accounts in the early 1980s, M1 shot up as people switched their funds from savings accounts to checking accounts. However, M2 remained fairly constant because the fall in savings account deposits and the rise in checking account balances were both part of M2, canceling each other out.

Beyond M2 Because a wide variety of financial instruments bear some resemblance to money, some economists have advocated including almost all of them as part of the money supply. For example, credit cards are used extensively in exchange. Everyone who has a credit card has a credit limit—you can charge only a certain amount on your card before you have to pay it off. One of the very broad definitions of money includes the amount of available credit on credit cards (your charge limit minus what you have charged but not paid) as part of the money supply.

There are no rules for deciding what is and is not money. However, *for our purposes, "money" will always refer to transactions money, or M1*. For simplicity, we will say that M1 is the sum of two *general* categories: currency in circulation and deposits. Keep in mind, however, that M1 has *four* specific components: currency held outside banks, demand deposits, traveler's checks, and other checkable deposits.

How Banks Create Money

So far we have described the general way that money works and the way the supply of money is measured in the United States, but how much money is available at a given time? Who supplies it, and how does it get supplied? We are now ready to analyze these questions in detail. In particular, we want to explore a process that many find mysterious: the way banks *create money*.

A Historical Perspective: Goldsmiths

To begin to see how banks create money, consider the origins of the modern banking system. In the fifteenth and sixteenth centuries, citizens of many lands used gold as money, particularly for large transactions. Because gold is both inconvenient to carry around and susceptible to theft, people began to place their gold with goldsmiths for safekeeping. On receiving the gold, a goldsmith would issue a receipt to the depositor, charging him a small fee for looking after his gold. After a time, these receipts themselves, rather than the gold that they represented, began to be traded for goods. The receipts became a form of paper money, making it unnecessary to go to the goldsmith to withdraw gold for a transaction. The receipts of the de Medici's, who were both art patrons and goldsmith-bankers in Italy in the Renaissance period, were reputedly accepted in wide areas of Europe as currency.

At this point, all the receipts issued by goldsmiths were backed 100 percent by gold. If a goldsmith had 100 ounces of gold in his safe, he would issue receipts for 100 ounces of gold, and no more. Goldsmiths functioned as warehouses where people stored gold for safekeeping. The goldsmiths found, however, that people did not come often to withdraw gold. Why should they, when paper receipts that could easily be converted to gold were "as good as gold"? (In fact, receipts were better than gold—more portable, safer from theft, and so on.) As a result, goldsmiths had a large stock of gold continuously on hand.

Because they had what amounted to "extra" gold sitting around, goldsmiths gradually realized that they could lend out some of this gold without any fear of running out of gold. Why would they do this? Because instead of just keeping their gold idly in their vaults, they could earn interest on loans. Something subtle, but dramatic, happened at this point. The goldsmiths changed from mere depositories for gold into banklike institutions that had the power to create money. This transformation occurred as soon as goldsmiths began making loans. Without adding any more real gold to the system, the goldsmiths increased the amount of money in circulation by creating additional claims to gold—that is, receipts that entitled the bearer to receive a certain number of ounces of gold on demand.[1] Thus, there were more claims than there were ounces of gold.

A detailed example may help to clarify what might look at first to you like a sleight of hand. Suppose you go to a goldsmith who is functioning only as a depository, or warehouse, and ask for a loan to buy a plot of land that costs 20 ounces of gold. Also suppose that the goldsmith has 100 ounces of gold on deposit in his safe and receipts for exactly 100 ounces of gold out to the various people who deposited the gold. If the goldsmith decides he is tired of being a mere goldsmith and wants to become a real bank, he will loan you some gold. You don't want the gold itself, of course; rather, you want a slip of paper that represents 20 ounces of gold. The goldsmith in essence "creates" money for you by giving you a receipt for 20 ounces of gold (even though his entire supply of gold already belongs to various other people).[2] When he does, there will be receipts for 120 ounces of gold in circulation instead of the 100 ounces worth of receipts before your loan and the supply of money will have increased.

People think the creation of money is mysterious. Far from it! The creation of money is simply an accounting procedure, among the most mundane of human endeavors. You may suspect the whole process is fundamentally unsound or somehow dubious. After all, the banking system began when someone issued claims for gold that already belonged to someone else. Here you may be on slightly firmer ground.

---

[1] Remember, these receipts circulated as money, and people used them to make transactions without feeling the need to cash them in—that is, to exchange them for gold itself.

[2] In return for lending you the receipt for 20 ounces of gold, the goldsmith expects to get an IOU promising to repay the amount (in gold itself or with a receipt from another goldsmith) with interest after a certain period of time.

ECONOMICS IN PRACTICE

A Run on the Bank: George Bailey, Mary Poppins, Wyatt Earp

Frank Capra's 1946 classic film, *It's a Wonderful Life*, stars Jimmy Stewart as George Bailey, the-salt-of-the- earth head of a small town building and loan bank. At one point late in the movie, as a result of some devilry by a competitor, the sound-ness of Bailey's bank comes to be questioned. The result? A classic run on the bank, shown in the movie by a mob trying to get their deposits back at the bank window. Stewart's explanation to his depositors could be straight out of an economics textbook. "I don't have your money here," he tells them. "Your money is being used to build your neighbor's new house. "Just like the goldsmiths of yore, George Bailey's banks lent out their deposits, creating money. Bailey's defense against the bank run was easier in a time when people knew their bankers. "What we need now," Bailey assured us with Jimmy Stewart's earnest acting, "is faith in each other." In today's market, faith in the government is the more typical defense against a bank run.

Another cinematic look at bank runs, by the way, comes in *Mary Poppins* when Tommy, one of Poppins' two young charges, loudly insists in the middle of the bank where his father works that he wants his tuppence back and the bank won't give it to him. The result? Another bank run, British style!

Finally, there is Wyatt Earp, in this case a true story. Earp in 1909, near the end of his colorful life, was hired by a bank in Los Angeles. Rumors were out that the bank had loaned more money than it had gold in its vaults. Depositors, we assume not understanding that this is common, were storming the bank to get their money out. Earp was hired to calm things down. His response was different from George Bailey's. He took empty money sacks from the bank, hired a wagon and driver, drove to a nearby iron works, and filled the sacks with iron slugs about the size of $20 gold pieces. He drove back to the bank, where police were holding back the mob. He announced that he had about a million dollars in the wagon and began unloading the bars into the bank. He told the police to tell the crowd that "any gent who thinks he can find a better bank to put his money

Wyatt Earp and some of his buddies were members of the Dodge City Peace Commission in 1883. From left to right (top row): William H. Harris, Luke Short, William Bat Masterson, (bottom row): Charles E. Bassett, Wyatt Earp, Frank McLain, Jerry Hausman

into to go and find it. But he'd better be damned careful he don't get hit over the head and robbed while he's doing it." As the bars were being loaded into the bank, the crowd dispersed.

THINKING PRACTICALLY

1. How do Earp's remarks illustrate the advantages of paper money over gold?

Casey Tefertiller, *Wyatt Earp: The Life Behind the Legend*, John Wiley & Sons, Inc., 1997.

Goldsmiths-turned-bankers did face certain problems. Once they started making loans, their receipts outstanding (claims on gold) were greater than the amount of gold they had in their vaults at any given moment. If the owners of the 120 ounces worth of gold receipts all presented their receipts and demanded their gold at the same time, the goldsmith would be in trouble. With only 100 ounces of gold on hand, people could not get their gold at once.

In normal times, people would be happy to hold receipts instead of real gold, and this problem would never arise. If, however, people began to worry about the goldsmith's financial safety, they might begin to have doubts about whether their receipts really were as good as gold. Knowing there were more receipts outstanding than there were ounces of gold in the goldsmith's vault, they might start to demand gold for receipts.

This situation leads to a paradox. It makes perfect sense for people to hold paper receipts (instead of gold) if they know they can always get gold for their paper. In normal times, gold-smiths could feel perfectly safe in loaning out more gold than they actually had in their posses-sion. But once people start to doubt the safety of the goldsmith, they are foolish not to demand their gold back from the vault.

run on a bank Occurs when many of those who have claims on a bank (deposits) present them at the same time.

A run on a goldsmith (or in our day, a **run on a bank**) occurs when many people present their claims at the same time. These runs tend to feed on themselves. If I see you going to the goldsmith to withdraw your gold, I may become nervous and decide to withdraw my gold as well. It is the *fear* of a run that usually causes the run. Runs on a bank can be triggered by a variety of causes: rumors that an institution may have made loans to borrowers who cannot repay, wars, failures of other institutions that have borrowed money from the bank, and so on. As you will see later in this chapter, today's bankers differ from goldsmiths—today's banks are subject to a "required reserve ratio." Goldsmiths had no legal reserve requirements, although the amount they loaned out was subject to the restriction imposed on them by their fear of running out of gold. The *Economics in Practice* box on page 193 describes several fictional bank runs, along with a description of Wyatt Earp's role in preventing a real bank run!

The Modern Banking System

To understand how the modern banking system works, you need to be familiar with some basic principles of accounting. Once you are comfortable with the way banks keep their books, you will see that the process is not so dissimilar to the world of the goldsmith.

A Brief Review of Accounting Central to accounting practices is the statement that "the books always balance." In practice, this means that if we take a snapshot of a firm—any firm, including a bank—at a particular moment in time, then by definition:

$$\text{Assets} - \text{Liabilities} \equiv \text{Net Worth}$$
$$\text{or}$$
$$\text{Assets} \equiv \text{Liabilities} + \text{Net Worth}$$

Assets are things a firm owns that are worth something. For a bank, these assets include the bank building, its furniture, its holdings of government securities, cash in its vaults, bonds, stocks, and so on. Most important among a bank's assets, for our purposes at least, are the loans it has made. A borrower gives the bank an *IOU*, a promise to repay a certain sum of money on or by a certain date. This promise is an asset of the bank because it is worth something. The bank could (and sometimes does) sell the IOU to another bank for cash.

Federal Reserve Bank (the Fed) The central bank of the United States.

Other bank assets include cash on hand (sometimes called *vault cash*) and deposits with the U.S. central bank—the **Federal Reserve Bank (the Fed)**. As we will see later in this chapter, federal banking regulations require that banks keep a certain portion of their deposits on hand as vault cash or on deposit with the Fed.

A firm's *liabilities* are its debts—what it owes. A bank's liabilities are the promises to pay, or IOUs, that it has issued. A bank's most important liabilities are its deposits. *Deposits* are debts owed to the depositors because when you deposit money in your account, you are in essence making a loan to the bank.

The basic rule of accounting says that if we add up a firm's assets and then subtract the total amount it owes to all those who have lent it funds, the difference is the firm's net worth. *Net worth* represents the value of the firm to its stockholders or owners. How much would you pay for a firm that owns $200,000 worth of diamonds and had borrowed $150,000 from a bank to pay for them? The firm is worth $50,000—the difference between what it owns and what it owes. If the price of diamonds were to fall, bringing their value down to only $150,000, the firm would be worth nothing.

reserves The deposits that a bank has at the Federal Reserve Bank plus its vault cash on hand.

We can keep track of a bank's financial position using a simplified balance sheet called a T-account. By convention, the bank's assets are listed on the left side of the T-account and its liabilities and net worth are on the right side. By definition, the balance sheet always balances, so that the sum of the items on the left side of the T-account is equal to the sum of the items on the right side.

The T-account in Figure 10.1 shows a bank having $110 million in *assets*, of which $20 million are **reserves**, the deposits the bank has made at the Fed, and its cash on hand (coins and currency). Reserves are an asset to the bank because it can go to the Fed and get cash for them.

	Assets	Liabilities	
Reserves	20	100	Deposits
Loans	90	10	Net worth
Total	110	110	Total

◀ FIGURE 10.1
T-Account for a Typical Bank (millions of dollars)
The balance sheet of a bank must always balance, so that the sum of assets (reserves and loans) equals the sum of liabilities (deposits) and net worth.

the same way you can go to the bank and get cash for the amount in your savings account. Our bank's other asset is its loans, worth $90 million.

Why do banks hold reserves/deposits at the Fed? There are many reasons, but perhaps the most important is the legal requirement that they hold a certain percentage of their deposit liabilities as reserves. The percentage of its deposits that a bank must keep as reserves is known as the **required reserve ratio**. If the reserve ratio is 20 percent, a bank with deposits of $100 million must hold $20 million as reserves, either as cash or as deposits at the Fed. To simplify, we will assume that banks hold all of their reserves in the form of deposits at the Fed.

On the liabilities side of the T-account, the bank has deposits of $100 million, which it owes to its depositors. This means that the bank has a net worth of $10 million to its owners ($110 million in assets − $100 million in liabilities = $10 million net worth). The net worth of the bank is what "balances" the balance sheet. Remember that when some item on a bank's balance sheet changes, there must be at least one other change somewhere else to maintain balance. If a bank's reserves increase by $1, one of the following must also be true: (1) Its other assets (for example, loans) decrease by $1, (2) its liabilities (deposits) increase by $1, or (3) its net worth increases by $1. Various fractional combinations of these are also possible.

required reserve ratio The percentage of its total deposits that a bank must keep as cash or reserves at the Federal Reserve.

The Creation of Money

Like the goldsmiths, today's bankers can earn income by lending money out at a higher interest rate than they pay depositors for use of their money. In modern times, the chances of a run on a bank are fairly small, and even if there is a run, the central bank protects the private banks in various ways. Therefore, banks if they choose to can make loans up to the reserve requirement restriction. A bank's required amount of reserves is equal to the required reserve ratio times the total deposits in the bank. If a bank has deposits of $100 and the required ratio is 20 percent, the required amount of reserves is $20. The difference between a bank's actual reserves and its required reserves is its **excess reserves**:

excess reserves The difference between a bank's actual reserves and its required reserves.

$$\text{excess reserves} \equiv \text{actual reserves} - \text{required reserves}$$

When a bank's excess reserves are zero, it can no longer make loans. Why is this? When a bank makes a loan, it creates a demand deposit for the borrower. That demand deposit, in turn, requires reserves to back it up, just like the other deposits in the bank. With excess reserves at zero, and no new cash coming in, the bank has no way to reserve against the new deposit.

An example will help to show the connection between loans and excess reserves more generally. Assume that there is only one private bank in the country, the required reserve ratio is 20 percent, and the bank starts off with nothing, as shown in panel 1 of Figure 10.2. Now suppose dollar bills are in circulation and someone deposits 100 of them in the bank. The bank deposits the $100 with the central bank, so it now has $100 in reserves, as shown in panel 2. The bank now has assets (reserves) of $100 and liabilities (deposits) of $100. If the required reserve ratio is 20 percent, the bank has excess reserves of $80.

How much can the bank lend and still meet the reserve requirement? For the moment, let us assume that anyone who gets a loan keeps the entire proceeds in the bank or pays them to

	Panel 1		Panel 2		Panel 3	
Assets	Liabilities	Assets	Liabilities	Assets	Liabilities
Reserves 0	0 Deposits	Reserves 100	100 Deposits	Reserves 100 Loans 400	500 Deposits

▲ **FIGURE 10.2** **Balance Sheets of a Bank in a Single-Bank Economy**
In panel 2, there is an initial deposit of $100. In panel 3, the bank has made loans of $400.

someone else who does. Nothing is withdrawn as cash. In this case, the bank can lend $400 and still meet the reserve requirement. Panel 3 shows the balance sheet of the bank after completing the maximum amount of loans it is allowed with a 20 percent reserve ratio. With $80 of excess reserves, the bank can have up to $400 of additional deposits. The $100 original deposit, now in reserves, plus $400 in loans (which are made as deposits) equals $500 in deposits. With $500 in deposits and a required reserve ratio of 20 percent, the bank must have reserves of $100 (20 percent of $500)—and it does. The bank can lend no more than $400 because that is all its $100 of reserves will support, given its initial deposit. Another way to see this is to recognize that the bank originally had $80 in excess reserves. That $80 would support $400 in new deposits (loans) because 20% of $400 equals the $80 excess reserve figure. The $400 in loans uses up all of the excess reserves. When a bank has no excess reserves and thus can make no more loans, it is said to be *loaned up*.

Remember, the money supply (M1) equals cash in circulation plus deposits. Before the initial deposit, the money supply was $100 ($100 cash and no deposits). After the deposit and the loans, the money supply is $500 (no cash outside bank vaults and $500 in deposits). It is clear then that when loans are converted into deposits, the supply of money will increase.

The bank whose T-accounts are presented in Figure 10.2 is allowed to make loans of $400 based on the assumption that loans that are made *stay in the bank* in the form of deposits. Now suppose you borrow from the bank to buy a personal computer and you write a check to the computer store. If the store also deposits its money in the bank, your check merely results in a reduction in your account balance and an increase to the store's account balance within the bank. No cash has left the bank. As long as the system is closed in this way—remember that so far we have assumed that there is only one bank—the bank knows that it will never be called on to release any of its $100 in reserves. It can expand its loans up to the point where its total deposits are $500.

Of course, there are many banks in the country, a situation that is depicted in Figure 10.3. As long as the banking system as a whole is closed, it is still possible for an initial deposit of $100 to result in an expansion of the money supply to $500, but more steps are involved when there is more than one bank.

To see why, assume that Mary makes an initial deposit of $100 in Bank 1 and the bank deposits the entire $100 with the Fed (panel 1 of Figure 10.3). All loans that a bank makes are withdrawn from the bank as the individual borrowers write checks to pay for merchandise. After Mary's deposit, Bank 1 can make a loan of up to $80 to Bill because it needs to keep only $20 of its $100 deposit as reserves. (We are assuming a 20 percent required reserve ratio.) In other words, Bank 1 has $80 in excess reserves.

Bank 1's balance sheet at the moment of the loan to Bill appears in panel 2 of Figure 10.3. Bank 1 now has loans of $80. It has credited Bill's account with the $80, so its total deposits are $180 ($80 in loans plus $100 in reserves). Bill then writes a check for $80 for a set of shock absorbers for his car. Bill wrote his check to Sam's Car Shop, and Sam deposits Bill's check in Bank 2. When the check clears, Bank 1 transfers $80 in reserves to Bank 2. Bank 1's balance sheet now looks like the top of panel 3. Its assets include reserves of $20 and loans of $80; its liabilities are $100 in deposits. Both sides of the T-account balance: The bank's reserves are 20 percent of its deposits, as required by law, and it is fully loaned up.

	Panel 1		Panel 2		Panel 3	
	Assets	Liabilities	Assets	Liabilities	Assets	Liabilities
Bank 1						
	Reserves 100	100 Deposits	Reserves 100 Loans 80	180 Deposits	Reserves 20 Loans 80	100 Deposits
Bank 2						
	Reserves 80	80 Deposits	Reserves 80 Loans 64	144 Deposits	Reserves 16 Loans 64	80 Deposits
Bank 3						
	Reserves 64	64 Deposits	Reserves 64 Loans 51.20	115.20 Deposits	Reserves 12.80 Loans 51.20	64 Deposits

Summary:	Loans	Deposits
Bank 1	80	100
Bank 2	64	80
Bank 3	51.20	64
Bank 4	40.96	51.20
⋮	⋮	⋮
Total	400.00	500.00

▲ **FIGURE 10.3   The Creation of Money When There Are Many Banks**
In panel 1, there is an initial deposit of $100 in Bank 1. In panel 2, Bank 1 makes a loan of $80 by creating a deposit of $80. A check for $80 by the borrower is then written on Bank 1 (panel 3) and deposited in Bank 2 (panel 1). The process continues with Bank 2 making loans and so on. In the end, loans of $400 have been made and the total level of deposits is $500.

Now look at bank 2. Because Bank 1 has transferred $80 in reserves to Bank 2, Bank 2 now has $80 in deposits and $80 in reserves (panel 1, Bank 2). Its reserve requirement is also 20 percent, so it has excess reserves of $64 on which it can make loans.

Now assume that Bank 2 loans the $64 to Kate to pay for a textbook and Kate writes a check for $64 payable to the Manhattan College Bookstore. The final position of Bank 2, after it honors Kate's $64 check by transferring $64 in reserves to the bookstore's bank, is reserves of $16, loans of $64, and deposits of $80 (panel 3, Bank 2).

The Manhattan College Bookstore deposits Kate's check in its account with Bank 3. Bank 3 now has excess reserves because it had added $64 to its reserves. With a reserve ratio of 20 percent, Bank 3 can loan out $51.20 (80 percent of $64, leaving 20 percent in required reserves to back the $64 deposit).

As the process is repeated over and over, the total amount of deposits created is $500, the sum of the deposits in each of the banks. Because the banking system can be looked on as one big bank, the outcome here for many banks is the same as the outcome in Figure 10.2 for one bank.[3]

The Money Multiplier

In practice, the banking system is not completely closed—there is some leakage out of the system, as people send money abroad or even hide it under their mattresses! Still, the point here is that an increase in bank reserves can lead to a greater than one-for-one increase in the money supply. Economists call the relationship between the final change in deposits and the change in reserves that caused this change the money multiplier. Stated somewhat differently, the **money multiplier** is the multiple by which deposits can increase for every dollar increase in reserves. Do not confuse the money multiplier with the spending multipliers we discussed in the last two chapters. They are not the same thing.

money multiplier   The multiple by which deposits can increase for every dollar increase in reserves; equal to 1 divided by the required reserve ratio.

---

[3] If banks create money when they make loans, does repaying a loan "destroy" money? The answer is yes.

In the example we just examined, reserves increased by $100 when the $100 in cash was deposited in a bank and the amount of deposits increased by $500 ($100 from the initial deposit, $400 from the loans made by the various banks from their excess reserves). The money multiplier in this case is $500/$100 = 5. Mathematically, the money multiplier can be defined as follows:[4]

$$\text{money multiplier} \equiv \frac{1}{\text{required reserve ratio}}$$

In the United States, the required reserve ratio varies depending on the size of the bank and the type of deposit. For large banks and for checking deposits, the ratio is currently 10 percent, which makes the potential money multiplier 1/.10 = 10. This means that an increase in reserves of $1 could cause an increase in deposits of $10 if there were no leakage out of the system.

It is important to remember that the money multiplier is derived under the assumption that banks hold no excess reserves. For example, when Bank 1 gets the deposit of $100, it loans out the maximum that it can, namely $100 times 1 minus the reserve requirement ratio. If instead Bank 1 held the $100 as excess reserves, the increase in the money supply would just be the initial $100 in deposits (brought in, say, from outside the banking system). We return to the question of excess reserves later in this chapter.

10.3 LEARNING OBJECTIVE

Describe the functions and structure of the Federal Reserve System.

The Federal Reserve System

We have seen how the private banking system can create money by making loans. However, private banks are not free to create money at will. We have already seen the way that their ability to create money is governed by the reserve requirements set by the Fed. We will now examine the structure and function of the Fed.

Founded in 1913 by an act of Congress (to which major reforms were added in the 1930s), the Fed is the central bank of the United States. The Fed is a complicated institution with many responsibilities, including the regulation and supervision of about 6,000 commercial banks. The organization of the Federal Reserve System is presented in Figure 10.4.

The *Board of Governors* is the most important group within the Federal Reserve System. The board consists of seven members, each appointed for 14 years by the president of the United States. The *chair* of the Fed, who is appointed by the president and whose term runs for 4 years, usually dominates the entire Federal Reserve System and is sometimes said to be the second most powerful person in the United States. The Fed is an independent agency in that it does not take orders from the president or from Congress. The United States is divided into 12 Federal Reserve districts, each with its own Federal Reserve bank. These districts are indicated on the map in Figure 10.4. The district banks are like branch offices of the Fed in that they carry out the rules, regulations, and functions of the central system in their districts and report to the Board of Governors on local economic conditions.

U.S. monetary policy is formally set by the **Federal Open Market Committee (FOMC)** The FOMC consists of the seven members of the Fed's Board of Governors; the president of the New York Federal Reserve Bank; and on a rotating basis, four of the presidents of the 11 other district banks. The FOMC sets goals concerning interest rates, and it directs the **Open Market Desk** in the New York Federal Reserve Bank to buy and/or sell government securities. (We discuss the specifics of open market operations later in this chapter.)

Federal Open Market Committee (FOMC) A group composed of the seven members of the Fed's Board of Governors, the president of the New York Federal Reserve Bank, and 4 of the other 11 district bank presidents on a rotating basis; it sets goals concerning the money supply and interest rates and directs the operation of the Open Market Desk in New York.

Open Market Desk The office in the New York Federal Reserve Bank from which government securities are bought and sold by the Fed.

---

[4] To show this mathematically, let *rr* denote the reserve requirement ratio, like 0.20. Say someone deposits 100 in Bank 1 in Figure 10.3. Bank 1 can create $100(1 - rr)$ in loans, which are then deposits in Bank 2. Bank 2 can create $100(1 - rr)(1 - rr)$ in loans, which are then deposits in Bank 3, and so on. The sum of the deposits is thus $100[1 + (1 - rr) + (1 - rr)^2 + (1 - rr)^3 + \ldots]$. The sum of the infinite series in brackets is $1/rr$, which is the money multiplier.

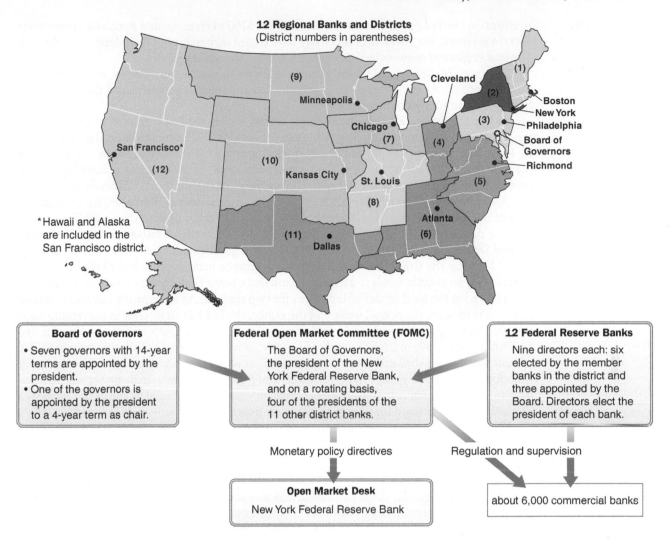

▲ FIGURE 10.4   **The Structure of the Federal Reserve System**

Functions of the Federal Reserve

The Fed is the central bank of the United States. Central banks are sometimes known as "bankers' banks" because only banks (and occasionally foreign governments) can have accounts in them. As a private citizen, you cannot go to the nearest branch of the Fed and open a checking account or apply to borrow money.

As we will see shortly, the Fed is responsible for monetary policy in the United States, but it also performs several important administrative functions for banks. These functions include clearing interbank payments, regulating the banking system, and assisting banks in a difficult financial position. The Fed is also responsible for managing exchange rates and the nation's foreign exchange reserves.[5] In addition, it is often involved in intercountry negotiations on international economic issues.

Clearing interbank payments works as follows. Suppose you write a $100 check drawn on your bank, the First Bank of Fresno (FBF), to pay for tulip bulbs from Crockett Importers of Miami, Florida. How does your money get from your bank in Fresno to Crockett's bank in Florida? The Fed does it. Both FBF and Banco de Miami have accounts at the Fed. When Crockett Importers receives your check and deposits it at Banco de Miami, the bank submits the check to the Fed, asking it to collect the funds from FBF. The Fed presents the check to FBF and is instructed to debit FBF's account for the $100 and to credit the account of Banco de Miami.

---

[5]*Foreign exchange reserves* are holdings of the currencies of other countries—for example, Japanese yen—by the U.S. government. We discuss exchange rates and foreign exchange markets at length in Chapter 19.

Accounts at the Fed count as reserves, so FBF loses $100 in reserves, and Banco de Miami gains $100 in reserves. The two banks effectively have traded ownerships of their deposits at the Fed. The *total* volume of reserves has not changed, nor has the money supply.

This way of clearing interbank payments allows banks to shift money around virtually instantaneously. All they need to do is wire the Fed and request a transfer, and the funds move from one computer account to another.

Besides facilitating the transfer of funds among banks, the Fed is responsible for many of the regulations governing banking practices and standards. For example, the Fed has the authority to control mergers among banks, and it is responsible for examining banks to ensure that they are financially sound and that they conform to a host of government accounting regulations. As we saw previously, the Fed also sets reserve requirements for all financial institutions.

An important responsibility of the Fed is to act as the **lender of last resort** for the banking system. As our discussion of goldsmiths suggested, banks are subject to the possibility of runs on their deposits. In the United States, most deposits of less than $250,000 are insured by the Federal Deposit Insurance Corporation (FDIC), a U.S. government agency that was established in 1933 during the Great Depression. Deposit insurance makes panics less likely but the Fed stands ready to provide funds to a troubled bank that cannot find any other sources of funds.

The Fed is the ideal lender of last resort for two reasons. As a nonprofit institution whose function is to serve the overall welfare of the public, the Fed has an interest in preventing catastrophic banking panics such as those that occurred in the late 1920s and the 1930s. The Fed also has an essentially unlimited supply of funds with which to help banks facing the possibility of runs since as we shall see, it can create reserves at will. These administrative and regulatory functions of the Fed are important, but its central function is to help manage the macroeconomy by setting the interest rate. To see how this process works we need to add to our analysis a discussion of the demand for money, to which we now turn.

lender of last resort One of the functions of the Fed: It provides funds to troubled banks that cannot find any other sources of funds.

10.4 LEARNING OBJECTIVE

Describe the determinants of money demand.

The Demand for Money

Think about the financial assets of a household. Some of those assets are held in what we have called in this chapter M1 money, cash and checking accounts offering little or no interest but great convenience in use. One can access these accounts by withdrawing money, but also by using a debit card or smartphone connected to a checking account. Other assets likely held by a household include interest-bearing savings accounts and securities which are less convenient to use, but do earn interest. In this section we consider how households think about dividing their assets between these two broad categories. What determines how much money people choose to hold?

As we have seen, one of the major functions of money is as a means of exchange, to facilitate transactions. We have already discussed the transactions use of money. Convenience in transactions is an obvious motive for people to hold some money, rather than keep all their assets in a harder-to-use savings account. In this section we consider what determines *how much* money people choose to hold. We will assume in this discussion that money as we are defining it earns no interest. It can take the form of either cash or deposits in non-interest-bearing checking accounts. Note that if debit cards or cell phones are used to pay for items in stores, deposits in checking accounts are needed to back this up. So "money" is being used for these kinds of payments.

Consider a simple example of how the decision to hold money versus an interest-bearing instrument might work. We will also assume for simplicity that there is only one other form other than money in which financial assets can be held, namely in a "savings account," which earns interest. Say at the end of the month the firm you work for deposits $5,000 in your checking account. If you leave the deposits in your checking account, you earn no interest. If you move some or all to your savings account, you earn interest on the amount moved. How much should you move? The gain from moving is the interest you earn on the amount moved. The constraint is that you may need the deposits in your checking account to support your transactions, via checks, debit card, or smartphone. The deposits in your checking account support your transactions. The more of your assets you move to your savings account, the more often you will have to move deposits back to your checking account as it is drawn down by your transactions.

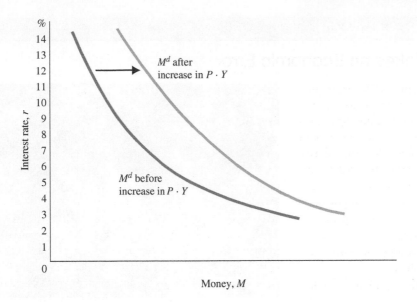

◀ **FIGURE 10.5** **The Demand for Money**
The quantity of money demanded (Md) depends negatively on the interest rate because the opportunity cost of holding money decreases as the interest rate falls. An increase in transactions ($P * Y$) shifts the money demand curve to the right.

We thus have a typical economic trade-off here. You gain interest by moving checking account deposits to your savings account, but the more you move, the more often you will have to move some back, which is costly in time. How much should you move? Here is where the interest rate plays a key role. The higher the interest rate, the more costly it is to keep deposits in your checking account. If the interest rate is close to zero, as it has been for a number of years, you earn very little by moving deposits to your savings account, so there is little reason to do so. There is a time cost of moving deposits back and forth, and there is no reason to bear this cost if you are earning practically nothing on your savings account. On the other hand, if the interest rate rises, the opportunity cost of keeping deposits in your checking account rises, and you should move some of the deposits to your savings account. The higher the interest rate, the more deposits you should keep on average in your savings account, other things being equal. Or, put another way, the higher the interest rate, the less on average you should hold in the form of money in your checking account. The amount of money you should hold thus depends negatively on the interest rate. Again, this is because a high interest rate means the opportunity cost of holding money is high because of the interest lost by not moving deposits to your savings account. You trade off convenience against an interest rate.

The amount of money you want to hold obviously also depends on the size of your transactions. The more you spend in a given period, the more deposits on average you will want to have in your checking account, other things being equal. If you hold very little in your checking account relative to the size of your transactions, the more time you will need to spend moving deposits from your savings account to your checking account, which is costly.

To summarize then, the demand for money depends positively on the size of total transactions in a period and negatively on the interest rate. In what follows we will use nominal income $P * Y$ as the measure of transactions. Figure 10.5 shows the demand for money schedule. The schedule slopes down because, as just discussed, the demand for money rises as the interest rate falls. The figure also shows that the demand for money curve shifts to the right as $P * Y$ increases because of the increase in transactions. The relationship between money demand and the interest rate will be an important part of our story of monetary policy and the Fed.

Interest Rates and Security Prices

Before we discuss how the Fed controls the interest rate, we need to briefly digress and consider the relationship between interest rates and security prices.

In our discussion thus far we have described the way in which households choose between holding money and holding their assets in interest-bearing securities or accounts. Interest-bearing

10.5 LEARNING OBJECTIVE

Define interest and discuss the relationship between interest rates and security prices.

ECONOMICS IN PRACTICE

Professor Serebryakov Makes an Economic Error

In Chekhov's play *Uncle Vanya*, Alexander Vladimirovitch Serebryakov, a retired professor, but apparently not of economics, calls his household together to make an announcement. He has retired to his country estate, but he does not like living there. Unfortunately, the estate does not derive enough income to allow him to live in town. To his gathered household, he thus proposes the following:

> Omitting details, I will put it before you in rough outline. Our estate yields on an average not more than two per cent, on its capital value. I propose to sell it. If we invest the money in suitable securities, we should get from four to five per cent, and I think we might even have a few thousand roubles to spare for buying a small villa in Finland.

This idea was not well received by the household, especially by Uncle Vanya, who lost it for a while and tried to kill Professor Serebryakov, but no one pointed out that this was bad economics. As discussed in the text, if you buy a bond and interest rates rise, the price of your bond falls. What Professor Serebryakov does not realize is that what he is calling the capital value of the estate, on which he is earning 2 percent, is not the value for which he could sell the estate if the interest rate on "suitable" securities is 5 percent. If an investor in Russia can earn 5 percent on these securities, why would he or she buy an estate earning only 2 percent? The price of the estate would have to fall until the return to the investor was 5 percent. To make matters worse, it may have been that the estate was a riskier investment than the securities, and if this were so,

a return higher than 5 percent would have been required on the estate purchase to compensate the investor for the extra risk. This would, of course, lower the price of the estate even more. In short, this is not a scheme by which the professor could earn more money than what the estate is currently yielding. Perhaps had Uncle Vanya taken an introductory economics course and known this, he would have been less agitated.

THINKING PRACTICALLY

1. What would happen to the value of the estate if the interest rate on the securities that Professor Serebryakov is talking about fell?

securities are issued by firms and the government seeking to borrow money. Short-term securities are usually called "bills," and long-term securities are usually called "bonds." Both types of securities work in similar ways. To induce lenders to buy these securities and provide funds, borrowers promise no only to return the funds borrowed at some later date but also to pay interest. For our discussion we will look at a 10-year U.S. Treasury security, a government bond.

Bonds are issued with a face value, typically in denominations of $1,000. They also come with a maturity date, which is the date the borrower agrees to pay the lender the face value of the bond. A bond also specifies a fixed dollar payment that will be paid to the bondholder each year. This payment is known as a coupon. Say that on January 2, 2015, the U.S. Treasury issued a 10-year bond that had a face value of $1,000 and paid a coupon of $20 per year. The bond was sold on this date in the bond market. The price at which the bond sold would be whatever price the market determined it to be. Say that the market-determined price was in fact $1,000. (The Treasury when issuing bonds tries to choose the coupon to be such that the price that the bond initially sells for is roughly equal to its face value.) The lender would give the Treasury a check for $1,000, and every January for the next 10 years the Treasury would send the lender a check for $20. Then on January 2, 2025, the Treasury would send the lender a check for the face value of the bond—$1,000—plus the last coupon payment—$20—and that would square all accounts.

In this example the interest rate that the lender receives each year on his or her $1,000 investment is 2 percent. In return for the $1,000 payment the lender receives $20 each year, or 2 percent of the market price of the bond.

Suppose that just before the government put its bond on the market, many other, identical-looking bonds were offered to lenders with coupons of $30, face values of $1,000, and maturity of 10 years. And suppose that these bonds were selling for $1,000. Could the Treasury still sell its bond? The answer is yes, but at a lower price. What would that price be? The other securities are offering lenders 3 percent interest, so the Treasury will have to do the same. With a coupon value fixed at $20, the only way to raise the interest rate to the required 3 percent is to lower the price of the bond. The market price of the bond will be less than $1,000.

A key relationship that we can see from this example and that we will use later in this chapter is that market-determined prices of existing bonds and interest rates are inversely related. When the Treasury (or a firm) issues a bond, the face value, coupon, and maturity are set. This means that the market price of the bond will change as market interest rates change. When interest rates rise, prices of existing bonds fall. We will use the inverse relationship between interest rates and bond prices as we explore monetary policy post 2008 near the end of the next section. We turn now to put money supply and money demand together to look at how monetary policy works through the Fed.

How the Federal Reserve Controls the Interest Rate

10.6 LEARNING OBJECTIVE
Understand how the Fed can change the interest rate.

Tools Prior to 2008

Traditionally the Fed had three tools available to it to control the interest rate via changing the money supply: open market operations, changing the reserve requirement ratio, and changing the discount rate that banks pay to the Fed to borrow reserves.

Consider again Figure 10.2. We see in this figure that if commercial bank reserves increase by $100 with a reserve requirement ratio of 20 percent, bank loans can increase by $400, with the money supply increasing by $500 ($400 in loans plus the initial $100 in reserves). This calculation assumes that no excess reserves are held. So one way the Fed can increase the money supply is by simply increasing reserves. How does the Fed do this? Its principal tool is to buy U.S. Treasury securities from the banks, which the banks hold. These securities do not count as reserves when held by the banks. If the Fed buys $100 in securities from a bank, it credits the bank with $100 in reserves. The bank's reserves have gone up by $100, so it can make loans of $400, thus increasing the money supply by $500. (We are assuming a single-bank economy, but the analysis goes through with many banks, as in Figure 10.3.) Conversely, if the Fed sells $100 in securities, the bank's reserves go down by $100 (the securities are paid for by the bank by a debit to the bank's reserves), and loans must be decreased by $400, thus decreasing the money supply by $500. This buying and selling of government securities by the Fed is called **open market operations**. Prior to 2008, when essentially no excess reserves were held by banks, it was the main way in which the Fed changed the money supply.

open market operations
The purchase and sale by the Fed of government securities in the open market.

Deposits in Figure 10.2 can also be increased if the reserve requirement ratio is lowered. We have already seen this in our discussion of the creation of money. If the reserve requirement ratio were 10 percent rather than 20 percent, loans of $900 could be made, thus increasing the money supply (deposits) to $1,000. Conversely, if the reserve requirement ratio were increased, loans would have to fall and thus the money supply (deposits) would fall. In the period before 2008, when banks rarely held excess reserves, changing the reserve requirement ratio was another tool the Fed could use to change the money supply, although it used this tool infrequently.

Banks also have the option to borrow reserves from the Fed, which they did now and again prior to 2008. Borrowed reserves are counted as reserves that can back loans, so when there is an increase in borrowed reserves, there is an increase in the money supply as banks increase their loans. Banks pay interest on the borrowed reserves, called the **discount rate**, and so a third way the Fed can increase the money supply is to lower the discount rate, inducing banks to borrow more and thus expand loans. Conversely, the Fed can raise the discount rate, inducing banks to pay back some of their borrowed reserves and thus contract loans. This third tool to change the money supply, changing the discount rate, was also infrequently used.

discount rate   The interest rate that banks pay to the Fed to borrow from it.

How do these tools give the Fed the ability to control the interest rate? We have just seen that when no excess reserves are held, the Fed can change the money supply through one of the three tools, the main tool being open market operations. The Fed can thus set the value of the money supply, the quantity of money, at whatever it wants. Assuming that the money market clears, which it does in practice, we can combine the demand for money schedule in Figure 10.5 with the money supply that the Fed chooses to determine the equilibrium value of the interest rate. This is done in Figure 10.6. Given the quantity of money that the Fed chooses to supply, the interest rate can simply be read off the money demand schedule. A value of M_0 leads to an interest rate of r_0 in the figure. Figure 10.6 also shows that if the Fed increases the money supply, from M_0 to M_1, the interest rate falls from r_0 to r_1. So any change in the money supply that the Fed might make leads to a change in the interest rate, with the magnitude of the interest rate change depending on the shape of the money demand function.

Prior to 2008 the preceding discussion would be the end of the story. Banks essentially held no excess reserves, and the Fed engaged in open market operations to change the money supply and the interest rate. This channel for monetary policy changed in 2008, as the Fed responded to the financial crisis.

Expanded Fed Activities Beginning in 2008

In March 2008, faced with many large financial institutions simultaneously in serious financial trouble, the Fed began to broaden its role in the banking system. No longer would it be simply a lender of last resort to banks, but it would become an active participant in the private banking system. How did this change come about?

Beginning in about 2003, the U.S. economy experienced rapidly rising housing prices, in what some called a "housing bubble." Financial institutions began issuing mortgages with less oversight, in some cases to households with poor credit ratings (so-called sub prime borrowers). Some households bought homes they could not afford based on their incomes, expecting to eventually "cash in" on the rising housing prices. Regulation, by the Fed or other federal or state agencies, was lax, and many financial firms took very large risks. When housing prices began to fall in late 2005, the stage was set for a financial crisis. Financial institutions, even large ones, began to experience very large losses, as home owners began defaulting on their loans, setting off a chain reaction that many people thought threatened the economic system.

The Fed responded to these events in a number of ways. In March 2008 it participated in an attempted bailout of Bear Stearns, a large financial institution, by guaranteeing $30 billion of Bear Stearns' liabilities to JPMorgan. On September 7, 2008, it participated in a government takeover of the Federal National Mortgage Association (Fannie Mae) and the Federal Home Loan Mortgage Corporation (Freddie Mac), which at that time owned or guaranteed about half of the $12 trillion mortgage market in the United States. On September 17, 2008, the Fed loaned $85 billion to the

▶ **FIGURE 10.6 The Equilibrium Interest Rate**
Given a value of the money supply that the Fed chooses, the equilibrium interest rate can be read off of the money demand schedule. If the Fed increases the money supply from M_0 to M_1, the interest rate falls from r_0 to r_1.

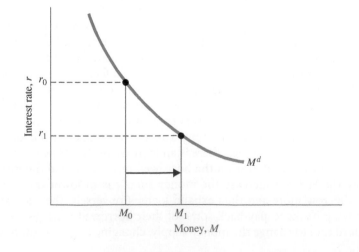

American International Group (AIG) insurance company to help it avoid bankruptcy. In mid-September, the Fed urged Congress to pass a $700 billion bailout bill, which was signed into law on October 3.

In the process of bailing out Fannie Mae and Freddie Mac, in September 2008 the Fed began buying securities of these two associations, called "federal agency debt securities." More remarkable, however, is that in January 2009 the Fed began buying mortgage-backed securities, securities that the private sector was reluctant to hold because of their perceived riskiness, and long-term government bonds. By September 2012 the Fed was buying mortgage-backed securities and long-term government bonds to the tune of $85 billion per month. This practice ended in November 2014. Most of these purchases ended up as an increase in excess reserves of commercial banks, as we will see in the next section.

As is not surprising, there has been much political discussion of whether the Fed should have regulated financial institutions more in 2003–2005 and whether its subsequent active role in the system was warranted. Whatever one's views, it is certainly the case that the Fed has taken a much more active role in financial markets since 2008.

The Federal Reserve Balance Sheet

The expanded Fed activities we have just described can be seen clearly by examining the way in which the Fed's balance sheet changed during the period after 2008.

Although the Fed is a special bank, it is similar to an ordinary commercial bank in that it has a balance sheet that records its asset and liability position at any moment of time. The balance sheet for April 9, 2015, is presented in Table 10.1.

On April 9, 2015, the Fed had $4,528 billion in assets, of which $11 billion was gold, $2,460 billion was U.S. Treasury securities, $37 billion was federal agency debt securities, $1,732 billion was mortgage-backed securities, and $288 billion was other.

Gold is trivial. *Do not think that this gold has anything to do with money in circulation.* Most of the gold was acquired during the 1930s, when it was purchased from the U.S. Treasury Department. Since 1934, the dollar has not been backed by (is not convertible into) gold. You cannot take a dollar bill to the Fed to receive gold for it; all you can get for your old dollar bill is a new dollar bill.[6] Although it is unrelated to the money supply, the Fed's gold counts as an asset on its balance sheet because it is something of value the Fed owns.

U.S. Treasury securities are the traditional assets held by the Fed. These are obligations of the federal government that the Fed has purchased over the years. As we discussed previously, when banks hold no excess reserves the buying and selling of Treasury securities (open market operations) is the way the Fed affects the money supply and the interest rate. Before the change in Fed behavior in 2008, almost all of its assets were in the form of U.S. Treasury securities. For

TABLE 10.1   Assets and Liabilities of the Federal Reserve System, April 9, 2015 (Billions of Dollars)

Assets			Liabilities
Gold	$ 11	$1,363	Currency in circulation
U.S. Treasury securities	2,460	2,793	Reserve balances (about 110 required)
Federal agency debt securities	37	62	U.S. Treasury deposits
Mortgage-backed securities	1,732	310	All other liabilities and net worth
All other assets	288	$4,528	Total
Total	$4,528		

Source: Federal Reserve Statistical Release, Factors affecting Reserve Balances, Board of Governors of the Federal Reserve System.

MyEconLab Real-time data

---

[6] The fact that the Fed is not obliged to provide gold for currency means it can never go bankrupt. When the currency was backed by gold, it would have been possible for the Fed to run out of gold if too many of its depositors came to it at the same time and asked to exchange their deposits for gold. If depositors come to the Fed to withdraw their deposits today, all they can get is dollar bills. The dollar was convertible into gold internationally until August 15, 1971.

example, in the ninth edition of this text, the balance sheet presented was for October 24, 2007, where total Fed assets were $885 billion, of which $780 billion were U.S. Treasury securities.

The new assets of the Fed (since 2008) are federal agency debt securities and mortgage-backed securities. (These were both zero in the October 24, 2007 balance sheet.) U.S. Treasury securities, federal agency debt securities, and mortgage-backed securities now total $4.229 trillion. The Fed's intervention in these markets has been huge. Of the Fed's liabilities, $1,363 billion is currency in circulation, $2,793 billion is reserve balances, $62 billion is U.S. Treasury deposits, and $310 billion is other. The Fed acts as a bank for the U.S. government, and so U.S. Treasury deposits are held by the U.S. government at the Fed. When the government needs to pay for something like a new aircraft carrier, it may write a check to the supplier of the ship drawn on its "checking account" at the Fed. Similarly, when the government receives revenues from tax collections, fines, or sales of government assets, it may deposit these funds at the Fed.

Currency in circulation accounts for about 30 percnt of the Fed's liabilities. The dollar bill that you use to buy a pack of gum is clearly an asset from your point of view. Because every financial asset is by definition a liability of some other agent in the economy, whose liability is the dollar bill? The dollar bill is a liability—an IOU—of the Fed. It is, of course, a strange IOU because it can only be redeemed for another IOU of the same type. It is nonetheless classified as a liability of the Fed.

Reserve balances account for about 62 percent of the Fed's liabilities. These are the reserves that commercial banks hold at the Fed. Remember that commercial banks are required to keep a certain fraction of their deposits at the Fed. These deposits are assets of the commercial banks and liabilities of the Fed. What is remarkable about the $2,793 billion in reserve balances at the Fed is that only about $110 billion are required reserves. The rest—more than $2,600 billion—are excess reserves, reserves that the commercial banks could lend to the private sector if they wanted to. The existence of these excess reserves complicates our story of the Fed's operations.

Tools After 2008

After 2008 we see that we are no longer in a world of zero excess reserves. Indeed, excess reserves on April 9, 2015, were more than $2.6 trillion, which is considerably above zero! What does this do to the Fed's ability to change the money supply and the interest rate?

Since the end of 2008 the short-term interest rate has been low, close to but not quite zero. However, by the spring of 2015 the financial markets expected that the Fed would begin raising the interest rate by at least the fall of 2015. How can the Fed do this? Not through the traditional tools of open market operations, reserve requirement ratio, and discount rate. Consider open market operations. Prior to 2008 the Fed would sell government securities, which would decrease reserves, contract bank loans, drive down the money supply, and thus increase the interest rate. Now, however, if the Fed sold government securities, the securities would mostly be bought by the banks with their excess reserves. Bank reserves would decrease, but with ample excess reserves remaining no contraction in bank loans is needed. Look at Table 10.1. If the Fed sold $1 trillion in U.S. Treasury securities, there would be a fall in U.S. Treasury securities of $1 trillion and a fall in Reserve balances of $1 trillion. Both Fed assets and liabilities would be lower by $1 trillion, but there would be no change in the interest rate! Banks would now have $1 trillion less in reserves, but still have more than $1.6 trillion in excess reserves. Just swapping Treasury securities for reserves does not change the interest rate. For the same reason, changing the reserve requirement ratio is also useless: the banks are already well over the requirement.

When the time comes that the Fed wants to raise the interest rate, the tool that it will probably use is to increase the rate it pays to banks on their reserves. Beginning in the post-2008 period, the Fed began paying a small interest rate on the bank reserves it holds. Indeed, this may help to explain why banks are holding these reserves rather than lending them out. The interest rate that the Fed pays on reserves is about the same as the interest rate on short-term U.S. Treasury securities (small, but not zero). (The following analysis is somewhat speculative because as of the time of this writing, September 2015, the Fed had not yet tried to increase the interest rate.) Suppose the Fed decided to raise the rate it pays banks on their reserves by 0.50 percentage points. What effect does this have on the short-term U.S. Treasury securities market? With some simplification, the story is roughly as follows. Banks hold both reserves and Treasury securities. Before the Fed increases the rate paid on bank reserves, the interest rate on reserves and short-term Treasury securities is roughly the same. After the Fed's move, the interest rate on reserves is 0.50 points higher. This higher rate induces banks to try to sell their now unattractive securities to the Fed. If the Fed won't buy, the price of the securities will fall because supply has increased and demand is unchanged. As we saw in the previous section, when the price of a security falls, the interest rate rises, so with security prices falling, the interest rate on the securities rises. The new equilibrium will be where the interest rate on the securities is also 0.50 points higher. The interest rate on short-term Treasury securities can thus be changed by the Fed simply increasing the rate it pays on bank reserves. This requires no change in the Fed's balance sheet.

Finally, we should add that when the Fed changes the short-term interest rate, this also changes longer-term interest rates. This is briefly explained in the appendix to this chapter. The appendix also discusses some of the key interest rates in the U.S. economy. Although in the text we are primarily focusing on one interest rate, denoted r, in practice there are many.

Looking Ahead

This has been a long chapter, but for future analysis we really only need one point, namely that the Fed has the ability to control the short-term interest rate. Before 2008 it did this primarily through open market operations, and in the future (2015 or later) it will probably do this by changing the rate it pays banks on their reserves with the Fed.

SUMMARY

10.1 AN OVERVIEW OF MONEY p. 188

1. Money has three distinguishing characteristics: (1) a *means of payment*, or *medium of exchange*; (2) *a store of value*; and (3) *a unit of account*. The alternative to using money is *barter*, in which goods are exchanged directly for other goods. Barter is costly and inefficient in an economy with many different kinds of goods.

2. *Commodity monies* are items that are used as money and that have an intrinsic value in some other use—for example, gold and cigarettes. *Fiat monies* are intrinsically worthless apart from their use as money. To ensure the acceptance of fiat monies, governments use their power to declare money *legal tender* and promise the public they will not debase the currency by expanding its supply rapidly.

3. There are various definitions of money. Currency plus demand deposits plus traveler's checks plus other checkable deposits compose M1, or *transactions money*—money that can be used directly to buy things. The addition of savings accounts and money market accounts (*near monies*) to M1 gives M2, or *broad money*.

10.2 HOW BANKS CREATE MONEY p. 192

4. The *required reserve ratio* is the percentage of a bank's deposits that must be kept as *reserves* at the nation's central bank, the *Federal Reserve*.

5. Banks create money by making loans. When a bank makes a loan to a customer, it creates a deposit in that customer's account. This deposit becomes part of the money supply. Banks can create money only when they have *excess reserves*—reserves in excess of the amount set by the required reserve ratio.

6. The *money multiplier* is the multiple by which the total supply of money can increase for every dollar increase in reserves. The money multiplier is equal to 1/required reserve ratio.

10.3 THE FEDERAL RESERVE SYSTEM p. 198

7. The Fed's most important function is controlling the short-term interest rate. The Fed also performs several other functions: It clears interbank payments, is responsible for many of the regulations governing banking practices and standards, and acts as a *lender of last resort* for troubled banks that cannot find any other sources of funds. The Fed also acts as the bank for the U.S. government.

10.4 THE DEMAND FOR MONEY p. 200

8. The demand for money depends negatively on the interest rate. The higher the interest rate, the higher the opportunity cost (more interest forgone) from holding money and the less money people will want to hold. An increase in the interest rate reduces the quantity demanded for money, and the money demand curve slopes downward.

9. The demand for money depends positively on nominal income. Aggregate nominal income is $P \cdot Y$, where P is the aggregate price level and Y is aggregate real income. An increase in either P or Y increases the demand for money.

10.5 INTEREST RATES AND SECURITY PRICES *p. 201*

10. Interest rates and security prices are inversely related. If market interest rates rise, prices of existing bonds fall.

10.6 HOW THE FEDERAL RESERVE CONTROLS THE INTEREST RATE *p. 203*

11. Prior to 2008 the Fed had three tools to control the money supply: (1) changing the required reserve ratio, (2) changing the *discount rate* (the interest rate member banks pay when they borrow from the Fed), and (3) engaging in *open market operations* (the buying and selling of already-existing government securities). To increase the money supply, the Fed could create additional reserves by lowering the discount rate or by buying government securities, or the Fed could increase the number of deposits that can be created from a given quantity of reserves by lowering the required reserve ratio. To decrease the money supply, the Fed could reduce reserves by raising the discount rate or by selling government securities or it could raise the required reserve ratio.

12. In the post-2008 period large quantities of excess reserves have been held by banks. The Fed is now paying interest on these reserves. When the Fed wants to raise interest rates in the future it will likely do so by increasing the interest rate it pays on bank reserves.

REVIEW TERMS AND CONCEPTS

barter, *p. 188*

commodity monies, *p. 190*

currency debasement, *p. 190*

discount rate, *p. 203*

excess reserves, *p. 195*

Federal Open Market Committee (FOMC), *p. 198*

Federal Reserve Bank (the Fed), *p. 194*

fiat, *or* token, money, *p. 190*

legal tender, *p. 190*

lender of last resort, *p. 200*

liquidity property of money, *p. 189*

M1, *or* transactions money, *p. 191*

M2, *or* broad money, *p. 191*

medium of exchange, *or* means of payment, *p. 188*

money multiplier, *p. 197*

near monies, *p. 191*

Open Market Desk, *p. 198*

open market operations, *p. 203*

required reserve ratio, *p. 195*

reserves, *p. 194*

run on a bank, *p. 194*

store of value, *p. 188*

unit of account, *p. 189*

Equations:

M1 $\equiv$ currency held outside banks + demand deposits + traveler's checks + other checkable deposits, *p. 191*

M2 $\equiv$ M1 + savings accounts + money market accounts + other near monies, *p. 191*

Assets $\equiv$ Liabilities + Net Worth, *p. 194*

Excess reserves $\equiv$ actual reserves $-$ required reserves, *p. 195*

Money multiplier $\equiv \dfrac{1}{\text{required reserve ratio}}$, *p. 198*

PROBLEMS

All problems are available on MyEconLab.

10.1 AN OVERVIEW OF MONEY

LEARNING OBJECTIVE: Define money and discuss its functions.

1.1 **[Related to the *Economics in Practice* on p. 189]** It is well known that cigarettes served as money for prisoners of war in World War II. Do an Internet search using the key word cigarettes and write a description of how this came to be and how it worked.

1.2 As king of Medivalia, you are constantly strapped for funds to pay your army. Your chief economic wizard suggests the following plan: "When you collect your tax payments from your subjects, insist on being paid in gold coins. Take those gold coins, melt them down, and remint them with an extra 10 percent of brass thrown in. You will then have 10 percent more money than you started with." What do you think of the plan? Will it work?

1.3 Why is M2 sometimes a more stable measure of money than M1? Explain in your own words using the definitions of M1 and M2.

1.4 After suffering two years of staggering hyperinflation, the African nation of Zimbabwe officially abandoned its currency, the Zimbabwean dollar, in April 2009 and made the U.S. dollar its official currency. Why would anyone in Zimbabwe be willing to accept U.S. dollars in exchange for goods and services?

1.5 Although the official currency of the United States is the U.S. dollar, some towns and cities actually issue their own money. In these communities, consumers are able to buy local currency at a discounted rate using U.S. dollars (for example, a consumer may spend 95 U.S. cents to buy one local dollar, thereby receiving a 5 percent discount), and then can spend the local currency at stores that have agreed to accept it. The idea is to help local consumers save money and at the same time give local businesses a boost. These local currencies are being issued in communities as diverse as small towns in North Carolina and Massachusetts to cities as large as Detroit, Michigan. Do these local currencies qualify as money based on the description of what money is in the chapter?

1.6 Suppose on your 21st birthday, your eccentric grandmother invites you to her house, takes you into her library, removes a black velvet painting of Elvis Presley from the wall, opens a hidden safe where she removes 50 crisp $100 bills, and hands them to you as a present, claiming you are her favorite grandchild. After thanking your grandmother profusely (and helping her rehang the picture of Elvis), you proceed to your bank and deposit half of your gift in your checking account and half in your savings account. How will these transactions affect M1 and M2? How will these transactions change M1 and M2 in the short run? What about the long run?"

10.2 HOW BANKS CREATE MONEY

LEARNING OBJECTIVE: Explain how banks create money.

2.1 For each of the following, determine whether it is an asset or a liability on the accounting books of a bank. Explain why in each case.
   - Cash in the vault
   - Demand deposits
   - Savings deposits
   - Reserves
   - Loans
   - Deposits at the Federal Reserve

2.2 The U.S. money supply (M1) at the beginning of 2015 was $2,683.3 billion broken down as follows: $1165.7 billion in currency, $3.5 billion in traveler's checks, and $1,514.1 billion in checking deposits. Suppose the Fed decided to decrease the money supply by increasing the reserve requirement from 10 percent to 12 percent. Assuming all banks were initially loaned up (had no excess reserves) and currency held outside of banks did not change, how large a change in the money supply would have resulted from the change in the reserve requirement?

2.3 Do you agree or disagree with each of the following statements? Explain your answers.
   a. When the Treasury of the United States issues bonds and sells them to the public to finance the deficit, the money supply remains unchanged because every dollar of money taken in by the Treasury goes right back into circulation through government spending. This is not true when the Fed sells bonds to the public.
   b. The money multiplier depends on the marginal propensity to save.

*2.4 When the Fed adds new reserves to the system, some of these new reserves find their way out of the country into foreign banks or foreign investment funds. In addition, some portion of the new reserves ends up in people's pockets and under their mattresses instead of in bank vaults. These "leakages" reduce the money multiplier and sometimes make it difficult for the Fed to control the money supply precisely. Explain why this is true.

2.5 You are given this account for a bank:

Assets			Liabilities
Reserves	$1,200	$8,000	Deposits
Loans	6,800		

The required reserve ratio is 10 percent.
   a. How much is the bank required to hold as reserves given its deposits of $8,000?
   b. How much are its excess reserves?
   c. By how much can the bank increase its loans?
   d. Suppose a depositor comes to the bank and withdraws $500 in cash. Show the bank's new balance sheet, assuming the bank obtains the cash by drawing down its reserves. Does the bank now hold excess reserves? Is it meeting the required reserve ratio? If not, what can it do?

2.6 Suppose Ginger deposits $12,000 in cash into her checking account at the Bank of Skidoo. The Bank of Skidoo has no excess reserves and is subject to a 4 percent required reserve ratio.
   a. Show this transaction in a T-account for the Bank of Skidoo.
   b. Assume the Bank of Skidoo makes the maximum loan possible from Ginger's deposit to Thurston and show this transaction in a new T-account.
   c. Thurston decides to use the money he borrowed to purchase a sail boat. He writes a check for the entire loan amount to Gilligan's Seagoing Vessels, which deposits the check in its bank, the Paradise Bank of Kona, Hawaii. When the check clears, the Skidoo Bank transfers the funds to the Paradise Bank. Show these transactions in a new T-account for the Skidoo Bank and in a T-account for the Paradise Bank.
   d. What is the maximum amount of deposits that can be created from Ginger's initial deposit?
   e. What is the maximum amount of loans that can be created from Ginger's initial deposit?

10.3 THE FEDERAL RESERVE SYSTEM

LEARNING OBJECTIVE: Define the functions and structure of the Federal Reserve System.

3.1 The United States is divided into 12 Federal Reserve districts, each with a District Bank. These Districts and the locations for the District Bank in each region are shown in Figure 10.4. Do some research to find out why the districts are divided as they are, why the District Banks are located in the 12 cities shown in Figure 10.4, and why so many districts are located in the Eastern portion of the United States.

10.4 THE DEMAND FOR MONEY

LEARNING OBJECTIVE: Describe the determinants of money demand.

4.1 What if, at a low level of interest rates, the money demand curve became nearly horizontal, as in the following graph. That is, with interest rates so low, the public would not find it attractive to hold bonds; thus, money demand would be very high. Many argue that this was the position of the U.S. economy in 2003. If the Fed decided to expand the money supply in the graph, what would be the impact on interest rates?

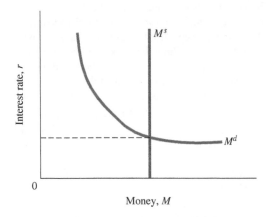

4.2 Explain why there is a negative relationship between the amount of money you should hold and the interest rate.

10.5 INTEREST RATES AND SECURITY PRICES

LEARNING OBJECTIVE: Define interest and discuss the relationship between interest rates and security prices.

5.1 [**Related to the** *Economics in Practice* **on p. 202**]
The *Economics in Practice* states that the capital value of Professor Serebryakov's estate is not the value for which he could sell the estate if the interest rate on "suitable" securities is higher than the average yield from the estate. What would happen to:
 a. the value of the estate if the interest rate on "suitable" securities rose?
 b. the value of the estate if investment in the estate was suddenly viewed as being less risky than investment in the securities?
 c. the yield on the securities if the securities were suddenly viewed as being more risky than was previously thought?

5.2 The United States entered a deep recession at the end of 2007. The Fed under Ben Bernanke used aggressive monetary policy to prevent the recession from becoming

another Great Depression. The Fed Funds target rate was 5.25 percent in the fall of 2007; by mid-2008, it stood at 2 percent; and in January 2009, it went to a range of 0 – 0.25 percent, where it still stood through mid-2015. Lower interest rates reduce the cost of borrowing and encourage firms to borrow and invest. They also have an effect on the value of the bonds (private and government) outstanding in the economy. Explain briefly but clearly why the value of bonds changes when interest rates change. Go to federalreserve.gov, click on "Economic Research & Data," and click on "Flow of Funds." Look at the most recent release and find balance sheet table B.100. How big is the value of Credit Market Instruments held by households?

5.3 Normally, people from the United States and from around the world think of highly rated corporate or government bonds as a safe place to put their savings relative to common stocks. Because the stock market had performed so poorly during the recession and because many foreigners turned to the United States as a safe place to invest, bond sales boomed.

If you were a holder of high-grade fixed-rate bonds that you purchased a few years earlier when rates were much higher, you found yourself with big capital gains. That is, as rates went lower, the value of previously issued bonds increased.
 a. Suppose you bought a $10,000 ten-year fixed-rate bond issued by the U.S. Treasury in July 2007 that paid 5% interest. In July 2010, new seven-year fixed-rate bonds were being sold by the Treasury that paid 2.43%. Explain clearly what was likely to have happened to the value of your bond which still has seven years to run paying 5%.
 b. Why would bond prices rise if people feared a recession was coming?

10.6 HOW THE FEDERAL RESERVE CONTROLS THE INTEREST RATE

LEARNING OBJECTIVE: Understand how the Fed can change the interest rate.

6.1 In the Republic of Doppelganger, the currency is the ditto. During 2015, the Treasury of Doppelganger sold bonds to finance the Doppelganger budget deficit. In all, the Treasury sold 80,000 ten-year bonds with a face value of 1,000 dittos each. The total deficit was 80 million dittos. The Doppelganger Central Bank reserve requirement was 16 percent and in the same year, the bank bought 10 million dittos' worth of outstanding bonds on the open market. All of the Doppelganger debt is held by either the private sector (the public) or the central bank.
 a. What is the combined effect of the Treasury sale and the central bank purchase on the total Doppelganger debt outstanding? On the debt held by the private sector?
 b. What is the effect of the Treasury sale on the money supply in Doppelganger?

c. Assuming no leakage of reserves out of the banking system, what is the effect of the central bank purchase of bonds on the money supply?

6.2 In 2000, the federal debt was being paid down because the federal budget was in surplus. Recall that surplus means that tax collections (*T*) exceed government spending (*G*). The surplus (*T* − *G*) was used to buy back government bonds from the public, reducing the federal debt. As we discussed in this chapter, the main method by which the Fed increases the money supply is to buy government bonds by using open market operations. What is the impact on the money supply of using the fiscal surplus to buy back bonds? In terms of their impacts on the money supply, what is the difference between Fed open market purchases of bonds and Treasury purchases of bonds using tax revenues?

6.3 If the head of the Central Bank of Brazil wanted to decrease the supply of money in Brazil in 2015, which of the following would do it? Explain your answer.
Increase the required reserve ratio
Decrease the required reserve ratio
Increase the discount rate
Decrease the discount rate
Buy government securities in the open market
Sell government securities in the open market

6.4 Suppose in the Republic of Sasquatch that the regulation of banking rested with the Sasquatchian Congress, including the determination of the reserve ratio. The Central Bank of Sasquatch is charged with regulating the money supply by using open market operations. In September 2015, the money supply was estimated to be 84 million yetis. At the same time, bank reserves were 12.6 million yetis and the reserve requirement was 15 percent. The banking industry, being "loaned up," lobbied the Congress to cut the reserve ratio. The Congress yielded and cut required reserves to 12 percent. What is the potential impact on the money supply? Suppose the central bank decided that the money supply should not be increased. What countermeasures could it take to prevent the Congress from expanding the money supply?

6.5 What are the three traditional tools the Fed can use to control the interest rate via changing the money supply? Briefly describe how the Fed can use each of these tools to either increase or decrease the money supply.

CHAPTER 10 APPENDIX

The Various Interest Rates in the U.S. Economy

LEARNING OBJECTIVE
Explain the relationship between a 2-year interest rate and a 1-year interest rate.

Although there are many different interest rates in the economy, they tend to move up or down with one another. Here we discuss some of their differences. We first look at the relationship between interest rates on securities with different maturities, or terms. We then briefly discuss some of the main interest rates in the U.S. economy.

The Term Structure of Interest Rates

The term structure of interest rates is the relationship among the interest rates offered on securities of different maturities. The key here is understanding issues such as these: How are these different rates related? Does a 2-year security (an IOU that promises to repay principal, plus interest, after 2 years) pay a lower annual rate than a 1-year security (an IOU to be repaid, with interest, after 1 year)? What happens to the rate of interest offered on 1-year securities if the rate of interest on 2-year securities increases?

Assume that you want to invest some money for 2 years and at the end of the 2 years you want it back. Assume that you want to buy government securities. For this analysis, we restrict your choices to two: (1) You can buy a 2-year security today and hold it for 2 years, at which time you cash it in (we will assume that the interest rate on the 2-year security is 3 percent per year), or (2) you can buy a 1-year security today. At the end of 1 year, you must cash this security in; you can then buy another 1-year security. At the end of the second year, you will cash in the second security. Assume that the interest rate on the first 1-year security is 2 percent.

Which would you prefer? Currently, you do not have enough data to answer this question. To consider choice (2) sensibly, you need to know the interest rate on the 1-year security that you intend to buy in the second year. This rate will not be known until the second year. All you know now is the rate on the 2-year security and the rate on the current 1-year security.

To decide what to do, you must form an expectation of the rate on the 1-year security a year from now. If you expect the 1-year rate (2 percent) to remain the same in the second year, you should buy the 2-year security. You would earn 3 percent per year on the 2-year security but only 2 percent per year on the two 1-year securities. If you expect the 1-year rate to rise to 5 percent a year from now, you should make the second choice. You would earn 2 percent in the first year, and you expect to earn 5 percent in the second year. The expected rate of return over the 2 years is about 3.5 percent, which is better than the 3 percent you can get on the 2-year security. If you expect the 1-year rate a year from now to be 4 percent, it does not matter much which of the two choices you make. The rate of return over the 2-year period will be roughly 3 percent for both choices.

We now alter the focus of our discussion to get to the topic we are really interested in—how the 2-year rate is determined. Assume that the 1-year rate has been set by the Fed and it is 2 percent. Also assume that people expect the 1-year rate a year from now to be 4 percent. What is the 2-year rate? According to a theory called the *expectations theory of the term structure of interest rates*, the 2-year rate is equal to the average of the current 1-year rate and the 1-year rate expected a year from now. In this example, the 2-year rate would be 3 percent (the average of 2 percent and 4 percent).

If the 2-year rate were lower than the average of the two 1-year rates, people would not be indifferent as to which security they held. They would want to hold only the short-term 1-year securities. To find a buyer for a 2-year security, the seller would be forced to increase the interest rate it offers on the 2-year security until it is equal to the average of the current 1-year rate and the expected 1-year rate for next year. The interest rate on the 2-year security will continue to rise until people are once again indifferent between one 2-year security and two 1-year securities.

Let us now return to Fed behavior. We know that the Fed can affect the short-term interest rate, but does it also affect long-term interest rates? The answer is "somewhat." Because the 2-year rate is an average of the current 1-year rate and the expected 1-year rate a year from now, the Fed influences the 2-year rate to the extent that it influences the current 1-year rate. The same holds for 3-year rates and beyond. The current short-term rate is a means by which the Fed can influence longer-term rates.

In addition, Fed behavior may directly affect people's expectations of the future short-term rates, which will then affect long-term rates. If the chair of the Fed testifies before Congress that raising short-term interest rates is under consideration, people's expectations of higher future short-term interest rates are likely to increase. These expectations will then be reflected in current long-term interest rates.

Types of Interest Rates

The following are some widely followed interest rates in the United States.

Three-Month Treasury Bill Rate   Government securities that mature in less than a year are called *Treasury bills*, or sometimes *T-bills*. The interest rate on 3-month Treasury bills is probably the most widely followed short-term interest rate.

Government Bond Rate   Government securities with terms of 1 year or more are called *government bonds*. There are 1-year bonds, 2-year bonds, and so on, up to 30-year bonds. Bonds of different terms have different interest rates. The relationship among the interest rates on the various maturities is the term structure of interest rates that we discussed in the first part of this Appendix.

Federal Funds Rate   Banks borrow not only from the Fed but also from each other. If one bank has excess reserves, it can lend some of those reserves to other banks through the federal funds market. The interest rate in this market is called the *federal funds rate*—the rate banks are charged to borrow reserves from other banks.

The federal funds market is really a desk in New York City. From all over the country, banks with excess reserves to lend and banks in need of reserves call the desk and negotiate a rate of interest. Account balances with the Fed are changed for the period of the loan without any physical movement of money.

This borrowing and lending, which takes place near the close of each working day, is generally for 1 day ("overnight"), so the federal funds rate is a 1-day rate. It is the rate on which the Fed has the most effect through its open market operations.

Commercial Paper Rate   Firms have several alternatives for raising funds. They can sell stocks, issue bonds, or borrow from a bank. Large firms can also borrow directly from the public by issuing "commercial paper," which is essentially short-term corporate IOUs that offer a designated rate of interest. The interest rate offered on commercial paper depends on the financial condition of the firm and the maturity date of the IOU.

Prime Rate   Banks charge different interest rates to different customers depending on how risky the banks perceive the customers to be. You would expect to pay a higher interest rate for a car loan than General Motors would pay for a $1 million loan to finance investment. Also, you would pay more interest for an unsecured loan, a "personal" loan, than for one that was secured by some asset, such as a house or car, to be used as collateral.

The prime rate is a benchmark that banks often use in quoting interest rates to their customers. A very low-risk corporation might be able to borrow at (or even below) the prime rate. A less well-known firm might be quoted a rate of "prime plus three-fourths," which means that if the prime rate is, say, 5 percent, the firm would have to pay interest of 5.75 percent. The prime rate depends on the cost of funds to the bank; it moves up and down with changes in the economy.

AAA Corporate Bond Rate   Corporations finance much of their investment by selling bonds to the public. Corporate bonds are classified by various bond dealers according to their risk. Bonds issued by General Motors are in less risk of default than bonds issued by a new risky biotech research firm. Bonds differ from commercial paper in one important way: Bonds have a longer maturity.

Bonds are graded in much the same way students are. The highest grade is AAA, the next highest AA, and so on. The interest rate on bonds rated AAA is the triple A corporate bond rate, the rate that the least risky firms pay on the bonds that they issue.

--- **APPENDIX PROBLEMS** ---

All problems are available on MyEconLab.

APPENDIX 10: THE VARIOUS INTEREST RATES IN THE U.S. ECONOMY

LEARNING OBJECTIVE: Explain the relationship between a 2-year interest rate and a 1-year interest rate.

1A.1 The following table gives three key U.S. interest rates in 1980 and again in 1993:

	1980 (%)	1993 (%)
Three-month U.S. government bills	11.39	3.00
Long-term U.S. government bonds	11.27	6.59
Prime rate	15.26	6.00

Provide an explanation for the extreme differences that you see. Specifically, comment on (1) the fact that rates in 1980 were much higher than in 1993 and (2) the fact that the long-term rate was higher than the short-term rate in 1993 but lower in 1980.

14

Financial Crises, Stabilization, and Deficits

We have seen in the last several chapters the way in which the government can use fiscal and monetary policies to affect the economy. And, yet, if you look back at Figure 5.5 on page 100 you can see that the unemployment rate still fluctuates widely. What accounts for these large fluctuations? Why can't policy makers do a better job of controlling the economy? This chapter covers a number of topics, but they are all concerned at least indirectly with trying to help answer this question.

In the next section we will consider the stock market and the housing market. Both of these markets have important effects on the economy through a household wealth effect. When stock prices or housing prices rise, household wealth rises, and households respond to this by consuming more. Economic models do a reasonably good job of estimating the effects of a wealth change on consumption. But they do a poor job of predicting the stock price and housing price changes that create that wealth change in the first place. Stock prices and housing prices are asset prices, and changes in these prices are, for the most part, unpredictable. Neither policy makers nor anyone else in the economy have the ability to predict how the stock and housing markets will behave in the future. This is then the first problem that policy makers face. If stock and housing prices are unpredictable, the best that policy makers can do is to try to react quickly to these changes once they occur. In this section we will also describe the way in which large unpredictable changes in these asset prices can lead to "financial crises" and what policy makers can and cannot do about them.

A second problem policy makers confront in stabilizing the economy is getting the timing right, which we cover in the second section of this chapter. We will see that there is a danger of overreacting to changes in the economy—making the fluctuations in the economy even worse than they otherwise would be. The third section of this chapter discusses government deficit issues. We learned at the end of Chapter 9 that it is important to distinguish between cyclical deficits and structural deficits. One expects that the government will run a deficit in a recession since tax revenue is down because of the sluggish economy and spending may be up as the government tries to stimulate the economy. If at full employment the government is *still* running a deficit, this part of the deficit is described as a structural deficit.

In 2015 many countries, including the United States, faced serious structural deficit problems. Many countries in the European Union struggled to meet the structural deficit targets set by the European Commission. We discuss various problems that may arise if a government runs large deficits year after year, including the possibility of a financial crisis. We will also look at some of the historical ways that have been used to control deficits in the United States.

The Stock Market, the Housing Market, and Financial Crises

Discuss the effects of historical fluctuations in stock and housing prices on the economy.

Introductory macroeconomic textbooks written before 1990 could largely ignore the stock and housing markets. The effects of these markets on the macroeconomy were small enough to be put aside in introductory discussions. In the 1990s this changed. The boom in the U.S. economy in the late 1990s and the subsequent recession owed a good deal to the rise and later fall in the stock market in that period. Similarly, in the period after 2000, the rise and later fall in housing prices contributed to cycles in the real economy. Now even introductory macroeconomics courses must spend some time looking at these two markets. We first turn to some background material on the stock market.

Stocks and Bonds

It will be useful to begin by briefly discussing the three main ways in which firms borrow or raise money to finance their investments. How do firms use financial markets in practice?

When a firm wants to make a large purchase to build a new factory or buy machines, it often cannot pay for the purchase out of its own funds. In this case, it must "finance" the investment. One way to do this is to borrow from a bank. The bank loans the money to the firm, the firm uses the money to buy the factory or machine, and the firm pays back the loan (with interest) to the bank over time.

Another possible way for a firm to borrow money is for the firm to issue a bond. If you buy a bond from a firm, you are making a loan to the firm. Bonds were discussed in Chapter 10 in our discussion of U.S. Treasury securities. We noted in that chapter that a bond is a promise to pay a fixed coupon periodically during the term of the bond and then to repay the full amount of the bond at the end of its term. Bonds issued by firms are called corporate bonds and are part of a firm's debt.

A third way for a firm to finance an investment is for it to issue additional shares of **stock**. Just as with bonds, typically only corporations have the ability to issue stock. When a firm issues new shares of stock, it does not add to its debt. Instead, it brings in additional owners of the firm, owners who agree to supply it with funds. Such owners are treated differently than bondholders, who are owed the amount they have loaned.

stock A certificate that certifies ownership of a certain portion of a firm.

A *share of common stock* is a certificate that represents the ownership of a share of a business, almost always a corporation. In some cases, firms pay a portion of their annual profits directly to their shareholders in the form of a *dividend*. For example, General Electric is a large, well-established diversified firm with its headquarters in Fairfield, Connecticut. GE has more than 10 billion shares outstanding and generates just over $15 billion in profits each year. GE shares are owned by many endowment and pension funds as well as by individuals. Major shareholders in 2015 included Vanguard and Blackrock. In 2015, GE paid just over one half of its $1.50 a share earnings out in dividends. The remainder was retained for firm investments. Stockholders who own stocks that increase in value earn what are called **capital gains**. **Realized capital gains** (or losses) are increases (or decreases) in the value of assets, including stocks, that households receive when they actually sell those assets. The government considers realized capital gains net of losses to be income, although their treatment under the tax code has been complex and subject to change every few years. The total return that an owner of a share of stock receives is the sum of the dividends received and the capital gain or loss.

capital gain An increase in the value of an asset.

realized capital gain The gain that occurs when the owner of an asset actually sells it for more than he or she paid for it.

Determining the Price of a Stock

What determines the price of a stock? If a share of stock is selling for $25, why is someone willing to pay that much for it? As we have noted, when you buy a share of stock, you own part of the firm. If a firm is making profits, it may be paying dividends to its shareholders. If it is not paying dividends but is making profits, people may expect that it will pay dividends in the future. Microsoft, for example, only began paying dividends in 2003 as it entered a more mature phase of its business. Apple began paying dividends in 2012. Dividends are important in thinking about stocks because dividends are the form in which shareholders receive income from the firm. So one thing that is likely to affect the price of a stock is what people expect its future dividends will be. The larger the expected future dividends, the higher the current stock price, other things being equal.

Another important consideration in thinking about the price of a stock is when the dividends are expected to begin to be paid. A $2-per-share dividend stream that is expected to start 4 years from now is worth less than a $2-per-share dividend that starts next year. In other words, the farther into the future the dividend is expected to be paid, the more it will be "discounted." The amount by which expected future dividends are discounted depends on the interest rate. The higher the interest rate, the more expected future dividends will be discounted. If the interest rate is 10 percent, I can invest $100 today and receive $110 a year from now. I am thus willing to pay $100 today to someone who will pay me $110 in a year. If instead, the interest rate were only 5 percent, I would be willing to pay $104.76 today to receive $110 a year from now because the alternative of $104.76 today at a 5 percent interest rate also yields $110.00 at the end of the year. I am thus willing to pay more for the promise of $110 a year from now when the interest rate is lower. In other words, I "discount" the $110 less when the interest rate is lower.

When investors buy a bond, that bond comes with a fixed coupon. When investors buy a stock, they can look at the current and past dividends, but there is no guarantee that future dividends will be the same. Dividends are voted each year by the board of a company, and in difficult times a board may decide to reduce or even eliminate dividends. So dividend payments come with a risk and that risk affects the stock price. People prefer certain outcomes to uncertain ones for the same expected values. For example, I prefer a certain $50 over a bet in which there is a 50 percent chance I will get $100 and a 50 percent chance I will get nothing, even though the expected value of the two deals are equal. The same reasoning holds for future dividends. If, say, I expect dividends for both firms A and B to be $2 per share next year but firm B has a much wider range of possibilities (is riskier), I will prefer firm A. Put another way, I will "discount" firm B's expected future dividends more than firm A's because the outcome for firm B is more uncertain.

We can thus say that the price of a stock should equal the discounted value of its expected future dividends, where the discount factors depend on the interest rate and risk. If for some reason (say, a positive surprise news announcement from the firm) we expect a firm to increase its future dividends, this should lead to an increase in the price of the stock. If there is a surprise fall in the interest rate, this decrease should also lead to a stock price increase. Finally, if the perceived risk of a firm falls, this perception should increase the firm's stock price.

Some stock analysts talk about the possibility of stock market "bubbles." Given the preceding discussion, what might a bubble be? Assume that given your expectations about the future dividends of a firm and given the discount rate, you value the firm's stock at $20 per share. Is there any case in which you would pay more than $20 for a share? We noted previously that the total return to an owner of a share of stock includes any capital gains that come from selling the stock. If the stock is currently selling for $25, which is above your value of $20, but you think that the stock will rise to $30 in the next few months, you might buy it now in anticipation of selling it later for a higher price and reap these capital gains. If others have similar views, the price of the stock may be driven up.

In this case, what counts is not the discounted value of expected future dividends, but rather your view of what others will pay for the stock in the future. You will recall we suggested that stock prices cannot be predicted. Sometimes stocks rise and give their owners capital gains, while other times they fall and there are capital losses. One way to define a bubble is a time in which everyone expects that everyone else expects that stock prices in general will be driven up. This expectation of general price appreciation itself fuels the market as people come to expect capital gains as part of the return on their investments. When a firm's stock price has risen rapidly, it is difficult to know whether the reason is that people have increased their expectations of the firm's future dividends or that there is a bubble. Because people's expectations of future dividends are not directly observed, it is hard to test alternative theories.

The Stock Market Since 1948

Most investors are interested in following the fortunes of individual firms. Macroeconomists, tracking the connection between stocks and overall levels of economic activity, need instead a measure of the stock market in general. There are several indices available. If you follow

▲ **FIGURE 14.1   The S&P 500 Stock Price Index, 1948 I–2014 IV**

the stock market at all, you know that much attention is paid to two stock price indices: the **Dow Jones Industrial Average** and the **NASDAQ Composite**. From a macroeconomic perspective, however, these two indices cover too small a sample of firms. One would like an index that includes firms whose total market value is close to the market value of all firms in the economy. For this purpose a much better measure is the **Standard and Poor's 500** stock price index, called the **S&P 500**. This index includes most of the larger companies in the economy by market value.

The S&P 500 index is plotted in Figure 14.1 for 1948 I–2014 IV. What perhaps stands out most in this plot is the huge increase in the index between 1995 and 2000. Between December 31, 1994, and March 31, 2000, the S&P 500 index rose 226 percent, an annual rate of increase of 25 percent. This is by far the largest stock market boom in U.S. history, completely dominating the boom of the 1920s. Remember that we are talking about the S&P 500 index, which includes most of the firms in the U.S. economy by market value. We are not talking about just a few dot-com companies. The entire stock market went up 25 percent per year for 5 years! This boom added roughly $14 trillion to household wealth, about $2.5 trillion per year.[1]

What caused this boom? You can see from Figure 12.7 in Chapter 12 that interest rates did not change much in the last half of the 1990s, so the boom cannot be explained by any large fall in interest rates. Perhaps profits rose substantially during this period, and this growth led to a large increase in expected future dividends? We know from the preceding discussion that if expected future dividends increase, stock prices should increase. Figure 14.2 plots for 1948 I–2014 IV the ratio of after-tax profits to GDP. It is clear from the figure that nothing unusual happened to profits in the last half of the 1990s. The share of after-tax profits in GDP rose from the middle of 1995 to the middle of 1997, but then generally fell after that through 2000. Thus, there does not appear to be any surge of profits that would have led people to expect much higher future dividends.

It could be that the perceived riskiness of stocks fell in the last half of the 1990s. This change would have led to smaller discount rates for stocks and thus, other things being equal, to higher stock prices. Although this possibility cannot be completely ruled out, there is no strong independent evidence that perceived riskiness fell.

The stock market boom is thus a puzzle, and many people speculate that it was simply a bubble. For some reason, stock prices started rising rapidly in 1995 and people expected that other people expected that prices would continue to rise. This led stock prices to rise further, thus fulfilling the expectations, which led to expectations of further increases, and so on. Bubble believers note that once stock prices started falling in 2000, they fell a great deal. It is not the case that stock prices just leveled out in 2000; they fell rapidly. People of the bubble view argue that this was simply the bubble bursting.

Dow Jones Industrial Average   An index based on the stock prices of 30 actively traded large companies. The oldest and most widely followed index of stock market performance.

NASDAQ Composite   An index based on the stock prices of more than 5,000 companies traded on the NASDAQ Stock Market. The NASDAQ market takes its name from the National Association of Securities Dealers Automated Quotation System.

Standard and Poor's 500 (S&P 500)   An index based on the stock prices of 500 of the largest firms by market value.

---

[1] It is worth noting that S&P changes the firms that are in its index as firms either prosper or fade. This selection tells us that the index will overestimate actual stock market gains as a result of survivor bias.

▲ FIGURE 14.2 **Ratio of After-Tax Profits to GDP, 1948 I–2014 IV**

The first problem then for the stability of the macroeconomy is the large and seemingly unpredictable swings in the stock market. As we will see, these swings induce behavior changes by households and firms that affect the real economy. Before we explore this link, however, we turn to a second volatile series: housing prices.

Housing Prices Since 1952

Figure 14.3 plots the relative price of housing for 1952 I–2014 IV. The plotted figure is the ratio of an index of housing prices to the GDP deflator. When this ratio is rising, it means that housing prices are rising faster than the overall price level, and vice versa when the ratio is falling.

The plot in Figure 14.3 is remarkable. Housing prices grew roughly in line with the overall price level until about 2000. The increase between 2000 and 2006 was then huge, followed by an equivalent fall between 2006 and 2009. Between 2000 I and 2006 I the value of housing wealth increased by about $13 trillion, roughly $500 billion per quarter. Between 2006 II and 2009 I the fall in the value of housing wealth was about $7 trillion, more than $600 billion per quarter. Once again, it is hard to find a cogent reason for this based on the use value of housing. Rental prices, for example, did not rise and fall in this way.

▲ FIGURE 14.3 **Ratio of a Housing Price Index to the GDP Deflator, 1952 I–2014 IV**

Household Wealth Effects on the Economy

We see that both the stock market and the housing market have periods of large unpredictable ups and downs. How are these swings felt in the real economy? We mentioned in Chapter 8 that one of the factors that affects consumption expenditures is wealth. Other things being equal, the more wealth a family has, the more it spends. Much of the fluctuation in household wealth in the recent past is because of fluctuations in stock prices and housing prices. When housing and stock values rise, households feel richer and they spend more. As a rough rule of thumb, a $1.00 change in the value of wealth (either stocks or housing) leads to about a $0.03 to $0.04 change in consumer spending per year. With unpredictable wealth changes, we end up with unpredictable consumption changes and thus unpredictable changes in GDP.

An increase in stock prices may also increase investment. If a firm is considering an investment project, one way in which it can finance the project is to issue additional shares of stock. The higher the price of the firm's stock, the more money it can get per additional share. A firm is thus likely to undertake more investment projects the higher its stock price. The cost of an investment project in terms of shares of stock is smaller the higher the price of the stock. This is the way a stock market boom may increase investment and a stock market contraction may decrease investment. Stock price changes affect a firm's cost of capital.

Financial Crises and the 2008 Bailout

It is clear that the stock market boom in the last half of the 1990s contributed to the strong economy in that period and that the contraction in the stock market after that contributed to the 2000–2001 recession. It is also clear that the boom in housing prices in the 2000–2005 period contributed to the expansion that followed the 2000–2001 recession and that the collapse of housing prices between 2006 and 2009 contributed to the 2008–2009 recession. This is just the household wealth effect at work combined in the case of stock prices with an effect on the investment spending of firms.

The recession of 2008–2009 was also characterized by some observers as a period of financial crisis. Although there is no precise definition of a financial crisis, most financial writers identify financial crises as periods in which the financial institutions that facilitate the movement of capital across households and firms cease to work smoothly. In a financial crisis, macroeconomic problems caused by the wealth effect of a falling stock market or housing market are accentuated.

Many people consider the large fall in housing prices that began at the end of 2006 to have led to the financial crisis of 2008–2009. We discussed briefly in Chapter 10 some of the reasons for this fall in housing prices. Lax government regulations led to excessive risk taking during the housing boom, with many people taking out mortgages that could only be sustained if housing prices kept rising. People bought houses expecting capital gains from those houses once they sold. The problem was exacerbated by low "teaser-rate" mortgage loans in which people paid very low interest rates for the first few years of home ownership. Once housing prices started to fall, the possibility of capital gains from a house sale lessened and it became clear that many households would not be able to afford their homes once teaser rates expired. With no prospect of a profitable house sale and higher mortgage interest rates, many people defaulted on those mortgages and the value of many mortgage-backed securities dropped sharply. Many large financial institutions were involved in the mortgage market, and they began to experience financial trouble. With the exception of Lehman Brothers, which went bankrupt, most of the large financial institutions were bailed out by the federal government—a $700 billion bailout bill that was passed in October 2008. These institutions included Goldman Sachs, Citigroup, Morgan Stanley, J.P. Morgan Chase, and A.I.G. The government provided capital to these firms to ease their financial difficulties. The Federal Reserve also participated in the bailout, buying huge amounts of mortgage-backed securities. We saw in Chapter 10 that in mid-April 2015, the Fed held about $1,732 billion in mortgage-backed securities, many of which it purchased in 2008 and 2009. Many other countries had similar issues with their own financial institutions, in part because many of them had purchased U.S. mortgage-backed securities as an investment.

What would have happened had the U.S. government not bailed out the large financial institutions? This is a matter of debate among economists and politicians. But some effects are clear. Absent intervention, the negative wealth effect would have been larger. Some of the financial institutions would have gone bankrupt, which would have wiped out their bondholders.

ECONOMICS IN PRACTICE

Predicting Recessions

How good are economists at predicting recessions? The answer is: not always that good. The 2008–2009 recession is a good example. A study by the Federal Reserve Bank of New York (FRBNY)[1] documents the failure of both policy makers and private economists to forecast the recession. The forecast errors were quite large. The unemployment rate rose from 4.8 percent in 2007 to 6.9 percent in 2008 and then to 10.0 percent in 2009. In late 2007 the FRBNY predicted that the unemployment rate would be 4.6 percent in 2008, an error of 2.3 points. Private forecasters were not much better, predicting a rate of 4.9 percent.[2] But even worse, in April 2008 the FRBNY forecast that the unemployment rate would be 5.6 percent in 2009, an error of 4.4 points. Private forecasters were essentially the same, predicting a rate of 5.5 percent. Even in November 2008 the FRBNY was forecasting an unemployment rate of only 8.1 percent for 2009. Private forecasters were forecasting only 7.7 percent. It wasn't until early 2009 that the severity of the recession was being predicted.

The fact that recessions can be hard to forecast means that the recognition lag discussed in the text can be long. It may take time for policy makers to realize how the economy is doing if their forecasts are no good. This being said, the Fed reacted faster to the 2008–2009 recession than might have been expected given the lag in predicting the severity of the recession. Figure 12.7 in Chapter 12 shows the quarterly path of the 3-month Treasury bill rate, which the Fed essentially controls. It is hard to see the exact numbers from the figure, but the bill rate fell from 4.7 percent in the second quarter of 2007 to 4.3 percent in the third, 3.4 percent in the fourth, 2.0 percent in the first quarter of 2008, 1.6 percent in the second, 1.5 percent in the third, and then roughly zero in the fourth quarter of 2008 and beyond. The Fed thus began to move in a fairly aggressive way near the end of 2007, even though the unemployment rate was not yet predicted to rise very much. And the Fed moved aggressively in 2008, reaching essentially zero by the end, again even though the severity of the recession was not yet forecast by the end of 2008.

The Fed was thus ahead of the curve regarding the 2008–2009 recession. One possibility is that the Fed governors were more pessimistic about the economy that the forecasts were and reacted accordingly. They may have thought there was more downside risk than upside risk in the forecasts

at the time. On the other hand, the forecasts were predicting increases in the unemployment rate, not just as large as turned out to be the case, and it could be that the Fed was simply responding to these predicted increases. When it then reached the zero lower bound at the end of 2008, it could go no further. At any rate, the Fed's timing looks pretty good in this period, especially given the forecast errors.

Why was the 2008–2009 recession so poorly predicted? A characteristic of the recession is that much of it was driven by the fall in housing and stock prices. This led to a negative wealth effect, which exacerbated the recession. The problem with predicting this recession was that it is difficult to predict changes in asset prices like housing prices and stock prices. Changes in these prices are essentially unpredictable. So if much of the recession was driven by unpredictable changes in asset prices, the recession itself will be unpredictable, which it was.

THINKING PRACTICALLY

1. Why might it have been hard to predict the boom in the U.S. economy in the last half of the 1990s?

[1] Simon Potter, "The Failure to Forecast the Great Recession," *Liberty Street Economics*, Federal Reserve Bank of New York, November 25, 2011.
[2] The private forecasters used here are those responding to the Blue Chip Survey.

Many of these bonds are held by the household sector, so household wealth would have fallen from the loss in the value of the bonds. The fall in overall stock prices would also likely have been larger, thus contributing to the negative wealth effect. The government bailout thus reduced the fall in wealth that took place during this period. Some people also argue that lending to businesses would have been lower had there been no bailout. This would have forced businesses to cut investment, thereby contributing to the contraction in aggregate demand. It is not clear how important this effect is since, as seen in Chapter 10, much of the Fed's purchase of mortgage-backed securities ended up as excess reserves in banks, not as increased loans.

It is important to distinguish between the stimulus measures the government took to fight the 2008–2009 recession, which were tax cuts and spending increases, and the bailout activity, which was direct help to financial institutions to keep them from failing. Putting aside the stimulus measures, was the bailout a good idea? On the positive side, it lessened the negative wealth effect and possibly led to more loans to businesses. Also, much of the lending to the financial institutions has or will be repaid; so the final total cost will be less than $700 billion. On the negative side, there were political and social costs. Most of the people who benefited from the bailout were wealthy—certainly wealthier than average. The bond holders of financial institutions tend to come from the top end of the income distribution. Many people noted that expenditures bailing out the financial institutions that made bad loans dwarfed expenditures to help home owners who took out those bad loans. Also, the jobs in the financial institutions that were saved were mostly jobs of high-income earners. People who will pay for the bailout in the long run are the U.S. taxpayers, who are on average less wealthy than those who benefited from the bailout. The bailout thus likely had, or at least was perceived by many to have had, bad income distribution consequences, which put a strain on the body politic.

We have seen how difficult it is to predict changes in asset prices like stock and housing prices, and we have also seen how much impact these changes can have on the real economy. But many have noted that while the government may not be able to predict asset bubbles, it does influence those fluctuations through other policies. In the case of housing, at least some of the fuel driving the bubble was likely lax credit standards, credit standards controlled in part by government agencies. Recent asset bubbles also may have reflected risk taking by financial institutions, risk behavior that is also under the control of government agencies. The substantial macroeconomic costs of the most recent recession stimulated numerous calls for regulatory reform in the financial market. In 2010 a financial regulation bill, known as the *Dodd-Frank bill*, was passed to try to tighten up financial regulations in the hope of preventing a recurrence of the 2008–2009 financial crisis.

Time Lags Regarding Monetary and Fiscal Policy

We have so far seen that the unpredictability of asset-price changes is difficult for policy makers to deal with. At best, policy makers can only react to these changes. The goal of **stabilization policy** is to smooth out fluctuation in GDP as much as possible. Consider the two possible time paths for aggregate output (income) (*Y*) shown in Figure 14.4. Path A (the dark blue line) represents GDP absent stabilization policies by the government; Path B (the light blue line) shows the smoother path that stabilization policy aims to produce. Stabilization policy is also concerned with the stability of prices. Here the goal is not to prevent the overall price level from rising at all, but instead to achieve an inflation rate that is as close as possible to a target rate of about 2 percent given the government's other goals of high and stable levels of output and employment.

14.2 LEARNING OBJECTIVE

Explain the purpose of stabilization policies and differentiate between three types of time lags.

stabilization policy Describes both monetary and fiscal policy, the goals of which are to smooth out fluctuations in output and employment and to keep prices as stable as possible.

◀ **FIGURE 14.4 Two Possible Time Paths for GDP**
Path *A* is less stable—it varies more over time—than path *B*. Other things being equal, society prefers path *B* to path *A*.

Time

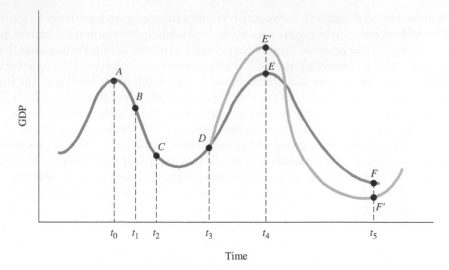

▲ **FIGURE 14.5** **Possible Stabilization Timing Problems**

Attempts to stabilize the economy can prove destabilizing because of time lags. An expansionary policy that should have begun to take effect at point A does not actually begin to have an impact until point D, when the economy is already on an upswing. Hence, the policy pushes the economy to points E' and F' (instead of points E and F). Income varies more widely than it would have if no policy had been implemented.

time lags Delays in the economy's response to stabilization policies.

Stabilization goals are not easy to achieve, particularly in the light of various kinds of **time lags**, or delays in the response of the economy to stabilization policies. Economists generally recognize three kinds of time lags: recognition lags, implementation lags, and response lags.

Figure 14.5 shows timing problems a government may face when trying to stabilize the economy. Suppose the economy reaches a peak and begins to slide into recession at point A (at time t_0). Given the need to collect and process economic data, policy makers do not observe the decline in GDP until it has sunk to point B (at time t_1). By the time they have begun to stimulate the economy (point C, time t_2), the recession is well advanced and the economy has almost bottomed out. When the policies finally begin to take effect (point D, time t_3), the economy is already on its road to recovery. The policies push the economy to point E'—a much greater fluctuation than point E, which is where the economy would have been without the stabilization policy. Sometime after point D, policy makers may begin to realize that the economy is expanding too quickly. By the time they have implemented contractionary policies and the policies have made their effects felt, the economy is starting to weaken. The contractionary policies therefore end up pushing GDP to point F' instead of point F.

Because of the various time lags, the expansionary policies that should have been instituted at time t_0 do not begin to have an effect until time t_3, when they are no longer needed. The light blue line in Figure 14.5 shows how the economy behaves as a result of the "stabilization" policies. The dark blue line shows the time path of GDP if the economy had been allowed to run its course and no stabilization policies had been attempted. In this case, stabilization policy makes income more erratic, not less—the policy results in a peak income of E' as opposed to E and a trough income of F' instead of F.

Critics of stabilization policy argue that the situation in Figure 14.5 is typical of the interaction between the government and the rest of the economy. This claim is not necessarily true. We need to know more about the nature of the various kinds of lags before deciding whether stabilization policy is good or bad.

Recognition Lags

It takes time for policy makers to recognize a boom or a slump. Many important data—those from the national income and product accounts, for example—are available only quarterly. It usually takes several weeks to compile and prepare even the preliminary estimates for these figures. If the economy goes into a slump on January 1, the recession may not be detected until the data for the first quarter are available at the end of April.

Moreover, the early national income and product accounts data are only preliminary, based on an incomplete compilation of the various data sources. These estimates can, and often do, change as better data become available. (For example, when the Bureau of Economic Analysis first announced the results for the fourth quarter of 2012, it indicated that the economy had negative growth, –0.1%. This announcement was at the end of January 2013. At the end of February the growth rate was revised to plus 0.1%. Then at the end of March it was further revised to plus 0.4%.) This situation makes the interpretation of the initial estimates difficult, and **recognition lags** result.

Recognition lag also kicks in on the upside of the cycle as the economy recovers from slow growth in response to government policy. When has the government done enough to stimulate the economy and when will further efforts lead to over stimulation? Janet Yellen, current chair of the Fed, spoke of exactly this concern as she contemplated changing the Fed's easy monetary policy in the spring of 2015 in a speech in San Francisco. "We need to keep in mind the well-established fact that the full effects of monetary policy are felt only after long lags. This means that policymakers cannot wait until they have achieved their objectives to begin adjusting policy. I would not consider it prudent to postpone the onset of normalization until we have reached, or are on the verge of reaching, our inflation objective. Doing so would create too great a risk of significantly overshooting *both* our objectives of maximum sustainable employment and 2 percent inflation, potentially undermining economic growth and employment if the FOMC is subsequently forced to tighten policy markedly or abruptly."

> **recognition lag** The time it takes for policy makers to recognize the existence of a boom or a slump.

Implementation Lags

The problems that lags pose for stabilization policy do not end once economists and policy makers recognize that the economy is in a boom or a slump. Even if everyone knows that the economy needs to be stimulated or reined in, it takes time to put the desired policy into effect, especially for actions that involve fiscal policy. **Implementation lags** result.

Each year Congress decides on the federal government's budget for the coming year. The tax laws and spending programs embodied in this budget are hard to change once they are in place. If it becomes clear that the economy is entering a recession and is in need of a fiscal stimulus during the middle of the year, there is a limited amount that can be done. Until Congress authorizes more spending or a cut in taxes, changes in fiscal policy are not possible.[2]

Monetary policy is less subject to the kinds of restrictions that slow down changes in fiscal policy. As we saw in Chapter 10, the Fed's current tool for changing the interest rate is to change the rate it pays on bank reserves. This change can be made very quickly, and there is in effect no implementation lag once the decision has been made to make the change.

> **implementation lag** The time it takes to put the desired policy into effect once economists and policy makers recognize that the economy is in a boom or a slump.

Response Lags

Even after a macroeconomic problem has been recognized and the appropriate corrective policies have been implemented, there are **response lags**—The time that it takes for the economy to adjust to the new conditions after a new policy is implemented; lags that occur because of the operation of the economy itself. Even after the government has formulated a policy and put it into place, the economy takes time to adjust to the new conditions. Although monetary policy can be adjusted and implemented more quickly than fiscal policy, it takes longer to make its effect felt on the economy because of response lags. What is most important is the total lag between the time a problem first occurs and the time the corrective policies are felt.

> **response lag** The time that it takes for the economy to adjust to the new conditions after a new policy is implemented; the lag that occurs because of the operation of the economy itself.

Response Lags for Fiscal Policy One way to think about the response lag in fiscal policy is through the government spending multiplier. This multiplier measures the change in GDP caused by a given change in government spending or net taxes. It takes time for the multiplier to reach its full value. The result is a lag between the time a fiscal policy action is initiated and the time the full change in GDP is realized.

The reason for the response lag in fiscal policy—the delay in the multiplier process—is simple. During the first few months after an increase in government spending or a tax cut, there

---

[2] Do not forget, however, about the existence of automatic stabilizers (Chapter 9). Many programs contain built-in countercyclical features that expand spending or cut tax collections automatically (without the need for congressional or executive action) during a recession.

is not enough time for the firms or individuals who benefit directly from the extra government spending or the tax cut to increase their own spending. Neither individuals nor firms revise their spending plans instantaneously. Until they can make those revisions, the increase in government spending does not stimulate extra private spending.

Changes in government purchases are a component of aggregate expenditure. When G rises, aggregate expenditure increases directly; when G falls, aggregate expenditure decreases directly. When personal taxes are changed, however, an additional step intervenes, giving rise to another lag. Suppose a tax cut has lowered personal income taxes across the board. Each household must decide what portion of its tax cut to spend and what portion to save. This decision is the extra step. Before the tax cut gets translated into extra spending, households must take the step of increasing their spending, which usually takes some time.

With a business tax cut, there is a further complication. Firms must decide what to do with their added after-tax profits. If they pay out their added profits to households as dividends, the result is the same as with a personal tax cut. Households must decide whether to spend or to save the extra funds. Firms may also retain their added profits and use them for investment, but investment is a component of aggregate expenditure that requires planning and time.

In practice, it takes about a year for a change in taxes or in government spending to have its full effect on the economy. This response lag means that if we increase spending to counteract a recession today, the full effects will not be felt for 12 months. By that time, the state of the economy might be different.

Response Lags for Monetary Policy Monetary policy works by changing interest rates—assuming that interest rates are not at the zero lower bound—which then change planned investment. Interest rates can also affect consumption spending, as we discuss further in Chapter 15. For now, it is enough to know that lower interest rates usually stimulate consumption spending and that higher interest rates decrease consumption spending.

The response of consumption and investment to interest rate changes takes time. Even if interest rates were to rise by 5 percent overnight, firms would not immediately decrease their investment purchases. Firms generally make their investment plans several years in advance. If General Motors (GM) wants to respond to an increase in interest rates by investing less, it will take time—perhaps up to a year—for the firm to come up with plans to scrap some of its investment projects. The response lags for monetary policy are even longer than response lags for fiscal policy. When government spending changes, there is a direct change in the sales of firms, which would sell more as a result of an increase in government purchases. When interest rates change, however, the sales of firms do not change until households change their consumption spending and/or firms change their investment spending. It takes time for households and firms to respond to interest rate changes. In this sense, interest rate changes are like tax-rate changes. The resulting change in firms' sales must wait for households and firms to change their purchases of goods.

Summary

Stabilization is thus not easily achieved even if there are no surprise asset-price changes. It takes time for policy makers to recognize the existence of a problem, more time for them to implement a solution, and yet more time for firms and households to respond to the stabilization policies taken. Monetary policy can be adjusted more quickly and easily than taxes or government spending, making it a useful instrument in stabilizing the economy. However, because the economy's response to monetary changes is probably slower than its response to changes in fiscal policy, tax and spending changes may also play a useful role in macroeconomic management.

14.3 LEARNING OBJECTIVE

Discuss the effects of government deficits and deficit targeting.

Government Deficit Issues

If a government is trying to stimulate the economy through tax cuts or spending increases, this, other things being equal, will increase the government deficit. One thus expects deficits in recessions—cyclical deficits. These deficits are temporary and do not impose any long-run problems, especially if modest surpluses are run when there is full employment. If, however, at full employment the deficit—the structural deficit—is still large, this can have negative long-run consequences.

Figure 9.6 in Chapter 9 shows that the U.S. government deficit as a percentage of GDP rose rapidly beginning in 2008. In 2009 the deficit as a percentage of GDP was about 9 percent. This is huge, but most of it was cyclical because of the sharp recession. Earlier, in 2005–2007, there was roughly full employment, and during this period the deficit was about 2 percent of GDP, which we can think of as a structural deficit given that it occurred in a full employment period. By the end of 2014, with the economy close to but not quite at full employment, the deficit was at 3 percent of GDP. At that point, the deficit had both structural and (small) cyclical elements.

The large deficits beginning in 2008 led to a large rise in the ratio of the federal government debt to GDP. Figure 9.7 in Chapter 9 shows that the ratio peaked at the end of 2012, where it was 68.4 percent. (This is up from about 46 percent in 2007). By the end of 2014, the ratio had fallen to 63.6 percent. Deficits and debts are always hot political issues. Should anything be done to lower the deficit or not? If action is needed, should we raise taxes or lower spending? Sometimes there are threats to shut down the government. A significant change in policy was made at the end of 2012. The Bush tax cuts, which had been in effect for 12 years, were not extended for high-income tax payers. These many debates about the deficit in fact led to a change in policy at the end of 2012. In addition, the payroll tax cut, which had been in effect for 2 years, was not extended. You can see from Figure 9.7 that the debt/GDP ratio has roughly flattened out since 2012, due in part to these changes.

One concern about a rising debt-to-GDP ratio for a country is that at some point investors may begin to perceive that the bonds the country is selling to finance its deficits are now more risky. This will increase the interest rate that the country must pay on its bonds, which will add further to the deficit as interest payments rise. This may in turn force the country to drastically cut spending or increase taxes, which may have large negative effects on the economy.

Deficit Targeting

Debates about deficits have been around for a long time. In the 1980s the U.S. government was spending much more than it was receiving in taxes. In response to the large deficits, in 1986 the U.S. Congress passed and President Reagan signed the **Gramm-Rudman-Hollings Act** (named for its three congressional sponsors), referred to as GRH. It is interesting to look back on this in the context of the current deficit problem. GRH set a target for reducing the federal deficit by a set amount each year. As Figure 14.6 shows, the deficit was to decline by $36 billion per year between 1987 and 1991, with a deficit of zero slated for fiscal year 1991. What was interesting about the GRH legislation was that the targets were not merely guidelines. If Congress, through its decisions about taxes and spending programs, produced a budget with a deficit larger than the targeted amount, GRH called for automatic spending cuts. The cuts were divided proportionately among most federal spending programs so that a program that made up 5 percent of total spending was to endure a cut equal to 5 percent of the total spending cut.[3]

In 1986, the U.S. Supreme Court declared part of the GRH bill unconstitutional. In effect, the Court said that Congress would have to approve the "automatic" spending cuts before they could take place. The law was changed in 1986 to meet the Supreme Court ruling and again in 1987, when new targets were established. The new targets had the deficit reaching zero in 1993

Gramm-Rudman-Hollings Act
Passed by the U.S. Congress and signed by President Reagan in 1986, this law set out to reduce the federal deficit by $36 billion per year, with a deficit of zero slated for 1991.

◀ FIGURE 14.6 **Deficit Reduction Targets under Gramm-Rudman-Hollings**
The GRH legislation, passed in 1986, set out to lower the federal deficit by $36 billion per year. If the plan had worked, a zero deficit would have been achieved by 1991.

---

[3] Programs such as Social Security were exempt from cuts or were treated differently. Interest payments on the federal debt were also immune from cuts.

instead of 1991. The targets were revised again in 1991, when the year to achieve a zero deficit was changed from 1993 to 1996. In practice, these targets never came close to being achieved. As time wore on, even the revised targets became completely unrealistic, and by the end of the 1980s, the GRH legislation was not taken seriously.

Although the GRH legislation is history, it is useful to consider the stabilization consequences of deficit targeting. What if deficit targeting is taken seriously? Is this good policy? The answer is probably not. We will now show how deficit targeting can make the economy more unstable.

In a world with no deficit targeting, the Congress and the president make decisions each year about how much to spend and how much to tax. The federal government deficit is a result of these decisions and the state of the economy. However, with deficit targeting, the size of the deficit is set in advance. Taxes and government spending must be adjusted to produce the required deficit. In this situation, the deficit is no longer a consequence of the tax and spending decisions. Instead, taxes and spending become a consequence of the deficit decision.

What difference does it make whether Congress chooses a target deficit and adjusts government spending and taxes to achieve that target or decides how much to spend and tax and lets the deficit adjust itself? The difference may be substantial. Consider a leftward shift of the AD curve caused by some negative demand shock. A negative demand shock is something that causes a negative shift in consumption or investment schedules or that leads to a decrease in U.S. exports.

We know that a leftward shift of the AD curve lowers aggregate output (income), which causes the government deficit to increase. In a world without deficit targeting, the increase in the deficit during contractions provides an **automatic stabilizer** for the economy. (Review Chapter 9 if this point is hazy.) The contraction-induced decrease in tax revenues and increase in transfer payments tend to reduce the fall in after-tax income and consumer spending because of the negative demand shock. Thus, the decrease in aggregate output (income) caused by the negative demand shock is lessened somewhat by the growth of the deficit [Figure 14.7(a)].

In a world with deficit targeting, the deficit is not allowed to rise. Some combination of tax increases and government spending cuts would be needed to offset what would have otherwise been an increase in the deficit. We know that increases in taxes or cuts in spending are contractionary in themselves. The contraction in the economy will therefore be larger than it would have been without deficit targeting because the initial effect of the negative demand shock is worsened by the rise in taxes or the cut in government spending required to keep the deficit from rising. As Figure 14.7(b) shows, deficit targeting acts as an **automatic destabilizer**.

automatic stabilizers
Revenue and expenditure items in the federal budget that automatically change with the economy in such a way as to stabilize GDP.

automatic destabilizers
Revenue and expenditure items in the federal budget that automatically change with the economy in such a way as to destabilize GDP.

▶ **FIGURE 14.7 Deficit Targeting as an Automatic Destabilizer**
Deficit targeting changes the way the economy responds to negative demand shocks because it does not allow the deficit to increase. The result is a smaller deficit but a larger decline in income than would have otherwise occurred.

a. Without Deficit Targeting

b. With Deficit Targeting

It requires taxes to be raised and government spending to be cut during a contraction. This reinforces, rather than counteracts, the shock that started the contraction.

Deficit targeting thus has undesirable macroeconomic consequences. It requires cuts in spending or increases in taxes at times when the economy is already experiencing problems. This drawback does not mean, of course, that a government should ignore structural deficit problems. But locking in spending cuts or tax increases during periods of negative demand shocks is not a good way to manage the economy. Moving forward, policy makers around the globe will have to devise other methods to control growing structural deficits.

—————————— SUMMARY ——————————

14.1 THE STOCK MARKET, THE HOUSING MARKET, AND FINANCIAL CRISES *p. 265*

1. A firm can finance an investment project by borrowing from banks, by issuing *bonds*, or by issuing new shares of its stock. People who own shares of *stock* own a fraction of the firm.

2. The price of a stock should equal the discounted value of its expected future dividends, where the discount factors depend on the interest rate and risk.

3. A bubble exists when the price of a stock exceeds the discounted value of its expected future dividends. In this case what matters is what people expect that other people expect about how much the stock can be sold for in the future.

4. The largest stock market boom in U.S. history occurred between 1995 and 2000, when the S&P 500 index rose by 25 percent per year. The boom added $14 trillion to household wealth.

5. Why there was a stock market boom in 1995–2000 appears to be a puzzle. There was nothing unusual about earnings that would predict such a boom. Many people believe that the boom was merely a bubble.

6. Housing prices rose rapidly between 2000 and 2006 and fell rapidly between 2006 and 2009. Many consider that the fall in housing prices beginning in 2006 led to the recession and financial crisis of 2008–2009.

7. Changes in stock prices and housing prices change household wealth, which affects consumption and thus the real economy. Changes in stock and housing prices are largely unpredictable, which makes many fluctuations in the economy unpredictable.

14.2 TIME LAGS REGARDING MONETARY AND FISCAL POLICY *p. 271*

8. *Stabilization policy* describes both fiscal and monetary policies, the goals of which are to smooth out fluctuations in output and employment and to keep prices as stable as possible. Stabilization goals are not necessarily easy to achieve because of the existence of certain *time lags*, or delays in the response of the economy to macroeconomic policies.

9. A *recognition lag* is the time it takes for policy makers to recognize the existence of a boom or a slump. An *implementation lag* is the time it takes to put the desired policy into effect once economists and policy makers recognize that the economy is in a boom or a slump. A *response lag* is the time it takes for the economy to adjust to the new conditions after a new policy is implemented—in other words, a lag that occurs because of the operation of the economy itself. In general, monetary policy can be implemented more rapidly than fiscal policy but fiscal policy generally has a shorter response lag than monetary policy.

14.3 GOVERNMENT DEFICIT ISSUES *p. 274*

10. The U.S. debt-to-GDP ratio has flattened out since 2012, due in part to policy changes that were made at the end of 2012.

11. In 1986 Congress passed and President Reagan signed the *Gramm-Rudman-Hollings Act (GRH)*, which set deficit targets for each year. The aim was to reduce the large structural deficit that existed.

12. Deficit-targeting measures that call for automatic spending cuts to eliminate or reduce the deficit, like the GRH legislation, may have the effect of destabilizing the economy.

—————————— REVIEW TERMS AND CONCEPTS ——————————

MyEconLab Visit **www.myeconlab.com** to complete these exercises online and get instant feedback. Exercises that update with real-time data are marked with art 🔾.

PROBLEMS

All problems are available on MyEconLab.

14.1 THE STOCK MARKET, THE HOUSING MARKET, AND FINANCIAL CRISES

LEARNING OBJECTIVE: Discuss the effects of historical fluctuations in stock and housing prices on the economy.

1.1 In July 2009, the S&P 500 index was at 1,000.
   a. What is the S&P 500 index?
   b. Where is the S&P today?
   c. If you had invested $10,000 in July 2009 and your investments had increased in value by the same percentage as the S&P 500 index had increased, how much would you have today?
   d. Assume that the total stock market holdings of the household sector were about $20 trillion and that the entire stock market went up/down by the same percentage as the S&P. Evidence suggests that the "wealth effect" of stock market holdings on consumer spending is about 4 percent of wealth annually. How much additional or reduced spending would you expect to see as a result of the stock market moves since July 2009? Assuming a multiplier of 2 and a GDP of $18,000 billion, how much additional/less GDP would you predict for next year if all of this was true?

1.2 During 1997, stock markets in Asia collapsed. Hong Kong's was down nearly 30 percent, Thailand's was down 62 percent, and Malaysia's was down 60 percent. Japan and Korea experienced big drops as well. What impacts would these events have on the economies of the countries themselves? Explain your answer. In what ways would you have expected these events to influence the U.S. economy? How might the spending of Asians on American goods be affected? What about Americans who have invested in these countries?

14.2 TIME LAGS REGARDING MONETARY AND FISCAL POLICY

LEARNING OBJECTIVE: Explain the purpose of stabilization policies and differentiate between three types of time lags.

2.1 Some states are required to balance their budgets. Is this measure stabilizing or destabilizing? Suppose all states were committed to a balanced-budget philosophy and the economy moved into a recession. What effects would this philosophy have on the size of the federal deficit?

2.2 Explain why stabilization policy may be difficult to carry out. How is it possible that stabilization policies can actually be destabilizing?

2.3 [Related to the *Economics in Practice* on p. 270] The *Economics in Practice* states that since recessions can be hard to forecast, the recognition lag can be long, as was the case with the recession of 2008–2009. Assuming that the recognition lag with regards to this recession was the same for both federal government and Federal Reserve policy makers, explain which type of policy, fiscal or monetary, should have been the quickest to take effect in the economy and with which of these policies should the economy have most rapidly adjusted to the newly implemented conditions.

14.3 GOVERNMENT DEFICIT ISSUES

LEARNING OBJECTIVE: Discuss the effects of government deficits and deficit targeting

3.1 Explain why the government deficit rises as the economy contracts and why the government deficit falls when the economy expands.

3.2 You are given the following information about the economy in 2015 (all in billions of dollars):

Consumption function:	$C = 100 + (.8 \times Y_d)$
Taxes:	$T = -150 + (.25 \times Y)$
Investment function:	$I = 60$
Disposable income:	$Y_d = Y - T$
Government spending:	$G = 80$
Equilibrium:	$Y = C + I + G$

Hint: Deficit is $D = G - T = G - [-150 + (.25 \times Y)]$.

   a. Find equilibrium income. Show that the government budget deficit (the difference between government spending and tax revenues) is $5 billion.
   b. Congress passes the Foghorn-Leghorn (F-L) amendment, which requires that the deficit be zero this year. If the budget adopted by Congress has a deficit that is larger than zero, the deficit target must be met by cutting spending. Suppose spending is cut by $5 billion (to $75 billion). What is the new value for equilibrium GDP? What is the new deficit? Explain carefully why the deficit is not zero.
   c. Suppose the F-L amendment was not in effect and planned investment falls to $I = 55$. What is the new value of GDP? What is the new government budget deficit? What happens to GDP if the F-L amendment is in effect and spending is cut to reach the deficit target? (*Hint:* Spending must be cut by $21.666 billion to balance the budget.)

3.3 Since the year 2000, several countries have defaulted on their sovereign bonds. Do some research to find information on three countries that have defaulted since 2000. For each of the three countries you have researched, explain when the default occurred, how much debt was involved in the default, what interest rates each government had to pay on its bonds immediately following the default, and what interest rates the government is now paying on its bonds. How do these interest rates compare to the interest rates being paid on current U.S. government bonds?

3.4 Suppose the government decides to decrease spending and increase taxes in an attempt to decrease its deficit.

Is it possible for the Fed to ease the macroeconomic effects of the spending and tax changes? Explain.

3.5 If the government implements a spending and tax policy in which it promises to neither increase nor decrease spending and taxes, is it still possible for the budget deficit to increase or decrease? Explain.

3.6 In January 2015, the Congressional Budget Office (CBO) issued a report estimating that the federal budget deficit for 2015 was expected to fall slightly to $468 billion, or 2.6 percent of GDP. Working under the assumption that current laws affecting the budget will not change (i.e., no revisions in planned tax changes or fiscal stimulus spending), the CBO also estimated that the deficit as a percentage of GDP would hold steady at 2.6 percent through 2018 but rise thereafter, with a projected deficit of 4.0 percent of GDP in 2025. Go to www.cbo.gov and look up the current and estimated deficit-to-GDP ratios. Were the CBO's estimates accurate, and have its projections changed? Explain whether any policy changes enacted since January 2015 might have been responsible for changes in the CBO's projections.

Glossary

absolute advantage   A producer has an absolute advantage over another in the production of a good or service if he or she can produce that product using fewer resources (a lower absolute cost per unit). *p. 25*

absolute advantage   The advantage in the production of a good enjoyed by one country over another when it uses fewer resources to produce that good than the other country does. *p. 333*

accelerator effect   The tendency for investment to increase when aggregate output increases and to decrease when aggregate output decreases, accelerating the growth or decline of output. *p. 290*

actual investment   The actual amount of investment that takes place; it includes items such as unplanned changes in inventories. *p. 147*

adjustment costs   The costs that a firm incurs when it changes its production level—for example, the administration costs of laying off employees or the training costs of hiring new workers. *p. 290*

aggregate behavior   The behavior of all households and firms together. *p. 90*

aggregate income   The total income received by all factors of production in a given period. *p. 141*

aggregate output (income) (Y)   A combined term used to remind you of the exact equality between aggregate output and aggregate income. *p. 141*

aggregate output   The total quantity of goods and services produced (or supplied) in an economy in a given period. *pp. 91, 141*

aggregate production function   A mathematical relationship stating that total GDP (output) depends on the total amount of labor used and the total amount of capital used. *p. 303*

aggregate saving (S)   The part of aggregate income that is not consumed. *p. 143*

aggregate supply (AS) curve   A graph that shows the relationship between the aggregate quantity of output supplied by all firms in an economy and the overall price level. *p. 215*

aggregate supply   The total supply of all goods and services in an economy. *p. 215*

animal spirits of entrepreneurs   A term coined by Keynes to describe investors' feelings. *p. 289*

appreciation of a currency   The rise in value of one currency relative to another. *p. 367*

automatic destabilizer   Revenue and expenditure items in the federal budget that automatically change with the state of the economy in such a way as to destabilize GDP. *p. 178*

automatic destabilizers   Revenue and expenditure items in the federal budget that automatically change with the economy in such a way as to destabilize GDP. *p. 276*

automatic stabilizers   Revenue and expenditure items in the federal budget that automatically change with the economy in such a way as to stabilize GDP. *pp. 178, 276*

balance of payments   The record of a country's transactions in goods, services, and assets with the rest of the world; also the record of a country's sources (supply) and uses (demand) of foreign exchange. *p. 357*

balance of trade   A country's exports of goods and services minus its imports of goods and services. *p. 358*

balance on current account   The sum of income from exports of goods and services and income from investments and transfers minus

payments for imports of goods and services and payments for investments and transfers. *p. 358*

balanced-budget multiplier   The ratio of change in the equilibrium level of output to a change in government spending where the change in government spending is balanced by a change in taxes so as not to create any deficit. The balanced-budget multiplier is equal to 1: The change in Y resulting from the change in G and the equal change in T are exactly the same size as the initial change in G or T. *p. 271*

barter   The direct exchange of goods and services for other goods and services. *p. 188*

base year   The year chosen for the weights in a fixed-weight procedure. *p. 114*

binding situation   State of the economy in which the Fed rule calls for a negative interest rate. *p. 235*

black market   A market in which illegal trading takes place at market-determined prices. *p. 77*

brain drain   The tendency for talented people from developing countries to become educated in a developed country and remain there after graduation. *p. 386*

budget deficit   The difference between what a government spends and what it collects in taxes in a given period: $G - T$. *p. 164*

business cycle   The cycle of short-term ups and downs in the economy. *p. 91*

capital   Those goods produced by the economic system that are used as inputs to produce other goods and services in the future. *p. 22*

capital flight   The tendency for both human capital and financial capital to leave developing countries in search of higher expected rates of return elsewhere with less risk. *p. 385*

capital gain An increase in the value of an asset. *p. 265*

capital market The input/factor market in which households supply their savings, for interest or for claims to future profits, to firms that demand funds to buy capital goods. *p. 44*

catch-up The theory stating that the growth rates of less developed countries will exceed the growth rates of developed countries, allowing the less developed countries to catch up. *p. 303*

ceteris paribus, or all else equal A device used to analyze the relationship between two variables while the values of other variables are held unchanged. *p. 8*

change in business inventories The amount by which firms' inventories change during a period. Inventories are the goods that firms produce now but intend to sell later. *p. 108*

circular flow A diagram showing the flows in and out of the sectors in the economy. *p. 94*

command economy An economy in which a central government either directly or indirectly sets output targets, incomes, and prices. *p. 36*

commodity monies Items used as money that also have intrinsic value in some other use. *p. 190*

comparative advantage A producer has a comparative advantage over another in the production of a good or service if he or she can produce that product at a lower *opportunity cost*. *p. 26*

comparative advantage The advantage in the production of a good enjoyed by one country over another when that good can be produced at lower cost in terms of other goods than it could be in the other country. *p. 334*

compensation of employees Includes wages, salaries, and

various supplements—employer contributions to social insurance and pension funds, for example—paid to households by firms and by the government. *p. 109*

complements, complementary goods Goods that "go together"; a decrease in the price of one results in an increase in demand for the other and vice versa. *p. 49*

constrained supply of labor The amount a household actually works in a given period at the current wage rate. *p. 285*

consumer goods Goods produced for present consumption. *p. 28*

consumer price index (CPI) A price index computed each month by the Bureau of Labor Statistics using a bundle that is meant to represent the "market basket" purchased monthly by the typical urban consumer. *p. 129*

consumer sovereignty The idea that consumers ultimately dictate what will be produced (or not produced) by choosing what to purchase (and what not to purchase). *p. 36*

consumer surplus The difference between the maximum amount a person is willing to pay for a good and its current market price. *p. 82*

consumption function The relationship between consumption and income. *p. 142*

contraction, recession, *or* slump The period in the business cycle from a peak down to a trough during which output and employment fall. *p. 92*

Corn Laws The tariffs, subsidies, and restrictions enacted by the British Parliament in the early nineteenth century to discourage imports and encourage exports of grain. *p. 333*

corporate bonds Promissory notes issued by firms when they borrow money. *p. 96*

corporate profits The income of corporations. *p. 109*

correlated Two variables are correlated if their values tend to move together. *p. 401*

cost shock, or supply shock A change in costs that shifts the short-run aggregate supply (AS) curve. *p. 217*

cost-of-living adjustments (COLAs) Contract provisions that tie wages to changes in the cost of living. The greater the inflation rate, the more wages are raised. *p. 252*

cost-push, *or* supply-side, inflation Inflation caused by an increase in costs. *p. 238*

currency debasement The decrease in the value of money that occurs when its supply is increased rapidly. *p. 190*

current dollars The current prices that we pay for goods and services. *p. 111*

cyclical deficit The deficit that occurs because of a downturn in the business cycle. *p. 179*

cyclical unemployment Unemployment that is above frictional plus structural unemployment. *p. 129*

cyclical unemployment The increase in unemployment that occurs during recessions and depressions. *p. 246*

deadweight loss The total loss of producer and consumer surplus from underproduction or overproduction. *p. 84*

deflation A decrease in the overall price level. *p. 93*

demand curve A graph illustrating how much of a given product a household would be willing to buy at different prices. *p. 47*

demand schedule Shows how much of a given product a household would be willing to buy at different prices for a given time period. *p. 46*

demand-pull inflation Inflation that is initiated by an increase in aggregate demand. *p. 238*

depreciation of a currency The fall in value of one currency relative to another. *p. 367*

depreciation The decline in an asset's economic value over time, or the amount by which an asset's value falls in a given period. *p. 108*

depression A prolonged and deep recession. *p. 91*

desired, *or* optimal, level of inventories The level of inventory at which the extra cost (in lost sales) from lowering inventories by a small amount is just equal to the extra gain (in interest revenue and decreased storage costs). *p. 291*

difference-in-differences Difference-in-differences is a method of identifying causality by looking at the way in which the average change over time in the outcome variable is compared to the average change in a control group. *p. 406*

discouraged-worker effect The decline in the measured unemployment rate that results when people who want to work but cannot find jobs grow discouraged and stop looking, thus dropping out of the ranks of the unemployed and the labor force. *pp. 126, 295*

discretionary fiscal policy Changes in taxes or spending that are the result of deliberate changes in government policy. *p. 163*

disembodied technical change Technical change that results in a change in the production process. *p. 308*

disposable personal income or after-tax income Personal income minus personal income taxes. The amount that households have to spend or save. *p. 111*

disposable, *or* after-tax, income (Y_d) Total income minus net taxes: $Y - T$. *p. 163*

dividends The portion of a firm's profits that the firm pays out each period to its shareholders. *p. 96*

Doha Development Agenda An initiative of the World Trade Organization focused on issues of trade and development. *p. 345*

Dow Jones Industrial Average An index based on the stock prices of 30 actively traded large companies. The oldest and most widely followed index of stock market performance. *p. 267*

dumping A firm's or an industry's sale of products on the world market at prices below its own cost of production. *p. 342*

durable goods Goods that last a relatively long time, such as cars and household appliances. *p. 106*

economic growth An increase in the total output of an economy. Growth occurs when a society acquires new resources or when it learns to produce more using existing resources. *pp. 10, 32*

economic integration Occurs when two or more nations join to form a free-trade zone. *p. 345*

economics The study of how individuals and societies choose to use the scarce resources that nature and previous generations have provided. *p. 1*

efficiency In economics, allocative efficiency. An efficient economy is one that produces what people want at the least possible cost. *p. 10*

efficiency wage theory An explanation for unemployment that holds that the productivity of workers increases with the wage rate. If this is so, firms may have an incentive to pay wages above the market-clearing rate. *p. 248*

efficient market A market in which profit opportunities are eliminated almost instantaneously. *p. 3*

embodied technical change Technical change that results in an improvement in the quality of capital. *p. 307*

empirical economics The collection and use of data to test economic theories. *p. 8*

employed Any person 16 years old or older (1) who works for pay, either for someone else or in his or her own business for 1 or more hours per week, (2) who works without pay for 15 or more hours per week in a family enterprise, or (3) who has a job but has been temporarily absent with or without pay. *p. 124*

entrepreneur A person who organizes, manages, and assumes the risks of a firm, taking a new idea or a new product and turning it into a successful business. *p. 43*

equilibrium The condition that exists when quantity supplied and quantity demanded are equal. At equilibrium, there is no tendency for price to change. In the macroeconomic goods market, equilibrium occurs when planned aggregate expenditure is equal to aggregate output. *p. 148*

equity Fairness *p. 10*

European Union (EU) The European trading bloc composed of 28 countries (of the 28 countries in the EU, 17 have the same currency—the euro). *p. 345*

excess demand *or* shortage The condition that exists when quantity demanded exceeds quantity supplied at the current price. *p. 60*

excess labor, excess capital Labor and capital that are not needed to produce the firm's current level of output. *p. 290*

excess reserves The difference between a bank's actual reserves and its required reserves. *p. 195*

excess supply *or* surplus The condition that exists when quantity supplied exceeds quantity demanded at the current price. *p. 62*

exchange rate The price of one country's currency in terms of another country's currency; the ratio at which two currencies are traded for each other. *pp. 339, 356*

exogenous variable A variable that is assumed not to depend on the state of the economy—that is, it does not change when the economy changes. *p. 153*

expansion or boom The period in the business cycle from a trough up to a peak during which output and employment grow. *p. 92*

expenditure approach A method of computing GDP that measures the total amount spent on all final goods and services during a given period. *p. 106*

explicit contracts Employment contracts that stipulate workers' wages, usually for a period of 1 to 3 years. *p. 251*

export promotion A trade policy designed to encourage exports. *p. 392*

export subsidies Government payments made to domestic firms to encourage exports. *p. 342*

factor endowments The quantity and quality of labor, land, and natural resources of a country. *p. 341*

factors of production (*or* factors) The inputs into the process of production. Another term for *resources*. Land, labor, and capital are the three key factors of production. *pp. 23, 44*

favored customers Those who receive special treatment from dealers during situations of excess demand. *p. 76*

Fed rule Equation that shows how the Fed's interest rate decision depends on the state of the economy. *p. 220*

federal budget The budget of the federal government. *p. 173*

federal debt The total amount owed by the federal government. *p. 176*

Federal Open Market Committee (FOMC) A group composed of the seven members of the Fed's Board of Governors, the president of the New York Federal Reserve Bank, and four of the other 11 district bank presidents on a rotating basis; it sets goals concerning the money supply and interest rates and directs the operation of the Open Market Desk in New York. *p. 198*

Federal Reserve Bank (the Fed) The central bank of the United States. *p. 195*

federal surplus (+) *or* (−) deficit Federal government receipts minus expenditures. *p. 173*

fiat, or token, money Items designated as money that are intrinsically worthless. *p. 190*

final goods and services Goods and services produced for final use. *p. 105*

fine-tuning The phrase used by Walter Heller to refer to the government's role in regulating inflation and unemployment. *p. 97*

firm An organization that transforms resources (inputs) into products (outputs). Firms are the primary producing units in a market economy. *p. 43*

fiscal drag The negative effect on the economy that occurs when average tax rates increase because taxpayers have moved into higher income brackets during an expansion. *p. 178*

fiscal policy Government policies concerning taxes and spending. *pp. 96, 161*

fixed-weight procedure A procedure that uses weights from a given base year. *p. 114*

floating, *or* market-determined, exchange rates Exchange rates that are determined by the unregulated forces of supply and demand. *p. 364*

foreign direct investment (FDI) Investment in enterprises made in a country by residents outside that country. *p. 306*

foreign exchange All currencies other than the domestic currency of a given country. *p. 357*

frictional unemployment The portion of unemployment that is due to the normal turnover in the labor market; used to denote short-run job/skill-matching problems. *pp. 129, 246*

full-employment budget What the federal budget would be if the economy

were producing at the full-employment level of output. *p. 178*

General Agreement on Tariffs and Trade (GATT) An international agreement signed by the United States and 22 other countries in 1947 to promote the liberalization of foreign trade. *p. 344*

Global South Developing nations in Asia, Africa, and Latin America. *p. 383*

government consumption and gross investment (*G*) Expenditures by federal, state, and local governments for final goods and services. *p. 109*

government spending multiplier The ratio of the change in the equilibrium level of output to a change in government spending. *p. 168*

Gramm-Rudman-Hollings Act Passed by the U.S. Congress and signed by President Reagan in 1986, this law set out to reduce the federal deficit by $36 billion per year, with a deficit of zero slated for 1991. *p. 275*

Great Depression The period of severe economic contraction and high unemployment that began in 1929 and continued throughout the 1930s. *p. 97*

gross domestic product (GDP) The total market value of all final goods and services produced within a given period by factors of production located within a country. *p. 104*

gross investment The total value of all newly produced capital goods (plant, equipment, housing, and inventory) produced in a given period. *p. 108*

gross national income (GNI) GNP converted into dollars using an average of currency exchange rates over several years adjusted for rates of inflation. *p. 117*

gross national product (GNP) The total market value of all final goods and services produced within a given period by factors of production owned by a country's citizens, regardless of where the output is produced. *p. 105*

gross private domestic investment (*I*) Total investment in capital—that is, the purchase of new housing, plants, equipment, and inventory by the private (or nongovernment) sector. *p. 108*

Heckscher-Ohlin theorem A theory that explains the existence of a country's comparative advantage by its factor endowments: A country has a comparative advantage in the production of a product if that country is relatively well endowed with inputs used intensively in the production of that product. *p. 341*

households The consuming units in an economy. *p. 43*

hyperinflation A period of very rapid increases in the overall price level. *p. 93*

identity Something that is always true. *p. 143*

implementation lag The time it takes to put the desired policy into effect once economists and policy makers recognize that the economy is in a boom or a slump. *p. 273*

import substitution An industrial trade strategy that favors developing local industries that can manufacture goods to replace imports. *p. 391*

income The sum of all a household's wages, salaries, profits, interest payments, rents, and other forms of earnings in a given period of time. It is a flow measure. *p. 49*

income approach A method of computing GDP that measures the income—wages, rents, interest, and profits—received by all factors of production in producing final goods and services. *p. 106*

indirect taxes minus subsidies Taxes such as sales taxes, customs duties, and license fees less subsidies that the government pays for which it receives no goods or services in return. *p. 109*

Industrial Revolution The period in England during the late eighteenth and early nineteenth centuries in which new manufacturing technologies and improved transportation gave rise to the modern factory

system and a massive movement of the population from the countryside to the cities. *p. 3*

infant industry A young industry that may need temporary protection from competition from the established industries of other countries to develop an acquired comparative advantage. *p. 350*

inferior goods Goods for which demand tends to fall when income rises. *p. 49*

inflation An increase in the overall price level. *p. 93*

inflation rate The percentage change in the price level. *p. 253*

inflation targeting When a monetary authority chooses its interest rate values with the aim of keeping the inflation rate within some specified band over some specified horizon. *p. 242*

informal economy The part of the economy in which transactions take place and in which income is generated that is unreported and therefore not counted in GDP. *p. 116*

innovation The use of new knowledge to produce a new product or to produce an existing product more efficiently. *p. 309*

input *or* factor markets The markets in which the resources used to produce goods and services are exchanged. *p. 44*

inputs *or* resources Anything provided by nature or previous generations that can be used directly or indirectly to satisfy human wants. *p. 23*

intention to treat A method in which we compare two groups based on whether they were part of an initially specified random sample subjected to an experimental protocol. *p. 403*

intermediate goods Goods that are produced by one firm for use in further processing by another firm. *p. 105*

invention An advance in knowledge. *p. 309*

inventory investment The change in the stock of inventories. *p. 291*

investment The process of using resources to produce new capital. New capital additions to a firm's capital stock. Although capital is measured at a given point in time (a stock), investment is measured over a period of time (a flow). The flow of investment increases the capital stock. *p. 28*

IS curve Relationship between aggregate output and the interest rate in the goods market. *p. 219*

J-curve effect Following a currency depreciation, a country's balance of trade may get worse before it gets better. The graph showing this effect is shaped like the letter J, hence the name J-curve effect. *p. 370*

labor demand curve A graph that illustrates the amount of labor that firms want to employ at each given wage rate. *p. 246*

labor force The number of people employed plus the number of unemployed. *p. 124*

labor market The input/factor market in which households supply work for wages to firms that demand labor. *p. 44*

labor productivity growth The growth rate of output per worker. *p. 301*

labor supply curve A curve that shows the quantity of labor supplied at different wage rates. Its shape depends on how households react to changes in the wage rate. A graph that illustrates the amount of labor that households want to supply at each given wage rate. *p. 247*

Laffer curve With the tax rate measured on the vertical axis and tax revenue measured on the horizontal axis, the Laffer curve shows that there is some tax rate beyond which the supply response is large enough to lead to a decrease in tax revenue for further increases in the tax rate. *p. 322*

laissez-faire economy Literally from the French: "allow [them] to do." An economy in which individual people and firms pursue their own self-interest without any central direction or regulation. *p. 36*

land market   The input/factor market in which households supply land or other real property in exchange for rent. *p. 44*

law of demand   The negative relationship between price and quantity demanded: *Ceteris paribus*, as price rises, quantity demanded decreases; as price falls, quantity demanded increases. *p. 47*

law of one price   If the costs of transportation are small, the price of the same good in different countries should be roughly the same. *p. 368*

law of supply   The positive relationship between price and quantity of a good supplied: An increase in market price will lead to an increase in quantity supplied, and a decrease in market price will lead to a decrease in quantity supplied. *p. 56*

least squares estimates   Least squares estimates are those that correspond to the smallest sum of squared distances, or errors. *p. 410*

legal tender   Money that a government has required to be accepted in settlement of debts. *p. 190*

lender of last resort   One of the functions of the Fed: It provides funds to troubled banks that cannot find any other sources of funds. *p. 200*

life-cycle theory of consumption A theory of household consumption: Households make lifetime consumption decisions based on their expectations of lifetime income. *p. 281*

liquidity property of money   The property of money that makes it a good medium of exchange as well as a store of value: It is portable and readily accepted and thus easily exchanged for goods. *p. 189*

Lucas supply function   The supply function embodies the idea that output

(*Y*) depends on the difference between the actual price level and the expected price level. *p. 326*

M1, *or* transactions money Money that can be directly used for transactions. *p. 191*

M2, *or* broad money   M1 plus savings accounts, money market accounts, and other near monies. *p. 191*

macroeconomics   Deals with the economy as a whole. Macroeconomics focuses on the determinants of total national income, deals with aggregates such as aggregate consumption and investment, and looks at the overall level of prices instead of individual prices. The branch of economics that examines the economic behavior of aggregates—income, employment, output, and so on—on a national scale. *p. 90*

marginal propensity to consume (*MPC*)   That fraction of a change in income that is consumed, or spent. *p. 143*

marginal propensity to import (*MPM*)   The change in imports caused by a $1 change in income. *p. 361*

marginal propensity to save (*MPS*)   That fraction of a change in income that is saved. *p. 143*

marginal rate of transformation (*MRT*)   The slope of the production possibility frontier (ppf). *p. 30*

marginalism   The process of analyzing the additional or incremental costs or benefits arising from a choice or decision. *p. 2*

market   The institution through which buyers and sellers interact and engage in exchange. *p. 36*

market demand   The sum of all the quantities of a good or service demanded per period by all the households buying in the market for that good or service. *p. 53*

market supply   The sum of all that is supplied each period by all producers of a single product. *p. 59*

medium of exchange, or means of payment   What sellers generally accept and buyers generally use to pay for goods and services. *p. 188*

microeconomics   Examines the functioning of individual industries and the behavior of individual decision-making units—firms and households. The branch of economics that examines the functioning of individual industries and the behavior of individual decision-making units—that is, firms and households. *p. 90*

minimum wage laws   Laws that set a floor for wage rates—that is, a minimum hourly rate for any kind of labor. *p. 249*

model   A formal statement of a theory, usually a mathematical statement of a presumed relationship between two or more variables. *p. 7*

monetary policy   The behavior of the Federal Reserve concerning interest rates. The tools used by the Federal Reserve to control the short-term interest rate. *pp. 96, 162*

money multiplier   The multiple by which deposits can increase for every dollar increase in reserves; equal to 1 divided by the required reserve ratio. *p. 197*

movement along a demand curve   The change in quantity demanded brought about by a change in price. *p. 53*

movement along a supply curve The change in quantity supplied brought about by a change in price. *p. 58*

multiplier   The ratio of the change in the equilibrium level of output to a change in some exogenous variable. *p. 153*

NAIRU   The nonaccelerating inflation rate of unemployment. *p. 258*

NASDAQ Composite   An index based on the stock prices of over 5,000 companies traded on the NASDAQ Stock Market. The NASDAQ market takes its name from the National

Association of Securities Dealers Automated Quotation System. *p. 267*

national income and product accounts Data collected and published by the government describing the various components of national income and output in the economy. *p. 103*

national income The total income earned by the factors of production owned by a country's citizens. *p. 109*

natural experiment Selection of a control versus experimental group in testing the outcome of an intervention is made as a result of an exogenous event outside the experiment itself and unrelated to it. *p. 394*

natural rate of unemployment The unemployment rate that occurs as a normal part of the functioning of the economy. Sometimes taken as the sum of the frictional unemployment rate and the structural unemployment rate. *p. 129*

natural rate of unemployment The unemployment that occurs as a normal part of the functioning of the economy. Sometimes taken as the sum of frictional unemployment and structural unemployment. *p. 257*

near monies Close substitutes for transactions money, such as savings accounts and money market accounts. *p. 191*

net business transfer payments Net transfer payments by businesses to others. *p. 109*

net exports (EX − IM) The difference between exports (sales to foreigners of U.S.- produced goods and services) and imports (U.S. purchases of goods and services from abroad). The figure can be positive or negative. *p. 109*

net exports of goods and services (EX − IM) The difference between a country's total exports and total imports. *p. 361*

net interest The interest paid by business. *p. 109*

net investment Gross investment minus depreciation. *p. 100*

net national product (NNP) Gross national product minus depreciation; a nation's total product minus what is required to maintain the value of its capital stock. *p. 110*

net taxes (T) Taxes paid by firms and households to the government minus transfer payments made to households by the government. *p. 163*

new Keynesian economics A field in which models are developed under the assumptions of rational expectations and sticky prices and wages. *p. 327*

nominal GDP Gross domestic product measured in current dollars. *p. 111*

nominal wage rate The wage rate in current dollars. is the wage rate in current dollars. *p. 283*

nondurable goods Goods that are used up fairly quickly, such as food and clothing. *p. 106*

nonlabor, or nonwage, income Any income received from sources other than working—inheritances, interest, dividends, transfer payments, and so on. *p. 284*

nonresidential investment Expenditures by firms for machines, tools, plants, and so on. *p. 108*

normal goods Goods for which demand goes up when income is higher and for which demand goes down when income is lower. *p. 49*

normative economics An approach to economics that analyzes outcomes of economic behavior, evaluates them as good or bad, and may prescribe courses of action. Also called *policy economics*. *p. 7*

North American Free Trade Agreement (NAFTA) An agreement signed by the United States, Mexico, and Canada in which the three countries agreed to establish all North America as a free-trade zone. *p. 345*

not in the labor force A person who is not looking for work because he or she does not want a job or has given up looking. *p. 124*

Ockham's razor The principle that irrelevant detail should be cut away. *p. 7*

Okun's Law The theory, put forth by Arthur Okun, that in the short run the unemployment rate decreases about 1 percentage point for every 3 percent increase in real GDP. Later research and data have shown that the relationship between output and unemployment is not as stable as Okun's "Law" predicts. *p. 295*

Open Market Desk The office in the New York Federal Reserve Bank from which government securities are bought and sold by the Fed. *p. 198*

open market operations The interest rate that banks pay to the Fed to borrow from it. *p. 203*

opportunity cost The best alternative that we forgo, or give up, when we make a choice or a decision. *p. 2*

opportunity cost The best alternative that we give up, or forgo, when we make a choice or decision. *p. 24*

output growth The growth rate of the output of the entire economy. *pp. 133, 301*

outputs Goods and services of value to households. *p. 23*

per-capita output growth The growth rate of output per person in the economy. *pp. 233, 301*

perfect price discrimination Occurs when a firm charges the maximum amount that buyers are willing to pay for each unit. *p. 278*

perfect substitutes Identical products. *p. 49*

permanent income The average level of a person's expected future income stream. *p. 282*

personal consumption expenditures (C) Expenditures by consumers on goods and services. *p. 106*

personal income The total income of households. *p. 111*

personal saving   The amount of disposable income that is left after total personal spending in a given period. *p. 111*

personal saving rate   The percentage of disposable personal income that is saved. If the personal saving rate is low, households are spending a large amount relative to their incomes; if it is high, households are spending cautiously. *p. 111*

Phillips Curve   A curve showing the relationship between the inflation rate and the unemployment rate. *p. 253*

planned aggregate expenditure (AE)   The total amount the economy plans to spend in a given period. Equal to consumption plus planned investment: $AE \equiv C + I$ *p. 149*

planned investment (I)   Those additions to capital stock and inventory that are planned by firms. *p. 147*

positive economics   An approach to economics that seeks to understand behavior and the operation of systems without making judgments. It describes what exists and how it works. *p. 7*

post hoc, ergo propter hoc   Literally, "after this (in time), therefore because of this." A common error made in thinking about causation: If Event A happens before Event B, it is not necessarily true that A caused B. *p. 8*

potential output *or* potential GDP   The level of aggregate output that can be sustained in the long run without inflation. *p. 226*

price ceiling   A maximum price that sellers may charge for a good, usually set by government. *p. 75*

price feedback effect   The process by which a domestic price increase in one country can "feed back" on itself through export and import prices. An increase in the price level in one country can drive up prices in other countries. This in turn further increases the price level in the first country. *p. 364*

price floor   A minimum price below which exchange is not permitted. *p. 79*

price rationing   The process by which the market system allocates goods and services to consumers when quantity demanded exceeds quantity supplied. *p. 73*

price surprise   Actual price level minus expected price level. *p. 326*

privately held federal debt   The privately held (non-government-owned) debt of the U.S. government. *p. 177*

producer price indexes (PPIs)   Measures of prices that producers receive for products at various stages in the production process. *p. 130*

producer surplus   The difference between the current market price and the cost of production for the firm. *p. 83*

product or output markets   The markets in which goods and services are exchanged. *p. 44*

production possibility frontier (ppf)   A graph that shows all the combinations of goods and services that can be produced if all of society's resources are used efficiently. *p. 29*

production   The process by which inputs are combined, transformed, and turned into outputs. *p. 23*

productivity, *or* labor productivity   Output per worker hour. *p. 294*

productivity growth   The growth rate of output per worker. *p. 133*

profit   The difference between total revenue and total cost. *p. 56*

proprietors' income   The income of unincorporated businesses. *p. 109*

protection   The practice of shielding a sector of the economy from foreign competition. *p. 342*

purchasing-power-parity theory   A theory of international exchange holding that exchange rates are set so that the price of similar goods in different countries is the same. *p. 368*

p-value   The probability of obtaining the result that you find in the sample data if the null hypothesis of no relationship is true. *p. 408*

quantity demanded   The amount (number of units) of a product that a household would buy in a given period if it could buy all it wanted at the current market price. *p. 45*

quantity supplied   The amount of a particular product that a firm would be willing and able to offer for sale at a particular price during a given time period. *p. 56*

quantity theory of money   The theory based on the identity $M \times V \equiv P \times Y$ and the assumption that the velocity of money (V) is constant (or virtually constant). *p. 319*

queuing   Waiting in line as a means of distributing goods and services: a nonprice rationing mechanism. *p. 75*

quota   A limit on the quantity of imports. *p. 343*

random experiment   (Sometimes referred to as a randomized experiment.) A technique in which outcomes of specific interventions are determined by using the intervention in a randomly selected subset of a sample and then comparing outcomes from the exposed and control group. *p. 394*

ration coupons   Tickets or coupons that entitle individuals to purchase a certain amount of a given product per month. *p. 76*

rational-expectations hypothesis   The hypothesis that people know the "true model" of the economy and that they use this model to form their expectations of the future. *p. 324*

real business cycle theory   An attempt to explain business cycle fluctuations under the assumptions of complete price and wage flexibility and rational expectations. It emphasizes shocks to technology and other shocks. *p. 327*

real interest rate   The difference between the interest rate on a loan and the inflation rate. *p. 132*

real wage rate The amount the nominal wage rate can buy in terms of goods and services. *p. 283*

real wealth effect The change in consumption brought about by a change in real wealth that results from a change in the price level. *p. 225*

realized capital gain The gain that occurs when the owner of an asset actually sells it for more than he or she paid for it. *p. 265*

recession A period during which aggregate output declines. Conventionally, a period in which aggregate output declines for two consecutive quarters. *p. 91*

regression discontinuity Identifies the causal effects of a policy or factor by looking at two samples that lie on either side of a threshold or cutoff. *p. 405*

recognition lag The time it takes for policy makers to recognize the existence of a boom or a slump. *p. 273*

relative-wage explanation of unemployment An explanation for sticky wages (and therefore unemployment): If workers are concerned about their wages relative to the wages of other workers in other firms and industries, they may be unwilling to accept a wage cut unless they know that all other workers are receiving similar cuts. *p. 251*

rental income The income received by property owners in the form of rent. *p. 109*

required reserve ratio The percentage of its total deposits that a bank must keep as reserves at the Federal Reserve. *p. 195*

reserves The deposits that a bank has at the Federal Reserve bank plus its cash on hand. *p. 194*

residential investment Expenditures by households and firms on new houses and apartment buildings. *p. 108*

response lag The time that it takes for the economy to adjust to the new conditions after a new policy is implemented; the lag that occurs because of the operation of the economy itself. *p. 273*

run on a bank Occurs when many of those who have claims on a bank (deposits) present them at the same time. *p. 194*

scarce Limited. *p. 2*

selection bias Selection bias is when the sample used is not random. *p. 400*

services The things we buy that do not involve the production of physical things, such as legal and medical services and education. *p. 106*

shares of stock Financial instruments that give to the holder a share in the firm's ownership and therefore the right to share in the firm's profits. *p. 96*

shift of a demand curve The change that takes place in a demand curve corresponding to a new relationship between quantity demanded of a good and price of that good. The shift is brought about by a change in the original conditions. *p. 53*

shift of a supply curve The change that takes place in a supply curve corresponding to a new relationship between quantity supplied of a good and the price of that good. The shift is brought about by a change in the original conditions. *p. 58*

Smoot-Hawley tariff The U.S. tariff law of the 1930s, which set the highest tariffs in U.S. history (60 percent). It set off an international trade war and caused the decline in trade that is often considered one of the causes of the worldwide depression of the 1930s. *p. 343*

social overhead capital Basic infrastructure projects such as roads, power generation, and irrigation systems. *p. 388*

social, *or implicit*, contracts Unspoken agreements between workers and firms that firms will not cut wages. *p. 570*

stability A condition in which national output is growing steadily, with low inflation and full employment of resources. *p. 10*

stabilization policy Describes both monetary and fiscal policy, the goals of which are to smooth out fluctuations in output and employment and to keep prices as stable as possible. *p. 591*

stagflation A situation of both high inflation and high unemployment. The simultaneous increase in unemployment and inflation. *pp. 98, 237*

Standard and Poor's 500 (S&P 500) An index based on the stock prices of 500 of the largest firms by market value. *p. 267*

statistical discrepancy Data measurement error. *p. 110*

statistical significance A result is said to be statistically significant if the computed p-value is less than some presubscribed number, usually 0.05. *p. 408*

sticky prices Prices that do not always adjust rapidly to maintain equality between quantity supplied and quantity demanded. *p. 90*

sticky wages The downward rigidity of wages as an explanation for the existence of unemployment. *p. 250*

stock A certificate that certifies ownership of a certain portion of a firm. *p. 265*

store of value An asset that can be used to transport purchasing power from one time period to another. *p. 188*

structural deficit The deficit that remains at full employment. *p. 179*

structural unemployment The portion of unemployment that is due to changes in the structure of the economy that result in a significant loss of jobs in certain industries. *pp. 129, 246*

substitutes Goods that can serve as replacements for one another; when the price of one increases, demand for the other increases. *p. 49*

supply curve A graph illustrating how much of a product a firm will sell at different prices. *p. 56*

supply schedule Shows how much of a product firms will sell at alternative prices. *p. 56*

surplus of government enterprises Income of government enterprises. *p. 110*

survivor bias Survivor bias exists when a sample includes only observations that have remained in the sample over time making that sample unrepresentative of the broader population. *p. 400*

tariff A tax on imports. *p. 342*

tax multiplier The ratio of change in the equilibrium level of output to a change in taxes. *p. 170*

terms of trade The ratio at which a country can trade domestic products for imported products. *p. 338*

theory of comparative advantage Ricardo's theory that specialization and free trade will benefit all trading parties (real wages will rise), even those that may be "absolutely" more efficient producers. *pp. 24, 333*

time lags Delays in the economy's response to stabilization policies. *p. 272*

trade deficit Occurs when a country's exports of goods and services are less than its imports of goods and services. *pp. 338, 358*

trade feedback effect The tendency for an increase in the economic activity of one country to lead to a worldwide increase in economic activity, which then feeds back to that country. *p. 363*

trade surplus The situation when a country exports more than it imports. *p. 333*

transfer payments Cash payments made by the government to people who do not supply goods, services, or labor in exchange for these payments. They include Social Security benefits, veterans' benefits, and welfare payments. *p. 94*

Treasury bonds, notes, *and* bills Promissory notes issued by the federal government when it borrows money. *p. 96*

U.S.-Canadian Free Trade Agreement An agreement in which the United States and Canada agreed to eliminate all barriers to trade between the two countries by 1998. *p. 345*

unconstrained supply of labor The amount a household would like to work within a given period at the current wage rate if it could find the work. *p. 285*

unemployed A person 16 years old or older who is not working, is available for work, and has made specific efforts to find work during the previous 4 weeks. *p. 124*

unemployment rate The number of people unemployed as a percentage of the labor force. *pp. 93, 124, 246*

unit of account A standard unit that provides a consistent way of quoting prices. *p. 189*

value added The difference between the value of goods as they leave a stage of production and the cost of the goods as they entered that stage. *p. 104*

variable A measure that can change from time to time or from observation to observation. *p. 7*

velocity of money The number of times a dollar bill changes hands, on average, during a year; the ratio of nominal *GDP* to the stock of money. *p. 318*

vicious-circle-of-poverty Suggests that poverty is self-perpetuating because poor nations are unable to save and invest enough to accumulate the capital stock that would help them grow. *p. 385*

wealth *or* net worth The total value of what a household owns minus what it owes. It is a stock measure. *p. 49*

weight The importance attached to an item within a group of items. *p. 113*

World Trade Organization (WTO) A negotiating forum dealing with rules of trade across nations. *p. 344*

zero interest rate bound The interest rate cannot go below zero. *p. 235*

Index

*Notes: Key terms and the page on which they are defined appear in **boldface.** Page numbers followed by *n* refer to information in footnotes.

Photo Credits